The Journal of Negro History

(Volume VIII)

Carter G. Woodson

Alpha Editions

This edition published in 2020

ISBN : 9789354043208

Design and Setting By
Alpha Editions
www.alphaedis.com
email - alphaedis@gmail.com

As per information held with us this book is in Public Domain.
This book is a reproduction of an important historical work. Alpha Editions uses the best technology to reproduce historical work in the same manner it was first published to preserve its original nature. Any marks or number seen are left intentionally to preserve its true form.

THE JOURNAL

OF

NEGRO HISTORY

CARTER G. WOODSON
EDITOR

VOLUME VIII

1923

THE ASSOCIATION FOR THE STUDY OF NEGRO LIFE
AND HISTORY, Inc.
LANCASTER, PA., AND WASHINGTON, D. C.
1923

CONTENTS OF VOLUME VIII

No. 1. January, 1923

L. P. Jackson: *The Educational Efforts of the Freedmen's Bureau and Freedmen's Aid Societies in South Carolina, 1862–1872*	1
G. R. Wilson: *The Religion of the American Negro Slave: His Attitude toward Life and Death*	41
G. Smith Wormley: *Prudence Crandall*	72
Documents:	81
Extracts from Newspapers and Magazines. Anna Murray-Douglass—*My Mother as I Recall Her.* Frederick Douglass in Ireland.	
Book Reviews:	108
Bragg's *The History of the Afro-American Group of the Episcopal Church;* Haynes's *The Trend of the Races;* Hammond's *In the Vanguard of a Race;* The Chicago Commission on Race Relations, *The Negro in Chicago.*	
Notes:	115
Proceedings of the Annual Meeting of the Association for the Study of Negro Life and History	116

No. 2. April, 1923

J. W. Bell: *The Teaching of Negro History*	123
Paul W. L. Jones: *Negro Biography*	128
George W. Brown: *Haiti and the United States*	134
H. N. Sherwood: *Paul Cuffe*	153
Documents:	230
The Will of Paul Cuffe.	
Book Reviews:	233
Wiener's *Africa and the Discovery of America;* Detweiler's *The Negro Press in the United States;* McGregor's *The Disruption of Virginia;* Johnston's *A Comparative Study of the Bantu and Semi-Bantu Languages.*	
Notes:	243

No. 3. July, 1923

T. R. Davis: *Negro Servitude in the United States*	247
Gordon B. Hancock: *Three Elements of African Culture*	284

J. C. HARTZELL: *Methodism and the Negro in the United States* 301
WILLIAM RENWICK RIDDELL: *Notes on the Slave in Nouvelle France* 316
DOCUMENTS: 331
    Banishment of the Free People of Color from Cincinnati.
    First Protest against Slavery in the United States.
    A Negro Pioneer in the West.
    Concerning the Origin of Wilberforce.
COMMUNICATIONS: 338
    A Letter from Mr. J. W. Cromwell bearing on the Negro in West Virginia.
    A Letter from Dr. James S. Russell giving Information about Peter George Morgan of Petersburg, Virginia.
    A Letter from Captain A. B. Spingarn about early Education of the Negroes in New York.
BOOK REVIEWS: 346
    JONES'S *Piney Woods and its Story*; JOHNSON'S *American Negro Poetry*; RHODES'S *The McKinley and Roosevelt Administrations*; GUMMERE'S *Journal of John Woolman*.
NOTES: 351
THE SPRING CONFERENCE.................................. 353

No. 4. October, 1923

ALBERT PARRY: *Abram Hannibal, the Favorite of Peter the Great* 359
ALRUTHEUS A. TAYLOR: *The Movement of the Negroes from the East to the Gulf States from 1830 to 1850*........ 367
ELIZABETH ROSS HAYNES: *Negroes in Domestic Service in the United States* 384
DOCUMENTS: 443
    Documents and Comments on Benefit of Clergy as applied to Slaves, by Wm. K. Boyd.
COMMUNICATIONS: 448
    A Letter from A. P. Vrede giving an Account of the Achievements of the Rev. Cornelius Winst Blyd of Dutch Guiana.
    A Letter from Captain T. G. Steward throwing Light on various Phases of Negro History.
BOOK REVIEWS: 455
    FROBENIUS'S *Das Unbekannte Africa*; OBERHOLTZER'S *History of the United States since the Civil War*; LUCAS'S *Partition of Africa*; JACKSON'S *Boy's Life of Booker T. Washington*.
NOTES: 465
ANNUAL REPORT OF THE DIRECTOR FOR THE YEAR 1922–23.... 466

THE JOURNAL OF NEGRO HISTORY

Vol. VIII., No. 1   January, 1923.

THE EDUCATIONAL EFFORTS OF THE FREEDMEN'S BUREAU AND FREEDMEN'S AID SOCIETIES IN SOUTH CAROLINA, 1862–1872[1]

INTRODUCTION

Slavery in the United States was abolished by force of circumstances. The appeal to arms in April, 1861, was made by the North for the purpose of saving the Union, but only within a few months after the breaking out of hostilities "what shall we do with the slaves within our lines" was the cry heard from all sections of the invaded territory. Deserted by their masters or endeavoring to obtain freedom, the Negroes came into the Union camps in such large numbers that humanitarian as well as military reasons demanded that something be done to change their status and alleviate their physical suffering.[2] In the ab-

[1] This dissertation was submitted in partial fulfilment of the requirements for the degree of Master of Arts in the Faculty of Education of Columbia University in 1922.

[2] I. The sources for this dissertation are:
1. PUBLIC DOCUMENTS. *Senate: 38 Cong., 1 Sess., Vol. 1, No. 1—Letter from freedmen's aid societies, Dec. 17, 1863. 39 Cong., 1 Sess., Vol. 2, No. 27—Reports of assistant commissioners, Dec. 1, 1865, to March 6, 1866. 39 Cong., 2 Sess., Vol. 1, No. 6—Reports of assistant commissioners, Jan. 3, 1867.* HOUSE EXECUTIVE DOCUMENTS. *39 Cong., 1 Sess., Vol. 7, No. 11; 39 Cong., 2 Sess., Vol. 3, No. 1; 40 Cong., 2 Sess., Vol. 2, No. 1; 40 Cong., 3 Sess., Vol. 3, No. 1; 41 Cong., 2 Sess., Vol. 6, No. 142; 41 Cong., 3 Sess., Vol. 1, No. 1; 42 Cong., 2 Sess., Vol. 1, No. 1—Reports of*

sence of a uniform national policy on the matter, the several commanding generals settled the question according to their own notions. Butler, at Fortress Monroe, for example, refused to return the group of fugitive slaves and cleverly styled them "contraband of war."

Howard as Commissioner, Dec. 1865–Dec. 1871. United States Statutes at Large, Vols. 13–17. (Boston).

2. Reports of General Superintendent and the Societies. J. W. Alvord, *Schools and Finances of Freedmen* (Washington, 1866); J. W. Alvord, *Semi-annual reports, 1867–'70;* J. W. Alvord, *Letters from the South, relating to the condition of freedmen Addressed to General O. O. Howard* (Washington, 1870); American Missionary Association, *Annual report, 1862–1872;* Educational Commission for freedmen, *Annual report, No. 1, 1862–'63* (Boston, 1863); and New England Freedmen's Aid Society, *annual report, No. 2, 1863–'64;* New York National Freedmen's Relief Association, *Annual report, 1865–'66* (N. Y., 1866). *Ibid., Brief History with 4th annual report, 1865;* Friends Association of Philadelphia for the Aid and Elevation of Freedmen, *Annual report, 1866–71;* Freedmen's Aid Society of the Methodist Episcopal Church, *Annual report, 1869–'72;* American Baptist Home Mission Society, *Annual report, 1863–'72;* and Board of Missions for Freedmen of the Presbyterian Church, *Annual report, 1869–'70.*

3. NEWSPAPERS AND PERIODICALS. *The New York Times; The New York Tribune; The Charleston Daily Courier. The Darlington New Era; The Columbia Phoenix; The Nation. The Atlantic Monthly,* vol. XII (Sept., 1863). Edward L. Pierce—"The Freedmen at Port Royal"; *Atlantic Monthly,* vol. XII (May–June, 1864). Charlotte S. Forten, *Life on the Sea Islands, The North American Review,* vol. CI (July, 1865); William C. Gannet, *The Freedmen at Port Royal; The Southern Workman,* vol. XXX (July, 1901). Laura M. Towne, *Pioneer Work on the Sea Islands; The American Missionary,* 1862–'72, organ of the American Missionary Association; *The American Freedman,* 1866–'68 (incomplete), organ of American Freedmen's Union Commission; *The National Freedman,* 1865–66 (incomplete), organ of New York National Freedmen's Relief Association; *Pennsylvania Freedmen's Bulletin,* 1866–'67 (incomplete), organ of Pennsylvania Freedmen's Relief Association; *Freedmen's Record and Freedmen's Journal,* 1865–'68 (incomplete), organ of New England Freedmen's Aid Society; *The Freedman,* London, 1866 (incomplete), organ of London Freedmen's Aid Society; and *The Baptist Home Mission Monthly,* 1878–'80, organ of American Baptist Home Mission Society.

4. DIARY, REMINISCENCES, AND AUTOBIOGRAPHY. Eliza Ware Pearson (editor), *Letters from Port Royal, written at the time of the Civil War* (Boston, 1906); Rupert S. Holland (editor), *Letters and Diary of Laura M. Towne, written from the sea islands of South Carolina, 1862–1884* (Cambridge, 1912); Henry N. Sherwood (editor), *Journal of Mrs. Susan Walker, March 3d to June 6th, 1862. Quarterly publication of the Historical and Philosophical Society of Ohio,* vol. 1, No. 1, 1912; Eliz Hyde Botume, *First days among the Contrabands* (Boston, 1893); Oliver O. Howard, *Autobiography,* 2 vols., vol. 2 (New York, 1907); and A. Toomer Porter. *The History of a Work of Faith and Love in Charleston, S. C.* (New York, 1882).

5. Description and Travel. Charles Nordhoff, *The Freedmen of South Carolina; some account of their appearance, condition and peculiar customs* (New York, 1863); Whitelaw Reid, *After the War, A Southern Tour,* May 1, 1865, to May 1, 1866 (New York, 1866); and Sidney Andrews, *The South Since the War as Shown by 14 Weeks Travel in Georgia and the Carolinas,* 1866.

II. SECONDARY SOURCES. Myrta L. Avary, *Dixie After the War* (New York, 1906); Laura J. Webster, *Operation of the Freedmen's Bureau in South Carolina, Smith College Studies in History,* vol. 1, 1915–'16; Paul S. Pierce, *The Freedmen's Bureau, University of Iowa Studies* (Iowa City, 1904); Thomas Jesse Jones, *Negro Education, U. S. Bureau of Education, Bulletins,* 1916, Nos. 38 and 39; Colyer Meriwether, *History of Higher Education in South Carolina, U. S. Bureau of Education, Circular of Information,* No. 3, 1888; William W. Sweet, *The Methodist Episcopal Church and the Civil War* (Cincinnati, 1912); Amory D. Mayo, *Work of*

It was under these circumstances that voluntary benevolent associations or freedmen's aid societies sprang up in quick succession all over the North as agencies first to relieve physical suffering and finally to administer to the religious and educational needs of the blacks and white refugees. Missionary efforts were rapidly pushed by them to all Confederate States just as fast as the Union armies advanced into the invaded territory. These private philanthropic efforts which began in 1861 finally led toward the close of the war to the establishment by the United States Government of the Bureau of Refugees, Freedmen and Abandoned Lands—an agency which carried on the work already begun by the societies and at the same time cooperated with them until changed conditions were reached about 1870.

The military event in South Carolina which called forth immediate relief was the capture of Hilton Head and the adjacent sea islands on November 7, 1861, by Commodore Dupont and General T. W. Sherman.[3] The agencies formed to succor the blacks on these islands were the New England Freedmen's Aid Society, the New York National Freedmen's Relief Association, and the Pennsylvania Freedmen's Relief Association. These several bodies were non-sectarian in character. Cooperating with them were some regular church organizations.

At some time during the seven years existence of the Freedmen's Bureau it embraced a six-fold program: (1) distributing rations and medical supplies; (2) establishing schools and aiding benevolent associations; (3) regulating labor contracts; (4) taking charge of confiscated lands; (5) administering justice in cases where blacks were con-

Northern Churches in the Education of the Freedmen. Advanced sheets. U. S. Bureau of Education. Chapter V, 1903; Bowyer Stewart, *The Work of the Church in the South during the Period of Reconstruction* (Episcopalian). *Hale Memorial Sermon, 1913* (Chicago, 1913) ; J. P. Hollis, *Early Period of Reconstruction in South Carolina. Johns Hopkins University. History and Political Studies*, 1905; *Negro Year Book, 1918–'19* (Tuskegee, Alabama) ; *Charleston Year Book,* 1880; and W. E. B. DuBois, *Souls of Black Folk* (Chicago, 1903).

[3] Not to be confused with the more familiar Gen. W. T. Sherman mentioned later.

cerned, and (6) the payment of bounties to soldiers. The societies likewise exercised various physical functions, but it is only the educational activities of all parties concerned that are of primary interest here.

The chosen period of ten years, 1862–1872, represents a rise and fall. During the war the non-sectarian societies operated with all the vigor that the military situation would permit. At its close in 1865 and lasting through 1866 their greatest efforts were expended. Beginning about 1867, signs of retrenchment appear; and in 1868 their operations practically cease. At the same time, both as a cause and as a result of the dissolution of the non-sectarian societies, the church organizations took up the work and carried it not only until the end of this decade but down to the present time. The Freedmen's Bureau, as guardian over all, had no funds the first year or two, but in 1867 and especially in 1868 and 1869 when the societies weakened, it did its greatest work. After 1870 the Freedmen's Bureau had but a nominal existence. By Congressional action the institution expired in 1872. With this ending and one or two important developments by the church organizations in 1871 and 1872, this essay likewise closes.

This educational campaign is thus one conducted by outside parties. The several organizations adopted the policy of "no distinction on account of race or color"; but, inasmuch as the schools were conducted primarily for the blacks, these ten years represent an effort for this race with automatically very little attention to the native whites. The subject, then, lends itself to the following organization: The Port Royal Experiment, the organization and relationship, the establishment and work of schools, the difficulties and complications, and self-help and labor among the freedmen.

THE PORT ROYAL EXPERIMENT

The sea islands of South Carolina are located between Charleston and Savannah on the Atlantic seaboard. In the group connected with the capture of Hilton Head are St. Helena, Port Royal, Morgan, Paris and Phillips. Collectively, as a military designation, these were known as Port Royal. On these islands in 1861 there were about nine thousand slaves,—the lowest in America.[4] As laborers on the cotton and rice plantations these slaves for generations had been removed from all the influences that tended to elevate the bondmen elsewhere. They were densely illiterate, superstitious and in general but little removed from African barbarism.[5] To add to the general low stage of these slaves their language was a jargon hardly understandable by those who came to teach them.[6] For example, some of them would say: "Us aint know nothin' an' you is to larn we."

Upon the capture of Hilton Head by the Federals, the white masters fled to Charleston and the up-country and abandoned all of their property.[7] The control of abandoned property at this time rested with the Treasury Department. Accordingly, Secretary Chase sent Edward L. Pierce, of Milton, Massachusetts, to Port Royal to report on the amount of cotton and also to make recommendations for its collection and sale. The findings of Pierce together with that of Sherman in command of the military forces introduce us to our main story. At the suggestion of Chase, Pierce and Sherman sent appeals broadcast to the North for the immediate relief of the abandoned slaves. In February, 1862, Sherman issued this General Order No. 9: "The helpless condition of the blacks inhabiting the vast area in the occupation of the forces of this command, calls for immediate action on the part of a highly favored and philanthropic people. . . . Hordes of totally uneducated,

[4] Gannet, *North American Review*, vol. 101 (1865), p. 2.

[5] Laura M. Towne, *Southern Workman*, July, 1901, "Life on the Sea Islands"; *Journal of Mrs. Susan Walker;* Charles Nordhoff, *The Freedmen of South Carolina*.

[6] *The Nation*, vol. I (1865), p. 744. Sidney Andrews, *The South Since the War*, p. 228.

[7] Charlotte S. Forten, in *The Atlantic Monthly*, vol. XIII (May, 1864), p. 593; Botume, *First Days among the Contrabands*, p. 11.

ignorant and improvident blacks have been abandoned by their constitutional guardians, not only to all the future chances of anarchy and starvation, but in such a state of abject ignorance and mental stolidity as to preclude all possibility of self-government and self-maintenance in their present condition. . . . To relieve the Government of a burden that may hereafter become insupportable . . . a suitable system of culture and instruction must be combined with one providing for their physical wants. In the meanwhile . . . the service of competent instructors will be received whose duties will consist in teaching them, both young and old, the rudiments of civilization and Christianity."[8]

In response to this appeal there was organized in Boston, on February 7, 1862, the Boston Education Commission, later known as the New England Freedmen's Aid Society or the New England Society, and on the twenty-second of the same month, at a mass meeting held at the Cooper Institute in New York City, the New York National Freedmen's Relief Association was organized. At this meeting the following rules were adopted with reference to the abandoned slaves:

  1. "They must be treated as free men.

  2. "They must earn their livelihood like other freemen and not be dependent upon charity.

  3. "Schools and churches shall be established among them, and the sick shall be cared for."[9]

Following in the wake of Boston and New York came Philadelphia in March with the Port Royal Relief Committee, later known as the Pennsylvania Freedmen's Relief Association or the Pennsylvania Society. Carrying out the resolutions mentioned above, there assembled on the third of March, 1862, at the port of New York, a party of fifty-three teachers and superintendents of labor, including twelve women, who set sail on the same day for Port

[8] New York National Freedmen's Relief Association, *Annual Report,* 1866, pp. 5–6.
[9] *Ibid.,* pp. 8–9.

Royal.[10] The salaries of these persons were to be paid by their respective societies, while transportation and military protection were afforded by the United States Government. Following this original party in March and April, came twenty more representatives from the New England Society and likewise added increments from New York, Philadelphia and elsewhere all through the year. In the Fall the American Missionary Association of New York added a corps of thirty-one teachers. It must be remarked at this point that these individuals represented the flower of New England culture. The first party, "Gideonites" as they were called, was made up in part of recent graduates of Harvard, Yale, Brown and the divinity schools of Andover and Cambridge.[11] Furthermore, they were sent forward on their mission by William Cullen Bryant, William Lloyd Garrison, Francis G. Shaw and Edward Everett Hale, with the sanction and close cooperation of the Secretary of the Treasury, S. P. Chase.

The voluntary steps taken by these parties attracted considerable attention and concern from the best minds of Europe, as well as the United States. Articles on the subject appeared in English and French periodicals.[12] The result of these efforts to aid and elevate the sea island Negroes was to be considered as an index as to their ability to learn and likewise would indicate the possibility of general development of slaves in other States. The labors of the United States Government and the societies here, therefore, came to be known as the "Port Royal Experiment."

The United States Government and the regulation of the abandoned territory for three years, until the close of the war, underwent a number of changes. Prior to the arrival of the Gideonites on March 9th, the territory was controlled by the special cotton agent, E. L. Pierce, as directed by the Treasury Department. In June, in response to Congressional action, control passed to the War

[10] *Journal of Susan Walker*, p. 11; Boston Ed. Commission, *Annual Report*, 1863, p. 7; *Letters from Port Royal*, pp. 2–3.
[11] Pierce, in *The Atlantic Monthly*, vol. XII, 1863, p. 299.
[12] *Ibid.*, p. 292.

Department. Pierce was displaced and Major Rufus Saxton was made the administrator with headquarters at Beaufort on Port Royal. His duties were to supervise the growth and sale of cotton, to regulate labor, to direct the activities of new comers and settle them at suitable points over the several islands. At the same time the military forces stationed at Hilton Head passed successively under the command of Sherman and General David Hunter.

Pursuant to the Congressional Act of June 7, 1862, "for the collection of direct taxes in insurrectionary states" the abandoned property was bought in by the United States Government and private individuals. In September, 1863, the Government relinquished its purchases whereby the "freedmen," as they were now called, could buy property in twenty-acre lots and at the same time establish school farms of six thousand acres, the proceeds from which were to be used for educational purposes. According to the plan laid out by Pierce, the islands were divided into four districts which contained a total of one hundred and eighty-nine plantations.[13] Over each district was placed a general superintendent with a local superintendent for each plantation. W. C. Gannet and John C. Zachas of the New England Society were placed in charge of the schools.[14]

School work had already begun prior to the arrival of the main party through the initiative taken by Pierce and his coworkers. On the eighth of January, 1862, Rev. Solomon Peck, of Roxbury, Massachusetts, established a school for the contrabands at Beaufort. Another was opened at Hilton Head by Barnard K. Lee of Boston the same month.[15] In February there was organized still another at Beaufort, which was taught for a short while by an agent of the American Missionary Association.[16] In estimating what was accomplished by these preliminary disorganized efforts we can assume that it was no more than learning the alphabet.

[13] Nordhoff, *The Freedmen of South Carolina*, p. 12.
[14] *Journal of Susan Walker*, p. 14.
[15] *Congressional Globe*, 41 Cong., 3 Sess., vol. I, No. 1.
[16] J. W. Alvord, *Fifth Semi-annual Report* (Jan. 1, '68), p. 4.

After their arrival in March those persons who had come in the capacity of teachers began their work immediately. By the eighth of May there were eight schools in operation.[17] The improvised school houses consisted of cotton barns, sheds or old kitchens and "praise houses."[18] Some had classes in tents.[19] The furniture correspondingly was equally as crude. The desks were mere boards thrown across old chairs. A fair idea of the general informal state of affairs both as to the time and place of teaching is gained by this recital of one teacher's experience: "I leave town about 6 o'clock A. M. and arrive at the first plantation about 9, and commence teaching those too young to labor. About 11 the task is done, and the field hands come in for their share. About 1 P. M. I go to the other three plantations one and a half miles. They assemble at the most central one for instruction. This lasts about two hours, first teaching the young then the older persons . . . there being no buildings suitable for a school on any plantation, I teach them under the shadow of a tree, where it is more comfortable than any house could be in hot weather."[20] In only one or two instances were there buildings erected specifically for school purposes. One interesting case is that of a building sent from the North in sections and likewise erected piece by piece. An estimate of what was done as a whole during the first year of the "experiment" may be made from the fact that 35,829 books and pamphlets were sent to Port Royal by northern agencies, and 3,000 scholars were put under instruction. In addition to this purely educational effort there were distributed 91,834 garments, 5,895 yards of cloth, and $3,000 worth of farming implements and seeds.[21]

Further light on the general nature and progress of the work is gained through a return visit made by Pierce to Port Royal in March, 1863. At this time he reported that

[17] *New York Tribune*, June 17, 1862.
[18] "Cabins of slaves for religious meetings."
[19] Botume, *First Days among the Contrabands*, p. 42.
[20] *The American Missionary*, vol. VI (Aug., 1862), p. 186.
[21] *House Executive Documents*, 41 Cong., 2 Sess., vol. VI, No. 142, p. 4.

there were more than 30 schools conducted by about 40 or 45 teachers. The average attendance was 2,000 pupils and the enrollment 1,000 more. The ages ranged from 8 to 12.[22] As to the studies "the advanced classes were reading simple stories and mastered some passages in such common school books, as Hillard's *Second Primary Reader,* Wilson's *Second Reader,* and others of similar grade." Some few were having elementary lessons in arithmetic, geography and writing.

A very large part of the school exercises consisted of utilizing what the teachers found the scholars endowed with by nature—an abundance of feeling as expressed in their folk songs and crude religion. An insight into their inwardly depressed condition is gained by the fact that these songs were usually cast in the minor mode, although they were sung in a joyful manner.[23] "In their lowest state singing was the one thing they could always do well. At first they sang melody alone, but after having once been given an idea of harmony, they instantly adopted it. Their time and tone were always true."[24] They took particular delight in ringing out "Roll Jordan Roll." Along with the singing the general atmosphere of the instruction was religious. Indeed, the New Testament was used as a text-book. After the pupils had learned to read a little they were set to work learning the Psalms and the Ten Commandments.

One teacher of the Port Royal group, herself of African descent, was Charlotte S. Forten of Philadelphia. She was a graduate of the State Normal School, Salem, Massachusetts, and had taught in the same city. Refusing a residence in Europe, she joined one of the parties for Port Royal to teach among her own people. This woman enjoyed the friendship of Whittier and, as a beautiful singer herself, the poet sent her directly his *Hymn* written for the scholars of St. Helena Island which she taught them to

---

[22] Pierce, in *The Atlantic Monthly*, vol. XII (1863), p. 303.

[23] *The Nation*, vol. I (1865), p. 745.

[24] Laura M. Towne, *Southern Workman*, July, 1901, p. 337. Nordhoff, p. 10.

sing for the Emancipation Proclamation exercises of January 1, 1863.[25]

The banner school on "St. Helen's Isle" and Port Royal was the one in charge of Laura M. Towne, of Philadelphia, and supported by the Philadelphia Society. After three years' work this school had reached a fair degree of organization. The school was conducted in the building sent in sections as referred to above and was known as the "Penn School" in honor of the society which supported it. Classes were grouped as primary, intermediate, and higher, each in charge of one teacher in a separate room. The branches of study, however, were the same in all—reading, spelling, writing, geography, and arithmetic.[26] The situation here described represents in the embryo the present day Penn Normal and Agricultural Institute.

Similarly well housed was the school taught by Elizabeth Hyde Botume, of Boston, under the auspices of the New England Society. It commands interest for the reason that it was the beginning in industrial training on these islands. As plantation laborers the pupils knew little or

[25] "Oh, none in all the world before
Were ever glad as we!
We're free on Carolina's shore,
We're all at home and free.

"We hear no more the driver's horn
No more the whip we fear,
This holy day that saw Thee born
Was never half so dear.

"The very oaks are greener clad,
The waters brighter smile;
Oh, never shone a day so glad
On sweet St. Helen's Isle.

"Come once again, O blessed Lord!
Come walking on the sea!
And let the mainlands hear the word
That sets the islands free!"

See Pierce, in *The Atlantic Monthly*, vol. XII, p. 305; *Letters from Port Royal*, p. 133.

[26] *The Nation*, vol. I (1865), p. 747.

nothing of sewing. To supply this need Miss Botume solicited the necessary apparatus from her northern friends and began work on some old contraband goods stored in an arsenal. She reported that sewing was a fascination to all and that "they learned readily and soon developed much skill and ingenuity."[27] This school has come down today as the Old Fort Plantation School. The work of these two women thus took on a permanent character and to this extent largely formed an exception to the general informality of the schooling at Port Royal.

Obviously, the heroic efforts of the several societies to assist the blacks amounted to far more than school-room procedure. Indeed, this was a very small part of the work of the teachers and it was so regarded by them. They visited the little cabins, counselled and advised their wards, attended church, and taught them in the Sabbath Schools. Three years of this intermingling between the culture of New England and the most degraded slaves in America resulted in some promising signs for the latter. There was some improvement in manners and dress and an increase in wants. At the stores set up on the islands they were buying small articles for the improvement of their surroundings.[28] For the first time they were now being paid wages. At the tax sales in March, 1863, when 16,479 acres were up for auction they purchased about 3,500 acres at the price of $93\frac{1}{2}$ cents an acre. Shortly afterwards they had doubled this amount.[29] As free laborers, however, they were somewhat disappointing to their new employers since old habits still persisted. All in all, with some three thousand or one-third of the whole number having received "more or less" instruction in books the societies were well satisfied with the experiment and at the close of the war increased their efforts at Port Royal and throughout the State.

[27] Botume, *First Days among the Contrabands*, p. 64.
[28] *The Nation*, vol. I (1865), p. 746.
[29] N. E. Freedman's Aid Society, *Annual Report*, 1864, p. 15.

Organization and Relationship

The Freedmen's Bureau as established by Act of Congress March 3, 1865, "with the supervision and management of all abandoned lands and the control of all subjects relating to refugees and freedmen from rebel states," was an outgrowth of the Port Royal experiment and other such enterprises carried on elsewhere. Social conditions in the South at the close of the war called for increased efforts on the part of northern benevolence, but this was only possible through governmental aid and supervision. The societies already at work during the war made appeals to the government toward this end. One committee, for example, on December 1, 1863, stated that the needs represented "a question too large for anything short of government authority, government resources, and government ubiquity to deal with."[30]

The organization of the Freedmen's Bureau as affecting South Carolina consisted of a commissioner at Washington, an assistant commissioner for the State at large with headquarters at Charleston, and sub-assistant commissioners— one for each of the five districts into which the State was divided. Furthermore, there was a subdivision of each district with agents in charge. For the educational work of the Freedmen's Bureau there was a corps consisting of a general superintendent on the commissioner's staff, a State superintendent correspondingly on the assistant commissioner's staff at Charleston, and the various sub-assistant commissioners and agents who combined the supervision of schools with their other duties. The personnel of this hierarchy consisted of General O. O. Howard, Commissioner, J. W. Alvord, general superintendent of education, General Rufus Saxton, General R. K. Scott, Colonel J. R. Edie, successively, assistant commissioners, and Reuben Tomlinson, Major Horace Neide, Major E. L. Deane, successively, State superintendents of education. These officers, beginning with the lowest, made to their respective

[30] *Senate Executive Documents*, 38 Cong., 1 Sess., vol. I, No. 1, pp. 2–6.

chiefs monthly, quarterly or semi-annual reports which were finally submitted to the commissioner at Washington, who was required to make "before the commencement of each regular session of Congress, a full report of his proceedings."

The duties of the general superintendent were to "collect information, encourage the organization of new schools, find homes for teachers and supervise the whole work."[31] Similarly, the State superintendent was to take cognizance of all that was "being done to educate refugees and freedmen, secure proper protection to schools and teachers, promote method and efficiency, and correspond with the benevolent agencies . . . supplying his field."[32] On October 5, 1865, Tomlinson sent out this notice to the people of the whole State: "I request all persons in any part of this state . . . to communicate with me furnishing me with all the facilities for establishing schools in their respective neighborhoods."[33]

Between the Freedmen's Bureau and the several aid societies there was perfect understanding. Howard announced: "In all this work it is not my purpose to supersede the benevolent agencies already engaged, but to systematize and facilitate them."[34] So close was the cooperation between the efforts of the Bureau and the societies that it is hard in places to separate the work of the two.

Prior to the supplementary Freedmen's Bureau Act of July 16, 1866, the Commission had no funds appropriated to it for educational purposes. It was able to help only by supervision, transportation of teachers and occupation of buildings in possession of the Freedmen's Bureau. This action of the first year met the full approval of Congress, for in the Act of July 16, 1866, it was stated "that the commissioner . . . shall at all time cooperate with private

[31] *House Executive Documents*, 41 Cong., 2 Sess., vol. VI, No. 142, p. 11.
[32] *Ibid.*, 39 Cong., 1 Sess., vol. VII, No. 11, p. 49.
[33] *National Freedman*, Oct., 1865, p. 300.
[34] Howard, *Autobiography*, vol. II, p. 221.

benevolent agencies of citizens in aid of freedmen . . . and shall hire or provide by lease buildings for purposes of education whenever such association shall without cost to the government, provide suitable teachers and means of instruction, and he shall furnish such protection as may be required for the safe conduct of such schools." Further, "the commissioner of this bureau shall have power to seize, hold, use, lease or sell all buildings and tenements . . . and to use the same or appropriate the proceeds derived therefrom to the education of the freed people."[35] In the following March, 1867, $500,000 was appropriated by Congress for the Freedmen's Bureau "for buildings for schools and asylums; including construction, rental and repairs."[36]

The aid societies which under these provisions operated in South Carolina may be classified in three groups:

1. Non-sectarian: The New York National Freedmen's Relief Association, the New England Freedmen's Aid Society and the Pennsylvania Freedmen's Relief Association (as enumerated above).

2. Denominational: (*a*) The American Baptist Home Mission Society; (*b*) the Freedmen's Aid Society of the Methodist Episcopal Church; (*c*) the Presbyterian Committee of Missions for Freedmen; (*d*) the Friends Association of Philadelphia for the Aid and Elevation of the Freedmen; (*e*) and the Protestant Episcopal Freedman's Commission.

3. Semi-denominational: The American Missionary Association.

To the non-sectarian societies might be added the London Freedmen's Aid Society and the Michigan Freedmen's Relief Association, although the latter supported only one school and for a short time only. The American Missionary Association, during the war, served as the agency for the Free Will Baptists, Wesleyan Methodists, and Congregationalists, at which time its work was non-sectarian; but

[35] *Statutes at Large*, XIV, p. 176.
[36] *Ibid.*, p. 486.

as the first two drew out at the close of the war, this association became very largely a congregational agency, establishing churches along with its schools. None of these several agencies confined their attention exclusively to South Carolina, although two of them, the New York and New England societies, did their best work in this State.

The spirit of good will that existed between the Freedmen's Bureau and the societies, however, did not exist among the societies themselves, particularly among the church organizations. For the purpose of bringing about coordination and unity of action from 1863 to 1866, the New York, New England and Pennsylvania societies joined hands with various western societies operating in other States. Each year and oftener these bodies underwent reorganization until in May, 1866, at Cleveland, all non-sectarian societies in all parts of the country united and formed the American Freedmen's Union Commission.[37] To this general body the local societies sustained a relationship of local autonomy. They were now known as the New York, New England, and Pennsylvania "Branches."

In addition to the organization already mentioned, there were attached to each of the branches or local bodies numerous auxiliaries which usually made themselves responsible for some one teacher or group of teachers. In 1867 the New England Society had a total of 187 auxiliaries, 104 in Massachusetts, 75 in Vermont, 6 in New Hampshire, 1 in Connecticut and 1 in Georgia.[38] The strongest New England auxiliary was that at Dorchester, while that of New York was at Yonkers. The London Freedmen's Aid Society with its many branches raised one-half a million of dollars for the cause of the freedmen in America. England reasoned that since America had given so freely toward the Irish famine that it was now her duty and opportunity to return the favor.[39] South Carolina's share in this sum

[37] *U. S. Bureau of Ed. Bulletin*, 1916, No. 38, pp. 269-271; *Annual Reports of Societies*, 1863-1868.

[38] *The Freedmen's Record* (1865-1874), quoted in *Bulletin*, 1916, No. 38, p. 297.

[39] *The Freedman*, August, 1865, p. 12.

was the support of a school at Greenville and one at St. Helena.[40]

During the war the several church bodies supported the non-sectarian societies, but toward the close of the war they began by degrees to withdraw support and take independent action.[41] To their regular missionary departments was now added this new "Freedmen's Aid Society" and to support it a "Freedmen's Fund." Several of the churches also had their Woman's Home Missionary Society which established and conducted schools in conjunction with the parent organization. The efforts of the Presbyterians, Friends, and Episcopalians were similarly directed in that they established the parochial type of school as an annex to the church. With some exceptions, this policy militated against the progress of their schools.[42] Among all the different classes of societies the American Missionary Association (New York City) was the best prepared for its work. This association was organized in 1846 and prior to the war had already established schools and missions.

The several groups of societies had elements in common. They were one on the question of the treatment of the Negro, there being scarcely any difference in their purposes as stated in their constitutions. They felt that the National Government was too silent on the principles of freedom and equality and that the State Governments, North as well as South, had laws inimical to the Negro that should be abolished. The two groups differed in personnel, the non-sectarian consisting largely of business men, particularly the New York Society, and the denominational of clergymen. In the selection of teachers the former made no requirements as to church affiliation, whereas the latter usually upheld this principle.

The ultimate aim of the church bodies was usually religious. They endeavored to institute the true principles of Christianity among the blacks, but in order to do this,

[40] J. W. Alvord, *Semi-annual Report*, July 1, 1869, p. 81.
[41] W. W. Sweet, *Methodist Episcopal Church and the Civil War*, p. 175.
[42] A. D. Mayo, *Northern Churches and the Freedmen*, p. 300.

in order to raise up ministers and Christian leaders among them, schools were necesasry.[43] The Baptists in particular emphasized the training of ministers and the reports of their agents in the field always included the number baptized along with the number of schools and students.

ESTABLISHMENT AND WORK OF SCHOOLS

The schools established during this period may be roughly classified as primary and higher, under the auspices of the non-sectarian and denominational bodies respectively. They include day schools, night schools, and Sabbath schools.

The term "higher" includes secondary and college instruction, although within this decade only two or three schools were even doing secondary work while another which reports "classical" students was really of secondary rank. Some of the church schools were graced with the name "college" and "university" which in reality merely represents the expectation of the promoters. In later years at least two of the institutions begun at this time reached college rank.[44]

The Freedmen's Bureau assumed general charge and supervision of education for the State in the fall of 1865, under the direction of Superintendent Reuben Tomlinson. Schools were in operation, however, before this time— those at Port Royal and the Beaufort district, as mentioned above, continued in operation and in increased numbers. At Charleston schools were opened under the control of the military government on the fourth of March, 1865, only a few weeks after the surrender of the city. James Redpath was appointed as superintendent of these schools. Outside of these two places no regularly organized schools were begun until the Fall, when they were extended over all the State.

The Charleston and Columbia schools are of chief interest. On March 31, 1865, after the schools had just

[43] A. D. Mayo, *Northern Churches and the Freedmen*, p. 291.
[44] *U. S. Bureau of Education Bulletin* (1916), No. 39, p. 16.

opened, Redpath reported the following in operation with the attendance of each:

Morris Street School	962
Ashley Street School	211
Saint Phillip Street School	850
Normal School	511
King Street School (boys)	148
Meeting Street School	211
Saint Michael's School	221
Total	3,114

There were employed eighty-three teachers, seventy-five of whom, white and colored, were natives of Charleston. The salaries of these teachers were paid by the New York and New England societies and cooperating with Redpath in organizing these schools were agents of these societies, one of whom served as a principal of one school. Within a month or two another school was added to this list, and during the same time there sprang up five night schools for adults. The students were made up of both white and Negro children and were taught in separate rooms. The whites, however, represented a very small proportion of the total number.[45]

In the fall of the year, with the reopening of the schools, the general organization underwent considerable changes due to the restoration of the regular civil government in charge of the ex-Confederates. Most of the schools mentioned above were now conducted for white children and taught by the native whites as of old. The Morris Street School, however, was kept for Negro children and taught by the native whites. The Normal School in time became the Avery Institute. The New England Society, which in the Spring had supported the Morris Street School, moved to the Military Hall and subsequently built the Shaw Memorial School. This school was named in the honor of Colonel Robert G. Shaw, who was killed during the war in the assault on Fort Wagner (Morris Island) while leading his Negro troops. The funds for the erection of the school

[45] *National Freedman*, May 1, 1865, p. 122; *Ibid.*, April 30, 1865, p. 150. *American Freedman*, May, 1866, p. 29.

were contributed by the family of Colonel Shaw and they retained a permanent interest in it. In 1874, when the New England Society dissolved, the school was bought by the public school authorities and used for Negro children.[46] During the course of four or five years other schools were established here or in the vicinity of Charleston by the several church organizations.

Charleston thus made a commendable start in education partly for the reason that the city had a school system before the war and for a while during the conflict. The free Negroes of this city likewise had been instructed under certain restrictions during slavery time.[47] The schools which were controlled or supported by the northern agencies were by 1868 offering an elementary grade of instruction corresponding to about the fourth or fifth grade with classes in geography, English composition and arithmetic. Just here, however, it must be said that the personnel of the student body was constantly changing or at least during 1865 and 1866. Charleston was merely a sort of way station for the blacks, who, returning from the up-country where they had fled or had been led during the war, were on their way to the sea islands to take up land as offered by Sherman's order.[48] During April, 1865, Redpath reported that at least five hundred pupils "passed through" the schools, remaining only long enough to be taught a few patriotic songs, to keep quiet and to be decently clad. Others in turn came and in turn were "shipped off."[49]

Columbia, though behind Charleston in point of time, made an equally good beginning in spite of annoying handicaps. There was a fertile field here for teaching, since the blacks were crowding in from all the surrounding territory. Sherman having destroyed about all the suitable buildings, T. G. Wright, representative of the New York Society, in company with three northern ladies, started a school on November 6, 1865, in the basement of a Negro church with

---

[46] *Charleston Year Book* (1880), p. 122.
[47] See Carter G. Woodson, *Education of the Negro Prior to 1861*, p. 129.
[48] Sidney Andrews, *The South Since the War*, p. 98.
[49] *National Freedman*, June 1, 1865, p. 150.

243 scholars. Soon thereafter, on November 7th, another was begun in the small room of a confiscated building "very unsuitable for a school room." On the same day two other schools were begun at similar places, one of them at General Ely's headquarters and taught by his daughters. On the ninth another school started on Arsenal Hill in an old building rented for a church by the freedmen and on the thirteenth still another was opened in one of the government buildings. These schools were numerically designated as "No. 1," "No. 2," etc., being nine in all. In addition to these there were two night schools begun about the same time, one of them enrolling fifty adult males and the other 121.[50] The Columbia schools were taught wholly under the control of the New York Society by northern ladies with the assistance of a few Negro instructors who were competent to assist them. They had a large attendance and consequently there were many changes made in the location of schools in the course even of the first few months.

Fortunately these temporary congested quarters gave way in the fall of 1867 when the Howard School was completed. This school was erected by the New York Society and the Freedmen's Bureau at a cost of about $10,000. It contained ten large class rooms. At the close of the school year (1868) it had an attendance of 600. The closing exercises of the year seemed to have attracted considerable attention inasmuch as the officers of the city, Tomlinson, and newspaper men all attended. The examinations at the close embraced reading, spelling, arithmetic, geography, history and astronomy. *The Columbia Phoenix* (a local paper) said of the exercises: "We were pleased with the neat appearance and becoming bearing of the scholars . . . and the proficiency exhibited in the elementary branches was respectable."[51]

The New York Society did its best work in Columbia. At Beaufort this same organization had schools which oc-

[50] *National Freedman*, Nov. 15, 1865, p. 314; *Ibid.*, May, 1866, pp. 139–140.
[51] J. W. Alvord, *Report*, Jan. 1, 1868, p. 27. *American Freedman*, July-August, 1868, p. 442.

cupied the large buildings formerly used by the whites. The New England Society was best represented at Charleston and Camden. The Philadelphia Society was best represented at St. Helena. Some notion of the exact location of the schools fostered by these societies (May, 1866) may be gained from the following table:[52]

Town	Number of teachers	Support
Ashdale	1	New York Branch
Combahee	1	New York Branch
Columbia	10	New York Branch
Edgerly	1	New York Branch
Greenville	6	New York Branch
Gadsden	2	New York Branch
Hopkins	1	New York Branch
James Island	5	New York Branch
Mitchellville	2	New York Branch
Lexington	2	New York Branch
Pineville	1	New York Branch
Perryclear	1	New York Branch
Pleasant Retreat	2	New York Branch
Red House	1	New York Branch
Rhett Place	2	New York Branch
River View	1	New York Branch
Woodlawn	2	Michigan Branch
Camden [53]	2	New England Branch
Darlington	2	New England Branch
Edisto Island	2	New England Branch
Hilton Head	6	New England Branch
Jehosse's Island	2	New England Branch
Johns Island	1	New England Branch
Marion	2	New England Branch
Orangeburg	3	New England Branch
Summerville	3	New England Branch
Port Royal Island	2	Pennsylvania Branch
Rockville	2	Pennsylvania Branch
St. Helena	5	Pennsylvania Branch
Beaufort	9	New York Branch 7
		New England Branch 2
Charleston	36	New York Branch 13
		New England Branch 23
Georgetown	4	New York Branch 1
		New England Branch 3

[53] The school at Camden increased in size the next year.

[52] *The American Freedman*, May, 1866, p. 261. This does not, however, indicate in all cases the number of schools at each town.

With some exceptions the schools enumerated here and elsewhere unfortunately had only a short existence for the reason that the societies which supported them gradually became short of funds. The New York Society, for example, in 1868, found itself hardly able to bring its teachers home. The efficiency of other societies likewise began to wane. By January 1, 1870, or within a few months afterwards, the Freedmen's Bureau passed out of existence. Alvord and his whole staff thereby were discharged from duty. The non-sectarian societies ceased to exist because the aid societies of the several northern churches claimed the allegiance of their members. A stronger reason, as given by them, was that the freedmen were now (1868) in a position to help themselves politically through the provision of Negro Suffrage for the new State government, under the Congressional plan of reconstruction. The Freedmen's Bureau was discontinued for similar reasons.

A few of the schools so well begun either passed into the hands of the State under regular State or municipal control of schools, as, for example, the Shaw Memorial at Charleston, or they became private institutions with other means of northern support. Before expiration, however, during 1869, the Freedmen's Bureau used its remaining funds to establish new schools and repair buildings throughout the State. A graphic picture of the Bureau's activity during the latter part of 1869 is thus shown:[54]

SCHOOL HOUSES ERECTED

Location	Cost	Size	Material	Value of lot	Ownership of lot
Bennettsville	$1,000	30 x 40	Wood	$100	Freedmen
Gadsden	800	25 x 40	"	50	"
Laurens	1,000	30 x 40	"	100	"
Newberry	2,500	2 stories 26 x 50	"	300	"
Walterboro	1,000	30 x 40	"	100	"
Manning	500	25 x 40	"	50	"
Lancaster	500	25 x 30	"	50	"
Graniteville	700	25 x 40	"	100	"
Blackville	500	25 x 30	"	50	"
	$8,500				

[54] J. W. Alvord, *Report*, Jan. 1, 1870, p. 25.

SCHOOL HOUSES REPAIRED AND RENTED

Locality	Ownership	Amount expended
Conkem	Freedmen	$ 500
Beaufort	Freedmen	1,000
Columbia	Bureau	100
Charleston (Orphan Asylum)	Protestant Episcopal	2,400
Charleston (Shaw School)	Bureau	100
Charleston (Meeting St. Post Office)	Rented	40
Charleston	Protestant Episcopal	8,000
Chester	Rented	30
Darlington	Bureau	100
Eustis Place	Bureau	800
Florence	Freedmen	35.75
Marion	Bureau	150
Mt. Pleasant	Bureau	40
Sumter	Freedmen	500
Shiloh	Freedmen	100
Winnsboro	Bureau	50
Orangeburg	Methodist Episcopal Church	2,500
Total		$16,445.75

After all, the real significance of this educational movement was the policy adopted by the denominational bodies that they should establish permanent institutions—colleges and normal schools to train teachers for the common schools and also in time that the Negroes themselves should run these institutions.[55] South Carolina under the Negro-Carpet-Bag rule in 1868, then, for the first time ventured to establish a school system supported by public taxation. For this object there were practically no competent teachers to serve the Negroes. The only sources of supply were the persons trained in the schools herein described and a few of the northern teachers who remained behind.[56] Very small and crude it was in the beginning, but the policy adopted here at least furnishes the idea upon which ever since the public schools of the State have been mainly justified. By 1870 the Penn School at St. Helena was sending out teachers in response to calls from the State.[57] In the

[55] Freedmen's Aid Society of the M. E. Church, *Annual Report*, 1871, pp. 19-20.
[56] Mayo, *Northern Churches and the Freedmen*, p. 300.
[57] *Letters and Diary of Laura M. Towne*, p. 221.

same year the principal of the Avery Institute reported that he was asked by the State to furnish fifty teachers.[58] This school was perhaps the best fitted to perform this function.

The American Missionary Association supported, at Port Royal and other points in the State, schools which, along with many others, had only a temporary existence. The lasting and best contribution of this association to this movement was the Avery Institute, its second best was the Brewer Normal. Avery was established at Charleston on October 1, 1865, in the State Normal School building, which was offered by General Saxton. The school commenced with twenty teachers and one thousand scholars with every available space taken, one hundred being crowded in the dome. The next year, having been turned out of this building, the school was held for two years in the Military Hall in Wentworth Street. On May 1, 1869, the school entered its present new large building on Bull Street when it dropped the name of the Saxton School for Avery in honor of the philanthropist from a portion of whose bequest $10,000 was spent by the American Missionary Association for the grounds and a mission home. The building proper was erected by the Freedmen's Bureau at a cost of $17,000.[59]

Avery very soon dropped its primary department and concentrated its efforts on the normal or secondary department where it had from the beginning a comfortable number of students. These students came largely from the free Negro class. Under the guidance of their well-trained Negro principal the boys and girls here were reading Milton's "L'Allegro," translating Caesar, and solving quadratic equations.[60] From the standpoint of grade of instruction, Avery was the banner school of the State. With a less pretentious beginning Brewer was established by the American Missionary Association at Greenwood in 1872 on school property valued at $4,000.

[58] *American Missionary Ass'n Annual Report*, 1870, p. 221.
[59] *History of the A. M. A.*, p. 36; *Annual Report*, 1868, p. 47; Mayo, p. 287.
[60] *The Nation*, vol. I (1865), p. 778.

The Baptist Home Mission Society, following in the wake of the American Missionary Association, made a beginning at Port Royal with the labor of Rev. Solomon Peck, at Beaufort. This society in 1871 established Benedict at Columbia. The school property consisted of eighty acres of land with one main building—"a spacious frame residence," two stories, 65 x 65. This property cost $16,000 with the funds given by Mrs. Benedict, a Baptist lady of New England. During the first year the school had sixty-one students, most of whom were preparing for the ministry.[61] In 1868, Mrs. Rachel C. Mather established the Industrial School at Beaufort which now bears her name. This school came under the auspices of the Women's American Baptist Home Mission Society.

The Freedmen's Aid Society of the Methodist Episcopal Church conducted primary schools at Charleston, Darlington, Sumter, John's Island, Camden, St. Stephens, Gourdins' Station, Midway and Anderson; but, like the Baptists, its substantial contribution was Claflin University. This institution was established in 1869 in the building formerly used by the Orangeburg Female Academy. The property was purchased through the personal efforts of its first president, Dr. A. Webster. The University was granted a charter by the State and named in honor of Hon. Lee Claflin of Massachusetts, by whose liberality it came into existence. The attendance the first year was 309 and by 1872 the institution had a college department, a normal department, a theological department, and a preparatory department.[62] The Women's Home Missionary Society of this same church had the excellent policy of establishing homes for girls where, in addition to purely classroom work, they would be taught the principles of home making and Christian womanhood. In pursuance of this object in 1864 Mrs. Mather of Boston established a school at Camden which in later years became known as the Browning Industrial Home.

[61] American Baptist Home Mission Society, *Annual Report*, 1872, p. 26.
[62] Merriwether, *History of Higher Education in South Carolina*, p. 125; *Annual Report* (1872) *F. A. S.*, p. 17.

The Presbyterian Church, through its Committee of Missions for Freedmen, in 1865 established the Wallingford Academy in Charleston at a cost of $13,500, the Freedmen's Bureau paying about one-half of this amount. In 1870 the number of pupils was 335. In later years this school, like others planted by the churches, was doing creditable secondary work and training teachers for the city and different parts of the State.[63] At Chester in 1868 this Committee established the Brainerd Institute and in the same year the Goodwill Parochial School at Mayesville.

The Protestant Episcopal Freedmen's Commission in cooperation with its South Carolina Board of Missions to Negroes established a school at Charleston (1866) in the Marine Hospital through the effort of Rev. A. Toomer Porter, a native white man of Charleston. Two years later this institution had a corps of thirteen teachers and about six hundred pupils.[64] Smaller efforts were likewise made by this commission at Winnsboro and other parts of the State.

The Friends (Pennsylvania Quakers) made a most valuable contribution to this general educational movement in 1868 through the efforts of Martha Schofield in establishing at Aiken the Schofield Normal and Industrial School. This institution in time became one of the most influential, not only in South Carolina but in the entire South. The Friends' Association of Philadelphia for the Aid and Elevation of the Freedmen, established, in 1865, at Mt. Pleasant (Charleston) the school which later became known as the Laing Normal and Industrial School.[65] Miss Abbey D. Munro, in 1869, became its principal.

DIFFICULTIES AND COMPLICATIONS.

As a result of these efforts an observer said: "In South Carolina where, thirty years ago, the first portentious

---

[63] *Charleston Year Book* (1880), pp. 126–127; *Annual Report* (1870) *Presbyterian Committee*, p. 12.

[64] Porter, *Work of Faith and Love*, p. 6; Stewart, *Work of the Church during Reconstruction*, p. 63.

[65] *Annual Report* (1866) *Friends Ass'n*, p. 8.

rumblings of the coming earthquake were heard and where more recently the volcanic fires of rebellion burst forth . . . our missionaries and teachers have entered to spread their peaceful and healing influence. . . . The Sea Islands have been taken possession of in the name of God and humanity. . . . King Cotton has been dethroned and is now made humbly to serve for the enriching and elevating of the late children of oppression."[66] Another said: "New England can furnish teachers enough to make a New England out of the whole South, and, God helping, we will not pause in our work until the free school system . . . has been established from Maryland to Florida and all along the shores of the Gulf."[67] They came to the South with the firm belief in the capacity of the Negro for mental development and on a scale comparable to the white man. The letters written by teachers to northern friends abound in reports to this effect. Such was the spirit in which the northern societies entered the South.

The northern societies, however, failed "to make a New England out of the South"; but due credit must be given them for their earnestness and enthusiasm. They entered the State while the war was in progress and thus imperiled their lives. The planters at Port Royal who had abandoned their property certainly looked forward to the restoration of the same and to this end they struggled by force of arms. The freedmen themselves, as well as their northern benefactors under these conditions, lived in fear lest the restored planters should successfully reestablish the old regime. One teacher at Mitchelville on Hilton Head reported one week's work as "eventful." A battle only twelve miles away at Byrd's Point was raging while her school was in session. The cannonading could be heard and the smoke of the burning fields was visible.[68]

There were other difficulties. In view of the fact that the missionaries associated with the freedmen in a way totally

[66] *A. M. A. Annual Report* (1864), p. 16.
[67] *Freedmen's Journal*, Jan. 1, 1865, p. 3.
[68] *Ibid.*, p. 7.

unknown to southern tradition, they were met with social ostracism. It was impossible to obtain boarding accommodations in a native white family and in line with the same attitude the lady teachers were frequently greeted with sneers and insults and a general disregard for the courtesies of polite society. One teacher said: "Gentlemen sometimes lift their hats to us, but the ladies always lift their noses."[69]

Social contact with the Negroes, however, was a necessity.[70] The letter of instruction to teachers from the Pennsylvania Branch contained this rule: "All teachers, in addition to their regular work, are encouraged to interest themselves in the moral, religious and social improvement of the families of their pupils; to visit them in their homes; to instruct the women and girls in sewing and domestic economy; to encourage and take part in religious meetings and Sunday schools."[71] Thus it was that a very large part of the activities of the teachers were what we call "extracurricular." They were not confined to the school room but went from house to house.[72]

The spirit of informality which seemed to pervade the whole work, along with that of the Freedmen's Bureau, moreover, serves to explain in part their misfortune resulting from poor business methods. The reports which Howard and Alvord have left us reveal unusually important facts. Their funds were limited and what monies they did raise were not always judiciously expended. The salaries of the teachers usually ranged from $25 to $50 a month. One society paid $35 a month without board and $20 with board. These salaries, the personal danger, the social ostracism and unhealthy climate, all lead one to feel, however, that the motive behind these pioneering efforts was strictly missionary. Some of the teachers worked without a salary and a few even contributed of their means to further the work.

[69] *National Freedman*, Feb., 1866, p. 49.
[70] *Letters from Port Royal; Letters and Diary of Laura M. Towne.*
[71] *Pennsylvania Freedmen's Bulletin*, Oct., 1866, p. 1.
[72] *Baptist Home Mission Monthly* (1879), p. 6.

The campaign of education for the elevation of the freedmen was a product of war time and as such was conducted in the spirit engendered by war conditions. In addition to the purely school exercises of the three R's was the political tenor of the instruction. As staunch Republicans no little allusion was made to "Old Jeff Davis" and the "Rebels." Besides the native songs with which the scholars were so gifted there was frequent singing of *John Brown* and *Marching through Georgia*. The Fourth of July and the first of January were carefully observed as holidays. Several of the teachers in the schools and officers of the Freedmen's Bureau—Tomlinson, Cardoza, Jillson, Mansfield, French, and Scott—became office holders in the Negro-carpetbagger government of 1868.

There was another handicap. The Civil War left South Carolina "Shermanized." The story of this invader's wreck of the State is a familiar one. Barnwell, Buford's Bridge, Blackville, Graham's Station (Sato), Midway, Bamberg, and Orangeburg were all more or less destroyed. Three-fifths of the capital was committed to the flames and Charleston, although this city escaped the invader, had been partially burned already in 1861.[73] With millions of dollars in slave property lost, added to the above, the native whites were in no frame of mind to approve this philanthropic effort of the northern teachers. Furthermore, on the question of education the State had no substantial background by which it could encourage any efforts at this time. Free schools had been established prior to the war, but owing to the eleemosynary stigma attached to them and the permissive character of the legislative acts very little had been accomplished for the whites even, in the sense that we understand public education today.[74]

There ran very high the feeling that the Yankees were fostering social equality and that if they were allowed to educate the freedmen the next thing would be to let them vote.[75] Some reasoned that since the North had liberated

---

[73] *Columbia Phoenix*, March 21, 1865.

[74] Merriwether, *History of Higher Education in South Carolina*, p. 115.

[75] *Hohse Executive Documents*, 39 Cong., 1 Sess., vol. VII, No. 11, p. 13.

the slaves, it was now its business to care for them. It is safe to say that without the protection of the United States military forces during the first year at least the efforts to enlighten the ex-slaves would have been impossible. The native white attitude, however, appears to have undergone a change from year to year and from locality to locality.

At Orangeburg, the superintendent of education reported that a night school was fired into on one or two occasions, and the attempt to discover the perpetrators of this outrage was without success.[76] A. M. Bigelow, a teacher of a colored school at Aiken, was compelled by curses and threats to leave the town in order to save his life.[77] In the town of Walhalla a school conducted by the Methodist church was taught by a lady from Vermont. A number of white men tried to break it up by hiring a drunken vagabond Negro to attend its sessions and accompany the young lady through the village street. The attempted outrage was frustrated only by the intercession of a northern gentleman. At Newberry, about the same time, a man who was building a school for the freedmen was driven by armed men from the hotel where he was staying and his life threatened. These occurrences the superintendent reported as "specimen" cases.[78]

In other sections of the State where the planters sustained amicable relations to all the functions of the Freedmen's Bureau, there was little opposition to the elevation of the freedmen. In the districts of Darlington, Marion, and Williamsburg there was a fair spirit of cordiality. At Darlington the Yankee editor of *The New Era* in its first edition probably thus expressed the feeling of the community: "Let the excellent work be sustained wherever it shall be introduced and the happiest results will be witnessed."[79]

Charleston and Columbia, despite the wreck of these cities, as already shown, proved to be an open field for

[76] J. W. Alvord, *Semi-annual Report* (July 1, 1867), p. 25.
[77] *The Nation*, vol. III, Oct. 25, 1866.
[78] Alvord, *Semi-annual Report* (Jan. 1, 1870), p. 26.
[79] *The New Era*, July 28, 1865.

educational endeavor. In the former city where it was no new thing to see the blacks striving for education, the opposition expressed itself in the occupation of the buildings formerly used for the whites.[80] A correspondent of *The New York Times* reported that in Columbia "the whites extend every possible facility and encouragement in this matter of education."[81] There is one instance of actual initiative in the education of the freedmen in the case of Rev. A. Toomer Porter of the Episcopal Church in Charleston as already mentioned. This gentleman went North to solicit the necessary funds and while there visited Howard and President Johnson. For his purpose the president himself contributed one thousand dollars.[82] For this deed *The Charleston Courier* remarked that it was "a much more substantial and lasting token of friendship to the colored race than all the violent harangues of mad fanatics." Finally in enumerating here and there cases of a favorable attitude, Governor Orr's remarks cannot be overlooked. To the colored people at Charleston he said: "I am prepared to stand by the colored man who is able to read the Declaration of Independence and the Constitution of the United States. I am prepared to give the colored man the privilege of going to the ballot-box and vote."[83]

The length of service for most of the teachers was one year. In the original Port Royal party of March 3, 1862, several of the party returned home before summer. The American Missionary Association which sent thirty-five teachers to Port Royal reported "eight for a short time only." From these facts it is to be inferred, despite the glowing reports of success, that the teachers met with discouragement and disappointment. Some of them were unfit for their duties and some no doubt committed acts of indiscretion with reference to the relationship of the races.

[80] Alvord, *Report*, Aug. 6, 1866, p. 5.
[81] *New York Times*, Aug. 14, 1866.
[82] Porter, *Work of Faith and Love*, p. 6; *The Nation*, vol. II (1866); p. 770.
[83] *Charleston Courier*, Feb. 15, 1867; *American Freedman*, April, 1867, p. 204.

The difficulties and complications of this movement were a part of the war itself. Calmer moments of reflection which it is ours now to enjoy, however, reveal the great value of the educational efforts of the northern missionaries. Unfortunately, the efforts to uplift were directed to only one race, but in a larger sense the work done has been for the welfare of all. South Carolinians to-day will all pay tribute to the work of Abbey D. Munro, Martha Schofield and Laura M. Towne. These women, with others, gave their lives for the elevation of the Negro race and what they did is merely a representation of that common battle against ignorance and race prejudice. "She (Miss Towne) came to a land of doubt and trouble and led the children to fresh horizons and a clearer sky. The school she built is but the symbol of a great influence; there it stands, making the desert blossom and bidding coming generations look up and welcome ever-widening opportunities. Through it she brought hope to a people and gave them the one gift that is beyond all price to men."[84]

SELF–HELP AND LABOR AMONG THE FREEDMEN

Were the Negroes there in such numbers and condition as to help themselves? South Carolina in 1860 had a white population of 291,300, a slave population of 402,406 and a free colored population of 9,914.[85] Having this large number of slaves, the dominant race in its efforts to maintain control passed its police laws by which the evils of slavery existed there in their worst form. One of these laws was that of 1834 which made it a punishable offense to teach any slave to read and write.[86] This law, however, was often violated and free Negroes and even slaves attended school long enough to develop unusual power.

[84] The school referred to here is the one already mentioned, the Penn Normal and Agricultural School. It is an excellent community school and one especially fitted for St. Helena, the population of which is still largely colored. See *United States Bureau of Education Bulletin* (1916), No. 39, p. 483. Miss Towne remained in service 39 years, Miss Schofield 48 years, and Miss Munro at Mt. Pleasant 45 years.

[85] *United States Census*, 1860.

[86] Hurd, *Law of Freedom and Bondage*, II, p. 98.

After generations of oppression the dawn of freedom brought with it a social upheaval. The freedmen now proceeded to taste the forbidden fruit and the people who brought learning to them they received with open arms.[87] The Yankee school master was not only to the freedmen a teacher but his deliverer from bondage. Happily in the enthusiasm of the "late children of oppression" for learning they proved themselves to be not objects of charity but actual supporters and promoters of the educational movement.

It was a principle of some of the societies to open no new school unless a fair proportion of its expenses could be met by the parents of the pupils.[88] There were made various arrangements by which the freedmen could help sustain the schools. In some instances they boarded the teachers and met the incidental expenses of the school while the societies paid the salaries and traveling expenses. In this way nearly one-half of the cost was sustained by them and in some instances nearly two-thirds of it.[89] As the foregoing tables have helped to show in part, in some cases the freedmen met the entire expenses, bought the lot, erected the school house, and paid the salary of the teacher.

During 1866, Tomlinson reported five houses had been built by them and others were under the course of erection. These were located at the following places:

```
Kingstree .................................size 20 x 37 ft.
Darlington ...............................size 30 x 72 ft.
Florence .................................size 35 x 45 ft.
Timmonsville .............................size 14 x 24 ft.
Marion ...................................size 20 x 50 ft.
```

During 1867 twenty-three school houses were reported to have been built by the freedmen aided by the Freedmen's Bureau and northern societies. For the support of school teachers this year they contributed $12,200. This with $5,000 for school houses made an aggregate of $17,200.[90]

[87] *Baptist Home Mission Monthly*, June, 1879, p. 182.
[88] *Freedmen's Record*, April, 1868, p. 50.
[89] Freedmen's Aid Society, *Annual Report* (1871), p. 13.
[90] *H. Ex. Docs.*, 40 Cong., 2 Sess., vol. II, No. 1, p. 8.

The school houses were placed in the hands of trustees selected from among themselves and were to be held permanently for school purposes.[91]

The means by which the freedmen offered their support was not always in cash but in kind. During the early years following the war there was a scarcity of money in circulation. The employers of the blacks, the planters, were themselves unable always to pay in cash, and as a substitute a system of barter grew up.[92] Directing attention to this situation and the general question of self-help, Governor Andrews of Massachusetts, president of the New England Society, sent out the following circular to the freedmen of the South: "The North must furnish money and teachers— the noblest of her sons and daughters to teach your sons and daughters. We ask you to provide for them, wherever possible, school houses and subsistence. Every dollar you thus save us will help to send you another teacher . . . you can supply the teachers' homes with corn, eggs, chickens, milk and many other necessary articles. . . . Work an extra hour to sustain and promote your schools."[93] The value of such labor averaged only about eight dollars a month, but Governor Andrews' recommendation was carried out in so many cases that much good was thereby accomplished.

The campaign of education for the freedmen was temporary in character and was so regarded by the Freedmen's Bureau and the societies. It was merely an effort to place the ex-slaves on their own feet and afterwards it was their task. In line with this policy the Freedmen's Bureau and the military authorities seized every opportunity of instituting self-government among them, especially where they were congregated in large numbers. Such a case was Mitchelville.

Sherman's field order 15 called for the laying aside of

[91] J. W. Alvord, *Report on Schools and Finances of Freedmen*, July, 1866, p. 6.
[92] *American Freedman*, July, 1868, p. 446.
[93] *National Freedman*, Oct., 1865, p. 299.

a vast stretch of territory exclusively for the freedmen. In the same manner in 1864 the military officers at Hilton Head laid out a village for them near the officers' camps and introduced measures of self-government. The village was called Mitchelville in honor of General Ormsby Mitchell who had been like a father to the multitude of fifteen hundred or more occupying the village. The place was regularly organized with a Mayor and Common Council, Marshal, Recorder and Treasurer, all black, and all elected by Negroes, except the Mayor and Treasurer. Among the powers of the Common Council, which concern us here, was the compulsory provision that "every child between the ages of six and fifteen years . . . shall attend school daily, while they are in session, excepting only in cases of sickness . . . and the parents and guardians will be held responsible that said children so attend school, under the penalty of being punished at the discretion of the Council of Administration."[94] We may or may not call this South Carolina's first compulsory school law.

With a view to training teachers from among themselves the northern teachers seized every opportunity to pick out a bright student who would ultimately assume full responsibility. Accordingly, the schools were taught by persons of both races. In addition those Negroes who already had some learning were pressed into service. This arrangement had its obvious disadvantages as well as advantages. The Negro teacher understood the environment and the character and nature of the pupils to a far greater extent than the northern coworker; but, as could be expected, the native teacher was lacking in preparation. As one of the northern journals expressed the situation, the "men and women from the North carry much more than their education. They carry their race, moral training, their faculty, their character, influence of civilization, their ideas, sentiments and principles that characterize northern society."[95] Occasionally native white teachers were employed, but not

---

[94] Whitelaw Reid, *After the War*, pp. 89-91.
[95] *National Freedman*, June, 1866, p. 169.

always to the satisfaction of either the Yankee teachers or their pupils.

Besides the regular organized schools that came under the control of the Freedmen's Bureau and the societies, the freedmen in their eagerness to learn opened what Alvord styles "native schools" where some man or woman who had just learned to read and write a very little set about for the smallest pittance to teach his neighbors' children. Such teaching, though possibly arising from a commendable spirit, was a travesty on education. The white teachers characterized these native schools "so far as any intelligent result goes" as "worse than useless." They would rather receive "their pupils totally ignorant than with the bad habits of reading, pronunciation and spelling of these schools."[96] However, there were among the Negro teachers a few who deserve special mention as showing signs of an endeavor to help the movement and at the same time may serve as a test of the value of the missionary movement by their northern friends.

Some of the Negro teachers were from the North, as in the case of Charlotte S. Forten already mentioned. There was also Mrs. C. M. Hicks who was sent South by the New York Society and supported by an auxiliary association in Albany. Her school was located at Anderson and contained nearly two hundred pupils. After mentioning the good order and decorum of the school, *The Anderson Intelligencer,* a local white paper, says: "We were gratified with the proficiency and success attained and trust that they will persevere in their efforts to make better citizens and become more worthy of the high privileges now granted to the race. This school is presided over by a colored female (Mrs. Hicks) . . . she is intelligent and capable and devotes all her energies to the school."[97]

At Greenville there was Charles Hopkins who taught a school for the support of which his white neighbors con-

[96] *Freedmen's Record,* April, 1868, p. 52.
[97] *Anderson Intelligencer,* July, 1867, quoted in *The American Freedman,* Aug., 1867, p. 264.

tributed $230. He bought at his own risk the building from the State arsenal and moved it two miles on a piece of ground which he had leased for one year. The school opened with about two hundred scholars among whom were "boys and girls with rosy cheeks, blue eyes and flaxen hair, though lately slaves, mingled with the black and brown faces."[98] A visitor characterized the school as having "good order, rapid progress in learning and a great deal more." After supporting the school as long as possible Hopkins was relieved by the Freedmen's Bureau which assumed the responsibility he had incurred, and he was further aided by the accession of three additional teachers. His salary was contributed by the New York Branch. Frank Carter at Camden was making similar efforts during this period.

Down on Hilton Head at Mitchelville in connection with the Port Royal experiment there was Lymus Anders, a full-blooded African, who, prior to the coming of the northern teachers, was unable to read and write. Although fifty years old and having a family, he managed to learn to read by having one of the teachers give him lessons at night and at odd intervals. He was enterprising and after only a year or two had managed to save four or five hundred dollars. He bought land at the tax sales; and, in the efforts of his people at Mitchelville to have churches and schools, he succeeded in erecting a church and a school house with help from the whites and Negroes. The building cost nearly $350 and in time there was added a teachers' home. The school was taught by ladies from Northampton, Massachusetts, who always had the cooperation and assistance of Anders. They characterized him as a "black Yankee," not very moral or scrupulous, but a man who led all the others of his race in enterprise and ambition.[99]

Ned Lloyd White, who had picked up clandestinely a knowledge of reading while still a slave, was an assistant to two ladies at St. Helena, who had a school of ninety-two

[98] *American Freedman*, Feb., 1867, p. 168.
[99] *Letters from Port Royal*, p. 37; *The Freedmen's Journal*, Jan. 1, 1865, pp. 13-15; W. C. Gannet, *North American Review*, vol. CI (1865), p. 24.

pupils made up largely of refugees from a neighboring island. Likewise engaged was "Uncle Cyrus," a man of seventy, who, in company with one Ned, assembled one hundred and fifty children in two schools and taught them the best they could until teachers were provided by the relief societies.[100]

The brightest light among the Negro teachers was F. L. Cardoza. He was a native of Charleston and received his primary and common school education there under the instruction of the free Negroes of that city. Being unable at his own expense to pursue his studies at home as far as he desired, he attended the University of Glasgow. He returned to Charleston and became a leader in the educational affairs of the city immediately at the close of the war. He was employed by the American Missionary Association and became principal of the Saxton School, later known as Avery Institute. In conformity with his classical training, he offered his advanced pupils languages and in time they were ready for Howard University in Washington. There were some four thousand children in the city of school age. Seeing the need of a permanent graded school system supported by public taxation, he used his influence to bring about this result. With regard to this project Governor Orr said: "I heartily approve of the scheme of Mr. Cardoza to educate thoroughly the colored children of Charleston. . . . I am satisfied he will devote himself to the work earnestly and faithfully, and merits, and should receive the confidence of the public in his laudable undertaking." Other public officials spoke in the same vein. One of the northern teachers said of him: "He is the right man in the right place and I am very thankful that it has fallen my lot to be placed under him."[101]

Conclusion

Most of the work of the Bureau and the societies as already shown was temporary in character and perhaps

---

[100] Pierce, in *Atlantic Monthly*, vol. 12 (1863), p. 305.

[101] *A. M. A. Annual Report*, 1866, p. 27; 1867, pp. 32-33; *National Freedman*, May, 1866, p. 142.

rightly so. In Howard's own words, "it was but a beginning—a nucleus—an object lesson." Not more than one-sixth of the total black population of school age was reached. The movement only inaugurated a system of educational pioneering in the benighted South. Scientific data as to exactly what was accomplished unfortunately cannot be obtained owing to the inaccuracy of the Freedmen's Bureau reports. For example, in the report of July 1, 1868, the superintendent gives a total of sixty-two schools in operation with an additional "estimated" number of 451. Again, the amount of work done by the separate individual societies does not always tally with the reports of the Freedmen's Bureau.

Notwithstanding the fact that the efforts put forth failed to reach our modern ideal of the education of all the people, yet the movement did accomplish at least these three things: (1) By penetrating almost every county or district in the State, the schools served to awaken the Negroes to the need of education and to demonstrate to all persons that it was practicable to educate them; (2) it led up to the establishment of the public schools and left for this system material equipment in the form of school buildings and furniture; and (3), greatest of all, the combined efforts of the Freedmen's Bureau and the societies left the State with institutions of higher grade—the principal source of teachers for the common schools.

LUTHER P. JACKSON

THE RELIGION OF THE AMERICAN NEGRO SLAVE: HIS ATTITUDE TOWARD LIFE AND DEATH

I propose to discuss the religious behavior of the American Negro slave, between 1619 and the close of the Civil War, first, by a brief discussion of the religion of the tribes in Africa, and the tendency of the old habits and traditions to maintain themselves among the American slave; second, by a consideration of what the slave found in America, and his contact with another religious culture called Christianity; and third, by a description of the slave's reaction to a Christian environment, or what the slave's religious behavior really was.[1] My thesis is that the religion of Africa disappeared from the consciousness of the American slave; that the slave himself, by contact with a new environment, became a decidedly different person, having a new religion, a primitive Christianity, with the central emphasis, not upon this world, but upon heaven.[2]

[1] This dissertation was submitted to the Faculty of the Graduate School of Arts and Literature of the University of Chicago in candidacy for the degree of Bachelor of Divinity, March, 1921, by Gold Refined Wilson.

[2] Working toward this end, I have examined a vast amount of material on slavery, much of which is controversial, having been written by men who favored slaves, or by abolitionists and slaves who were able to see only one side of the question discussed. Such literature, being biased, so distorts the truth that it is extremely difficult to discover what is social fact. As sources, however, I have used books and magazine-articles, written from a more scientific point of view. There are a few representative ones. Kingsley's *West African Studies*, which, although expressing the attitude of the author, gives us a comprehensive picture of what the life in Africa is. Washington, in the *Story of the Negro*, in a simple, sincere manner, sets forth the struggles of the Negro in his contact with a higher civilization. Woodson's *Education of the Negro prior to 1861* shows to what extent effort was made by the whites to bring the slaves into contact with the white civilization. *The Religious Development of the Negro in Virginia*, by Earnest, shows how the church of the Negro slave, beginning in the church of the whites, grew to be an independent organization. Fragmentary evidence in the histories of the religious denominations shows the same progressive development. A few of the stories of fugitive slaves, though written for other purposes, still speak very clearly of how dependent the slave was upon his cultural surroundings

My task is to show that the religion of the Negro slave between 1619 and the Civil War did not originate in Africa, but was something totally different from the prevailing religion of the black continent in that it placed emphasis upon heaven; and that this distinctive element in the religion of the slave grew out of his contact with Christianity in America. In taking this position I have tried to give due weight to those considerations which tend to support a contrary position, such as the inertia of African habits and traditions in the life of the American slave, and the hostile tendency of his social surroundings to religious development.[3] On the other hand, I have considered the disinte-

for his religious ideas. The stories of the lives of Nat Turner, the Virginia slave insurrectionist, and of *Harriet, the Moses of Her People*, are filled with apocalyptic imagery. Concerning the phenomena of cultural contacts, the most scholarly piece of work yet produced is that by Prof. Park, which shows the tendency of one civilization to accommodate itself to another, by assimilation of concepts, expressed in language and custom. For a study of the religion of the slave, however, the best of all the sources is that spontaneous, naive body of literature consisting of the slave-songs, sometimes called "spirituals," which were sung by individuals upon various occasions, and by shouting groups of religious enthusiasts. Krehbiel, who set many of these primitive verses to printed scales, made of them a psychological interpretation that has given the slave-mood. Colonel T. W. Higginson, the commander of a "black regiment" in South Carolina, during the Civil War, an eyewitness of many of the slave religious meetings, gives the circumstances under which a number of the "spirituals" arose. But Odum, in Volume III of the *Journal of Religious Psychology and Education*, makes of all the classes of slave-songs a psychological interpretation that is unsurpassed. The value of these collections is the common longing found therein, a burning enthusiasm to live in heaven.

[3] In the preparation of this dissertation the following works were used: R. H. Nassau, *Fetichism in West Africa*, 1904; Mary H. Kingsley, *West African Studies* (London, 1901); J. B. Earnest, *The Religious Development of the Negro in Virginia* (Charlottesville, Va., 1914); H. M. Henry, *Slavery in South Carolina* (Emory, Va., 1914); Ivan E. McDougle, *Slavery in Kentucky, 1792–1865* (Reprinted from THE JOURNAL OF NEGRO HISTORY, vol. III, No. 3, July, 1918); H. A. Trexler, *Slavery in Missouri, 1804–1865, Being a Dissertation in Johns Hopkins University Studies* (Baltimore, 1914); J. C. Ballagh, *Slavery in Virginia, Johns Hopkins University Studies, vol. XXIX, 1902* (Baltimore); J. H. Russell, *Free Negro in Virginia, 1619–1865, Johns Hopkins University Studies, Series 31, No. 3* (Baltimore, Johns Hopkins University Press, 1913); J. R. Brackett, *Negro in Maryland* (Baltimore, 1889); G. H. Moore, *Slavery in Massachusetts* (New York, 1866); R. Q. Mallard, *Plantation Life before Emancipation* (Richmond, Virginia, 1892); Frances Anne Kemble, *Journal of a Residence on a Georgian Plantation in 1838–9* (New York, 1863); C. G. Woodson, *The Education of the Negro Prior to 1861* (New York, 1915); *The Journal of Negro History*, edited by C. G. Woodson, vols. I–IV, 1916–1919 (The Association for the Study of Negro Life and History, Inc., Washington, D. C.); Alcee Fortier,

grating effects of the American slave system upon black groups that originated in Africa, together with the American slave's new social contacts, which produced in him the religious attitude found, and out of which arose the early slave-preacher and church. Finally, I have attempted to show that the naive imagery and emphasis in the "spirituals" are selected elements that helped the slave adjust himself to his particular world.

Our beginning is with the prevailing religion of Africa, Fetishism. Authorities use the term "Fetishism" as the "(a) worship of inanimate objects, often regarded as purely African; (b) Negro religion in general; (c) the worship of inanimate objects conceived as the residence of spirits not inseparably bound up with, nor originally connected with, such objects; (d) the doctrine of spirits embodied in, or attached to, or conceiving influence through certain material objects;[4] (e) the use of charms, which are not wor-

History of Louisiana, 4 vols. (New York, 1904); Code Noir, I (Published 1724); M. W. Jernegan, *Slavery and Conversion in the American Colonies* (Reprinted from *The American Historical Review*, vol. XXI, No. 3, April, 1916); G. M. West, *Status of the Negro in Virginia during the Colonial Period* (New York); L. A. Chamerorzow, *Slave Life in Georgia; Narrative of John Brown* (London, 1865); B. T. Washington, *Story of the Negro*, 2 vols. (New York, 1909); *Baptist Annual Register;* A. N. Waterman, *A Century of Caste* (Chicago, 1901); Geo. Thompson, *Prison Life and Reflections*, 3d Edition (Hartford, 1849); Jacobs, *Incidents in the Life of a Slave Girl* (Boston, 1861); Sarah H. Bradford, *Harriet, The Moses of Her People* (New York, 1861); Thos. W. Higginson, *Life of a Black Regiment* (Boston, 1870); Jas. B. Avirett, *The Old Plantation, Great House and Cabin before the War, 1817–65* (New York, Chicago, London, 1901); Jno. S. Abbott, *South and North* (New York, 1860). Lucius P. Little, *Ben Harding, His Times and Contemporaries* (Louisville, 1867); *De Bow's Commercial Review* (New Orleans, 1847); *Life of Josiah Henson* (Boston, 1849); *Baptist Home Missions in America* (New York, 1883); *Presbyterian Magazine*, I (Philadelphia, 1851); *Methodist Magazine*, X (New York, 1827); W. L. Grissom, *History of Methodism in North Carolina, 1772–1805*, vol. I; *Sermons by John Wesley*, 3d Edition, vols. I–II (New York); B. F. Riley, *History of Baptists in Southern States East of Mississippi* (Philadelphia, 1888); John Rankin, *1793–1886, Letters on Slavery* (Boston, 1833); W. G. Hawkins, *Lunsford Lane* (Boston, 1863); Frederick Douglass, *My Bondage and Freedom* (New York, 1857); K. E. R. Pickard, *The Kidnapped and the Ransomed, Recollections of Peter Still and His Wife Vina*, 3d Ed. (Syracuse, 1865); *Fifty Years in Chains, Life of an American Slave* (New York); H. E. Krehbiel, *Afro-American Folk-Songs*, R. E. Park, *Education, Conflicts, and Fusions, American Sociological Society*, vol. XIII (Sept. 3, 1918); *Journal of American Folk-Lore*, vol. XIV (1901), pp. 1–11, vol. XXVII (1914), pp. 241–5, vol. XXIII, p. 435, vol. XXIV, p. 255; *Songs by Thos. P. Fenner;* W. F. Allen, *Slave Songs of the United States* (New York, 1867); *Twenty-two Years Work of Hampton Normal and Agricultural Institute* (Hampton, 1893); T. P. Fenner, *Hampton and its Students by Two of its Teachers, with 50 Cabin and Plantation Songs* (New York, 1875); *American Journal of Religious Psychology and Education*, vol. III, pp. 265–365; *Negro Year-Book;* E. W. Pearson, *Letters from Port Royal* (1916); C. H. Jones, *Instruction of Negro Slave* (1842).

[4] Tylor's *Anthropology*.

shipped, but derive their magical power from a god or spirit; (*f*) the use as charms of objects regarded as magically potent in themselves.''

All of the elements embodied in this definition are found, generally, in the primitive religions of the African peoples. Believing that persons and objects of this world were inhabited by spirits, the African necessarily accounted for the phenomena of the universe by the arbitrary will of spiritual beings, whom he feared, and, therefore, worshipped, or sought to control by magic. Unable thus to find companionship with these unseen, mysterious personalities, the men of Africa knew no land of sunshine beyond the dreadful shadow of the grave; but the American slave, who experienced death as a short period of darkness before a day of eternal glory, did not inherit the fears of Africa.

Now what did the slave bring from Africa? In answering this question let us consider what is commonly referred to as the inertia of African heritage. American missionaries reported that it was harder to teach the slaves who were born in Africa than those born in this country. This quotation from the Calendar of State Papers, Colonial America and West Indies, 1699, Section 473, supports this view: "Negroes born in this country were generally baptized, but for Negroes imported, the gross barbarity and rudeness of their manners, the variety and strangeness of their language, and the weakness and shallowness of their minds rendered it in a manner impossible to attain to any progress in their conversion."[5]

Two definite cases bear a similar testimony, the one being that of Phyllis Wheatley, a girl brought here from Africa, who spoke of how her mother there worshipped the rising sun, the other, this story related by a man concerning his grandfather: "He was an old man, nearly 80 years old," he said, "and he manifested all the fondness for me that I could expect from one so old. . . . He always expressed contempt for his fellow slaves, for when young he was an African of rank. . . . He had singular religious no-

[5] Earnest, p. 28.

tions, never going to meeting, or caring for the preachers he could, if he would, occasionally hear. He retained his native traditions respecting the deity and hereafter."[6]

Other cases, though few, clearly demonstrate that among the American slaves also there existed a belief in ghosts and a lurking fear of the denizens of a mysterious world. But what was religion in Africa was generally regarded by the American slaves themselves as mere superstition.

The hostility of masters to new slave-contacts had some bearing on the situation. Whatever superstition, whether from Africa or another source, we find among the slaves, had a tendency to maintain itself the more because of the attitude of some masters toward the religious education of their bondmen. Slaves of those owners, who, through love of money, were indifferent toward education, encouraged in vice and superstition, had no time for religious training. Although, ever since 1619, and especially after the rebellion of Nat Turner, there were some slaves whose eagerness to learn occasioned State-laws against the education or assembling of slaves, nevertheless, during the entire period there was a countless number of slaves who were absolutely disinterested in their own education. They were also handicapped in religious advancement, because many owners believed that baptism made the slave free, which belief was prevalently held until 1729, when the Christian nations finally reached the decision that baptism did not mean manumission, and that even a Christian could be a slave.[7] Such a sentiment against the contact of slaves with the Christian religion, beyond doubt, tended to keep them in ignorance and superstition, and to develop among them religious habits and attitudes peculiar to an isolated group, but the point can be over-emphasized, in view of all that actually happened.

Dr. Park says: "Coming from all parts of Africa and having no common language, and common tradition, the memories of Africa which they brought with them were

[6] *Fifty Years in Chains*, p. 14.
[7] Jernegan, pp. 506–7.

soon lost. . . . The fact that the Negro brought with him from Africa so little tradition which he was able to transmit and perpetuate on American soil makes that race unique among all peoples of our cosmopolitan population."[8] In connection herewith, moreover, we must also take into account that slave-groups, upon reaching America, were broken up and the members thereof sold into different parts of the country, where new habits had to be formed, because of a different environment. Contrasting the life in Africa with that of slaves in America, Washington better expresses the idea in these words: "The porters, carrying their loads along the narrow forest paths, sing of the loved ones in their far-away homes. In the evening the people of the villages gather around the fire and sing for hours. These songs refer to war, to hunting, and to the spirits that dwell in the deep woods. In them all the wild and primitive life of the people is reflected. . . .

"There is a difference, however, between the music of Africa and that of her transplanted children. There is a new note in the music which had its origin in the Southern plantations, and in this new note the sorrow and the sufferings which came from serving in a strange land find expression."[9]

Let us direct attention to what the Negro slave found in America, a Christian atmosphere. With their various groups broken into fragments and scattered by the American slave-trade, as the slaves here learned the English language, they were more able to assimilate the elements of Christianity found in American life. Sold into Christian homes, but gathered with their masters around the family altar, they became actual participants in the singing and praying that broke the morning and evening silence of those eventful days. The old records show that from the very beginning of American slavery[10] slaves experienced Christianity through the conscious help of some masters, and later,

[8] *Education, Conflicts, and Fusion*, p. 47.
[9] Washington, *Story of the Negro*, pp. 260–261.
[10] Earnest, p. 19.

as the whites saw that the Christian religion made the Negroes better slaves and did not set them free, the blacks secured more favorable opportunities for religious instruction. In some States masters were required even by legislation to look after the religious education of their slaves.[11] In Louisiana, for example, planters were obliged by the Code Noir to have their Negroes instructed and baptized, to give them Sundays and holidays for rest and worship. But, even when not required by law, a few owners established schools for their slaves, and either taught or hired others to teach them "the way of eternal life."

So it is reported that by the 19th century: "Few Negroes escaped some religious instruction from those good people. Usually on Sunday afternoons, but sometimes in the morning, the slaves would be gathered in the great house and lessons in the catechism had to be learned. The Apostles' Creed, the Lord's Prayer, and the Ten Commandments were also taught. Hymns were sung and prayers rose to Heaven. Many good masters read sermons to their slaves. Other masters hired ministers.... Others preached themselves."[12]

Another source of contact with Christianity was that resulting from the attitude of persons who worked, not for the religious development of their own slaves alone, but who, with a larger human interest, unmindful of the benefits that might come to their individual households, gave their lives to bless all slaves. One of the very purposes of American slavery being to benefit the slaves, one can readily see how missionary work among them grew with the system of slavery itself.

"After 1716," Woodson tells us, "when Jesuits were taking over slaves in large numbers, and especially after 1726, when Law's Company was importing many to meet the demand for laborers in Louisiana, we read of more instances of the instruction of Negroes by the Catholics.

---

[11] Woodson, *Education of Negro Prior to 1861*, p. 23.
[12] Earnest, p. 60.
[13] Woodson, *Education of Negro Prior to 1861*, p. 21.

. . . Le Petit spoke of being 'settled to the instruction of the boarders, the girls who live without, and the Negro women.' In 1738 he said, 'I instruct in Christian morals the slaves of our residence, who are Negroes, and as many others as I can get from their masters.' "

Awakened by what the zealous French in Louisiana were doing, English missionaries made progressive plans for preaching the gospel to the blacks. During the 18th century numerous missionaries, catechists, and school-masters, sent from England to America, founded schools for the slaves, and distributed many sermons, lectures, and Bibles among them. In 1705 Thomas counted among his communicants in South Carolina twenty Negroes who could read and write. Later, making a report of the work he and his associates were doing, he said: "I have here presumed to give an account of 1,000 slaves so far as they know of it and are desirous of Christian knowledge and seem willing to prepare themselves for it, in learning to read, for which they redeem the time from their labor. Many of them can read the Bible distinctly, and great numbers of them were learning when I left the province."[14]

"After some opposition," Woodson further says, "this work began to progress somewhat in Virginia. The first school established in that colony was for Indians and Negroes. . . . On the binding out a 'bastard or pauper-child black or white,' churchwardens specifically required that he should be taught 'to read and write and calculate as well as to follow some profitable form of labor.' . . . Reports of an increase in the number of colored communicants came from Accomac County where four or five hundred families were instructing their slaves at home and had their children catechised on Sunday."[15]

Side by side with the work done by missionaries, men of different denominations vied with one another in bringing slaves into the light of a Christian atmosphere. Some founded Sunday schools, some preached of the "inner light

[14] Woodson, *Education of Negro Prior to 1861*, p. 26.
[15] *Ibid.*, p. 29.

in every man," others more successfully preached salvation by faith in the power of a risen Christ, who died for the sins of men. Soon after the first Negroes were placed upon the shores of Jamestown, slaves began to be baptized, and received into the Episcopal Church. Earnest says that "at least one Negro was baptized soon after the contact with the colonists in Virginia."[16] Washington says that only five years after slavery was introduced into Virginia a Negro child named William was baptized, and that from that time on the names of Negroes can be found upon the register of most of the churches. In the old record-book of Bruton Parish, 1,122[17] Negro-baptisms were recorded between 1746 and 1797.[18] In 1809 there were about 9,000 Negro Baptists in Virginia.[19] The African Baptist Church of Richmond alone subsequently increased from 1,000 to 3,832 in 24 years. The Methodist Magazine of October, 1827, reports that as early as 1817 there were 43,411 Negro members in the Methodist societies.[20]

"The Negro seems, from the beginning," says Washington, "to have been very closely associated with the Methodists in the United States. When the Reverend Thomas Coke was ordained by John Wesley, as Superintendent or Bishop of the American Society in 1784, he was accompanied on most of his travels throughout the United States by Harry Hosier, a colored minister who was at the same time the Bishop's servant and an evangelist of the Church. Harry Hosier, who was the first American Negro preacher of the Methodist Church in the United States, was one of the notable characters of his day."[21]

Let us now consider the effects of these early religious contacts upon the life of slave-preachers, some of whom

[16] Earnest, *Religious Development*, p. 17.
[17] *Ibid.*, p. 45.
[18] *Ibid.*, p. 66.
[19] Ballagh, p. 114.
[20] In 1841, there were 500,000 slaves who were church members, or $\frac{1}{5}$ of total number of slaves. 2,000,000 were regular attendants. J. C. Ballagh, p. 114.
[21] *Story of the Negro*, p. 257.

were comparatively well educated. Concerning Jack of
Virginia it is said that "his opinions were respected, his
advice followed, and yet he never betrayed the least symptoms of arrogance or self-conceit. His dwelling was a rude
log-cabin, his apparel was of the plainest, coarsest materials. . . . He refused gifts of better clothing, saying,
'These clothes are a great deal better than are generally
worn by people of my color, and, besides, if I wear them I
find I shall be obliged to think about them even at meetings.' "[22]

With an influence among the slaves equal to Jack's, two
other Negro messengers of the gospel, Andrew Bryan and
Samson, his brother, who earlier had appeared in Georgia,
were publicly whipped and imprisoned with 50 companions,
but they joyously declared that they would suffer death for
their faith found in Christ, whom they expected to preach
until death.[23] By their uncompromising attitude,[24] which
silenced opponents and raised up friends, they won for
themselves among the slaves that sacred esteem belonging
to saintly martyrs like Polycarp, Huss, and Fox.

There were other itinerant ministers in these days, who
were either given their freedom or purchased it by working
as common laborers while preaching. Being better educated, and more closely in contact with the religious life
of the whites than the masses of slaves, they were carriers
of Christian sentiment from the whites to the blacks, in-

[22] *Story of the Negro*, p. 268; Quoted from Ballagh.

[23] Washington, *Story of Negro*, p. 266.

[24] Quite different from the early experiences of Bryan and Samson, who made adversity serve them, the beginning of Jasper's Christian career was greatly aided by his master, a man with a similar conversion and a similar faith in Christ. Using the Bible as the norma of all truth, in his attack upon current scientific knowledge, Jasper impressed all men by his sincere conviction and devout Christian life. A contemporary said of him: "Jasper made an impression upon his generation, because he was sincerely and deeply in earnest in all that he said. No man could talk with him in private, or listen to him from the pulpit, without being thoroughly convinced of that fact. . . . He took the Bible in its literal significance; he accepted it as the inspired Word of God; he trusted it with all his heart and soul and mind; he believed nothing that was in conflict with the teachings of the Bible."—See Washington's *Story of the Negro*, p. 264.

spiring them with the hope of life in an unseen world. One day there arrived in Fayetteville, North Carolina, Henry Evans, a Methodist preacher, a free Negro from Virginia, who worked as a carpenter during the week and preached on Sunday. Forbidden by the Town Council of Fayetteville to preach, he made his meetings secret, changing them from time to time until he was tolerated. Just before his death, while leaning on the altar-rail, he said to his followers:

"I have come to say my last word to you. It is this: None but Christ. Three times I have had my life in jeopardy for preaching the gospel to you. Three times I have broken the ice on the edge of the water and swam across the Cape Fear to preach the gospel to you, and if in my last hour I could trust to that or anything but Christ crucified, for my salvation, all should be lost, and my soul perish forever."[25]

Some of these ministers led an independent movement. Six years after Richard Allen, with a few followers, withdrew in 1790 from the Free African Society in Philadelphia,[26] and started an independent Methodist Church in a blacksmith shop, Negro members of the Methodist Episcopal Church in New York began separate meetings. After pastoring a white church,[27] Josiah Bishop started the First Colored Baptist Church of Portsmouth in 1791. Finding accommodations in the white church of Richmond inadequate, the Negroes petitioned for separate meetings in 1823.[28] Harding, speaking of the opportunity of religious instruction and of divine worship allowed the slaves in Kentucky, says that "in every church-edifice, seats were set apart for the occupancy of colored worshippers. . . . Almost every neighborhood had its Negro preacher whose credentials, if his own assertion was to be taken, came directly from the Lord."[29]

[25] Washington, *Story of the Negro*, pp. 260–1.
[26] *Ibid.*, pp. 254–5.
[27] *Ibid.*, pp. 255–6.
[28] Earnest, p. 72.
[29] *Ben Harding, His Times and Contemporaries*, p. 544.
[30] Earnest, p. 73.

What were the results of these contacts? The most important was that with its charming stories of the creation of the universe, of the Egyptian bondage, and of the journey across the Red Sea, with its New Testament emphasis upon the power, death, and resurrection of Christ, with its apocalyptic imagery, the Bible became to the slave the most sacred book of books. Upon its pages he saw the tears of men and women constantly fall, and from its truths he saw the pious preacher choose words suitable for exhortation. The peculiar interest of the Negro-slave in reading this book was soon apparent.

One old man, being secretly taught by a slave-girl to read the Bible, said, with trembling voice, while tears were falling from his penetrating eyes: "Honey, it 'pears when I can read dis good book I shall be nearer to God."[31] Another slave prayed thus: "I pray de good massa Lord will put it into de niggers' hearts to larn to read de good book. Ah, Lord, make de letters in our spelling books big and plain, and make our eyes bright and shining, and make our hearts big and strong for to larn. . . . Oh, Hebbenly Fader, we tank De for makin' our massas willin' to let us come to dis school."[32]

Upon a battlefield of the Civil War, another, a soldier, said: "Let me lib wid dis musket in one hand an' de Bible in de oder,—dat if I die at de muzzle ob de musket, die in de water, die on de land, I may know I hab de bressed Jesus in my hand an' hab no fear."[33]

How the text from Hebrews 2:9, "That He, by the grace of God, should taste of death for every man," became a part of his life, was told by Josiah Henson after becoming free: "This was the first text of the Bible to which I had ever listened, knowing it to be such. I have never forgotten it, and scarce a day has passed since, in which I have not recalled it, and the sermon that was preached from it. The divine character of Jesus Christ, his life and teach-

---

[31] Jacobs, *Life of a Slave-Girl*, p. 112.
[32] Coffin, p. 60.
[33] Higginson, p. 26.

ings, his sacrifice of himself for others, his death and resurrection were all alluded to, and some of the points were dwelt upon with great power. . . . I was wonderfully impressed, too, with the use which the preacher made of the last words of the text, 'for every man' . . . the bond as well as the free; and he dwelt on the glad tidings of the Gospel to the poor, the persecuted . . . till my heart burned within me, and I was in a state of greatest excitement . . . that such a being . . . should have died for me . . . a poor slave. . . ."[34]

Contemporaries assert that often while following the plow, gathering up the frosty corn, or driving the ox-cart to the barn, slaves, burning with enthusiasm, talked of how much sermons satisfied their hungry souls. Household and plantation slaves, gray-haired fathers and mothers with their children, crowded eagerly to hear the gospel preached. Thus Earnest says of one man: "His slaves came 17 miles to reach Mr. Wright's nearest preaching place."[35] Concerning the spread of the Christian religion among the slaves on the seaboard of South Carolina, it is affirmed that "the scenes on the Sabbath were affecting. The Negroes came in crowds from two parishes. Often have I seen (a scene, I reckon, not often witnessed) groups of them 'double-quicking' in the roads, in order to reach the church in time. . . . The white service being over, the slaves would throng the seats vacated by their masters. . . ."[36] John Thompson, in the story of his life, says that, "As soon as it got among the slaves, it spread from plantation to plantation, until it reached ours, where there were but few who did not experience religion."[37]

From the blighting, superstitious fears of a heartless universe, the heralds of Christianity brought to the slave words of hope and salvation, a message of companionship with a heavenly father. "You are poor slaves and have a

---

[34] Henson, *Life of Josiah Henson*, p. 12.
[35] Earnest, p. 42.
[36] *Plantation Life before Emancipation*, p. 164.
[37] *Life of John Thompson*, p. 19. See *Methodists in N. C.*, p. 238.

hard time of it here," said they, "but I can tell you the blessed Savior shed his blood for you as much as for your masters. . . . Break off from all your wicked ways, your lying, stealing, swearing, drunkenness, and vile lewdness; give yourselves to prayer and repentance and fly to Jesus, and give up your heart to him in true earnest; and flee from the wrath to come."[38]

Fred Douglass relates that "the preaching of a white Methodist minister, named Hanson, was the means of causing me to feel that in God I had such a friend. He thought that all men, great and small, bond and free, were sinners in the sight of God: that they were by nature rebels against his government; and that they must repent of their sins, and be reconciled to God through Christ. . . . I was wretched."[39]

Besides definite principles of morality which included humble submission to the divine right of masters, Negro slaves were also taught that "parents who meet their children in heaven will be more than consoled for their early death." "You can not imagine," said they, "what happiness is in reserve for you from this source. . . . When you have entered heaven you will probably be met by a youthful spirit who will call you father! mother! Perhaps you have a little family there, expecting your arrival . . . save your own soul."[40]

Exactly what was this religion of the slave? Thus coming into contact with this Christian environment, the slave consciously lived a new life, which definitely began with conversion, the phenomenon marked by a feeling of remorse, inner conflict, prayer, and release of tension, or what was felt to be "freedom from hell." Prior to conversion he had been a member of the "disobedient servant-group," perhaps lying, stealing, drinking, and using profanity; but after conversion, being initiated into a new

[38] Earnest, *Religious Development*, p. 54.
[39] *Life of Douglass*, p. 82.
[40] *Presbyterian Magazine* : 1831, p. 27; See vol. 6, pp. 8–9; Woodson, *Education of Negro Prior to 1861*, p. 49; *Sermons of Wesley and Whitefield*.

group, he had to live a circumspect life. Conversion, then, meant to the slave that experience by which he turned his back toward hell and began the journey toward heaven. Very often it signified retiring to some lonely spot, where the slave struggled with an unseen power, until freed by Christ, with whom, no longer a child of fear, he afterwards lived in filial companionship, hopefully asking and joyfully securing aid in an unfriendly world.

"I always had a natural fear of God from my youth," declared one slave, describing his feelings leading up to conversion, "and was often checked in conscience with thoughts of death, which barred me from my sins and bad company. I knew no other way at that time to hope for salvation but only in the performance of my good works. . . . If it was the will of God to cut me off at that time, I was sure I should be found in hell, as sure as God was in heaven. I saw my condemnation in my own heart, and I found no way which I could escape the damnation of hell, only through the merits of my dying Lord and Savior Jesus Christ; which caused me to make intercession with Christ, for the salvation of my poor immortal soul. . . . After this I declared before the congregation of believers the work which God had done for my soul."[41]

The slaves used to express it thus in song:[42]

> "One day when I was walkin' along,
> De element opened, an' de love came down,
> I never shall forget dat day,
> When Jesus washed my sins away."

They also sang such words as these:[43]

> "Jesus snatched me from de doors of hell,
> An' took me in with him to dwell."
> "Jesus told you . . . go in peace an' sin no mo'."
> "Soul done anchored in Jesus Christ."

With reference to the wilderness, where, without food, they overcame the spirit of evil by the aid of Jesus, and

[41] *Journal of Negro History*, vol. I, p. 70.
[42] *Twenty-two Years Work at Hampton*.
[43] *Journal of Religious Psychology and Education*, vol. 3, pp. 290-1.

with reference to the life led after having this experience, the slaves sang with much feeling:[44]

"All true children gwine in de wilderness,
Gwine in de wilderness, gwine in de wilderness,
True believers gwine in de wilderness,
To take away de sins ob de world."

"Stay in the field, stay in the field, stay in the field, till de war is ended." [45]

"You say your Jesus set-a you free;
View de land, view de land,
Why don't you let-a your neighbor be,
Go view de heavenly land.
You say you're aiming for de skies,
Why don't you stop-a your telling lies?" [46]

Another ceremonial feature of slave-conversion was the shout, in which the prospective convert, upon the "mourners' bench," surrounded by a group of singing dancers, prayed continually, until convinced of perfect relief from damnation, when he leaped and ran to proclaim the joyous news. When shouting, whether for making converts or for mere group-response, these noisy, black singers of antiphonal songs preferred to be alone in some cabin or in the praise-house, where they could express themselves with absolute freedom.

Just how they disturbed the peace is expressed in the following words: "Almost every night there is a meeting of these noisy, frantic worshippers. . . . Midnight! Is that the season for religious convocation? . . . is that the accepted time?"[47] Concerning worship by a light-wood fire another said: "But the benches are pushed back to the wall when the formal meeting is over, and old and young, men and women . . . begin, first walking and by and by shuffling around, one after the other, in a ring. The foot is hardly taken from the floor and the progression is mainly due to a jerking, hitching motion

[44] Higginson, *Life of a Black Regiment*, p. 133.
[45] *Twenty-two Years at Hampton.*
[46] *Hampton and its Students*, p. 182.
[47] Henry, p. 141.

which agitates the entire shouter and soon brings out streams of perspiration. Sometimes they dance silently; sometimes as they shuffle they sing the course of the spiritual, and sometimes the song itself is also sung by the dancers. But more frequently a band, composed of some of the best singers and of tired shouters, stand at the side of the room to 'face' the others singing the body of the song and dropping their hands together or on their knees. Song and dance are alike extremely energetic and often, when the shout lasts into the middle of the night, the monotonous thud, thud of the feet prevents sleep within half a mile of the praise-house.''[48]

"And all night, as I waked at intervals, I could hear them praying and 'shouting' and chattering with hands and heels," relates Colonel T. W. Higginson. "It seemed to make them very happy, and appeared to be at least an innocent Christian dissipation . . . the dusky figures moved in the rythmical barbaric dance the Negroes called a 'shout,' chanting, often harshly, but always in the most perfect time, some monotonous refrain."[49]

"By this time every man within hearing, from oldest to youngest, would be wriggling and shuffling, as if through some piper's bewitchment; for even those who at first affected contemptuous indifference would be drawn into the vortex ere long."[50]

Whatever may be said about the "shout," the fact remains, that whether this ceremony was mere play, or relaxation after a day of repressing toil, or whether it served to drive away a hostile spirit by creating within the members of the group the feeling of being possessed with the power of God, it became an indispensable part of the slave religious worship. In this Christian dance, the slave sang:

[48] *Life of Black Regiment*, by Higginson, pp. 51-2.
[49] *Ibid.*, pp. 35, 198.
[50] My position is that the shout was a natural and spontaneous creation of group-phenomena. It differed from the whites' behavior in ceremonial emphasis. Neither the shout nor the antiphonal song was brought from Africa. The real religious significance of both, however, is not in external behavior, but in content.

"O shout, shout, de debbil is about, O shut yo' do' an' keep him out." Through it he expected to destroy the kingdom of Satan, and thereby make the assurance of reaching heaven more complete. The feeling gained thereby became spiritual balm for the aches of by-gone and coming days.[51]

The songs, also, used by the slave in these meetings and sung generally by the individuals thereof, tell in a very definite way what the religious attitude of the American Negro slave was. They relate the sorrows of this world, and the joys felt by the slave, who anticipated a home in heaven. They describe in naive imagery the rugged journey of the weary traveler and the land of his happy destination. "Nothing," says Washington, "tells more truly what the Negro's life in slavery was, than the songs in which he succeeded, sometimes, in expressing his deepest thoughts and feelings. What, for example, could express more eloquently the feelings of despair which sometimes overtook the slave than these simple and expressive words:[52] " 'O Lord, O my Lord! O my good Lord! keep me from sinking down.'"

Unable to sing or pray during the lifetime of their master, after his death, by permission of their mistress, a crowd of Negro slaves sang the following hymn:

> "Oh walk togedder, children,
> Don't yer get weary,
> Walk togedder, children,
> Don't yer get weary,
> Walk togedder, children,
> Don't yer get weary,
> Dere's a great camp meetin' in de Promised Land.
> Gwine to mourn an' nebber tire . . .
> Mourn an' nebber tire,
> Mourn an' nebber tire,
> Dere's a great camp meetin' in de Promised Land."[53]

With longing for that mother who used to carry him upon her back to the dewy fields, where she, setting her babe upon the springing grass at the end of the row, began

[51] *Am. J. Rel. Psy. and Ed.*, 3: 287.
[52] *Story of the Negro*, p. 260.
[53] Fenner, *Hampton and its Students*, p. 223.

her daily task with the hoe, returning now and then to give him of her breast; for her whose beaming eyes turned back until the coming of the night, when she again held him in her arms, the slave sang in bitter tears. Her tender help was gone. Father's smile was no more.[54]

> "My mother's sick an' my father's dead,
> Got nowhere to lay my weary head."

> "My mother an' my father both are dead . . .
> Good Lord, I cannot stay here by myself.
> I'm er pore little orphan chile in de worl',
> I'm er pore little orphan chile in de worl' . . ."[55]

> "My mother'n yo' mother both daid an' gone,
> "My mother'n yo' mother both daid an' gone,
> Po' sinner man he so hard to believe.
> My folks an' yo' folks both daid an' gone,
> Po' sinner man he so hard to believe.
> My brother an' yo' brother both daid an' gone,
> Po' sinner man he so hard to believe."[56]

With great hope the slave sang:

> "Gwine to see my mother some o' dese mornin's,
> See my mother some o' dese mornin's,
> See my mother some o' dese mornin's,
> Look away in de heaven,
> Look away in de heaven, Lord,
> Hope I'll jine de band.
> Look away in de heaven, Lord,
> Hope I'll jine de band."[57]

To express his sorrow and his longing for relief from the burdens of his condition the slave sang:

> "One more valient soldier here,
> One more valient soldier here,
> One more valient soldier here,
> To help me bear de cross."[58]

---

[54] *Am. J. Rel. Psy. and Ed.*, 3: 303.
[55] *Ibid.*, 340.
[56] *Ibid.*, 3: 321.
[57] Fenner, *Hampton and its Students*, p. 190.
[58] Higginson, *Black Regiment of South Carolina*, 200-1.

"My trouble is hard,
O yes,
My trouble is hard,
O yes,
Yes indeed my trouble is hard." [59]

"Nobody knows the trouble I've seen,
Nobody knows but Jesus.
Nobody knows the trouble I've seen,
Glory halleluyah!
Sometimes I'm up, sometimes I'm down!
O yes, Lord!
Sometimes I'm almost to de groun'!
O yes, Lord!
What makes old Satan hate me so?
O yes, Lord,
Because he got me once, but he let me go;
O yes, Lord!" [60]

"Ever since my Lord done set me free,
Dis ole worl' been a hell to me,
I am de light un de worl'." [61]

"Oh, what a hard time,
Oh, what a hard time,
Oh, what a hard time,
All God's children have a hard time.

"Oh, what a hard time,
Oh, what a hard time,
Oh, what a hard time,
My Lord had a hard time too." [62]

"I'm a-trouble in de mind,
O I'm a-trouble in de mind.
I'm a-trouble in de mind,
What you doubt for?
I'm a-trouble in de mind." [63]

"I'm in trouble, Lord,
I'm in trouble.
I'm in trouble, Lord,
Trouble about my grave,
Trouble about my grave,
Trouble about my grave.

[59] *Am. J. Rel. Psy. and Ed.*, 3: 351.
[60] Krehbiel, p. 75.
[61] *Am. J. Relig. Psy. and Ed.*, 3: 304.
[62] *Ibid.*, 320.
[63] Allen, 30–1.

> Sometimes I weep, sometimes I mourn,
> I'm in trouble about my grave;
> Sometimes I can't do neither one,
> I'm in trouble about my grave." [64]

> "My father, how long,
> My father, how long,
> My father, how long,
> Poor sinner suffer here?
> And it won't be long,
> And it won't be long,
> And it won't be long,
> Poor sinner suffer here.
> We'll soon be free,
> De Lord will call us home.
> We'll walk de miry road
> Where pleasure never dies.
> We'll walk de golden streets
> Of de new Jerusalem . . .
> We'll fight for liberty
> When de Lord will call us home." [65]

> "Gwine rock trubbel over,
> I b'lieve,
> Rock trubbel over,
> I b'lieve,
> Dat Sabbath has no end." [66]

> "My fader's done wid de trouble o' de world,
> Wid de trouble o' de world,
> Wid de trouble o' de world,
> My fader's done wid de trouble o' de world,
> Outshine de sun." [67]

Although the songs above tell the slave's dissatisfaction with the present world, there are other songs that relate his definite experiences of joy arising from a feeling of triumph over this world of sorrow by assurances of a future world of bliss. Some of these songs of joy are the following:

> "I started home, but I did pray,
> An' I met ole Satan on de way;
> Ole Satan made a one grab at me,
> But he missed my soul, an' I went free.

[64] Allen, *Slave Songs*, 113, p. 94.
[65] *Ibid.*, 112, p. 93.
[66] *Am. J. Relig. Psy. and Ed.*, 3: 304.
[67] Allen, *Slave Songs*, 124, p. 101.

My sins went a-lumberin' down to hell,
An' my soul went a-leapin' up Zion's hill." [68]

"Ole Satan's church is here below.
Up to God's free church I hope to go.
Cry Amen, cry Amen, cry Amen to God!" [69]

"I'm so glad, so glad;
I'm so glad, so glad,
Glad I got religion, so glad,
Glad I got religion, so glad.
I'm so glad, so glad;
I'm so glad, so glad,
Glad I bin' changed, so glad,
Glad I bin' changed, so glad." [70]

"My brudder have a seat and I so glad,
Good news member, good news;
My brudder have a seat and I so glad,
And I heard from heav'n today." [71]

"Brudder, guide me home, an' I am glad,
Bright angels biddy me to come;
Brudder, guide me home, an' I am glad,
Bright angels biddy me to come.
What a happy time, chil'n,
What a happy time, chil'n,
What a happy time, chil'n,
Bright angels biddy me to come.
Let's go to God, chil'n,
Bright angels biddy me to come." [72]

"I jus' got home f'um Jordan,
I jus' got home f'um Jordan,
I jus' got home f'um Jordan,
'Ligion's so—o—o sweet.
My work is done an' I mus' go,
My work is done an' I mus' go,
My work is done an' I mus' go,
'Ligion's so—o—o sweet." [73]

"Shout an' pray both night an' day;
How can you die, you in de Lord?
Come on, chil'n, let's go home;
O I'm so glad you're in de Lord." [74]

---

[68] *Am. J. Relig. Psy. and Ed.*, 3: 288.
[69] Jacobs, p. 109.
[70] *Am. J. Relig. Psy. and Ed.*, 3: 309.
[71] Allen, *Slave Songs*, 120, p. 98.
[72] *Ibid.*, 107, p. 86.
[73] *Am. J. Relig. Psy. and Ed.*, 3: 365.
[74] Allen, *Slave Songs*, 80, p. 60.

"Little children, then won't you be glad,
Little children, then won't you be glad,
That you have been to heav'n, an' you gwine to go again,
For to try on the long white robe, children,
For to try on the long white robe." [75]

Even a slave, when dying, cried: "I am going home! Oh, how glad I am!" [76] The following hymns also vividly set forth what happy anxiety the slave felt about his journey "home."

"Gwine to weep, gwine to mourn,
Gwine to get up early in de morn,
Fo' my soul's goin' to heaven jes' sho's you born,
Brother Gabriel goin' ter blow his horn.
Goin' to sing, goin' to pray,
Goin' to pack all my things away,
Fo' my soul's goin' to heaven jes' sho's you born,
Brother Gabriel gwine ter blow his horn." [77]

"I want to go to Canaan,
I want to go to Canaan,
I want to go to Canaan,
To meet 'em at de comin' day." [78]

"I'm goin' home fer to see my Lord,
Bear yo' burden, sinner,
An' don't you wish you could go 'long
Bear yo' burden, let in the heat." [79]

"Oh, my mudder's in de road,
Most done trabelling;
My mudder's in de road,
Most done trabelling,
My mudder's in de road,
Most done trabelling,
I'm bound to carry my soul to de Lord." [80]

"Run, Mary, run,
Run, Mary, run,
Oh, run, Mary, run,
I know de oder worl' 'm not like dis.
Fire in de east an' fire in de west,
I know de oder worl' 'm not like dis,
Bound to burn de wilderness,

[75] Allen, *Slave Songs*, 108, p. 87.
[76] *Plantation Life Before Emancipation*, p. 168.
[77] *Am. J. Relig. Psy. and Ed.*, 3: 331.
[78] Atlantic Monthly, 19: 687.
[79] *Am. J. Relig. Psy. and Ed.*, 3: 317.
[80] Fenner, *Hampton and its Students*, p. 215.

I know de oder worl' 'm not like dis.
Jordan's ribber is a ribber to cross,
I know de oder worl' 'm not like dis,
Stretch your rod an' come across,
I know de oder worl' 'm not like dis.'' [81]

"We will march through the valley in peace,
We will march through the valley in peace;
If Jesus himself be our leader,
We will march through the valley in peace.'' [82]

"My sister's goin' to heaven fer to see my Lord,
To see my Lord, to see my Lord;
Well, my sister's goin' to heaven, to see my Lord,
What's de onbelievin' soul?'' [83]

"Bend-in' knees a-ach-in'
Body racked wid pain,
I wish I was a child of God,
I'd git home bim-by.
Keep prayin; I do believe
We're a long time waggin o' de crossin,
Keep prayin; I do believe
We'll git home to heaven bim-by.
O yonder's my old mudder,
Been a-waggin' at the hill so long;
It's about time she cross over,
Git home bim-by.
O hear dat lumerin' thunder
A-roll from do' to do',
A-callin' de people home to God;
Dey'll git home bim-by.'' [84]

"When the roll is called up yonder,
I'll be there.
By the grace of God up yonder,
I'll be there.
Yes my home is way up yonder,
An' I'll be there.
I got a mother way up yonder,
I'll be there.
I got a sister way up yonder,
I'll be there.'' [85]

Although this world was a hell to the slave, still he could

[81] Fenner, *Hampton and Its Students*, p. 188.
[82] Allen, *Slave Songs*, p. 73.
[83] *Am. J. Relig. Psy. and Ed.*, 3: 334.
[84] Krehbiel, p. 99.
[85] *Am. J. Relig. Psy. and Ed.*, 3: 362.

wait here with patience until the time of death, after which he would see the real home of his inner longing. To the slave heaven was a beautiful, comfortable place beyond the sky. It had golden streets and a sea of glass, upon which angels danced and sang in praise to Him upon the golden throne. There was no sun to burn one in that bright land of never-ending Sabbath. There kindred and friends reunited in the happiest relationships. The slave was poor, hampered, and sorrowful in this world; but in that world above, whose glory falling stars and melting elements would signify in the day of judgment, he would be rich and free to sing, shout, walk, and fly about carrying the news. There he would know no tears or the sorrow of parting, but only rest from toil and care, in the delightful companionship of the heavenly groups.

> "Dere's no rain to wet you,
> O, yes, I want to go home.
> Dere's no sun to burn you,
> O, yes, I want to go home.
> O, push along believers,
> O, yes, I want to go home.
> Dere's no hard trials,
> O, yes, I want to go home.
> Dere's no whips a crackin'
> O, yes, I want to go home."[86]

> "Oh de hebben is shinin', shinin',
> O Lord, de hebben is shinin' full ob love.
> Oh, Fare-you-well, friends,
> I'm gwine to tell you all,
> Gwine to leave you all a-mine eyes to close;
> De hebben is shinin' full ob love."[87]

> "How sweet a Sabbath thus to spend,
> In hope of one that ne'er shall end."[88]

> "Yes my mother's goin' to heaven to outshin the sun,
> An it's way beyon' the moon."[89]

[86] Atlantic Monthly, XIX, 687.
[87] Fenner, *Hampton and Its Students*, p. 219.
[88] *Am. J. Rel. Psy. and Ed.*, 3: 279.
[89] *Ibid.*, 337.

"Po' man goin' to heaven,
   Rich man goin' to hell,
   For Po' man got his starry crown,
   Rich man got his wealth." [90]

"Well there are sinners here and sinners there,
   An' there are sinners everywhere,
   But I thank God that God declare,
   That there ain't no sinners in heaven." [91]

O join on, join my Lord,
   Join de heaven wid the angels;
   O join on, join my Lord,
   Join de heaven wid de angels." [92]

"I'm gwin to keep a climbin' high
   Till I meet dem angels in de sky.
   Dem pooty angels I shall see—
   Why doan de debbil let a me be?
   O when I git to heaven goin sit an' tell,
   Three archangels gwin er ring dem bells
   Two white angels come a walkin' down,
   Long white robes an' starry crown.
   What's dat yonder, dat I see?
   Big tall angels comin' after me." [93]

The following spirituals emphasize what the slave felt that he would do in heaven.

"Heaven, heaven,
   Everybody talkin' bout heaven an' goin' there
   Heaven, heaven,
   Goin' to shine all 'round God's heaven." [94]

"Oh, I wish I was there,
   To hear my Jesus' orders,
   Oh, how I wish I was there, Lord,
   To wear my starry crown." [95]

"A golden band all 'round my waist,
   An' de palms of victory in-a my hand,
   An' de golden slippers on to my feet,
   Gwine to walk up and down o' dem golden street.

[b] *Am. J. Rel. Psy. and Ed.*, 336.
[91] *Ibid.*, 328.
[92] *Ibid.*, 332.
[93] *Ibid.*, 298.
[94] *Ibid.*, 328.
[95] *Life before Emancipation*, p. 163.

Oh, wait till I put on my robe.
An' a golden crown-a placed on-a my head,
An' my long white robe a-com a dazzlin' down,
Now wait till I get on my gospel shoes,
Gwine to walk about de heaven an' a-carry de news,
Oh, wait till I put on my robe."[96]

"You can hinder me here but you can't hinder me dere
For de Lord in Heaven gwin' hear my prayer.
De evening's great but my Cap'n is strong,
U'm fightin' fer de city an' de time ain't long."[97]

"Well, my mother's goin' to heaven,
She's goin' to outshine the sun, O Lord,
Well, my mother's goin' to heaven,
She's going to outshine the sun, O Lord,
Yes, my mother's goin' to heaven to outshine the sun,
An' its way beyon' the moon.
The crown that my Jesus give me,
Goin' outshine the sun,
You got a home in the promise lan',
Goin' outshine the sun,
Goin' to put on my crown in glory,
An' outshine the sun, O Lord.
'Way beyon' de moon."[98]

"Gwine hab happy meetin',
Gwine shout in hebben,
Gwine shout an' nebber tire,
O slap yo' han's chilluns,
I feels de spirit movin',
O now I'm gittin' happy."[99]

"Gwine to march a-way in de gold band,
In de army bye-and-bye;
Gwine to march a-way in de gold band,
In de army by-and-bye.
Sinner, what you gwine to do dat day?
Sinner, what you gwine to do dat day?
When de fire's a-rolling behind you,
In de army bye-and-bye.
Sister Mary gwine to hand down the robe,
In the army bye-and-bye;
Gwine to hand down the robe and the gold band,
In the army, bye-and-bye."[100]

[96] *Hampton and its Students*, p. 187.
[97] *Am. J. Relig. Psy. and Ed.*, 3: 323.
[98] *Ibid.*, 337.
[99] *Ibid.*, 299.
[100] Allen, *Slave Songs*, Song 103, p. 83.

> "You got a robe, I got a robe,
> All God's children got a robe,
> Goin' try on my robe an' if it fits me,
> Goin' to wear it all round God's heaven."[101]

> "We'll walk up an' down dem golden streets,
> We'll walk about Zion.
> Gwine sit in de kingdom,
> I really do believe, where sabbath have no end.
> Look way in de heaven—hope I'll jine de band,—
> Sittin' in de kingdom.
> I done been to heaven an' I done been tried.
> Dere's a long white robe in de heaven for me,
> Dere's a golden crown, golden harp, starry crown, silver slippers,
> In de heaven for me I know."[102]

> "I want to go to heaven when I die,
> To shout salvation as I fly.
> You say yer aiming fer de skies,
> Why don't yer quit yer tellin' lies.
> I hope I git dere bye-an' bye,
> To jine de number in de sky.
> When I git to heaven gwine to ease, ease,
> Me an' my God goin' do as we please,
> Sittin' down side o' de holy Lamb.
> When I git to heaven goin' set right down,
> Gwiner ask my Lord fer starry crown.
> Now wait till I gits my gospel shoes,
> Gwin-er walk 'bout heaven an' carry de news."[103]

A boy of ten, being sold from his mother, said,

> "I'm gwine to sit down at the welcome table,
> Den my little soul's gwine to shine.
> I'm gwine to feast off milk and honey,
> Den my little soul's gwine to shine.
> I'm gwine to tell God how-a you sarved me,
> Den my little soul's gwine to shine."[104]

The place that heaven must have had in the attitude of the slave we shall now consider, by an examination of the slave's mental world. To do so we must feel the hand of slavery holding him in subjection to the will of the master.

[101] *Am. J. Relig. Psy. and Ed.*, 3: 328.
[102] *Ibid.*, 294.
[103] *Ibid.*, 293.
[104] *Hampton and its Students*, p. 173.

The inner voices that called the black slave at his task, clothed in simple garb, and living on homely fare, we also must hear speaking to us, and invoking the same response. Then we shall be able to appreciate the religious significance of the situations.

The bell upon the white pole in the great-house yard summons the slaves to their daily tasks in the fields. Quickly, the slave-mother, rising from the cabin-floor, and taking her babe upon her back, sets out to join the crowd. With brawny arms around his mother's neck, the young child glares at the red rising of the sun, until he is left at the end of the row. Then as mother's hoe cuts grass from the tender corn, he hears her foot-steps blend with those of the plowman, her voice of love mingle with the mumble of slaves, and the songs of birds, that play in the warm sunlight of the morning. With longing eyes the child watches her who, last night, when her work was done, fed him from her breast, as she sat upon the cabin-floor, murmuring of a better world, where child and mother would know no weary sun. Sitting upon the green grass that fringes the end of the long rows, he watches her toiling, disappearing into the distance.

Taken from his mother at the age of seven, the child is transferred to the great-house yard, where the harsh voices of slave-children, conscious of their lot, fill the air. Yesterday he sat in the cabin-door, upon grandmother's knee, listening to the grinding of the big mill down by the pond, and watching the squirrels drop acorns from the old oak tree. Last night he opened the door for father, who, worn from being away so long, brought few potatoes and corn. Then there was a great time. Father, in overalls, grandmother with a "slat-bonnet" upon her gray head, mother with a "grass-sack" around her waist, all knelt upon their knees in prayer to God above, father leading mournfully. "Get up in heaven by-and-by," he said, until all were filled with joy. How different things are today. The old mill by the pond is now seen lifting its white, bird-like wings into heaven, where mother, father and grandmother may be. They may be up there in the sunlight, singing and shouting with the angels.

The dawn of another day comes in the life of the slave. Now all must help kill the "fatted hogs." The knives have been sharpened, the scaffolds built, the ashes brought up from the ash-heap. The slaves are gathered around the fire, warming themselves and waiting for the water in the big black pots to boil. They hear the shrill voice of the cock and the noise of the mules heralding the coming of day, when the presence of old master will stop their friendly discussions. While fading stars twinkle in the pines that cast ghost-like shadows upon the white-washed cabins, the slaves talk of their religious experiences, how they "overcame the devil in the wilderness" through the help of Christ. The stars were shining thus a year ago, when Aunt Lucinda died. She had been a good woman, never receiving a flogging. She used to make cakes for the neighbors and tell them when to plant their crops. When she died a bright star, like an angel, lit upon the cabin-roof, to take her soul away. This morning she is in heaven, wearing golden slippers, long, white robe, and starry crown, about which she used to sing in the camp-meetings.

The big hogs killed and put into the "smoke-house" and the coming of night ending the slave's work, he is now allowed to attend the camp-meeting, in the log-house, down by the side of the river, that lies behind the big woods. In the leaves of the old red oak, that stands upon the shore and that is said to be the place of ghosts, he hears the noise of the wood owl, calling to him, as he takes his boat and glides silently away amid the solemn shadows that lie upon the deep, moon-lit waters. Unconsciously he sings the words of his comrades as they marched last night to the grave-yard:

> "I know moon-rise;
> I know star-rise;
> Lay dis body down
> I march to the grave-yard,

> I march through the grave-yard
> Lay dis body down
> I lay in de grave-yard and stretch out my arms,
> Lay, dis body down."

At the meeting-house, not only does he sing and shout, but each slave for some sinner-friend or relative who has been sold away, sincerely asks the prayers of the other. There parent prays for child and child for parent. "Sister Martha," dressed in gingham, is there, that gray-haired woman, who goes each day to the river, hoping that some message may come floating from her "Tom." She is there to weep and to rejoice and to talk with "Brother Robert" about the cross of Christ. The slaves, singing and shouting, tearfully kiss each other's cheek, shake hands, and part. They were there to worship and not to play.

Inevitable then is the conclusion that the religion of the American slaves was decidedly different from the prevailing religion found among the peoples of Africa. We saw that fetishism was the prevailing religion found in Africa; that the few American slaves who maintained any of their African religious heritage were considered grossly superstitious by the American slaves generally; that the slave-groups brought to America from Africa were so broken up and scattered that the old group-habits did not continue to exist. We found on the other hand that the slaves of America, who were in contact with Christianity, became very enthusiastic over the Christian religion; that they developed a sorrow for this world and a joyous longing for heaven, as they showed by their shouts and songs. This emphasis upon a place of rest in heaven, we conclude, helped the American slave adjust himself to his particular environment. As it helped him to live, so it helped him also to die.

G. R. WILSON.

PRUDENCE CRANDALL

Prior to the Civil War, education for the American of color, was for the most part surreptitiously obtained. There were, however, a few fearless men and women of the white race, who, endowed with a magnanimous spirit and indomitable will, rose above the sordid plane of self-advancement and comfort, brooked the tide of social ostracism and censure to a realm of true altruism in behalf of the circumstantially weak and defenseless race.

Many of these noted benefactors belonged to that sect known in American history as Friends. True to their noble heritage, they faced the facts of social crises with intrepidity and strong convictions. They acted with unerring judgment and penetrating vision upon those principles sacred to the life and happiness of all mankind. In the vanguard of this honorable group, of martyrs to the cause of justice, stands an American school teacher, born of Quaker parentage, at Hopkinton, Rhode Island, September 3, 1803—Prudence Crandall. The noble purpose and sympathetic nature of this great teacher are clearly demonstrated in this extract from a letter addressed to William Lloyd Garrison, January 18th, 1833:[1]

"Now I will tell you why I write you, and the object is this: I wish to know your opinion respecting changing white scolars for colored ones. I have been for some months past determined if possible during the remaining part of my life to benefit the people of color. I do not dare tell any one of my neighbors anything about the contemplated change in my school and I beg of you, sir, that you will not expose it to any one; for if it was known, I have no reason to expect but it would ruin my present school. Will you be so kind as to write by the next mail and give me your opinion on the subject.

"Yours, with greatest respect,

"PRUDENCE CRANDALL."[2]

[1] Garrison's *Garrison*, I, Chap. X, p. 315; B. C. Steiner's *History of Slavery in Connecticut* (*Johns Hopkins University Studies*, XI, 415–422).
[2] May's *Antislavery Conflict*.

This letter shows clearly that Prudence Crandall foresaw that any undertaking of an educational nature in behalf of Negroes would meet with opposition, require personal sacrifices, and demand unfaltering courage and patience.

That she was willing to undergo these tests was proved when a young Negro girl applied for admission to the school which she was then conducting for white girls only. This ambitious pupil of color was Sarah Harris, seventeen years old, the daughter of a respectable man who owned a small farm near the village of Canterbury. Sarah had attended the same district school in which the majority of Prudence Crandall's students had received their elementary training and had proved herself a bright scholar and a pious young lady. So deeply impressed was the teacher with this girl's plea and her earnest desire to get a broader education to teach other girls of color, that Prudence Crandall admitted Sarah to her school.

The students themselves offered no opposition nor manifested any objection to her presence. Parents, however, began to complain and informed Prudence Crandall that her school would not be supported if she kept the Negro girl as a student. To this threat Prudence Crandall replied: "It might sink then for I should not turn her out." Soon the white girls began to leave the school, but the philanthropic teacher was determined to adhere to the principles of democratic education. She finally gave up the teaching of white girls entirely and brought a number of Negro children into her school, then situated in the most aristocratic part of the town of Canterbury. "If the Canterbury people," said Ellen D. Larned, "had quietly accepted the situation and left them in peace the difficulty would soon have ended. Even if the children had remained they would have given them little annoyance. Twenty Indian lads were received into Plainfield Academy a few years later, and few outside of the village even heard of them."[3]

---

[3] *Johns Hopkins University, Studies in Historical and Political Science,* XI, p. 417. Larned's *Windham County,* p. 493.

This step, however, aroused the most intense feeling of the town people and met with strong and immediate opposition. A committee of four of the chief men of the village, Adams, Frost, Fenner and Harris, visited Prudence Crandall and attempted to show her that such an undertaking was decidedly objectionable and seriously detrimental to the welfare of the whites of the community. One Esquire Frost intimated that Prudence Crandall's project fostered social equality and intermarriage of whites and blacks. To this insidious insinuation, she bluntly replied: "Moses had a black wife." To emphasize their decided opposition to this project, the people called a public meeting and drew up and adopted resolutions of a hostile nature. One of the leading politicians of that day, Andrew T. Judson, was so incensed at Miss Crandall's action that he denounced her in the most severe and scathing terms.

The Rev. Mr. May and Mr. Buffum, who were present on behalf of Miss Crandall, made several attempts to speak in her defense but were rudely and abruptly prohibited. Denied the privilege of espousing her cause in this meeting, Mr. May, upon adjournment, rose from his seat and addressed the people as they were leaving the hall: "Men of Canterbury, I have a word for you! Hear me!" A few turned to listen, and he pleaded with force and feeling the cause of the noble little teacher of Canterbury. He told them that Prudence Crandall was willing to move her school from its present situation, which was next door to the residence of Mr. Judson, her bitterest enemy, to some more retired part of the city.

May's arguments, however, were of no avail and only drew forth tirades of invective and abuse; for Mr. Judson responded: "Mr. May, we are not merely opposed to the establishment of that school in Canterbury; we mean there shall not be such a school set up anywhere in our state. The colored people can never rise from their menial condition in our country; they ought not to be permitted to rise here. They are an inferior race of beings, and never can or ought to be recognized as the equals of the whites.

Africa is the place for them. I am in favor of the colonization scheme. Let the niggers and their descendants be sent back to their fatherland and there improve themselves as much as they can. I am a colonizationist. You and your friend Garrison have undertaken what you cannot accomplish. The condition of the colored population of our country can never be essentially improved on this continent. You are fanatical about them. You are violating the constitution of our Republic, which settled forever the status of the black men in this land. They belong to Africa. Let them be sent back there or kept as they are here. The sooner you abolitionists abandon your project the better for our country, for the niggers and yourselves."[4]

In answer to this outburst of feeling, typical of ignorance and prejudice, though it came from the lips of a prospective judge of the Supreme Court, Mr. May replied: "Mr. Judson, there never will be fewer colored people in this country than there are now. Of the vast majority of them, this is their native land as much as it is ours. It will be unjust, inhuman in us to drive them out, or to make them willing to go by our cruel treatment of them . . . and the only question is whether we will recognize the rights which God gave them as men and encourage and assist them to become all he has made them capable of being, or whether we will continue wickedly to deny them the privileges we enjoy, condemn them to degradation, enslave and imbrute them; and so bring upon ourselves the condemnation of the Almighty, Impartial Father of all men and the terrible visitation of the God of the oppressed. I trust, sir, you well e're long come to see that we must accord to these men, their rights or incur justly the loss of our own. Education is one of the primal fundamental rights of all the children of men. Connecticut is the last place where this right should be denied."

These eloquent remarks truly portrayed the difference in the character of the two men. Encouraged by such noble characters as May and Garrison, Prudence Crandall was determined not to be deterred in her purpose by men like

[4] May's *Antislavery Conflict*, p. 47.

Judson. Her lofty ideals of service to humanity and to the humbler lot especially were evidenced in this extract from Garrison's letter to Isaac Knapp, April 11, 1833:

"She is a wonderful woman, as undaunted as if she had the whole world on her side. She has opened her school and is resolved to persevere. I wish brother Johnson to state this fact particularly in the next *Liberator* and urge all those who intend to send their children thither, to do so without delay."[5]

Despite all vicissitudes, Miss Crandall opened her school for girls of color early in April, with an enrollment of fifteen or twenty students. These for the most part came from Philadelphia, New York, Providence, and Boston.

The townspeople, greatly incensed, resorted to every foul means possible to destroy the school. At first, they searched for some obsolete vagrancy law for the purpose of intimidating those who came from other cities to attend school. One Negro girl, Anna Eliza Hammond, seventeen years of age, from Providence, was arrested, but Samuel May and other residents of Brooklyn gave bonds for $10,000 and thus defeated this plan. Frustrated in their first efforts, the townspeople held an indignation meeting at which they expressed their sentiment in the following resolutions:

"Whereas, it hath been publicly announced that a school is to be opened in this town, on the first Monday of April next, using the language of the advertisement, 'for young ladies and little misses of color,' or in other words for the people of color, the obvious tendency of which would be to collect within the town of Canterbury large numbers of persons from other States whose characters and habits might be various and unknown to us, thereby rendering insecure the persons, property, and reputations of our citizens. Under such circumstances our silence might be construed into an approbation of the project: Thereupon, Resolved That the locality of a school for the people of color at any place within the limits of this town, for the admission of persons of foreign jurisdiction, meets with our unqualified disapprobation, and it is to be understood, that the inhabitants of Canterbury protest against it in the most earnest manner.

[5] Garrison's *Garrison*, I, p. 341.

"Resolved, That a committee be now appointed to be composed of the Civil Authority and Selectmen, who shall make known to the persons contemplating the establishment of said school, the sentiments and objections entertained by this meeting in reference to said school—pointing out to her the injurious effects and incalculable evils resulting from such an establishment within this town, and persuade her to abandon the project."[6]

The people then influenced the Legislature to enact a disgraceful but well-named "Black Law,"[7] amid the ringing of church bells and great rejoicing. This act outlawed Miss Crandall's school. The people closed all shops and meeting houses to the teacher and her pupils. Stage drivers refused them transportation in the common carriers of the town. Physicians would not attend them. Miss Crandall's own family and friends were forbidden under penalty of heavy fines to visit her. The well near her house was filled with manure and water was denied her from other sources. The house itself was smeared with filth, assailed with rotten eggs, stormed with stones, and finally set afire.

Not only was Prudence Crandall herself assailed with threats of coming vengeance and ejection, but her father in the south part of the town was insulted and threatened. "When lawyers, courts and jurors are leagued against you," said one to him, "it will be easy to raise a mob and

[6] Larned's *Windham County, Connecticut*, II, 490–502.

[7] This law was:

Whereas, attempts have been made to establish literary institutions in this State, for the instruction of colored persons belonging to other States and counties, which would tend to the great increase of the colored population of the state, and thereby to the injury of the people: Therefore,

Section 1. Be it enacted by the Senate and House of Representatives, in General Assembly convened, that no person shall set up or establish in this State any school, academy or literary institution for the instruction or education of colored persons who are not inhabitants of this State; nor instruct or teach in any school, or other literary institution whatsoever, in this State; nor harbor or board, for the purpose of attending or being taught or instructed in any such school, academy, or literary institution, any colored person who is not an inhabitant of any town in this State, without the consent in writing first obtained, of a majority of the civil authority, and also of the Selectmen of the town, in which such school, academy, or literary institution is situated, etc. See *Superior Court, October Term, 1833*, and *Report of Arguments of Counsel in the Case of Prudence Crandall;* also *The Laws of Connecticut*, 1833.

tear down your house." "Mr. Crandall, if you go to your daughter," they said, "you are to be fined $100 for the first offense, $200 for the second and double it every time; Mrs. Crandall, if you go there, you will be fined and your daughter Almira will be fined, and Mr. May and those gentlemen from Providence (Messrs. George and Henry Benson), if they come there, will be fined at the same rate. And your daughter, the one that established the school for colored females, will be taken up the same way as for stealing a horse or for burglary. Her property will not be taken but she will be put in jail, not having the liberty of the yard. There is no mercy to be shown about it!"[8]

Miss Crandall was arrested and cast into prison, where she spent the night in a cell previously occupied by a murderer. She was twice tried. The first trial was held before the county court on August 22, 1833. The attorneys for the prosecution were Jonathan A. Welch, Andrew T. Judson and Ichabod Bulkley, while those for the defense were Calvin Goddard, W. W. Ellsworth and Henry Strong. The latter were secured by Samuel May and paid by Arthur Tappan.

The counsel for the defense argued that the "Black Law" conflicted with that article of the Federal Constitution which granted to citizens of each State all the privileges and immunities of citizens of the several States. The counsel for the prosecution argued that people of color were not and could not ever be citizens of any State. The judge, Mr. Eaton, gave the decision that the law was constitutional and binding upon the people of that State. The jurors, however, could not agree and so the case went over to the October term. It was then tried before the Superior Court of Windham County and its constitutionality again pronounced by Judge Daggett, who expressed himself as follows: "It would be a perversion of terms and the well-known rule of construction to say that slaves, free blacks, or Indians were citizens within the meaning of that term as

---

[8] Garrison's *Garrison*, I. ch. X, and Larned's *Windham County, Connecticut*, II, 490–502.

used in the constitution." The jurors thus influenced gave their verdict against the defendant. Prudence Crandall's counsel then appealed to the Court of Errors, where the decision was reversed, July 22, 1834, upon the ground of "insufficiency of the information," which omitted to allege that the school was opened without necessary license.[9]

[9] The report of this case was:

This information charges Prudence Crandall with harboring and boarding certain colored persons, not inhabitants of any town in this State, for the purpose of attending and being taught and instructed in a school, set up and established in said town of Canterbury, for the instruction and education of certain colored persons, not inhabitants of this State.

She is not charged with setting up a school contrary to law, not with teaching a school contrary to law; but with harboring and boarding colored persons, not inhabitants of this State, without license, for the purpose of being instructed in such school.

It is, however, not here alleged that the school was set up without license, or that the scholars were instructed by those who had no license.

If it is an offence within the statute to *harbor* or *board* such persons without license, under all circumstances, then this information is correct. But if the act, in the description of the defense itself, shows, that under some circumstances, it is no offence, then this information is defective.

The object in view of the legislature, as disclosed by the preamble, is to prevent injurious consequences resulting from the increase of the colored population, by means of literary institutions, attempted to be established for the instruction of that class of inhabitants of other States. Such institutions and instructors teaching such schools are prohibited, unless licensed, as are also persons from harboring or boarding scholars of that description, without license.

From the first reading of the Act, it might seem as if licenses must be obtained by each of these classes; by those who set up the school, those who instruct it and those who board the pupils; but, it is believed, this cannot have been intended. The object professedly aimed at is, to prevent the increase of this population, which, it is supposed, will take place by allowing them free education, and instruction; to prevent which it provides, 1st, That no person shall set up or establish any school for that purpose, without license: 2d, That no one shall instruct in any school, etc. without license: and 3rd, That no one shall board or harbor such persons, so to be instructed in any such school etc. without license. The object, evidently is to regulate the schools, not the boarding houses; the latter only is auxiliary to the former.

This information charges, that this school was set up in Canterbury, for the purpose of educating these persons of color, not inhabitants of this State, that they might be instructed and educated; but omits to state that it was not licensed. This omission is a fatal defect; as in an information on a penal statute, the prosecutor must set forth every fact that is necessary to bring the case within the statute; and every exception within the enacting clause of the

While the decision of the Court of Errors was pending, Prudence Crandall and her pupils were the victims of other fiendish acts of the townspeople. Having failed in their attempt to burn down her school, a number of them, with heavy clubs and iron bars, crept stealthily upon her house at midnight on the 9th of September, and simultaneously smashed in the windows with such force and suddenness that all the occupants were terror stricken. Even Prudence Crandall, for the first time, trembled with fear. Realizing that she and her pupils would ever be the object of insult and injury, she decided, upon the advice of Mr. May and other friends, to give up the school and send her girls back to their homes. Samuel May said that when he stood before Prudence Crandall and her pupils and advised them to leave, the words blistered his lips and his bosom glowed with indignation. "I felt ashamed of Connecticut," said he, "ashamed of my state, ashamed of my country, ashamed of my color."

The burden of these terrible ordeals was somewhat alleviated by the fidelity of her friends, the love and faith of her pupils and the devotion of her sister, father and husband. Having recently married the Rev. Calvin Philleo, a Baptist clergyman of Ithaca, New York, Prudence Crandall upon solicitation left Windham County never to return again. Tis true she had but little opportunity to teach the young women of color, nevertheless through sacrifice and service she taught the people of Connecticut a lesson of philanthropy and sacrifice.

G. SMITH WORMLEY.

act, descriptive of the offence, must be negated. See *Smith v. Mouse*, 6 Green 1, p. 274; and Judson's Remarks to the Jury, *Superior Court, October Term, 1833.*

DOCUMENTS
EXTRACTS FROM NEWSPAPERS AND MAGAZINES

Magazines and newspapers sometimes unconsciously give valuable facts not only as to sentiment but as to the actual achievements of persons and agencies through which they have worked. This is true of the extracts given below.

Endeavoring to set forth the part which Philadelphia played in African Colonization before the Civil War, *The Evening Bulletin* of that city carried the following, May 9, 1921:

THE LIBERIAN REPUBLIC

PHILADELPHIA'S PART IN FOUNDING THE NEGRO COMMONWEALTH

The visit to Philadelphia of the negro President of the Liberian Republic, recalls the important part which a small group of local philanthropists played a century ago in promoting the foundation of the only free country in Africa under republican rule. The Liberian enterprise owed its origin, not solely to pity for the condition of the enslaved blacks of the South but also to the desire of many northern friends of the negroes to ameliorate the hardships of the freed blacks of the north. Both Pennsylvania and New Jersey, in common with several other northern States, witnessed at close range the evils of slavery. During the Revolutionary War steps had been taken to liberate the blacks in Pennsylvania and the famous Act of March 1st, 1780, decreed the abolition of slavery throughout the colony. In this, as in other and later efforts to liberate the negroes the Philadelphia Quakers had an important part and the Pennsylvania Abolition Society, founded under the presidency of Benjamin Franklin, antedated the Revolutionary War by two years.

The plan for establishing an African Negro Republic, populated by emigrants from the United States, is credited to Dr. Robert Finley, one of the trustees of Princeton, who was well acquainted with the extent of slavery in New Jersey, where the census of 1810 revealed the presence of more than ten thousand slaves, and who also had knowledge of the miserable condition of the freed negroes in Pennsylvania. Late in 1816 he went to Washington, where his brother-in-law, Elias Boudinot Caldwell was a member of Congress, and endeavored to obtain national support for his project. A sympathetic response was not wanting, although Congress was not yet prepared for immediate action. Accordingly, Finley turned in another direction, secured the backing of Justice Bushrod Washington of the Supreme Court, aroused the interest of Henry Clay and other notables and, toward the end of 1816, succeeded in forming, at a public meeting in Washington presided over by Henry Clay, the American Colonization Society which immediately selected Justice Washington as its president.

As yet Dr. Finley had not hit upon any definite location for the proposed colony, although years before he began his efforts in behalf of the negroes. Thomas Jefferson had suggested that Virginia and other American Commonwealths might profitably imitate the example set in England by the Sierra Leone Company in populating that district of Africa. But the English plan of transporting the indigent negroes from London, started toward the close of the eighteenth century, was on an altogether different basis. Blacks and whites were mixed in the English colony, the emigrants were made up mainly of the idle and the dissolute, and the humanitarian motive, so strongly marked in the work of the American Colonization Society, was missing almost entirely.

Oddly enough, the free negroes of the North protested against the plans of the Colonization Society. In Philadelphia a number of negroes, meeting in the Bethel Church, adopted an indignant resolution of protest which Congressman Joseph Hopkinson presented in the House. But these incidents served also to arouse greater interest in the society's plan and led to the formation of several local auxiliaries, one of which was established promptly in Philadelphia, where the Friends and the Abolitionists were ready to give active support to any plan for the betterment of the negroes. Philadelphia money, representing the contributions of many local philanthropists, aided largely in strengthening the treasury of the national society, and, as an opportunity was afforded for the purchase of a number of smuggled slaves, put on sale by the State of Georgia, in 1817, and George Washington Parke Custis offered part of his lands for a refuge for the Colonization Society's purchases, an active effort was made again to arouse Congressional support, resulting this time in the founding of the African Republic by the Government of the United States.

While the Society was in the initial stages of development, two missionary agents, Samuel J. Mills and Ebenezer Burgess, had visited England and, after receiving a rebuff from Bathurst, the Secretary of State for the English Colonies, had gone down the African coast as far as Sherbro Island and selected a site for the American colony. Interest was aroused to such extent that Congress assented to the proposal for purchasing the Georgia blacks and shipping them to Africa and an appropriation of one hundred thousand dollars was granted for the purpose. A brig was chartered by the government to carry away the negroes, furnished by the Colonization Society, and the United States ship Cyane ordered to accompany the expedition as an armed guard. The vessels departed from New York in February, 1820, and after a five weeks voyage landed eighty-six men, women and children on Sherbro Island. The inclemency of the climate, however, proved disastrous to the little group, and, after a number had succumbed to malarial fever, the remainder fled to Sierra Leone. But the Society and its local auxiliaries kept at work and the next year sent out another party of negroes from Norfolk, this time seeking Cape Montserado as a place of settlement.

Success now attended the enterprise. Lieutenant Richard F. Stockton of the Navy arrived at Montserado in the autumn of 1821 and, in company with Dr. Ayres, the agent of the Colonization Society, succeeded in purchasing, for a few hundred dollars' worth of trinkets, the land on which Liberia was founded. Although the promoters had negotiated a favorable treaty with the natives the early settlers were attacked by hostile tribes and more than once they were on the point of abandoning the little town of Monrovia that had been named in honor of the American President and which is now the capital of the African Republic and a place of about six thousand inhabitants. A few years after this Philadelphia took up the work of colonization on a larger scale. At a meeting, held in the Franklin Institute in 1829, the Pennsylvania Colonization Society was formed, with Dr. Thomas C. James as its president and numbering among its founders many prominent citizens, including William White, Roberts Vaux, B. W. Richards, J. K. Mitchell, George W. Blight, James Bayard and Elliott Cresson, the latter becoming one of the most active assistants of the enterprise, in which he was joined by Mathew C. Carey, Solomon Allen and Robert Ralston, the last four contributing liberally to the colonization cause. For a time, too, a fortnightly journal, known as the Colonization Herald, was published in this city and local interest was aroused by reports of the parades of the State Fencibles, the Liberian imitation of Philadelphia's military organization, which assembled on fete days on Broad Street, the principal thoroughfare of Monrovia.

County and local societies to aid the project were formed throughout Pennsylvania. Philadelphia had a Young Men's Society fostered by the Methodists, the local Presbyterians endorsed the enterprise, the Bible societies backed it and the Quakers lent their friendly support. Ships were chartered and slaves transported at local expense and under Philadelphia direction a boat named the "Liberia" was built on the Delaware and employed in the work, while the manumission of slaves was freely encouraged. A colony on the St. John's River was assigned particularly to the care of the Pennsylvanians and African place names, such as Careysburg and Philadelphia, still commemorate the interest of Philadelphians. At first the government of Liberia was purely proprietary under the direction of the society's agents, the blacks being allowed to select only minor officials and it was not until 1847, when the colonization movement was losing ground before the growth of the abolition sentiment in this country, that the Free and Independent Republic of Liberia came into existence, after drafting a declaration of independence and adopting a constitutional form of government. But the dream of repatriating the negro had failed and now Liberia, extended in area by Anglo-Liberian and Franco-Liberian agreements of recent years until it is almost as large as Pennsylvania, numbers less than fifty thousand of the transplanted stock among a population of a million and a half.

On September 18, 1921, *The New Orleans States* displayed on its title page the following distorted sketch of the late Caesar Confucius Antoine by W. O. Hart:

A telegram to The States from Shreveport three days ago told of the death of C. C. Antoine, colored, who had been lieutenant-governor of Louisiana and sometimes acted as governor of the State.

The death of Antoine, widely known in New Orleans, cuts off another link with Reconstruction days.

At the request of The States, W. O. Hart, Louisiana historian, contributes the story telling how Antoine went from a barber's chair to power and affluence.

Caesar Confucius Antoine, who was a native of New Orleans, was in many respects one of the most remarkable of the colored politicians who thrived in reconstruction days in Louisiana.

He was a native of New Orleans, but appears to have been unknown until he was elected from the Parish of Caddo, a member of the Constitutional Convention of 1868.

He was a very small man and light in weight. He was coal-black in color and always dressed with the utmost neatness and simplicity.

When the Constitution was adopted he was elected to the State Senate from Caddo Parish and held that office for four years. In 1872 he was nominated for Lieutenant-Governor on the ticket headed by W. P. Kellogg, and though that ticket was defeated by the Democratic ticket which carried the names of John McEnery, of Ouachita, for Governor, and Davidson B. Penn, of New Orleans, for Lieutenant-Governor, Kellogg and all those returned as elected by the Returning Board, were recognized by President Grant and served out their full terms of four years.

Antoine like many of the other colored Legislators of those days acquired an almost perfect knowledge of parliamentary law and presided over the Senate with dignity and impartiality.

He was a man who, in general, had the respect of all parties. He was renominated on the ticket with S. B. Packard in 1876 and with Packard remained in the State House, which was the old St. Louis Hotel, until April, 1877, when President Hayes, having withdrawn the Federal troops, the semblance of Government which Packard established, disappeared and the Nicholls Government went into full possession of all the State Offices.

My recollection is that he held some Federal office after this but I am not certain what it was.

In a suit which he brought against D. D. Smith and the heirs of George L. Smith, reported in the 40th Annual (1888), beginning at page 560, considerable of the record of Antoine is given.

How He Made Money

The suit was brought after the death of George L. Smith, to recover two hundred shares of the capital stock of the Louisiana State Lottery Company, which at the time of the suit, had a very large value. The allegations of Antoine's petition and his evidence in the case were to the effect that on March 31st, 1873, he purchased from Charles T. Howard the lottery stock at sixty cents on the dollar, that is twelve thousand dollars for all, and that he was induced by George L. Smith, who also owned 225 shares of the stock, to transfer it to D. D. Smith, a cousin of George L. Smith, because as Smith said to Antoine: "We are both engaged in politics, and it would not do to have the stock in our name—more especially myself, as I was Lieutenant-Governor, and President of the Senate; that questions in regard to the charter of the Lottery Company might come up, and that, in case of a tie vote, I would naturally have to vote on it; and, probably, my vote might be challenged."

Smith had been Tax Collector and also speculated in salary warrants for account of himself and Antoine and Antoine's profits therefrom were three or four thousand dollars.

Partner Of Pinchback

When Antoine first went into politics he was the proprietor of a barber shop in the city of Shreveport; a few years afterwards, he engaged in the cotton factorage business in New Orleans, in partnership with P. B. S. Pinchback; also once Lieutenant-Governor. He acquired an interest in a newspaper establishment; had a grocery store and purchased and operated a small plantation in Caddo Parish. He also purchased some city lots in Shreveport and a $1300 residence in this city, this in addition to the twelve thousand dollars he paid for the Lottery Stock.

The Supreme Court, after stating the above facts, commented thereon as follows:

"We cannot refrain from expressing some surprise at the auspicious good fortune that seemed to attend his efforts, whereby his hitherto slender income and limited means had yielded such a comfortable little fortune within so few years.

"Money matters appeared to have been so easy with him that he could loan a friend a thousand dollars, payable on call."

The opinion of the court was rendered by Mr. Justice L. B.

Watkins, and the court concluded that the acquisition of the stock by Antoine was so tainted with fraud that he was entitled to receive no redress at the hands of the courts and the judgment of the lower court which was rendered by Judge Albert Voohries, presiding in Division "E" of the Civil District Court, was affirmed.

Antoine was represented in the suit by Rouse and Grant and Thomas J. Semmes, America's greatest lawyer, while the defendants were represented by the firm of Leonard, Marks and Brueno. Everyone connected with the case is now dead except Pinchback who, over eighty years of age, is now living in Washington.

When under the Wheeler Compromise after the election of 1874, the Democrats secured a majority in the State House of Representatives, an effort was made to impeach Kellogg, which, if successful, would have made Antoine Governor, but what benefit the Democrats could have derived therefrom, it is impossible to say because even if Antoine had then resigned, as was thought possible, the President of the Senate, who would become Governor was or would be a Republican as the Democrats had but nine of the thirty-six members of that body. However, the impeachment trial properly speaking, was never held.

As soon as the Senate which had adjourned, heard of the impeachment resolution, it immediately reconvened and sent for the Chief Justice, John T. Ludeling, and the Court of Impeachment was opened without waiting for the presentation of the charges from the House of Representatives, and Kellogg was "triumphantly" acquitted.

The Item, a New Orleans newspaper, featured the following sketch of Isaiah T. Montgomery by Stanley Cisby Arthur in its Sunday magazine section on September 25, 1921:

One of the most interesting figures at the meeting of the secretaries of the Federal Farm Loan Association, was an aged negro, "Uncle" Isaiah T. Montgomery, of Mound Bayou City, Bolivar County, Mississippi. "Uncle" Isaiah is not only one of the wealthiest farmers in his district, but he founded the town of Mound Bayou, which is composed exclusively of colored people, who run the stores, the banks, the postoffice, the schools and the peace offices, but "Uncle" Isaiah was a former slave and a body servant of Jefferson Davis, president of the Confederacy.

Black of face, with white hair and a white chin beard "Uncle" Isaiah looks exactly the part of the regulation stage "Uncle" of the old regime. He looks every bit of his 74 years but his mind is exceedingly bright and he recounted the happenings of over half a century with the utmost clarity of speech and showed many evidences of his education, which he says he gave himself. When he took recourse to a piece of paper and a pen to estimate the ginnage of his community, he set down words and figures with Spencerian exactness. His handwriting was truly a revelation to the interviewer.

"I was born on Hurricane plantation, in Warren county, Mississippi, in 1847, and my father and I were owned by Joseph E. Davis, brother of Jefferson Davis. The plantation owned by the late president of the Confederacy adjoined the Hurricane, and was called Brierfield plantation," said the aged colored man and former slave who is now a prosperous banker in the town he founded. "I was about nine years old when I first remember Jefferson Davis real well. I was working in my master's office when his brother came back from Congress and I was told to meet the steamboat Natchez in a row boat and get Mr. Jeff.

"When the Natchez blew her whistle as she came around a bend of the river I rowed out and Mr. Jeff got in my boat with his grips and things and I took him to shore and toted all his things into the 'White Room' where Mr. Jeff staid for a considerable spell. While there I was his personal attendant, I blacked his shoes, kept his room in order, held his horse for him and other little things that a servant like I was was supposed to do. On one of his trips down the river on the Natchez (Mr. Jeff and Captain Tom P. Leathers, the historic commander of that boat, were close friends), he brought his wife and daughter, who was afterwards Mrs. Hayes, and they all were very kind to me because I was Mr. Jeff's personal servant all the time they were at the Hurricane.

"When the war between the states came I staid on the Joseph Davis plantation all during the fighting. In '62 or '63, anyway, after the battle of Corinth, the Yankees commenced overrunning the South and Mr. Joe, took all his stock and colored people to Jackson, and later on to Alabama. He had me return to the plantation with my mother and act as sort of caretakers and we were there when Admiral Porter's Mississippi squadron made its way up the river. It seems sometime before a gunboat, the Indianola, had been sunk in the river, just off the Hurricane plantation and folks in the neighborhood had dismantled her.

"When Admiral Porter came up the river he stopped at the plantation so as to look at the wreck and see if her guns could be found. But they had been thrown overboard and had gone down in the quicksand. The Admiral asked me if I wanted to go with him as cabin boy. I said yes, and ran to get my mammy's consent which was given. This was in April of '63 and a few months later I was with the Admiral in the siege of Vicksburg and later the battle at Grand Gulf. Soon afterwards I got a sickness from drinking Red River water and when I was sent back to Hurricane I found my parents had gone to Cincinnati and when I got word of this to Admiral Porter he secured transportation there for me.

"When the war was over Mr. Joe Davis got in touch with my father and had him come back to Hurricane plantation and after we got there he made a proposition that we could buy the two plantations, Hurricane, that Mr. Joe owned, and Brierfield, of 4,000 acres, that Mr. Jeff Davis owned. While he could not sell to colored people under the existing laws, through a court action by which my father, Benjamin T. Montgomery, and my brother William T. and myself, agreed to pay $300,000 for the combined properties, they were turned over to us and we were to pay six per cent a year on the whole until it was paid off.

"Our first year working the plantation resulted in almost disaster as we suffered from an overflow and when the first payment came around we were only able to pay $6,000. When we sent this to Mr. Joe Davis with our excuses he sent us back a canceled note for the rest of the $18,000. The Davis brothers, were gentlemen, sir. Well, we kept the plantation going for thirteen years and in that time we ranked as third in the production of cotton in Warren county. While we were growing cotton I became very well acquainted with Captain John W. Cannon, the commander of the famous steamboat the Robert E. Lee. He and Captain Tom Leathers, the commander of the Natchez, were always having some sort of a fight or another and I saw the famous race between the two when they actually settled the matter for good and all.

"The death of Mr. Joe Davis and taking over of his properties by his heirs lost us our holdings and I became interested in the Yazoo Delta. I heard that the Y. & M. V. was asking colored people to come in and open up the country and after going over the situation

I decided to select Mound Bayou for the seat of my future operations. This place was selected because between Big and Little Mound bayous there was an old Indian mound. This was in 1887 and it certainly was a wild territory, it had rich land but it was thickly grown over with oak and ash and gum, and acres and acres of cane. Well, I plundered around here and induced other colored folks to settle there. I founded Mound Bayou Settlement—the railroad folks wanted to name it Montgomery, a few years ago but I made the original name stick.

"Building up our community was slow work. All the colored folks bought their places on 10-year contracts and it was hard work for some of them in the face of a few crop failures, overflows, boll weevil and other set-backs but we succeeded. Mound Bayou Settlement is now a town of a little over 1,000 population and there are about 2,500 in the country nearby. The town is of wholly colored population and we have three big churches, one costing $25,000, another costing $15,000 and another $10,000. There are several other less pretentious places of worship, as well.

"We have two big mercantile establishments. The largest being the one I founded and known as the Mercantile Co-operative Company which now has a $20,000 stock. We also have the Mound Bayou State Bank, with $10,000 capital, a $3,000 surplus, with resources between $150,000 and $200,000. I am a member of the board of directors and we make a great many loans to our colored people to see they get out their crops, and being in the staple cotton belt, we make most of it on this crop.

"We have just completed a consolidated school house, 95 feet square, three stories high, with 16 large class rooms. It cost us $100,000 which was raised by a local bond issue. We have a seven to eight months' term and employ an agricultural expert, co-operating under the Smith-Lever national fund and a very fine domestic science class.

"The town has a mayor and a board of aldermen, all office holders being colored folks, and the present mayor, B. H. Green, was the first man born in the settlement. I was mayor for over four years, being the first to hold the office, resigning it to hold the office of receiver of public monies at Jackson, Miss.

"We have four gins that can handle over 5,000 bales and our people now feel that the upward trend of the cotton price will make for further prosperous times."

Uncle Isaiah Montgomery remembers his services with the Jefferson family, first as slave and afterwards as a trusted servant, with the kindliest feelings. He told of the periods in 1880 and 1883 when Jefferson Davis returned to the old Brierfield and Hurricane plantations, spending several weeks at the old home once or twice a year. He usually had Mrs. Davis with him and the aged negro said that Mrs. Davis was a remarkable woman.

"She displayed a wonderful interest in the future of the colored race," he said. "It was the impression made on me by this lovely woman that helped confirm my belief in the ultimate outcome of my work and efforts toward race betterment, education and uplift of the negro. Mrs. Jefferson Davis had a broader comprehension of the race's needs than anyone with whom I have ever come in contact with. With her death the negro lost one of his greatest friends.

"Mr. Jefferson Davis was a wonderful man, too. My thoughts frequently go back, now that I am approaching the end of my days, to the time I was his personal servant as a barefoot boy. I truly believe, when he got his last sickness, had I been near to nurse and care for him, that he would have lived many more years. I knew, and so did my wife, what he needed in the way of food and we could have done for him as no one else could.

"It was the influence of Jefferson Davis and his sweet life that has guided all my efforts in bettering the life of my colored brothers and if I have succeeded it was because of them."

The American Magazine in July, 1914, gave the following account, an achievement of "Comébacks" of recent date:

BEATEN ONCE, PERRY TRIED AGAIN—AND SUCCEEDED.

For years Heman E. Perry, a negro, traveled over Texas for white companies, selling old line life insurance to his people. But he had a vision of someday founding a company under negro management, to transact its business and make its investments among the colored race.

Finally, plans outlined and prospectus and other literature completed, he undertook the arduous task of organizing his company. He applied for a charter under the laws of Georgia, which require that the full $100,000 capital shall be raised in two years, or the charter be revoked.

To raise $100,000 among white men, or even $100,000,000, is a comparatively easy task, for they are accustomed to corporate investments. But Mr. Perry was to raise $100,000 among a people whose investments had taken the form of horses and houses, and who did not understand the value of commercial paper, especially when purchased for $150 with a par value of $100. In other words, he had to sell 1,000 shares of stock, one, two or three shares at a time, and he must do this among a people who had never before raised $100,000 for a business venture.

For two years, at his own expense, Perry traveled throughout the South. Then, with a scant thirty days left, he found himself with but two thirds of the money in hand. He hastened to New York hoping to obtain a loan from some bankers. They put him off until the last day slipped by. Then began Perry's heart-breaking task of returning the money he had collected. He returned every dollar with four per cent interest—money that he had spent all his own cash in collecting.

This was enough to crush any ordinary man. But after three months Perry met a selected assembly of negro business men in Atlanta, ready to begin all over again.

He retraced his first long journey, constantly hearing, "You failed once, you'll fail again." But he continued his fight, and on June 14th, 1913, after $105,000 had been paid for Georgia state bonds, the first and only old line legal reserve life insurance company in the world managed and operated by negroes formally began business. It now operates in nine states, and has over $2,000,000 insurance on the lives of negroes, because Heman E. Perry would not acknowledge defeat, and had the power to "come back" and conquer.

GEORGE F. PORTER

ANNA MURRAY-DOUGLASS—MY MOTHER AS I RECALL HER[1]

Looking backward over a space of fifty years or more, I have in remembrance two travelers whose lives were real in their activity; two lives that have indelibly impressed themselves upon my memory; two lives whose energy and best ability was exerted to make my life what it should be, and who gave me a home where wisdom and industry went hand in hand; where instruction was given that a cultivated brain and an industrious hand were the twin conditions that lead to a well balanced and useful life. These two lives were embodied in the personalities of Frederick Douglass and Anna Murray his wife.

They met at the base of a mountain of wrong and oppression, victims of the slave power as it existed over sixty years ago, one smarting under the manifold hardships as a slave, the other in many ways suffering from the effects of such a system.

The story of Frederick Douglass' hopes and aspirations and longing desire for freedom has been told—you all know it. It was a story made possible by the unswerving loyalty of Anna Murray, to whose memory this paper is written.

Anna Murray was born in Denton, Caroline County, Maryland, an adjoining county to that in which my father was born. The exact date of her birth is not known. Her parents, Bambarra Murray and Mary, his wife, were slaves, their family consisting of twelve children, seven of whom were born in slavery and five born in freedom. My mother, the eighth child, escaped by the short period of one month, the fate of her older brothers and sisters, and was the first free child.

Remaining with her parents until she was seventeen, she felt it time that she should be entirely self-supporting and with that idea she left her country home and went to Baltimore, sought employment in a French family by the name of Montell whom she served two years. Doubtless it was while with them she gained her first idea as to household management which served her so well

[1] This paper and the one which *follows* give valuable information about Frederick Douglass and his wife.

in after years and which gained for her the reputation of a thorough and competent housekeeper.

On leaving the Montells', she served in a family by the name of Wells living on S. Caroline Street. Wells was Post-master at the time of my father's escape from slavery. It interested me very much in one of my recent visits to Baltimore, to go to that house accompanied by an old friend of my parents of those early days, who as a free woman was enabled with others to make my father's life easier while he was a slave in that city. This house is owned now by a colored man. In going through the house I endeavored to remember its appointments, so frequently spoken of by my mother, for she had lived with this family seven years and an attachment sprang up between her and the members of that household, the memory of which gave her pleasure to recall.

The free people of Baltimore had their own circles from which the slaves were excluded. The ruling of them out of their society resulted more from the desire of the slaveholder than from any great wish of the free people themselves. If a slave would dare to hazard all danger and enter among the free people he would be received. To such a little circle of free people—a circle a little more exclusive than others, Frederick Baily was welcomed. Anna Murray, to whom he had given his heart, sympathized with him and she devoted all her energies to assist him. The three weeks prior to the escape were busy and anxious weeks for Anna Murray. She had lived with the Wells family so long and having been able to save the greater part of her earnings was willing to share with the man she loved that he might gain the freedom he yearned to possess. Her courage, her sympathy at the start was the mainspring that supported the career of Frederick Douglass. As is the condition of most wives her identity became so merged with that of her husband, that few of their earlier friends in the North really knew and appreciated the full value of the woman who presided over the Douglass home for forty-four years. When the escaped slave and future husband of Anna Murray had reached New York in safety, his first act was to write her of his arrival and as they had previously arranged she was to come on immediately. Reaching New York a week later, they were married and immediately took their wedding trip to New Bedford. In "My Bondage of Freedom," by Frederick Douglass, a graphic account of that trip is given.

The little that they possessed was the outcome of the industrial and economical habits that were characteristic of my mother. She had brought with her sufficient goods and chattel to fit up comfortably two rooms in her New Bedford home—a feather bed with pillows, bed linen, dishes, knives, forks, and spoons, besides a well filled trunk of wearing apparel for herself. A new plum colored silk dress was her wedding gown. To my child eyes that dress was very fine. She had previously sold one of her feather beds to assist in defraying the expenses of the flight from bondage.

The early days in New Bedford were spent in daily toil, the wife at the wash board, the husband with saw, buck and axe. I have frequently listened to the rehearsal of those early days of endeavor, looking around me at the well appointed home built up from the labor of the father and mother under so much difficulty, and found it hard to realize that it was a fact. After the day of toil they would seek their little home of two rooms and the meal of the day that was most enjoyable was the supper nicely prepared by mother. Father frequently spoke of the neatly set table with its snowy white cloth— coarse tho' it was.

In 1890 I was taken by my father to these rooms on Elm Street, New Bedford, Mass., overlooking Buzzards Bay. This was my birth place. Every detail as to the early housekeeping was gone over, it was splendidly impressed upon my mind, even to the hanging of a towel on a particular nail. Many of the dishes used by my mother at that time were in our Rochester home and kept as souvenirs of those first days of housekeeping. The fire that destroyed that home in 1872, also destroyed them.

Three of the family had their birthplace in New Bedford. When after having written his first narrative, father built himself a nice little cottage in Lynn, Mass., and moved his family there, previously to making his first trip to Europe. He was absent during the years '45 and '46. It was then that mother with four children, the eldest in her sixth year, struggled to maintain the family amid much that would dampen the courage of many a young woman of to-day. I had previously been taken to Albany by my father as a means of lightening the burden for mother. Abigail and Lydia Mott, cousins of Lucretia Mott, desired to have the care of me.

During the absence of my father, mother sustained her little family by binding shoes. Mother had many friends in the anti-slavery circle of Lynn and Boston who recognized her sterling qualities, and who encouraged her during the long absence of her husband. Those were days of anxious worry. The narrative of Frederick Douglass with its bold utterances of truth, with the names of the parties with whom he had been associated in slave life, so incensed the slaveholders that it was doubtful if ever he would return to this country and also there was danger for mother and those who had aided in his escape, being pursued. It was with hesitancy father consented to leave the country, and not until he was assured by the many friends that mother and the children would be carefully guarded, would he go.

There were among the Anti-Slavery people of Massachusetts a fraternal spirit born of the noble purpose near their heart that served as an uplift and encouraged the best energies in each individual, and mother from the contact with the great and noble workers grew and improved even more than ever before. She was a recognized co-worker in the A. S. Societies of Lynn and Boston, and no circle was felt to be complete without her presence. There was a weekly gathering of the women to prepare articles for the Annual A. S. Fair held in Faneuil Hall, Boston. At that time mother would spend the week in attendance having charge, in company of a committee of ladies of which she was one, over the refreshments. The New England women were all workers and there was no shirking of responsibility—all worked. It became the custom of the ladies of the Lynn society for each to take their turn in assisting mother in her household duties on the morning of the day that the sewing circle met so as to be sure of her meeting with them. It was mother's custom to put aside the earnings from a certain number of shoes she had bound as her donation to the A. S. cause. Being frugal and economic she was able to put by a portion of her earnings for a rainy day.

I have often heard my father speak in admiration of mother's executive ability. During his absence abroad, he sent, as he could, support for his family, and on his coming home he supposed there would be some bills to settle. One day while talking over their affairs, mother arose and quietly going to the bureau drawer produced a Bank book with the sums deposited just in the proportion father had sent, the book also containing deposits of her own earnings—and not a debt had been contracted during his absence.

The greatest trial, perhaps, that mother was called upon to endure, after parting from her Baltimore friends several years before, was the leaving her Massachusetts home for the Rochester home where father established the "North Star." She never forgot her old friends and delighted to speak of them up to her last illness.

Wendell Phillips, Wm. Lloyd Garrison, Sydney Howard Gay and many more with their wives were particularly kind to her. At one of the Anti-Slavery conventions held in Syracuse, father and mother were the guests of Rev. Samuel J. May, a Unitarian minister and an ardent Anti-Slavery friend. The spacious parlors of the May mansion were thrown open for a reception to their honor and where she could meet her old Boston friends. The refreshments were served on trays, one of which placed upon an improvised table made by the sitting close together of Wendell Phillips, Wm. Lloyd Garrison and Sydney Howard Gay, mother was invited to sit, the four making an interesting tableaux.

Mother occasionally traveled with father on his short trips, but not as often as he would have liked as she was a housekeeper who felt that her presence was necessary in the home, as she was wont to say "to keep things straight." Her life in Rochester was not less active in the cause of the slave, if anything she was more self-sacrificing, and it was a long time after her residence there that she was understood. The atmosphere in which she was placed lacked the genial cordiality that greeted her in her Massachusetts home. There were only the few that learned to know her, for, she drew around herself a certain reserve, after meeting her new acquaintances that forbade any very near approach to her. Prejudice in the early 40's in Rochester ran rampant and mother became more distrustful. There were a few loyal co-workers and she set herself assiduously to work. In the home, with the aid of a laundress only, she managed her household. She watched with a great deal of interest and no little pride the growth in public life of my father, and in every possible way that she was capable aided him by relieving him of all the management of the home as it increased in size and in its appointments. It was her pleasure to know that when he stood up before an audience that his linen was immaculate and that she had made it so, for, no matter how well the laundry was done for the family, she must with her own hands smooth the tucks in father's linen and when he was on a long journey she would forward at a given point a fresh supply.

Being herself one of the first agents of the Underground Railroad she was an untiring worker along that line. To be able to accommodate in a comfortable manner the fugitives that passed our way, father enlarged his home where a suite of rooms could be made ready for those fleeing to Canada. It was no unusual occurrence for mother to be called up at all hours of the night, cold or hot as the case may be, to prepare supper for a hungry lot of fleeing humanity.

She was greatly interested in the publication of the "North Star" or Frederick Douglass' paper as it was called later on, and publication day was always a day for extra rejoicing as each weekly paper was felt to be another arrow sent on its way to do the work of puncturing the veil that shrouded a whole race in gloom. Mother felt it her duty to have her table well supplied with extra provisions that day, a custom that we, childlike, fully appreciated. Our home was two miles from the center of the city, where our office was situated, and many times did we trudge through snow knee deep, as street cars were unknown.

During one of the summer vacations the question arose in father's mind as to how his sons should be employed, for them to run wild through the streets was out of the question. There was much hostile feeling against the colored boys and as he would be from home most of the time, he felt anxious about them. Mother came to the rescue with the suggestion that they be taken into the office and taught the case. They were little fellows and the thought had not occurred to father. He acted upon the suggestion and at the ages of eleven and nine they were perched upon blocks and given their first lesson in printer's ink, besides being employed to carry papers and mailing them.

Father was mother's honored guest. He was from home so often that his home comings were events that she thought worthy of extra notice, and caused renewed activity. Every thing was done that could be to add to his comfort. She also found time to care for four other boys at different times. As they became members of our home circle, the care of their clothing was as carefully seen to as her own children's and they delighted in calling her Mother.

In her early life she was a member of the Methodist Church, as was father, but in our home there was no family alter. Our custom was to read a chapter in the Bible around the table, each reading a verse in turn until the chapter was completed. She was a person who strived to live a Christian life instead of talking it.

She was a woman strong in her likes and dislikes, and had a large discernment as to the character of those who came around her. Her gift in that direction being very fortunate in the protection of father's interest especially in the early days of his public life, when there was great apprehension for his safety. She was a woman firm in her opposition to alcoholic drinks, a strict disciplinarian—her *no* meant *no* and *yes, yes,* but more frequently the *no's* had it, especially when I was the petitioner. So far as I was concerned, I found my father more yielding than my mother, altho' both were rigid as to the matter of obedience.

There was a certain amount of grim humor about mother and perhaps such exhibitions as they occurred were a little startling to those who were unacquainted with her. The reserve in which she held herself made whatever she might attempt of a jocose nature somewhat acrid. She could not be known all at once, she had to be studied. She abhorred shams. In the early 70's she came to Washington and found a large number of people from whom the shackles had recently fallen. She fully realized their condition and considered the gaieties that were then indulged in as frivolous in the extreme.

On one occasion several young women called upon her and commenting on her spacious parlors and the approaching holiday season, thought it a favorable opportunity to suggest the keeping of an open house. Mother replied: "I have been keeping open house for several weeks. I have it closed now and I expect to keep it closed." The young women thinking mother's understanding was at fault, endeavored to explain. They were assured, however, that they were fully understood. Father, who was present, laughingly pointed to the New Bay Window, which had been completed only a few days previous to their call.

Perhaps no other home received under its roof a more varied class of people than did our home. From the highest dignitaries to the lowliest person, bond or free, white or black, were welcomed, and mother was equally gracious to all. There were a few who presumed on the hospitality of the home and officiously insinuated themselves and their advice in a manner that was particularly disagreeable to her. This unwelcome attention on the part of the visitor would be grievously repelled, in a manner more forceful than the said party would deem her capable of, and from such a person an erroneous impression of her temper and qualifications would be given, and criticisms sharp and unjust would be made; so that altho she had her triumphs, they were trials, and only those who knew her intimately could fully understand and appreciate the enduring patience of the wife and mother.

During her wedded life of forty-four years, whether in adversity or prosperity, she was the same faithful ally, guarding as best she could every interest connected with my father, his life-work and the home. Unfortunately an opportunity for a knowledge of books had been denied her, the lack of which she greatly deplored. Her increasing family and household duties prevented any great advancement, altho' she was able to read a little. By contact with people of culture and education, and they were her real friends, her improvement was marked. She took a lively interest in every phase of the Anti-Slavery movement, an interest that father took full pains to foster and to keep her intelligently informed. I was instructed to read to her. She was a good listener, making comments on passing events, which were well worth consideration, altho' the manner of the presentation of them might provoke a smile. Her value was fully appreciated by my father, and in one of his letters to Thomas Auld, (his former master,) he says, "Instead of finding my companion a burden she is truly a helpmeet."

In 1882, this remarkable woman, for in many ways she was remarkable, was stricken with paralysis and for four weeks was a great sufferer. Altho' perfectly helpless, she insisted from her sick bed to direct her home affairs. The orders were given with precision and they were obeyed with alacrity. Her fortitude and patience up to within ten days of her death were very great. She helped us to bear her burden. Many letters of condolence from those who had met her and upon whom pleasant impressions had been made, were received. Hon. J. M. Dalzell of Ohio, wrote thus:

"You know I never met your good wife but once and then her welcome was so warm and sincere and unaffected, her manner altogether so motherly, and her goodby so full of genuine kindness and hospitality, as to impress me tenderly and fill my eyes with tears as I now recall it."

Prof. Peter H. Clark of Cincinnati, Ohio, wrote: "The kind treatment given to us and our little one so many years ago won for her a place in our hearts from which no lapse of time could move her. To us she was ever kind and good and our mourning because of her death, is heartfelt."

There is much room for reflection in the review in the life of such a woman as Anna Murray Douglass. Unlettered tho' she was, there was a strength of character and of purpose that won for her the respect of the noblest and best. She was a woman who strove to inculcate in the minds of her children the highest principles of morality and virtue both by precept and example. She was not well versed in the polite etiquette of the drawing room, the rules for the same being found in the many treatises devoted to that branch of literature. She was possessed of a much broader culture, and with discernment born of intelligent observation, and wise discrimination she welcomed all with the hearty manner of a noble soul.

I have thus striven to give you a glimpse of my mother. In so doing I am conscious of having made frequent mention of my father. It is difficult to say any thing of mother without the mention of father, her life was so enveloped in his. Together they rest side by side, and most befittingly, within sight of the dear old home of hallowed memories and from which the panting fugitive, the weary traveler, the lonely emigrant of every clime, received food and shelter.

ROSETTA DOUGLASS SPRAGUE.

FREDERICK DOUGLASS IN IRELAND

Few persons have any idea as to the connection between the abolition of slavery in the United States and the struggle of the Irish for freedom. According to *The Standard Union*, when in the decade 1830 Negro slavery existed in the British West Indies, a little party of liberal men in the British Parliament began to agitate in season and out of season for emancipation, Daniel O'Connell, with a few Irish members who supported him, threw his strength to this little party on every division. There was a West Indian interest pledged to maintain Negro slavery, and this interest counted twenty-seven votes in Parliament. They came to O'Connell and offered their twenty-seven votes to him on every Irish question if he would oppose Negro emancipation.

"It was," said Wendell Phillips, "a terrible temptation. How many a so-called statesman would have yielded!" O'Connell said: "Gentlemen, God knows I speak for the saddest nation the sun ever sees, but may my right hand forget its cunning and my tongue cleave to the roof of my mouth, if to serve Ireland, even Ireland, I forget the Negro one single hour."

The following account taken from *The Liberator*, including a letter from Frederick Douglass, shows the genuineness of this Irish friendship for the Negro in the United States:

A letter of extraordinary interest at this time from Mr. Frederick Douglass to Mr. William Lloyd Garrison has just come to light in the columns of *The True American*, a little anti-slavery paper published in Cortland Village, N. Y., in 1846. The letter, written with the eloquence and depth of feeling which characterized all Mr. Douglass's utterances on the subject of slavery and the abuse of the Negro in this country. The letter, which *The True American* copied from *The Boston Liberator*, Mr. Garrison's Paper, is introduced by the following editorial comment from *The Albany Journal* under date of February 11, 1846.

"It is scarcely necessary to direct attention to the letter of

Frederick Douglass which we copy from *The Boston Liberator*. It will be read with equal pleasure and amazement by those who remember that eight years ago he was a slave, and that he literally stole the elements of an education which now gives him rank among the most gifted and eloquent men of the age.

"We shall not blame those who refuse to believe that Frederick wrote this letter. Without the personal knowledge we possess of his extraordinary attainments, we too should doubt whether a fugitive slave, who, as but yesterday, escaped from a bondage that doomed him to ignorance and degradation, now stands up and rebukes oppression with a dignity and force scarcely less glowing than that which Paul addressed to Agrippa."

The letter is as follows:

VICTORIA HOTEL, BELFAST,
January 1st, 1846.

My dear Friend Garrison:

I am now about to take leave of the Emerald Isle, for Glasgow, Scotland. I have been here a little more than four months.—Up to this time, I have been given no direct expression of the views, feelings and opinions which I have formed, respecting the character and condition of the people of this land. I have refrained thus purposely. I wish to speak advisedly, and in order to do this, I have waited till I trust experience has brought my opinions to an intelligent maturity. I have been thus thankful, not because I think what I may say will have much effect in shaping the opinions of the world, but because whatever of influence I may possess, whether little or much, I wish it to go in the right direction, and according to truth.

I hardly need say that in speaking of Ireland, I shall be influenced by no prejudices in favor of America. I think my circumstances all forbid that. I have no end to serve, no creed to uphold, no government to defend; and as to nation, I belong to none. I have no protection at home, or resting place abroad. The land of my birth welcomes me to her shores only as a slave, and spurns with contempt the idea of treating me differently.—So that I am an outcast from the society of my childhood, and an outlaw in the land of my birth. "I am a stranger with thee, and a sojourner as all my fathers were." That men should be patriotic is to me perfectly natural; and as a philosophical fact, I am able to give it an intellectual recognition. But no further can I go. If ever I had any patriotism, or any capacity for the feeling, it was whipt out of me long since by the lash of the American souldrivers.

In thinking of America, I sometimes find myself admiring her bright blue sky—her grand old woods—her fertile fields—her beautiful rivers—her mighty lakes, and star crowned mountains. But my rapture is soon checked, my joy is soon turned to mourning. When I remember that all is cursed with the infernal spirit of slaveholding, robbery and wrong,—when I remember that with the waters of her noblest rivers, the tears of my brethren are borne to the ocean, disregarded and forgotten, and that her most fertile fields drink daily of the warm blood of my outraged sisters, I am filled with unutterable loathing, and led to reproach myself that anything could fall from my lips in praise of such a land. America will not allow her children to love her. She seems bent on compelling those who would be her warmest friends, to be her worst enemies. May God give her repentance before it is too late, is the ardent prayer of my heart. I will continue to pray, labor and wait, believing that she cannot always be insensible to the dictates of justice, or deaf to the voice of humanity.

My opportunities for learning the character and condition of the people of this land have been very great. I have travelled almost from the hill of "Howth" to the "Giant's Causeway, and from the Giant's Causeway to Cape Clear. During these travels, I have met with much in the character and condition of the people to approve, and much to condemn—much that has thrilled me with pleasure—and very much that has filled me with pain. I will not in this letter attempt to give any description of those scenes which have given me pain. This I will do hereafter. I have enough, and more than your subscribers will be disposed to read at one time, of the bright side of the picture. I can truly say, I have spent some of the happiest moments of my life since landing in this country. I seem to have undergone a transformation. I live a new life.

The warm and generous co-operation extended to me by the friends of my despised race—the prompt and liberal manner with which the press has rendered me its aid—the glorious enthusiasm with which thousands have flocked to hear the cruel wrongs of my down-trodden and long enslaved countrymen portrayed—the deep sympathy of the slave, and the strong abhorrence of the slaveholder, everywhere evinced—the cordiality with which members and ministers of various religious bodies, and of various shades of religious opinion, have embraced me and lent me their aid—the kind hospitality constantly proffered to me by persons of the highest rank in society—the spirit of freedom that seems to animate all with whom I come in contact—and the entire absence of everything that looked like prejudice against me, on account of the color of my skin—contrasting so strongly with my long and bitter experience in the United States, that I look with wonder and amazement on the transition.

In the Southern part of the United States I was a slave, thought of and spoken of as property. In the language of the law, "held, taken, reputed and adjudged to be chattel in the hands of my owners and possessors, and their executors, administrators, or assigns, to all intents, constructions, and purposes whatever."—Brev. Digest, 224. In the Northern States, a fugitive slave, liable to be hunted at any moment like a felon, and to be hurried into the terrible jaws of slavery—doomed by an inveterate prejudice against color to insult and outrage in every hand. (Massachusetts out of the question)—denied the privileges and courtesies common to others in the use of the most humble of conveyances—shut out from the cabins on steamboats—refused admission to respectable hotels—caricatured, scorned, scoffed, mocked and maltreated with impunity by any one (no matter how black his heart), so he has a white skin.

But now behold the change! Eleven days and a half gone, and I have crossed three thousand miles of the perilous deep. Instead of a democratic government, I am under a monarchical government. Instead of the bright blue sky of America, I am covered with the soft gray fog of the Emerald Isle. I breathe, and lo! the chattel becomes a man. I gaze around in vain for one who will question my equal humanity, claim me as his slave, or offer me an insult. I employ a cab—I am seated beside white people—I reach the hotel—I enter the same door—I am shown into the same parlor—I dine at the same table—and no one is offended. No delicate nose grows deformed in my presence. I have no difficulty here in obtaining admission into any place of worship, instruction or amusement, on equal terms with people as white as any I ever saw in the United States. I meet nothing to remind me of my complexion. I find myself regarded and treated at every turn with the kindness and deference paid to white people. When I go to church, I am met by no upturned nose and scorned lip to tell me, "We don't allow niggers in here!"

I remember about two years ago, there was in Boston, near the southwest corner of Boston Common, a menagerie. I had long desired to see such a collection as I understood were being exhibited there. Never having had an opportunity while a slave, I resolved to seize this, my first, since my escape. I went, and as I approached the entrance to gain admission, I was met and told by the doorkeeper in a harsh and contemptuous tone, "We don't allow niggers here!" I also remember attending a revival meeting in the Rev. Henry Jackson's meeting house, at New Bedford, and going up the broad aisle to find a seat. I was met by a good deacon, who told me in a pious tone, "We don't allow niggers here!" Soon after my arrival in New Bedford from the South, I had a strong desire to attend the Lyceum, but was told, "We don't allow niggers here!"

While passing from New York to Boston on the steamer Massachusetts, on the night of the 9th Dec., 1843, when chilled almost through with the cold, I went into the cabin to get a little warm, I was soon touched upon the shoulder and told, "We don't allow niggers here!" On arriving in Boston from an anti-slavery tour, hungry and tired I went into an eating house near my friend Mr. Campbell's, to get some refreshments. I was met by a lad in a white apron, "We don't allow niggers here!" A week or two before leaving the United States, I had a meeting appointed at Weymouth, the home of that glorious band of true abolitionists, the Weston family and others. On attempting to take a seat on the omnibus to that place, I was told by the driver (and I never shall forget the fiendish haste), "I don't allow niggers in here!"

Thank heaven for the respite I now enjoy! I had been in Dublin but a few days, when a gentleman of great respectability kindly offered to conduct me through all the public buildings of that beautiful city; and a little afterwards, I found myself dining with the Lord Mayor of Dublin. What a pity there was not some American Democratic Christian at the door of his splendid mansion, to bark out at my approach, "They don't allow niggers in here!" The truth is, the people here know nothing of the Republican Negro hate prevalent in our glorious land. They measure and esteem men according to their moral and intellectual worth, and not according to the color of their skin. Whatever may be said of the aristocracies here, there is none based on the color of a man's skin. This species of aristocracy belongs pre-eminently to "the land of the free, and the home of the brave." I have never found it abroad, in any but Americans. It sticks to them wherever they go. They find it almost as hard to get rid of as to get rid of their skins.

The second day after my arrival at Liverpool, in company with my friend Buffum, and several other friends I went to Eaton Hall, the residence of the Marquis of Westminster, one of the most splendid buildings in England. On approaching the door, I found several of our American passengers who came out with us in the Cambria, waiting at the door for admission, as but one party was allowed in the house at a time. We all had to wait till the company within came out. And of all the faces, expressive of chagrin, those of the Americans were pre-eminent. They looked as sour as vinegar, and as bitter as gall, when they found I was to be admitted on equal terms with themselves. When the door was opened I walked in, on an equal footing with my white fellow citizens, and from all I could see I had as much attention paid me by the servants who showed me through the house as any with a paler skin. As I walked through the building, the statuary did not fall down, the pictures did not leap from their places, the doors did not refuse to open, and the servants did not say, "We don't allow niggers in here!"

A happy new year to you and to all the friends of freedom.

Excuse this imperfect scrawl and believe me to be ever and always yours,

FREDERICK DOUGLASS

BOOK REVIEWS

The History of the Afro-American Group of the Episcopal Church. By GEORGE F. BRAGG, Rector St. James First African Church, Baltimore. With an Introduction by the Rt. Rev. T. DuBose Bratton, D.D., LL.D., Bishop of Mississippi. The Church Advocate Press, Baltimore, 1922, pp. 319.

This work is intended to supply the need of a volume tracing the connection of the Negro with the Protestant Episcopal Church in America. As this particular group of communicants has not the status of independent organization, its peculiar history has remained only in fragments. To embody these in the form of a handy volume to show how this denomination has influenced the life of the Negro and how members of the race have been affected thereby, will be a distinct service for which the public would feel thankful. Whether or not the author has accomplished this task the readers themselves will decide. He has undertaken the work with so much enthusiasm and found so many things to praise and such a few to condemn that the reader may find the work somewhat *ex parte*. The struggle of the Negro communicants in this demonination and its indifference toward the strivings of the race before the Civil War are not emphasized. Approaching the volume with reservation, however, the investigator will find the work of some value.

The volume begins with the early baptism of African children during the early days. He directs attention to the work of missionaries in South Carolina, Maryland, Georgia, and Virginia and brings his story down to the days of the independent movement among Negro communicants as it culminated in the organization of the Free African Society of Philadelphia out of which emerged the St. Thomas African Church under the leadership of Absalom Jones. He then discusses the rise of such churches as St. Phillips in New York, St. James in Baltimore, Christ Church in Providence, St. Luke in New Haven, The Church of the Crucifixion in Philadelphia, St. Matthews in Detroit, St. Phillips in New Jersey and St. Phillips in Buffalo. The renewed interest of the Protestant Episcopal Church in the uplift of the Negro is interwoven around his discussion of the Freedman's Commission organized in 1868 to Christianize and educate the Negroes recently emancipated in the South. He then discusses the further interest shown by the General Convention of 1871 and treats with some detail the efforts through mission schools in the South.

The remaining portion of the book consists of biographical sketches. It contains a list of the Negro clergy prior to 1866, mentioning such names as Absalom Jones, Peter Williams, William Levington, James C. Ward, Jacob Oson, Gustavus V. Caesar, Edward Jones, William Douglass, Isaiah G. DeGrasse, Alexander Crummell, Eli Worthington Stokes, William C. Munroe, Samuel Vreeland Berry, Harrison Holmes Webb, James Theodore Holly, William Johnson Alston, and John Peterson. Among these are accounts of such veteran friends as Bishops Atkinson, Lyman, Johns, Whittle, Smith, Quintard, Whittingham, Howe, Stevens, Young, and Dudley, along with Mr. Joseph Bryan, General Samuel C. Armstrong, and Mrs. Loomis L. White. He then gives sketches of some self-made strong characters like James E. Thompson, Cassius M. C. Mason, James Solomon Russell, James Nelson Denver, Henry Mason Joseph, Henry Stephen McDuffy, Primus Priss Alston, Paulus Moort, Henry L. Phillips, August E. Jensen, Joshua Bowden Massiah, William Victor Tunnell, and John W. Perry. Honorable mention is given to Samuel David Ferguson, John Payne, Edward T. Demby, Henry B. Delany, and T. Momolu Gardiner.

The Trend of the Races. By GEORGE E. HAYNES, Ph.D. With an introduction by JAMES H. DILLARD. Published jointly by Council of Women for Home Missions and Missionary Education Movement of the United States and Canada. New York, 1922, pp. 205.

This volume is at once both historical and sociological. It is interesting but might have been more readable if the materials had been better organized so as to avoid unnecessary repetition from chapter to chapter. It marks an epoch in the history of the Negro in the United States, however, in that it was written at the request of white persons constituting the Joint Committee on Home Mission Literature representing the Missionary Education Movement and the Council of Women for Home Missions and the Missionary Educational Boards. The aim of the work is to present to the white workers in the Church the achievements of the

Negro, believing that if the Negro becomes known to the white man, he will not be any longer hated by him; or, as the chairman of the committee herself says in the foreword to the volume: "Our seeking to know him must be on the basis of the broadest sympathy. In the friendliest and most helpful spirit we should sincerely desire to understand him in the place where he is and to apprehend something of the road by which he came and the direction of his highest and best aspirations, that we may, so far as we can, make it possible for him to attain his best in our common civilization. We should at the same time quite as earnestly seek to know ourselves in respect to our limitations, achievements, and goals in the building of the social order."

The book begins with a presentation of the case of the Negro, reviewing two methods of racial adjustment. It then discusses the conditions under which some choice of procedure must be made in view of the white and Negro public opinion. The author then endeavors to show what the Negro has accomplished during the sixty years emphasizing his achievements both economic and industrial. In this chapter he deals largely with the progress of Negro farmers, the growth of business enterprises, improvements in health, moral uplift, the development of homes, achievements in community life, education, inventions, scientific discovery, and religious life. The author then treats in some detail the mental capacity of the Negro, his feelings, his conduct, his humor and his dramatic ability. He shows how the Negro practices self-abnegation, toleration and optimism in spite of oppression and yet brings out the fact that there is a rising tide of race consciousness, increasing resentment and suspicion. The development of racial self-respect, and the forward looking program of self-assertion are also mentioned in showing how the Negroes are learning to depend upon their own leaders and to undertake to do for themselves what they have long requested others to accomplish for them.

One of the important features of the book is its emphasis on the part which the Negro has played in the various wars in the United States beginning with the American Revolution and bringing the story through all of our national and international struggles. Most space, however, is devoted to the Negro's participation in the World War and to the local economic situation in which the Negroes figured during the dearth of labor and the scarcity of money when they responded to the call to render non-combatant service and to lend the Government their means by purchasing Liberty Bonds. Following this the author finds it opportune to show the trend of the white world, bringing out its attitude and ways of action due to conscience. Here he discusses the influence of economic motives, survivals from the past, attitudes due to ideals of race, the effects of the principles and ideals of democracy and the interracial mind. The author believes that the way to interracial peace is through racial contacts, church cooperation, efficient reorganization in the division of labor, and through mutual economic and life interests, group interdependence between mental and social factors, educational institutions, popular government, and voluntary organizations coordinating interracial activities.

In the Vanguard of a Race. By L. H. HAMMOND. Published jointly by Council of Women for Home Missions and Missionary Education Movement of the United States and Canada. New York, 1922, pp. 176.

This is a volume not so serious as that of Dr. Haynes's but written for the purpose of presenting to the American public a number of useful leaders now shaping the destiny of the Negro race. Inasmuch as all famous workers of the race could not be mentioned, the author endeavored to select one typical of each particular thought and to portray them as the representatives of a large host of laborers rebuilding the civilization of a large portion of mankind. The persons sketched have worked as musicians, painters, sculptors, actors, singers, poets, educators, physicians, farmers, and clergymen. When one considers several of the selections made, however, he must be astounded at the lack of judgment shown as to who are the leading Negro workers doing something worth while. The author seems to have obtained advice from such friends and helpers as Miss Ida A. Tourtellot of the Phelps-Stokes Foundation, Miss Flora Mitchell of the Woman's Home Missionary Society of the Methodist Episcopal Church, Mrs. Booker T. Washington of Tuskegee, Mr. Jackson Davis of the General Education Board, Mr. N. C. Newbold of the North Carolina State Department of Education, Mr. W. T. B. Williams of the Jeanes and Slater Boards, Professor G. L. Imes of Tuskegee, and Dr. A. M. Moore of Durham, North Carolina, all of whom do not claim to be authorities in matter of this kind.

On the whole, however, the book has a value. In the first chapter, "A Long Ascent," there is an interesting sketch of the rising race showing unusual possibilities which must convince the world of the inherent worth and bright future of the Negro. The sketch of Booker T. Washington entitled "A Story of Service" is decidedly interesting and is written in such a style as to popularize the achievements of the great educator. Presented very much in the same way is the account of the valuable service of Dr. C. V. Roman whose efforts have not been restricted to medicine, inasmuch as he is an author and a lecturer of recognized standing. Miss Nannie H. Burroughs is properly presented to typify that part of the story known as "Saving an Idea." Herein is sketched the rise and the culmination of the career of one of the most useful women of our day. In the same style the work of Dr. William N. DeBerry of Springfield, Massachusetts, appears. There follows the sketch of the career of Mrs. Jane Barrett, a believer in happiness, then that of John B. Pierce, a builder of prosperity, and next that of Mrs. Maggie L. Walker, a woman banker. Much space is given also to the career of the famous composer, Harry T. Burleigh. This sketch is followed by two others directing attention to Miss Martha Drummer and James Dunston. The book closes with a brief biography of Joseph S. Cotter, Jr., the young poet who recently attained distinction in expressing the strivings of an oppressed people.

The Negro in Chicago. A study of race relations and a race riot. By the Chicago Commission on Race Relations. The University of Chicago Press, Chicago, Illinois, 1922, pp. 672.

It is generally admitted that this report of the Commission on Race Relations is the most important contribution to this interesting subject. The very organization of the commission deepens this impression. Before the end of this racial conflict in which 38 lives were lost and 537 persons injured between July 27 and August 6, 1919, representatives of 48 social, civic, commercial and professional organizations of Chicago met on the first of August and requested Governor Frank O. Lowden, of Illinois, to appoint an emergency State Committee "to study the psychological, social and economic causes underlying the conditions resulting in the present race riot and to make such recommendations as will tend to prevent a recurrence of such conditions in the future."

In response to this and other urgent requests, according to the report and pursuant to his personal knowledge of the situation derived from investigations made by him in Chicago during the riot, Governor Lowden appointed as a commission, Edgar A. Bancroft, William Scott Bond, Edward Osgood Brown, Harry Eugene Kelley, Victor F. Lawson, and Julius Rosenwald as representatives of the white race and Robert S. Abbott, George Cleveland Hall, George H. Jackson, Edward H. Morris, Adelbert H. Roberts, and Lacey Kirk Williams representing the Negroes, all to serve as a commission to undertake the work suggested by the memorialists. Mr. Bancroft was designated by the Governor as chairman but on account of his absence due to ill health, Dr. F. W. Shepardson, Director of the State Department of Registration and Education, was appointed to serve as acting chairman and on the return of Mr. Bancroft, Dr. Shepardson was added to the commission and made its Vice-Chairman. Inasmuch as the commission had no funds a committee consisting of Messrs. James B. Forgan, chairman, Abel Davis, Treasurer, Arthur Meeker, John J. Mitchell, and John G. Shedd, together with Messrs. R. B. Beach and John F. Bowman of the staff of the Chicago Association of Commerce, enabled the commission of inquiry to meet this emergency. The actual work was done under the direction of an Executive Secretary, Graham Romeyn Taylor and an Associate Executive Secretary, Charles S. Johnson, the latter assuming charge of the actual inquiries and investigation.

The report does not present any solution by which all racial troubles may be avoided. It well fulfills its mission, however, in finding facts which, if properly studied, will serve to guide others in promoting amicable relations between racial groups. It at once convinces the general public that causes of racial friction may be insignificant in themselves but are nevertheless capable of leading to serious results, although a little effort can easily effect their removal in time to avoid such fatal consequences. It shows, moreover, that grievances too often portrayed as justifiable reasons for self-help are generally exaggerated primarily for the purpose of inflaming the public mind and should such findings be given adequate publicity the effects of such unwise action may be counteracted in time. It is claimed for this commission, moreover, that its work has promoted an understanding between the two racial groups in the city of Chicago and removed misunderstandings which have been such prolific sources of trouble.

The report covers in some detail an informing account of the race riot itself and of other outbreaks in the State of Illinois. Going to the very causes of things, the commission studied the migration of the Negroes from the South, the Negro population in Chicago, directing attention to the housing of Negroes, racial contacts, vicious environments, and lines of industry. One of the most informing parts of the work is a treatment of public opinion in race relations, bringing out beliefs concerning Negroes and the background of such and public opinion as expressed by Negroes themselves. Adequate space is given to the instruments of opinion-making, such as Chicago newspapers and the Negro press as well as to rumors, myths, and propaganda. The recommendations of the Commission require careful attention. While the public will not generally accept these recommendations as final, they are at least suggestive and require careful consideration.

One defect of the work, however, if it has a defect, is that it fails to take into account one important cause, namely, the migration of many poor whites to the North during the period of scarcity of labor incident to the World War when these southerners brought north their own opinions about how to keep the Negro down and helped to aggravate the situation in Chicago.

NOTES

Mr. George W. Brown, a graduate of Howard University who, as a result of a year of graduate work in History and Political Science at Western Reserve University, has received the degree of Master of Arts, has been appointed Instructor in History at the West Virginia Collegiate Institute. Mr. Brown is the author of a dissertation entitled *Haiti and the United States*.

Mr. Miles Mark Fisher who contributed to the last issue of THE JOURNAL OF NEGRO HISTORY the valuable dissertation and documents bearing on the career of Lott Cary and who has written two other valuable works, *The History of the Olivet Baptist Church* and *The Master's Slave*, has been appointed an instructor at the Virginia Union University, Richmond, Virginia.

Mr. Luther P. Jackson, a graduate of Fisk University, who specialized at Columbia in History and Education leading to the degree of Master of Arts, and who contributes to the current number of THE JOURNAL OF NEGRO HISTORY the dissertation entitled *The Educational Efforts of the Freedmen's Bureau and Freedmen's Aid Societies in South Carolina*, 1862–1872, has been appointed an instructor in the Virginia Normal and Industrial Institute, Petersburg, Virginia.

The Macmillan Company has published *A Boys' Life of Booker T. Washington* by W. C. Jackson, Vice President of the North Carolina College for Women, Greensboro, and Professor of History.

The A. B. Caldwell Publishing Company, Atlanta, Georgia, has brought out an autobiography, *Echoes from a Pioneer Life* by Jared Maurice Arter, an instructor in Storer College, Harpers Ferry, West Va.

From the University of Chicago Press there has come another interesting volume on the Negro. This is entitled *The Negro Press in the United States* by Frederick G. Detweiler.

Sir Harry H. Johnston, G. C. M. G., K. C. B., Sc.D., has published through Oxford at the Clarendon Press his second volume of *A Comparative Study of the Bantu and Semi-Bantu Languages*.

THE PROCEEDINGS OF THE ANNUAL MEETING OF THE ASSOCIATION FOR THE STUDY OF NEGRO LIFE AND HISTORY

The Association met in annual session on the 22d, 23d and 24th of November in Louisville, Kentucky. The day sessions were held at the Chestnut Street Branch Library and the evening sessions at the Quinn Chapel A. M. E. Church. The meeting was a success from both the local and national points of view. Persons from afar came to take an active part and the citizens of Louisville and nearby cities of Kentucky attended in considerable numbers.

The meeting was opened at eight o'clock Wednesday evening at the Chestnut Street Branch Library with a stereopticon lecture on the History of the Negro by Dr. A. Eugene Thomson, principal of Lincoln Institute, Lincoln Ridge, Kentucky. This lecture covered the early history of the Negro in Egypt and Ethiopia with illustrations of the historic monuments exhibiting the progress of the natives in architecture and the fine arts. There followed an informing discussion of the importance of the study of this particular part of the past of the dark races.

On Thursday morning at ten o'clock a conference on "The Present State of the Negro" was held. Mr. E. E. Reed, principal of the Bowling Green High School, delivered an address on "The Social and Economic Status of the Negro." This was the main feature of the conference. The general discussion was opened by Mr. E. A. Carter, secretary of the Louisville Urban League, who discussed "The Political Status of the Negro." The views of the speakers were such as to present both the optimistic and the pessimistic sides of the question. They believed that while there have been some developments which indicate improvement in the status of the Negro, there have been also other changes which indicate a tendency of things to become static.

Early in the afternoon at 1:30 P. M. a special session was held at the William J. Simmons University. The aim here was to interest the students in the importance of the preservation of the records of the Negro. Several members of the Association discussed the history of the organization, its achievements and plans, and welcomed the cooperation of all as coworkers in this long neglected field. Dr. W. H. Steward, the editor of *The American Baptist*, then spoke from his experience on "The Value of a Written Record," mentioning several cases in Kentucky where important matters have been decided by such documentary evidence. He emphasized the importance of the work accomplished by the Association and encouraged the youth to connect themselves with it that the cause may be promoted more successfully.

At three o'clock Thursday afternoon with Professor W. B. Matthews, principal of the Central High School, presiding, there followed a session devoted to "The Teaching of Negro History." Many of the teachers from the local school system were present. In a very thoughtful and impressive manner Mr. J. W. Bell, principal of the Hopkinsville High School, discussed the teaching of Negro history as a matter of concern not only to the Negro himself but to the white man. He expressed the opinion that through the dissemination of such information the one race may become better acquainted with the other. He was then followed by Mr. P. W. L. Jones, instructor in History at the Kentucky Normal and Industrial Institute, Frankfort, Kentucky. Mr. Jones directed his attention to "The Value of Negro Biography" as a means of keeping before the race the records of a number of useful citizens who might otherwise be forgotten and as a means of inspiring the youth to useful endeavor and noble achievement. He took occasion to present brief sketches of a number of Negroes once prominent in the past but now almost forgotten because of the failure to pass their story on to the coming generation. Mr. Thomas F. Blue, librarian of the Chestnut Street Branch Library, then opened the general discussion showing from his experience the need for directing more attention to these neglected aspects of this peculiar problem of a race in the making.

The first evening session was held at the Quinn Chapel A. M. E. Church with Dr. Noah W. Williams presiding. On this occasion the Honorable C. C. Stoll, representing the Mayor of Louisville, welcomed the Association in words adequate to arouse interest and enthusiasm. Dr. L. G. Jordan, secretary emeritus of the National Baptist Foreign Mission Board, responded to this address on behalf of the Association. He took occasion, moreover, to make some interesting observations out of his experiences in America and in Africa. Then followed an address by Dr. C. G. Woodson who briefly connected the achievements of the Negro with such movements in history as the commercial revolution, the intellectual revival, the struggle for the rights of man, the industrial revolution, the reform movements of the nineteenth century, and the present effort to attain social justice.

On Friday morning at ten o'clock with Dr. James Bond presiding there followed a conference on the Negro slave. Mr. W. H. Fouse, principal of the Russell High School of Lexington, read an informing paper on "The Contribution of the Slave to Civilization." He emphasized especially the value of Negro labor as the basis upon which Southern society was established, showing that whatever valuable culture was developed was made possible by the work of the Negro slave. He did not, however, subscribe to the theory that it is necessary to enslave one part of the population that the other may apply itself to the study of science, philosophy and politics. Dr. R. S. Cotterill, instructor in History at the University of Louisville, then read a valuable dissertation entitled "The Use of Slaves in Building Southern Railroads." The speaker showed that he had made an extensive research into documentary material, and he presented an array of facts which unusually enlightened his audience in this neglected field. During the general discussion which followed some other important facts were brought forward, and much interest in the researches of these two speakers was generally expressed.

From Friday afternoon at two o'clock to 5:30 P. M. there were exhibited at the Chestnut Street Branch Library samples of the publications of the Association and a number of valuable engravings of the Antique Works of Art in Benin, West Africa. This offered the public an opportunity to judge the progress made by the Association since its organization in 1915 and to form an opinion as to the sort of work prosecuted and the manner in which it has been done. The engravings setting forth the achievements of an important group of African peoples of the 16th century convinced a large number that the Negro race has behind it a valuable record which can never be known except through such research and expeditions as will unearth these important contributions.

At three o'clock there was held the business session of the Association. The reports of the Director and the Secretary-Treasurer were read and, after favorable comment, were accepted and approved by vote of the Association. These reports follow:

THE REPORT OF THE DIRECTOR.

With respect to the most difficult task of the Director, that of raising money, the work of the Association has been eminently successful. Encouraged by the appropriation of $25,000 obtained from the Carnegie Corporation last year, the Director appealed to several boards for the same consideration. Last February one of these, the Laura Spelman Rockefeller Memorial, appropriated $25,000 to this work, payable in annual installments of $5,000, as in the case of that obtained from the Carnegie Corporation. It is to be regretted, however, that smaller contributions, heretofore yielding most of the income of the Association prior to obtaining the two appropriations, have diminished in number and amount. Appealed to repeatedly, many of these persons give the heavy income tax as an excuse, while not a few make the mistake of thinking that the other funds received by the Association are sufficient to take care of the general expenses. During the fiscal year 1921–1922, thirty-seven persons, most of whom were Negroes, contributed $25.00 each, whereas during the previous fiscal year the number was larger.

The following report of the Secretary-Treasurer shows how these funds have been used:

FINANCIAL STATEMENT OF THE SECRETARY-TREASURER

WASHINGTON, D. C., July 1, 1922

THE ASSOCIATION FOR THE STUDY OF
NEGRO LIFE AND HISTORY, INC.,
WASHINGTON, D. C.

Gentlemen:

I hereby submit to you a statement of the amount of money received and expended by the Association for the Study of Negro Life and History, Incorporated, from July 1, 1921, to June 30, 1922, inclusive:

Receipts		*Expenditures*	
Subscriptions	$ 1,772.63	Printing and Stationery	$ 4,929.97
Memberships	241.00	Petty Cash	670.00
Contributions	9,113.75	Stenographic service	990.23
Advertising	195.45	Rent and Light	714.67
Rent and Light	180.14	Salaries	3,450.00
Books	1.70	Traveling Expenses	468.09
Refunds	50.42	Miscellaneous	286.46
Total receipts	$11,555.09	Total expenditures	$11,509.42
Bal. on hand July 1, 1921	43.09	Bal. on hand June 30, 1922	88.76
	$11,598.18		$11,598.18

This report does not cover the $5,000 annually received for research into the Free Negro Prior to 1861 and Negro Reconstruction History. This fund was made available on the first of July, the beginning of the fiscal year, and has been apportioned so as to pay three investigators and a copyist employed to do this work.

Respectfully submitted,
(Signed) S. W. RUTHERFORD,
Secretary-Treasurer.

The appropriation of $25,000 obtained from the Laura Spelman Rockefeller Memorial requires the employment of investigators to develop the studies of the Free Negro Prior to 1861 and of Negro Reconstruction History. The annual allowance of $5,000 is devoted altogether to this work, inasmuch as special instructions received from the Trustees of the Laura Spelman Rockefeller Memorial prohibit the use of this money for any other purpose. The Association has, therefore, employed Dr. George Francis Dow to read the eighteenth century colonial newspapers of New England, C. G. Woodson to make a study of the Free Negro Prior to 1861, A. A. Taylor to study the Social and Economic Conditions of the Negro during the Reconstruction, and a clerk serving the investigators in the capacity of a copyist.

At present Mr. A. A. Taylor is spending only one-half of his time at this work, but after the first of next June he will have the opportunity to direct his attention altogether to this task. During this year it is expected that he will complete his studies of the Social and Economic Conditions in Virginia and South Carolina.

In the study of the Free Negro the Director has spent the year compiling a statistical report giving the names of free Negroes who were heads of families in the South in 1830 showing the number in each family and the number of slaves owned. Within a few months that part of the report dealing with Louisiana, South Carolina and North Carolina will be completed.

The Association is also directing attention to the work of training men for research in this field. The program agreed upon is to educate in the best graduate schools with libraries containing works bearing on Negro life and history at least three young men a year, supported by fellowships of $500 from the Association and such additional stipend as the schools themselves may grant for the support of the undertaking. One of these students will take up the study of Negro History, one will direct his attention to Anthropometric and Psychological measurements of Negroes, and one to African Anthropology and Archaeology. In this undertaking the Director has not only the cooperation of Prof. Carl Russell Fish, of the University of Wisconsin, and Prof. William E. Dodd, of the University of Chicago, who with him constitute the Committee on Fellowships, but also the assistance of Professors Franz Boas and E. L. Thorndike of Columbia University and of Professor E. A. Hooton of Harvard University.

Closely connected with these plans, moreover, are certain other projects to preserve Negro folklore and the fragments of Negro music. In this effort the Association has the cooperation of Mrs. Elsie Clews Parsons, the moving spirit of the American Folklore Society. She is now desirous of making a more systematic effort to embody this part of the Negro civilization and she believes that the work can be more successfully done by cooperation with the Association. As soon as the Director can obtain a special fund for this particular work, an investigator will be employed to undertake it.

The interest manifested in the study of Negro History in clubs and schools has been very encouraging. Most of the advanced institutions of learning of both North and South make use of *The Journal of Negro History* in teaching social sciences. The Director's two recent works, *The History of the Negro Church* and *The Negro in Our History* are being extensively used as textbooks in classes studying Sociology and History. The enthusiasm of some of these groups has developed to the extent that they now request authority to organize under the direction of the Association local bodies to be known as State Associations for the Study of Negro Life and History.

Respectfully submitted,
C. G. WOODSON,
Director.

Upon taking up the election of officers there prevailed a motion to cast the unanimous ballot of the Association for the following officers:

John R. Hawkins, *President*
S. W. Rutherford, *Secretary-Treasurer*
C. G. Woodson, *Director*

The following were elected members of the Executive Council:

John R. Hawkins	Henry C. King
S. W. Rutherford	William E. Dodd
Carter G. Woodson	E. A. Hooton
Julius Rosenwald	Bishop John Hurst
James H. Dillard	Alexander L. Jackson
Bishop R. A. Carter	Bishop R. E. Jones
Robert R. Church	Clement Richardson
Franz Boas	Robert C. Woods
Carl Russell Fish	

John R. Hawkins, S. W. Rutherford and C. G. Woodson were chosen as trustees of the Association. John R. Hawkins, S. W. Rutherford and A. L. Jackson were elected members of the Business Committee.

There then followed a brief discussion of plans and ways and means for the expansion of the work. Most of this discussion developed from the various items of the report of the Director. Mr. W. H. Fouse, of Lexington, Kentucky, proposed that the Association should authorize the organization of State Associations for the Study of Negro Life and History to cooperate with the national body in preserving local biographical records of Negroes in counties and cities inaccessible to national workers. This proposal was favorably received.

On Friday evening at 8:30 P. M. there took place the second evening session at the Quinn Chapel A. M. E. Church with Prof. H. C. Russell presiding. The chief feature of the occasion was the address of Dr. C. V. Roman entitled "The American Civilization and the Negro.'' Following the line of his researches and his opinions already expressed in various works, Dr. Roman discussed the meaning of culture and connected the achievements of the Negro therewith. He took occasion also to show how the history of the race has been neglected and how many records worth while have been accredited to the defamers of the Negro race. Mr. J. W. Bell, of Hopkinsville, Kentucky, then entertained the audience with a very eloquent address, speaking in general of the achievements of the Association and emphasizing the importance of close cooperation therewith. The meeting was then closed with a few remarks by the Director who thanked the people of Louisville and of Kentucky for their cooperation in making the meeting a success.

THE JOURNAL OF NEGRO HISTORY

THE TEACHING OF NEGRO HISTORY [1]

The teaching of Negro history will serve the two-fold purpose of informing the white man and inspiring the Negro. The untoward circumstances under which the Negro lives make the teaching of his history imperatively necessary. When the founders of this government brought forth a new nation conceived in liberty and dedicated to the proposition that all men are created equal, many thought that the Negro was not regarded as a man. Thomas Jefferson himself, the writer of that document, held the Negro as a slave. The Negro was regarded as mere property, as a mere beast of burden. It required four years of bloody war to transform him from the position of a thing and place him in the ranks of men with a mere chance to struggle for actual democracy. These circumstances have caused one of the most intricate problems, the race problem. They have placed the American Negro in a category by himself. They have brought about the peculiar situation of a nation within a nation.

The teaching of Negro history would contribute much to the solution of this complicated race problem. The solution of any problem depends upon an adequate understand-

[1] An address delivered before the Association for the Study of Negro Life and History at Louisville, November 23, 1922.

ing of it. The most illuminating approach to the race problem is the historical approach. The white man of this country must be supplied with the real facts pertaining to the Negro. If not, all of his generalizations will be mere verbiage based upon tradition inspired by prejudice. To prevent a distorted social perspective and to develop a wider community consciousness, the white man should read history from the Negro's point of view.

For more than four centuries the Negro has been brought into contact with the European white man. For the most part the Teutonic stocks have regarded the Negro as a negative factor in history. The Latin and Slavic races have been more kindly disposed toward him. They have been disposed to give honor to whom honor is due regardless of race or color. To them color has been an incident of birth, not a badge of inferiority. In the annals of Russia Alexander Pushkin is recognized as her national poet. France considered Toussaint L'Ouverture, one of the most commanding figures of any age, a conspicuous example of the possibilities of the pure-blooded Negro. She recognized Alexander Dumas as her most distinguished romancer. Today she places this mantle upon the shoulders of René Maran.

The white people of the United States consider their race to be men of a superior breed and have ignored the Negro in recording European and American history. In their desire to substantiate the theory of the superiority of the white man and the inferiority of the Negro, they have failed to publish or suppressed the truth about the achievements of the Negro. They have looked for nothing praiseworthy in him; they have widely proclaimed his faults and failures. Well did Macaulay say:

By exclusive attention to one class of phenomena, by exclusive taste for one species of excellence the human intellect was stunted. The best historians of later days have been seduced from truth, not by their imagination, but by their reason. They far excel their predecessors in the art of deducing general principles from facts, but unhappily they have fallen into the error of distorting the facts to suit the general principles. They arrive at a theory from looking at a part of the phenomena; the remaining phenomena they strain or curtail to suit the theory. In every human character and transaction there is a mixture of good and evil: a little exaggeration, a little suppression, a judicious use of epithets, a watching and searching skepticism with respect to the evidence on one side, a convenient credulity with respect to every report or tradition on the other side may easily make a saint of Laud or a tyrant of Henry IV.

The Negro's most important contribution to American history is his unparalleled progress—his rise from poverty to wealth, from ignorance to knowledge, from backwardness to civilization. No other race has achieved more under the same conditions. No authentic history of the United States, then, can ignore or exclude the Negro. The part which he has played in American history has served largely to make the nation what it is today.

The fidelity of the Negro slave to his master, his devotion and loyalty to his country should constitute interesting historical themes. Under the regime of slavery the Negro was literally bought and sold like the very soil. His life was but one unceasing round of toil and misery; his faith, his hope, and his ambition, were fettered down with chains which he had no power to rend. Under these circumstances he contributed two hundred and fifty years of unrequited toil. With the muscles of his brawny arms he cleared away the forests, tilled the soil, and made the wilderness to blossom like the rose. With his callous hands he has built railroads and cities in this country and has thus made this a goodly land in which to live.

Every time a foreign foe has threatened this nation, the Negro with unswerving patriotism and undaunted courage has contributed his full quota of protection. With profound sincerity he has offered his services to his country; with voluntary devotion he has laid himself upon her altar. It was Crispus Attucks who rushed upon the plains of Boston, struck the first blow and thus became the first martyr to the cause of American independence. It was the Negro soldiers who plunged dauntlessly into the face of death, scaled the heights of El Caney and San Juan and brought victory to the American flag. It was the black boys of the Ninth and the Tenth Cavalry that led the van and spilt their blood upon the troublous soil of Mexico in order that the dignity of the United States might be maintained. Negro soldiers were among the first to carry the stars and stripes into the trenches upon the gory field somewhere in France. These Negro soldiers have written their names high upon the scroll of fame.

You cannot erase their record without destroying some of the most important pages of American history. In the true annals of this nation their illustrious deeds of valor and patriotism cannot be hidden. Unobscured by prejudice these records shall shine forth and point out to posterity some of the most daring exploits and some of the most vicarious sacrifices. When the ponderous volumes of history rich with the spoils of time shall unroll their ample pages before the eyes of generations yet unborn, there in letters which he who runs may read should be inscribed the names of Johnson, Roberts, Butler, and many other black boys who staked their lives in the World War upon the contention that the world should be made safe for democracy.

Teaching of Negro history to the white people will give them a broader view. It will prove to them that the Negro has contributed a very considerable portion to the wealth, population and resources of the nation. It will engender a greater sympathy and a wider community consciousness. It will prove that the Negro is imbued with the white man's spirit and strives after his ideals. To the white man who truly studies Negro history will come views of tolerance and a spirit of justice, kindness, and helpfulness.

What benefit will accrue to the Negro from the teaching of Negro history? If the purpose of history teaching in our schools is to train for citizenship, what kind of a citizen will the Negro be, if the history he studies does not comprehend his race? The education of any race is incomplete unless it embodies the ideals of that race. The histories taught in Negro schools were not written in contemplation of the race. They were written for the white man and are the embodiment of his ideals and prejudices. The teaching of Negro history to the Negro youth is necessary to inspire race pride and arouse race consciousness. The study of what his race has done under adverse circumstances will animate the Negro youth to greater achievements. By contemplating the deeds of the worthy members of his own race the Negro youth will have his aspirations raised to attain the highest objective of life.

Because of existing conditions the inevitable conclusion is, that Negro history should be taught in all the schools of all races in the United States. The history outline should provide that Negro history supplement the regular text in United States history. The teaching of Negro history will bring a knowledge of those essential elements without which there can be no solution of the race problem. Standing upon the vantage ground of history retrospecting the past and prospecting the future, every real seeker of the truth can catch a glimmer of the glory in the realization of the prophetic utterance: "Princes shall come out of Egypt and Ethiopia shall soon stretch forth her hand to God."

J. W. BELL.

NEGRO BIOGRAPHY [1]

Twenty years ago I became interested in the study of Negro biography. I was anxious to know more about the personal histories of a score or more of Negro men and women whose part in helping to make the history of the Negro in the United States stood out pre-eminently. I did not desire detailed accounts of their lives at that time, but I did wish to know when and where they were born, how they made their way to front rank, how they suffered, fought, and sacrificed, where they spent their declining years, and when they passed away. I found the field of Negro biography a neglected one. I set to work, in my weak way, then, to bring to light the main facts in these personal histories.

The early Negro historians seem to have placed little emphasis on telling the interesting facts in the lives of the leaders of the race, and these persons themselves, with a few exceptions, were too modest, too busy, or too poor to publish their lives in book form. Josiah Henson, Samuel Ringgold Ward, Frederick Douglass, William Wells Brown, and a few others published their autobiographies. Unsatisfactory brief sketches of Phyllis Wheatley, Benjamin Banneker, Crispus Attucks, Lott Cary, and a score of others could be found here and there. Many writers have attempted to make known the part the Negro group has played in helping to make American history and civilization, but few have brought to light the stories of the Negro men and women of might and mark whose impress upon their generation gives evidence of our onward march of progress.

Looking over the field of American Negro historiography one sees a change in aspect and in tone. The early

[1] An address delivered before the Association for the Study of Negro Life and History at Louisville, November 23, 1922.

historian told the chronicled story of the race as a separate and distinct narrative, an independent, isolated tale of a people apart from the world. He endeavored to show the part the Negro had played in making possible his own progress. Today the Negro historian points to the fact that the Negro's advancement is a part of the forward movement of the world, and his progress in all the fields wherein he has labored is a part of the general progress of mankind. The historian of today is scientifically bringing to light the evidences as to the worth of the Negro and his contributions to the uplift of the World. More and more the historian is directing attention to the private lives of our leaders. More and more the leaders themselves are recording their own deeds, writing their autobiographies, and uncovering many inside facts connected with movements with which they were identified and in which they played conspicuous parts. But the personal histories of the old leaders, "the Old Guard" of the race, remain unknown. The stories of their lives, in addition to making rare literature, would shed light on the past, teach race loyalty and pride, and give inspiration to thousands of Negro youths who would find encouragement in their trials and battles.

"Biography," says Lossing, "is history teaching by example." Every race that has counted for much in history has had its heroes. Every nation that has helped to build civilization got its inspiration from within. Every nation that has left a record of value had its ideal men and women, its patriots, its martyrs—its examples of usefulness within itself. The white race seeks its ideals within its own ranks. The Red man's ideal is his group. The Greek youth imbibed the dare-and-do spirit from the tales of the Greek heroes. The Roman fashioned his life after those citizens who fought and achieved for Rome. Englishmen find their heroes among their own, and though they admire and praise genius and usefulness in men of other nationalities, their greatest men are those who played well their parts in helping to expand the influence of England

and to establish the British Empire. The German gets his inspiration from German history. The Japanese worships at the shrine of those of his country who have been factors in giving Japan "a place in the sun." The Frenchman sees his examples of true greatness in the men and women who sacrificed all for the glory of France.

No race, no nation, no people whose ideals of manhood and patriotism are without, can hope to be accorded full recognition by the world. The Negro's ideal must be a Negro if he is to appreciate keenly his own particular stock. The Negro's examples of achievement and devotion must be found within his group, if he is to learn to serve the race faithfully and intelligently. Its sages, its patriots, its heroes must all be persons of color, men whose faces show the mark of Africa, if the Negro youth is to develop that essential feeling commonly known as race pride. Negro achievements must be taught to the young men and women, if they are to learn to labor and to achieve, to do and to dare.

Negro biography stands out as the medium through which the youths of the race can be taught to love the race more and to serve it better. Negro biography is the main source from which the young Negro is to get inspiration and encouragement. Negro biography is the door through which he enters Negro history. Negro biography unlocks the past and explains the present effectively and impressively. If we want our children trained to love the race we must not only teach them what the world is, what nations have accomplished, and what individuals within the ranks of these nations have done toward helping to brighten the path of life, but we must tell them of the sturdy characters of Negro ancestry who have labored and struggled and triumphed and by their contributions enriched the history of civilization. The appreciation for the record of our own group will stimulate the youth to greater endeavor.

The histories of nations are but narratives of what their citizens have said and done. If, then, we would teach effectively the chronicles of the nations, we must be answering questions, incessantly responding to inquiries about the men and the women who blazed the way and led their kinsmen to toil and suffer to bring to pass a happier and a brighter day for themselves and their posterity. Such examples of devotion to the cause of humanity, examples of consecration to truth and righteousness, examples of goodness and greatness worthy of the praise of all races and creeds, are found everywhere in the ranks of the Negro race. If unearthed and popularized, these examples would shed light upon the history of the race in the United States, illuminate the general history of man, and inculcate a profound respect for the Negro.

In connection with the Negro's early efforts at freedom and culture mention is made of John Chavis, George Moses Horton, John Sella Martin, George Liele, John S. Rock, James Varick, Andrew Bryan, Daniel Coker, Peter Spencer, David Walker, John T. Hilton, David Ruggles, William Whipper, James Monroe Whitefield, James McCune Smith, James Madison Bell, Thomas Paul, Mary Shadd Carey, Jupiter Hammon, and Samuel Ringgold Ward, about whose personal histories, Ward excepted, little is known. And even in the case of Ward, his life after he left the United States is almost a blank. Few people know what work he did after making his home in Jamaica, and the circumstances under which he passed away there. Let it be remembered that Frederick Douglass called Ward the most brilliant Negro orator of the abolition cause. Would not the story of his remarkable career be a valuable addition to our history? He was one of the chief pillars of the anti-slavery movement.

Would not the true facts concerning the birth, education and early life of Lieutenant Colonel William N. Reed, First North Carolina Volunteers, or the Thirty-fifth United States Colored Troops, who fell mortally wounded in the battle of the Olustee in 1864, make interesting reading to arouse the imagination of the youth? A full narrative of the life of Dr. John V. DeGrasse, the first commissioned surgeon in the United States Army, would give a new idea of the versatility of the Negro patriot. The life of David Ruggles, told in detail, would be both informing and inspiring. His hatred of the slaveholder and his love of freedom brought him to deal sledge hammer blows at the institution of slavery and to oppose the colonization of free Negroes in Africa. His manly appeal to reason and his eloquent and convincing arguments against deportation did much to make friends for Negro freedom. James W. C. Pennington, an honor alumnus of the University of Heidelberg (Germany), deserves more consideration in our history than will ever be given him because we know so little about his life and labors. An eloquent preacher and a lover of justice and truth, he won the praise of the good and the great in both America and Europe.

How many American Negroes know the name of Joseph Colvis, a native of the United States who won distinction during the Franco-Prussian War, who was decorated by the French Government, and who retained till his death his American citizenship? What Negro of the United States knows the story of the last years of Edmonia Lewis, the sculptress, one of the truly great products of the race? Her name should be made to live by telling every youth of her wonderful career as an artist.

How many Negro youths know the names of C. H. J. Taylor, James Monroe Trotter, John H. Jackson and J. McHenry Jones, four men of our own time who successfully labored for the uplift of the race? Taylor and Trotter were among the first to preach Negro independence in politics, and Jackson and Jones infused new life into two State schools and made these institutions mighty instruments of service in the uplift of the race. What do we know of Whipper, Rock, Martin, Chavis, Jones, Whitefield, pioneers all? of Bell, Varick, Coker, Cary, Bryan, Liele, all but martyrs? What these men achieved, in spite of handicap, in an environment unfavorable to progress by peoples of dark skin, has won the admiration of the enemies of the race. Is there a student of history who does not wish to know more about them? Unbiased historians on both sides of the seas will some day find delight in doing them honor.

Shall these heroes go unsung? Shall these makers of the history of the race go unhonored? Should not their names become familiar to our children and their struggles for truth and right the epics of the fireside? Lest we forget, and lest our children never know them, let us do our best to chronicle their deeds and to perpetuate their memories. Let us do our part towards placing these heroes before the world, erecting in their honor monuments in song and in story to the end that coming generations may be inspired to serve their day faithfully and aspiring youths everywhere be shown the path to true worth and glory.

PAUL W. L. JONES.

HAITI AND THE UNITED STATES *

INTRODUCTORY

We do not generally speak of *American imperialism*. Such words are incompatible. Imperialism in the United States, the land of the free and the home of the brave, seems ironical. The degenerate, dying one, however, gave birth to the vital, growing other. Imperialism is the torch that fired the souls that flared and flamed forth in conquering righteous anger and tore in twain the bond which held the British Lion's restless brood intact and set one loose to roam apart a land in which to breed and suckle a stock after its kind. It was thus the United States had its beginning. Can it be the echo of that severed bond still faintly heard shall prematurely die? drown in the clamor of our near Imperialistic programme in the republics of Haiti and Santo Domingo? Be that as it may, the sovereignty of Haiti and Santo Domingo has been impaired, and their independence overthrown by the United States of America. This is a fact against which no one holds a brief.

Whether we accept the interpretation of our country's actions in the island republics by Earnest H. Gruening, Managing Editor of *The Nation*, or that of Carl Kelsey,[1] Professor of Sociology at the University of Pennsylvania,[2] whether we conclude with, what may be termed conveniently "public opinion," or with the Investigation Committee of the Senate,[3] is finally a matter of individual judicature. To accept or reject, establish or refute, either

---
* This dissertation was submitted to the Graduate School of Western Reserve University in 1922 in partial fulfilment of the requirements for the degree of Master of Arts.

[1] *Current History*, Vol. XV, No. 6, March, 1922.

[2] *Annals of the American Academy of Political and Social Science*, Vol. C, No. 189, March, 1922.

[3] *Treaties and Conventions between the United States and other Powers.*

interpretation or conclusion would require a thorough study of the character and motives of the men, and the nature, extent, and the conditions under which the facts were collected. Such a survey would lead us far afield in this dissertation.

Knowing as we do the importance of the Monroe Doctrine, we believe the basis of the present Haitian-Dominican relation with the United States to be found in our praccal interpretation of that unwritten law. There is another factor which, if possible, is paramount to the Monroe Doctrine, our economic interests. The strength of a nation is its wealth. In our economic interests upon which rests our political government, and in the Monroe Doctrine—time honored, versatile chaperon and guardian of them both at international fetes—are to be found the official justification and true motives of the foreign policy of the United States in Haiti and Santo Domingo.

Survey of Haiti

Before proceeding farther, let us briefly review Haiti up to the American Occupation. The story of the Santo-Dominican affair is singularly similar to that of Haiti, and it needs to be referred to only in the rare instances of dissimilarity.

Hispaniola or Haiti is the second largest island in the Antilles. It lies between Cuba and Porto Rico. It was discovered by Columbus, and the earliest Caucasian civilization in this hemisphere took root there. The tomb supposed to hold the ashes of Columbus is in the Cathedral of Santo Domingo. The eastern two-thirds of the island is occupied by the Dominican Republic, the western one-third by that of Haiti. The island was a French colony until 1804, although the French claims were frequently disputed by the Spaniards, who at various times established themselves in the eastern part, where language and culture remained Castilian. Following nearly fifteen years of struggle, which began when the Bastile fell, the natives achieved their independence.[4] This revolution was unique in that the revolutionaries, who had formerly been slaves, secured both the political independence of their country and their personal freedom. The republic of Haiti was established on January 1, 1804, the second republic in the Western Hemisphere. In 1844 the eastern two-thirds of the island seceded and set up the Dominican Republic.

The republic of Haiti continued free and independent until 1915. During that one hundred and eleven years it had a troublous history. The constitutional office for a president in Haiti is seven years, but President Salomon, who held office from 1879 to 1886, is apparently the only such functionary to fill out his term of office. He was overthrown within two years after his reelection for a second term in 1886.

This drama may be reduced to read thus: In 1804 Dessalines was crowned as emperor. Two years later he was assassinated; and war broke out between Christophe and Petion. In 1807 Christophe became king under the title of Henry I, but had upon his hands annoying strife. In 1811 Petion was made president of the southern part of

[4] In the preparation of this article the following works were used:

Tyranny by the United States in Haiti and Santo Domingo, by Earnest H. Gruening, Managing Editor of *The Nation*, in CURRENT HISTORY, Volume XV, No. 6, March, 1922; *Latin America, Clark University Addresses*, November, 1913, edited by George H. Blakeslee, Professor of History, Clark University; *Caribbean Interests of the United States*, by Chester Lloyd Jones, Professor of Political Science, University of Wisconsin; *The United States and Latin America*, by John Holladay Latané, Professor of History, Johns Hopkins University; *The American Intervention in Haiti and the Dominican Republic*, in THE ANNALS OF THE AMERICAN ACADEMY OF POLITICAL AND SOCIAL SCIENCE, Volume C, No. 189, March, 1922, by Carl Kelsey, Ph.D., Professor of Sociology, University of Pennsylvania; *The Monroe Doctrine and Its Application to Haiti*, by William A. MacCorkle, Former Governor of West Virginia, in THE ANNALS OF THE AMERICAN ACADEMY OF POLITICAL AND SOCIAL SCIENCE, Volume LIV, July, 1914; *The Haitian Revolution*, by T. G. Steward; THE JOURNAL OF NEGRO HISTORY, Vol. II, No. 4, October, 1917; *Independence of South American Republics*, by F. L. Paxson; and *Treaties and Conventions between the United States and Other Powers*, Government Printing Office, Washington, D. C.

the island and civil war ensued. Boyer was declared regent for life in 1820 and after tremendous insurrection and flow of blood Christophe committed suicide. In 1843 Boyer was deposed and exiled after a revolution. In 1844 Santo Domingo, the Spanish port of the island, became an independent republic in spite of the efforts of the French portion to subdue it. Herard, the next ruler, was exiled after a rule of one year. Then came Guerrier and Pierrot, each of whom could hold out one year only. In 1846 Riché was proclaimed president but he passed away within twelve months. In 1849 Soulouque was declared emperor after many wars and much bloodshed. He managed to rule in some way until he was exiled in 1859. Geffrad then became president and ruled until 1867 when he was exiled. From 1856 to 1867 there followed a dreadful revolution when Salnave revolted, taking refugees from the British consulates and killing them. An English ship drove them out and helped Geffrad who, however, was finally banished. Salnave was then made president with a new constitution; and the revolt was suppressed amidst torrents of blood. From 1868 to 1870 there was continual revolution, but Salnave massacred his enemies, proclaimed himself emperor, and thus reigned until he was finally defeated and shot. In 1874 after Nissage Saget had completed his term of four years, Domingue seized the government, but after bloody revolution he was exiled in 1876. Then came another bloody revolution when Canal seized power but after a stormy reign he was exiled in 1879, when Salomon was elected. Salomon was reelected in 1886 but was deposed and exiled in 1888. Then came civil war between Hippolyte and Légitime resulting in the temporary success of Légitime, who held sway for one year only. In 1889 Hippolyte was chosen chief executive and he died in office in 1896. Sam who became president that year had trouble with Germany and numerous disorders in the country. In 1902 Sam took all the funds and left the country. In 1902 General Alexis Nord was proclaimed president, and he was retired by revolution in 1908 when the powers sent warships to stop massacre. Cincinnatus Lecompte was elevated to the presidency in 1911 and was killed in 1912. Tancrede Auguste, who succeeded him, met the same fate the following year. Michall Oreste, the next unfortunate, served into the year 1914 when he was dethroned by the usual upheaval; and so suffered Zamor in 1914, and Guillaume who was killed in 1915. On July 28, 1915, United States forces landed at Port-au-Prince and began the present Occupation.[5]

Survey of Santo Domingo

National and domestic conditions of Haiti are popular knowledge. It is unnecessary to go into that upon which all students of Latin American countries are agreed. Accordingly we make no mention of the form of government and detailed exposition of its operation in this country.

It is not agreed that Santo Domingo is as well known. The total area of the Dominican Republic is over 19,000 square miles, or somewhat more than the combined areas of the States of Vermont and New Hampshire. The country is divided by a great central range whose highest peaks rise to 9,000 or 10,000 feet, forming valleys like Constanza, whose elevation is over 3,000 feet. The first census of the Dominican Republic ever taken was completed in the summer of 1921. This showed a total population of 894,587, a little over 45 a square mile, or about one-fourth the density of Haiti. The crop areas, rainfall being heavy in the vicinity of the central range, indicate fairly accurately the location of the mass of the population. The people are a mixture of Negro, Indian, and Spaniard with the Negro strain predominant. Among them, as in Haiti, the question of land ownership is important. There is no system of deeds by which titles are registered. As the country has never been surveyed, titles are in confusion.

The agricultural methods of the Dominicans do not

[5] These facts are well set forth in Steward's *Haitian Revolution*.

differ materially from those of the Haitians, but modern machinery is rapidly appearing. Conservatively it might be said that the Dominican farmers are more prosperous than the Haitian. One finds here the culture of cane, cacao, tobacco, and bananas to a greater extent than in Haiti, but these crops are not efficiently handled.

The most valuable crop of the country is sugar. Owing to the enormous cost of the mills, sugar is produced chiefly on large plantations. Of these there are about a dozen, most of which are today under American control. Two of the largest are La Romana in the east and Barahona in the west. In the former the investment is estimated at $7,000,000 with 16,000 acres in cane and a labor force of 7,000. Barahona is a new plantation which was grinding the winter of 1921 for the first time. The investment here is said to be over $10,000,000. A splendid plant with adequate provision for houses for the employees has been built. Besides sugar there are a few other industries including a little manufacturing. Factories are not numerous in the country, but at Puerto Plata, there are a match factory, a few distilleries, and two cigar factories turning out excellent products, and they are owned and operated by Dominicans. It is an open question whether forces and influences of this kind will do more to advance and stabilize these countries than all the resorts to force of military control and occupation.

Some transportation facilities and a few other economic factors of interest are observed. There are two lines of railroads doing a general business, with a combined mileage of about 150 miles. The Dominican Central Railway runs from Puerto Plata through Santiago to Moca, 60 miles. This was built by foreign interests but was taken over by the government in 1908. The second road, the Samaná and Santiago Railway, runs from Moca to Samaná with branches to San Fernando de Macoris and La Vega. No railroad runs from the northern to the southern part of the country. On the sugar estates in the south there are 225 miles of private roads. There is also a short line of some five miles connecting Azura with its ports. An excellent beginning had been made in road building. The engineers of the American forces since the occupation have carried it farther. There are docks at Puerto Plata, La Romana,[6] San Pedro de Macoris, Santo Domingo and Barahona. Elsewhere lighters are used. The Clyde Steamship Line has had a monopoly much of the time in the trade with the United States. Now at least two other lines send freight steamers regularly. The French line gives direct connection with Europe, and there is also frequent communication with Porto Rico.

A study of the statistical table of commerce indicates a very gratifying increase in the total foreign trade but a considerable part of the increase after 1914 was due to war time prices, just as the terrible slump which came in 1921, and had little relation to production. The output of sugar has been increased from 85,000 tons in 1910 to about 185,000 in 1920. A large part of this commerce is with the United States. For instance, in 1919-20 the United States trade represented 77 per cent of the imports and 87 per cent of the exports. 13 per cent more of the imports were from Porto Rico, and to that island went 26 per cent of the exports. The rapid increase in commerce brought great prosperity to the country. Then came the reaction, disastrous to creditors, many of whose accounts were settled for 35 cents on the dollar. The country, however, is relatively undeveloped, which means its day is yet ahead. Schvenrich is correct in speaking of Santo Domingo as the country with a future.

Religion, education, and politics come next in this hurried survey. The Roman Catholic Church is dominant in this country. With the exception of a few Franciscans all the priests are natives. The Protestant churches in the country are few and small.

Education is still in a backward state. In 1915 the

[6] This dock belongs to a sugar company, but it is open to others.

Dominican Republic did not own a single school building. Rural schools did not exceed eighty-four in number. The total school enrollment was about 18,000. While there were some public schools in rented buildings dependence seems to have been placed on the private subsidized schools, and the amount granted was determined wholly by political influence. The teachers were irregularly and poorly paid. A commission appointed by the government investigated thoroughly the educational situation and because of its findings prepared and recommended the following laws: (a) Compulsory school attendance; (b) school administration; (c) general studies, literary, law, and theological courses; and an (d) organic law of public education, and school revenues. The educational institutions now total: (a) 647 rural schools—enrollment 50,000, the chief work being in agriculture; (b) 194 primary schools; (c) 7 secondary and normal schools; (d) 6 industrial schools for girls; (e) 2 schools of fine arts; and (f) 2 correctional schools and the Central University at the capital. The total school attendance is 100,000, and the total number of teachers is 1,468.

The constitution establishes a representative form of government—a republic. The government is of executive, legislative, and judicial branches. The national congress meets annually at the capital, Santo Domingo, on February 27 for a period of 90 days, which may be extended 60 days if necessary. It is composed of a senate of 12 members, one from each province, and of a chamber of deputies of 24 members, two from each province. Senators are elected by indirect vote for a term of six years, and the senate is renewed by thirds every two years. Deputies are elected by indirect vote for a period of four years, and the chamber is renewed by half every two years. Suffrage is free to all male citizens over 18 years old. The President is the executive authority of the republic. He is elected for six years by indirect vote. There is no Vice-President. The cabinet is composed of seven functionaries: the Secretary of Interior and Police, Secretary of Foreign Affairs, Secretary of Treasury and Commerce, Secretary of War and Marine, Secretary of Justice and Public Instruction, Secretary of Agriculture and Immigration, and Secretary of Promotion and Communications.

The chief judicial power resides in the Supreme Court of Justice, which consists of a president and six justices chosen by Congress, and one Procurador Fiscal General appointed by the executive to serve for a term of four years, and sitting at Santo Domingo. The territory of the republic is divided into twelve judicial districts, each having its own civil and criminal tribunal and court of first instance. These districts are subdivided into communes, each with a local justice. There are two courts of appeal, one at Santiago de los Caballeros, and the other at Santo Domingo City. For administrative purposes these twelve provinces are subdivided into communes. The provinces are administered by governors appointed by the President as are the chief executive officers of other political divisions.

Early International Relations

Let us now direct attention to the early international relations of Haiti and Santo Domingo with the United States. For many years recognition of the little state by certain world powers fearing the disastrous effect on their slaves, was withheld. The French, moreover, under the constant threat of reinvasion, succeeded in exacting a 90,000,000 franc indemnity for the property of Frenchmen expelled in the Haitian war of independence. Charles X of France then recognized the republic. Recognition by the United States did not come until the presidency of Abraham Lincoln. Until recently, however, Haiti has had only one significant attraction for the United States. The important relations of Haiti with this country from then until 1915 amounted chiefly to negotiations and efforts to secure the cession of Mole St. Nicholas, a harbor, at the northwestern extremity of the island. It controls the

Windward Passage, and the United States desired it for a naval base.

Notwithstanding the insistence of the United States that Haiti grant her Mole St. Nicholas for naval use, the harbor did not change hands. The Haitians adhered firmly to the constitutional provision, which forbade the cession of territory. During 1914 and 1915 the United States began overtures of a different character. A treaty giving American control of the customs and finances was proposed. The cession of Mole St. Nicholas appears also in the early exchanges. In October, 1914, William J. Bryan, Secretary of State, wrote to President Wilson, urging the immediate increase of our naval forces in Haitian waters, "not only for the purpose of protecting foreign interests, but also as an evidence of the earnest intention of this Government to settle the unsatisfactory state of affairs which exists." More naval vessels were sent, and at the same time the United States offered to assist the President of Haiti to put down some threatened revolutionary disturbances. As certain conditions were attached to this assistance, it was refused. In November and December modifications of previous treaty drafts were again submitted. They proposed the control and administration of the Haitian customs by the United States, and were again refused for reasons similar to those given above. On December 13, 1914, American marines from the United States Ship Machias landed in the Haitian capital and removed property of the country without the consent of the people.

The recent Dominican situation may be said to have begun on November 19, 1915. A draft giving the United States military and financial control was presented to President Jimenez of the Dominican Republic one week after the final ratification by Haiti of its similar treaty. It was rejected. In the following April, impeachment proceedings were entered upon against the President in the Dominican Congress. On May 4, 1916, during some revolutionary disturbances, and without warning to the Dominican Government, American marines were landed near Santo Domingo. The American minister at that time gave assurance that these forces were solely for the purpose of protecting the American Legation.

On the eleventh of May Frederico Henrique Y Carvajol was nominated for president of the republic in the Chamber of Deputies and confirmed by the Senate on the twenty-third of May. On the thirteenth of May, the American minister formally notified the Dominican Government of the intention of the United States Government to land a large armed force and to occupy the capital, threatening bombardment of the city and unrestricted firing upon the natives, if in any way they interfered with the landing of the American forces. On the eighteenth of May the American minister notified the Dominican Congress that Carvajol was not acceptable to the United States as President. On the fifth of June the American minister gave a formal notice to the Dominican Government that the Receiver General of Customs would take charge of all the finances and funds of the Government. Under the treaty of 1907 with the United States one of its citizens appointed by this country was in charge of the collection of customs of the Dominican Republic. It was his duty under this treaty to turn in all but the sum of $100,000 monthly to the Dominican Government. All above this $100,000 was to go, one half to the Dominican Government for its own uses, the other half to the sinking fund of the loan contracted under the treaty. On the sixteenth of June, following orders from Washington the Receiver General of Customs took charge of all revenues,—internal as well as customs revenues which alone were stipulated in the treaty of 1907—and set himself up as disbursing agent of the republic. Then followed a series of protests, exchange of notes and the like. On November 26, 1916, there was issued a "proclamation of occupation" by the United States, followed by martial law, but the Dominicans refused to ratify the acts of the Military Government. The occupation here continued more than five years.

These and similar acts in both Haiti and Santo Domingo aside from questions of expediency, justification, or best interest have given rise to the present situation. Up to this time the United States Government has published no complete and comprehensive explanation of these acts. The answer to the question of motives is not to be found in surface considerations; not even the unlimited popular accounts convince us that this country is not adhering to a principle, to an accepted and subscribed policy, no matter how secret it may be.

THE UNITED STATES IN THE LARGER CANAL ZONE

When the United States secured Panama from Columbia she entered upon a new era. With the centralization of a large portion of our wealth in this section of Latin America came the recognition by statesmen that our political interests would have to expand accordingly. Then our attitude took on an air of aggression which, conflicting with our ideals, gives rise to varied conjectures upon our Latin American policy, and especially our policy in the Caribbean Sea.

There were steps made towards securing a coaling station or naval base even prior to our ownership of the Panama Canal Lands. In 1867 Admiral Porter and Mr. F. W. Seward, the assistant-secretary of state, were sent to Santo Domingo for the purpose of securing the lease of Samaná Bay as a naval station. Later President Grant sent Colonel Babcock to the island to report on the condition of affairs. Babcock, without diplomatic authority of any kind, negotiated a treaty for the annexation of the Dominican Republic and another for the lease of Samaná Bay.

The Spanish American War was the occasion for the advance of the United States into the Caribbean. From this conflict we acquired Porto Rico and a protectorate over Cuba. Furthermore, too much importance can not be attached to the Hay-Pauncefote treaty of 1901 in studying this expansion of the United States in that sphere. By this convention Great Britain abjured her claim to an equal voice with the United States in the control of an Isthmian Canal and withdrew her squadrons from the Caribbean Sea, leaving us the naval supremacy in this important strategic area.

Immediately following these occurrences came the episode of the Panama Canal. To review briefly a long told and well known story, the United States Government had not been successful in its attempt to secure from Columbia the treaty it sought for the building of the Isthmian Canal. In 1903 a revolution broke out in Panama, and Colombia failed to coerce effectively the insurgents, hindered, it is asserted, by the far reaching influence of the Roosevelt Administration. As soon as this revolution got in full swing the United States recognized Panama, and negotiated the long sought treaty. By the year 1903 we had acquired the canal zone. The determination to build a canal not only rendered inevitable the adoption of a policy of naval supremacy in the Caribbean Sea, but led also to the formulation of new political policies to be applied in the larger Canal Zone, that is, the West Indies, Mexico, Central America, Columbia, and Venezuela. These new policies are: (a) The establishment of protectorates, (b) the supervision of finances, (c) the control of naval routes, (d) the acquisition of naval stations, (e) and the policing and administration of disorderly countries. This program of policies has afforded this country many opportunities for expansion in these areas.

American Seas a Commercial Center

Prior to the completion of the Panama Canal the American Seas, the Gulf of Mexico and the Caribbean Sea, for many years had been silent waters. The Panama Canal has reversed these conditions. The important trade routes of the world will pass about these islands and over these seas, and they will be noisy with the whirl of the propeller and bright with the sail of ships. A great part of American commerce and a larger part of the traffic of the world will be through the American seas between the walls of this canal and by the shores of Haiti. These seas will become more popular with commerce than any other section of the world. They will be a gathering place and crossing point for the east and the west, and their possession, either forcibly or otherwise, will carry with it more potentiality than the possession of any other body of water on the face of the earth. It will be absolutely necessary, says this country, so to speak, that the outposts of the canal shall be in the hands of strong and stable governments, and it cannot be thought that the harbors necessary for that commerce and the islands by which it will pass, and in whose broad bays it will be compelled to anchor, shall be ripe with revolution and dangerous to that commerce. This country which is practically guardian of this commerce must allow to obtain no condition which will be a daily menace to this unusual trade.

In all of these communities the commercial diplomacy of our time will have a growing interest, an interest greatly enhanced by the fact that through the Caribbean, the traffic center of the American tropics, will pass the trade routes developed by the Panama Canal. Both the competition for the control of the trade which lies within their borders, and the fact that before their ports passes the commerce of distant countries, will give to Caribbean communities an importance in international affairs they have not had since the days when the Spanish Empire in America was at its height and the people of one of the great world powers depended for its prosperity on the arrival of the gold ships from its American colonies. The fortunes of the Caribbean are no matter of merely local interest. They involve, to a degree still unappreciated, the world at large and especially the American continents, both North and South. Upon the solution of the problems which arise there may depend the character of international and economic development in America. The importance of the new position in which the Caribbean region stands is brought home by almost every development in American international affairs.

Caribbean problems take on another important aspect when we remember the wonderful possibilities of economic development. Partly acting as a cause of this trade development, partly one of its results, there is going on a steady and rapid influx of foreign capital. The English financing of the Argentine is familiar to students of Latin-American history. In recent years, with the establishment of order in Mexico, that country has attracted large amounts of foreign investments. The departure of Spain from Cuba and Porto Rico was the signal for a rush of investors to these islands to develop resources which mistaken fiscal policies and local unrest had formerly kept unused. Foreign capital exploits the sugar, tobacco, coffee, cocoa, fruit, oil, and asphalt. These investments are scattered among all the great commercial nations. They give an international character even to purely internal improvements. Economic interests now tend to overflow national boundaries and to make the orderly development of every state truly a matter of general concern. Under the Monroe Doctrine we practically say to European nations they shall not for any cause lay their hands heavily upon a country in this hemisphere, which, with the added responsibility as trustee for the world in the possession of the Isthmian Canal, makes it dependent upon the United States, it is said, to keep order.

Haiti's Commercial Position

This policy of aggression has only one explanation. Next to Cuba, Haiti is the island of the greatest strategical influence in the Caribbean Sea and the Gulf of Mexico. The two important routes to the mouth of the canal from North America are, first the route by the Windward Passage between the island of Cuba and the island of Haiti; second, the route by the Mona Passage between the island of Haiti and the island of Porto Rico. This latter passage will be that chiefly used by the sailing vessels to and from the canal to the eastern portion of North America. The other important passage to the mouth of the canal is the Annegada Passage by the islands of St. Thomas and Porto Rico, and will be the route used from the isthmus to the Mediterranean and Central Europe. The travel to the British Islands and northern Europe will also use the Mona Passage between Haiti and Porto Rico. In other words, every ship sailing from Canada, New York, Philadelphia, Baltimore, Newport News, Charleston or the eastern coast of North America on its journey to the Latin American world of commerce will be compelled to pass by the island of Haiti, either through the Windward or the Mona Passage, and the travel to the greater part of Europe will use the Mona Passage by the east coast of Haiti. This world-wide commerce in case of stress and storm, according to the business world, must utilize this island in the necessities of sea life. It is the first convenient harboring place on its way to the Canal, and on its return it is the last stopping place. It will be as necessary to the commerce of this country as Malta or Aden or Gibraltar are to the Suez route. It lies athwart the greatest commerce that will cleave the seas. With the friendly influence of Cuba and Haiti the commerce of the United States will have a tremendous advantage in case of war or unfriendliness on the part of any nation, even if Jamaica is held by an unfriendly power. Modern nations with the shortening of trade routes, the touching of countries, and their demand for sure commercial conditions, are unfortunately arriving at the thought that there is no inalienable right on the part of any people to control any region to the detriment and injury of the world at large.

Summary

While many believe that the United States has thrown aside her lofty ideals to take on a program of imperialism, there is a growing colonial interest and expansion which does not, probably due to the very nature of conditions, extend these ideals. Whether the condition is one acceptable to us or not, says the business world, we are no longer merely a continental power. We already hold an Asiatic colony. A weak African state founded from this country has asked us for a protectorate and is already under our benevolent supervision. Toward the south we hold a colony, Porto Rico, and are the protectors of Cuba, Panama, the Dominican Republic, and Haiti. We have responsibilities in Nicaragua.

That the end of this development has come is highly unlikely. Political parties may differ as to national policies, internal and external, but they will bend before the natural cause of economic and political development. Our latest three administrations, those of Roosevelt, Taft, and Wilson, have represented widely divergent political views, but the general policy of all toward the Caribbean countries has been fundamentally the same, and the Harding administration has not yet departed therefrom. All have been willing to "assume increasing responsibilities toward our weaker neighbors" to secure economic advantage. It has been a development which is the response of the nation to its larger economic and political interests in the Larger Canal Zone.

Whilst this government disclaims any desire for conquest, yet the great advantage in the world movement and in the vital commercial affairs of the globe, the commercial world says, demand that the peace and safety of this hemisphere shall not be needlessly and wickedly broken, and that the peace, happiness and safety of this nation and the commerce of the world within the bounds of our governmental life shall not be imperiled in the future as they have been in the past. The tremendous impetus, which under the world movement of today has been so potent and plain, demands order in all the affairs and details of life. The conditions of the time and the dependence of one part of the globe upon the other, brought about by the easy interchange between the nations, mean that no disorder in that great world commerce can be tolerated. Unstable governments are unwelcome to a diplomacy which has as one of its controlling motives the creation of an extensive international exchange, especially when these governments are of races despised by the Teuton. Weakness of government may lead in the future, as it has in the past, to the rise of acute international questions. In recent years there have been many examples of the complications which may rise out of such conditions.

The areas referred to as the Larger Canal Zone have received great attention from this country. In fact our latest Latin-American diplomacy, which has as one of its controlling motives the creation of an extensive international exchange, is for these areas. Our economic interests have made demands upon our political life, the Monroe Doctrine has lighted the way and we have come forward with new policies. Haiti, it has been said, is not to be set apart and dealt with particularly in this new diplomatic program; it is but a factor in our "American Seas" interest, a vital economic and political part of our present-day American life. The subsequent questions of impaired sovereignty and overthrown independence, say the aggressors, should not obscure the real policies. Nor is it fair to accuse the United States of a lack of appreciation and respect for the governments of peoples of this section of the world.

Finally we are told: America stands at the dividing of the ways. Are we to pursue the ideals of "All men are created free and equal" with the equally idealistic form of government, or are we to keep pace with our commercial and economic expansion and accept the complementary program of economic imperialism? We are informed that the trend of our political policies is one of colonization; that colonization with respect to Western European Civilization is contradictory to democracy; and that a program of colonization at a time when racial and national antipathy exceed even individual expression, are all demonstrated by the refusal of our government to acknowledge and commit itself to any definite political program in these island republics. Our government, the defenders say, has occupied these republics apparently fearful of European intervention. Entering upon this policy committed to no program, with a lack of centralization of authority into one of the many departments of the government, it has caused much confusion. Obviously the position in which we find ourselves in Haiti is one of embarrassment and one which has affected the prestige of our country detrimentally. American statesmen are put to task. Shall our government admit and support its economic imperialistic policy inseparably from the added political burden accompanying our Panama Canal enterprise, profiting, thereby, upon the commercial importance of the canal; or shall it long continue the dexterous fête of keeping eyes and hands on democratic ideals with both feet in the path of imperialism? Our new policy is an economic imperialistic policy. The world wishes to know if we will admit it and announce our intentions in these regions, or whether we shall continue our imperialistic policy under the veil of the Monroe Doctrine held in position by the idealistic principles of democracy.

GEORGE W. BROWN.

PAUL CUFFE *

CHAPTER I

EARLY LIFE

The records tell us that on the sixteenth day of February, 1742, in consideration of the sum of one hundred and fifty pounds, Ebenezer Slocum of Dartmouth, Bristol County, Massachusetts, sold to John Slocum of the same city a Negro man.[1] He was about twenty-five years of age and a native African whom, doubtless, a slave trader had brought over some fifteen years before. This Negro was Cuffe by name (also spelled Cuff, Cuffee, and Cuffey) and, in conformity with the custom at that time was called Cuffe

* This biography is based on the original journal, letters, and papers of Paul Cuffe. They are preserved in the Public Library of New Bedford, Massachusetts. I am under obligations to the Librarian, George H. Pripp, for many favors in connection with the examination of these manuscripts.

The petitions referred to in Chapter II are with the Cuffe papers. A copy of the one presented to the Probate Court of Massachusetts Bay was furnished by Mr. James J. Tracey, Chief of the Archives Division, State House, Boston. The story of the lawsuit related in this same chapter is based on the original papers to be found in the records of the Bristol County, Taunton, Massachusetts, Probate Court. They were examined for me by my Harvard classmate, Professor Arthur Buffinton of Williams College.

I have previously published two articles bearing on this study. Early Negro Deportation Projects appeared in the *Mississippi Valley Historical Review* for March, 1916, the Formation of the American Colonization Society in the *Journal of Negro History* for July, 1917. A third article, PAUL CUFFE AND HIS CONTRIBUTIONS TO THE AMERICAN COLONIZATION SOCIETY, in volume six of the *Proceedings of the Mississippi Valley Historical Society*, was an attempt to bring together a full statement of his life and service. Since the publication of this study I found the original Cuffe Papers and have made use of them in this biography. Another source of great help was the *Life of William Allen with Selections from his Correspondence*, 2 vols., Philadelphia, 1847. A full account of the services in connection with the memorial monument erected by Mr. Horatio P. Howard is contained in the *New Bedford Morning Mercury* and the *New Bedford Standard* for June 16, 1917.

[1] *Cuffe Manuscripts*, New Bedford, Massachusetts, Public Library, from the bill of sale.

Slocum to indicate his master. While the name of the slave does not appear in the bill of sale yet, since the bill is a part of the family papers of his son, it must have been Cuffe.

There exists among the Negro's descendants a tradition that this slave with the aid of his master worked out his purchase price and obtained his liberty. It may have been that John Slocum purchased the Negro with this end in view. At any rate a grand-daughter relates how on a rainy morning when all, including Cuffe, were seated at the breakfast table, a justice of the peace appeared with papers of emancipation.[2] Having received his liberty at an unexpected moment, Cuffe knew not what to do. Seeing his bewilderment, the gracious squire and the quondam master gave him temporary employment and, when he was ready to leave, advised him to lead a steady life, take good care of his money, and get him a home. With this advice, two suits of clothes, and freedom, the manumitted slave went happily away.

Now it happened that about this time there came to Dartmouth an Indian girl called Ruth Moses. In due time the town clerk recorded: "Intention of marriage between Cuffe Slocum and Ruth Moses both of Dartmouth, was entered 3 January 1745."[3] The rest of the story is told by the minister of Dartmouth in these words: "July ye 7, 1746, Cuffe Slocum a Negro man and Ruth Moses an Indian woman both of Dartmouth were married by me Philip Taber."[4] These two records tell us all we know of the courtship and marriage of Cuffe Slocum.

Probably the newly-weds made their home in Chilsmark, Dukes County. The deed to some land which they bought in 1766 from David Brownell of Dartmouth refers to Cuffe Slocum of Chilsmark. The land was a farm of one hundred and twenty acres and sold for six hundred

[2] Ruth Cuffe to Joseph Congdon, February 12, 1851.
[3] *Dartmouth, Massachusetts, Town Book of Records for Entries of Intention of Marriage.*
[4] *Cuffe Manuscripts*, Memorandum of family marriages.

and fifty Spanish milled dollars. As indicated in the deed, the boundary was: "Northerly on the Country Road, Westerly on Land belonging to Jonathan Sowle, Southerly on Land Enos Gifford gave to his Daughter Rachel Wilbur, Easterly partly on said Gifford and partly on Philip Allen, or according to the Deed I had of Solomon Southwick."[5]

All of the children, except the youngest, were born previous to this purchase. There were six girls and four boys. The youngest boy and the seventh child born January 17, 1759, was Paul. Tradition holds that he was born on Cuttyhunk, one of the Elizabeth Islands, about nine miles from the main, and Cuffe himself says that he was born in the only house on the island.

About 1778, on the initiative of Paul, it is said, all of the children, except the youngest, dropped the slave name of Slocum. For their surname they used the given name of their father. In this way the Cuffe family came to be, and in this way we are introduced to its best known representative, Paul.

John, an older brother of Paul, made this memorandum which is preserved with the family papers: "My honored good old father Cuffe Slocum deceased in the month called March 1772—and our honored good old mother Ruth Slocum deceased the sixth day of January 1787 at 8 o'clock in the morning." The father left the farm jointly to Paul and his brother John. Later the brothers agreed to divide it between themselves. It was unproductive land and, no doubt, this fact caused the brothers to venture into commercial pursuits. The care of the family fell for the most part on them, for the older children had homes of their own.

At thirteen Paul was barely able to read and write. He kept at his studies, being assisted occasionally by a private tutor, and gave considerable time to the subject of navigation. On taking his first lesson in this subject he said it "was all black as midnight"; at the end of the second

[5] *Book of Bristol County Land Records*, Vol. 50, 478, 479.

lesson he saw "a little gleam of light"; after the third lesson he had more light. Finally, it was all plain to him. He told a certain Professor Griscom: "There were always three things that I paid attention to—latitude, lead, and lookout."

A Sea Captain

When about sixteen Paul secured employment as a common seaman on a vessel bound for the Gulf of Mexico on a whaling voyage. His next trip took him to the West Indies. On a third voyage, the Revolutionary War having broken out, he was captured by the British and held in New York for three months. On his release he repaired to Westport to engage in agricultural pursuits until the times were more propitious for life on the sea. In the meantime he carried on the study of arithmetic and navigation.

Having equipped himself for a life at sea both by study and service as a common seaman, Paul, aided by his brother David, built, at the age of twenty, an open boat to trade with the Connecticut people. But the hazard of the sea and the refugee pirates were too much for David. He left his younger brother and went to the farm, whereupon Paul had for the time being to give up the venture. Soon, however, he was at sea again but lost everything. The undaunted youth, nevertheless, would not give up. He made a boat himself from keel to gunwale, and in it he started to consult his brother concerning future undertaking. On the way he was discovered by the pirates who seized him and his vessel. He was lucky to reach home.

He was now no better off than when he first began. David, however, agreed to build a boat for him if he would furnish the material. When the boat was completed Paul, with borrowed money, bought a cargo and started for Nantucket. On the way he was chased by the pirates and compelled to return to Westport to refit his boat which was damaged by striking a rock. He still persevered, reached Nantucket, and sold his cargo. Financially it was not a profitable voyage.

On a second voyage the pirates robbed him of his cargo and inflicted personal injuries, but a third voyage netted good returns. Soon he procured a covered boat and employed a helper. From now on the business adventures of Cuffe brought him large profits. The war was over and the new Constitution was in operation—two reasons why the sea was safer and business more promising. With his new eighteen ton boat he sailed from his rented home on the Westport River for Saint George for a cargo of codfish. The voyage was the foundation for a profitable fishing industry near his home for many years.

At this time Michael Wainer, his brother-in-law, an Indian, entered his service. His brother-in-law was a good seaman and with a new twenty ton vessel, the *Sunfish*, the men made two trips to the Strait of Belle Isle and Newfoundland. With the profits from the ventures he built in connection with another person, the *Mary*, a forty-two ton schooner.

In the *Mary*, accompanied by two small boats, and with a crew of ten, they went on a whaling expedition to the Strait of Belle Isle. On reaching the Strait, Cuffe found four other vessels fully equipped with boats and harpoons. These vessels would not, as was customary, cooperate with Captain Cuffe, so he and his crew went at it alone. Now fearing they might get no whales the strangers fell in with the *Mary*. Seven whales were captured, six by the crew of the *Mary*. Two whales were the victims of Cuffe's own hand. Reaching Westport in the autumn of 1793 he proceeded to Philadelphia with his cargo of oil and bone and exchanged it for bolts and iron with which to build a new vessel.[6]

Accordingly the keel for a sixty-nine ton vessel was laid at Westport and in 1795 it was launched. He called it the *Ranger*. With a cargo valued at $2000, he sailed for Norfolk on the Chesapeake. From here he went to Vienna on Nanticoke River to buy corn. On reaching port it is said

---

[6] His commercial activities are well told in *Memoirs of Paul Cuffe*, York, 1812.

the townspeople "were filled with astonishment and alarm. A vessel owned and commanded by a black man, and manned with a crew of the same complexion, was unprecedented and surprising. Suspicions were raised, and several persons associated themselves for the purpose of preventing him from registering his vessel, or remaining among them. On examination, however, his papers proved to be correct and, therefore, the custom house officers could not legally oppose proceeding in a regular course. Paul combined prudence with resolution, and on this occasion conducted himself with candor, modesty, and firmness; his crew also behaved not inoffensively but with conciliating propriety. In a few days the inimical association vanished, and the inhabitants treated him and his crew with respect and even kindness."[7] Another writer affirms "Many of the principal people visited his vessel, and at the instance of one of them, Paul dined with his family in the town."[8] The investment in corn proved so profitable that a second voyage was made to Vienna. On the two trips Captain Cuffe cleared about $2000. The *Ranger* also made a trip to Passamaquoddy to get a cargo for James Brian of Wilmington.

In 1800 there was launched the *Hero*, a hundred and sixty-two ton bark, in which Captain Cuffe had one-half interest. This vessel, on one of its trips, rounded the Cape of Good Hope. In 1806 the *Alpha* was fitted out. This was a ship of two hundred and sixty-eight tons in which the Captain had three-fourths interest. Captain Cuffe with a crew of seven Negroes commanded the *Alpha* in a voyage from Wilmington to Savannah, thence to Gottenburg, Sweden, and from there to Philadelphia. Cuffe also owned one-half of the one hundred and nine ton brig, the *Traveller*, built in 1806. Of this ship more will be said elsewhere.

Captain Cuffe was now slightly beyond middle age. Instead of a small open boat, trading with the neighboring

---

[7] See W. J. Allison in *Non-Slaveholder*, December, 1850.
[8] *Ibid*.

townsmen, he had obtained a good sized schooner. "In this vessel," to quote from the funeral oration, "he enlarged the scope of his action, trading to more distant places, and in articles requiring larger capital, and thus, in the process of time, he became owner of one brig, afterwards of two, then he added a ship, and so on until 1806, at which time he was possessed of one ship, two brigs, and several smaller vessels, besides considerable property in houses and lands."[9]

FAMILY AFFAIRS

In the Cuffe manuscripts there is a laconic note chronicling this important event in Paul's life.

Bristol, Dartmouth. February 25, 1783. There personally appeared Paul Cuffe and Alice Pequit both of Dartmouth and was joined together in marriage by me.

BENJ. RUSSEL, *Justice of Peace.*

Other than that she was an Indian girl, little is known of this bride. She, like the groom's mother, probably belonged to the Wampanoag tribe. Paul's sister Mary married an Indian and there is reason for believing that his brother Jonathan also wedded an Indian. Certain it is that it was not uncommon for Negroes and Indians of this vicinity to intermarry.

For several years Captain Cuffe lived in a rented house. But in 1797, when he had such a successful venture in importing corn from Vienna, he purchased a $3500 farm on the shore of the Westport River, a few miles below Hip's Bridge. He soon built a wharf and a store house. At Westport Captain and Mrs. Cuffe made their home and reared their family of two sons and six daughters.

At the time of the purchase of the new farm the neighborhood was without educational facilities. There was neither school house nor tutor. This situation was displeasing to Cuffe. He called a meeting of the neighbors and proposed that steps be taken for adequate educational

[9] Peter Williams, *Discourse on the Death of Paul Cuffe, delivered before the New York African Institution, October 21, 1817.*

equipment. So much difference of opinion resulted that no agreement could be reached at this initial meeting. Subsequent efforts were alike unsuccessful. At last Cuffe built a school house with his own funds on his own farm and offered its use to the public.[12]

One wonders what books were read in his own home. Among his papers a few items relate to the purchase of books. A representative one reads:

Taylor's Concordance	$1.25
Perry's Dictionary	1.00
Clerk's Magazine	1.25
Bowditch Navigators	4.00
Paper	.53
	$8.03

The religious affiliation of the family was with the Friends. The parents of Captain Cuffe had attended the meetings of the Quakers and it was the natural course for the son to follow them. According to the records of the Westport monthly meeting of Friends, Cuffe requested membership with that body in 1808. He was faithful to his profession of Christ. He was considerate of the little folks, for he presented them with Bibles and good counsel and endeavored to set before them an example of righteous conduct. He must have believed that children should have something to do, for in a letter to his brother, he points out that his nephew Zacharis is lying around too much. Moreover, he writes:

I observe that my son Paul has brought home a gun that he borrowed of his Uncle John which I dare say his good uncle lent unto him out of pure love and good will for the want of due consideration, for in the first place I have two guns in order and make but littel use of them which is enough as Christ said unto Peter by the sword. My wife well knows that it is but littel time since Paul got my powder and loaded a logg and Charles fired it and it was wonderful that he had not been killied again he has lately sold his trunk to be abel to gratify himself in these unnecessary evils which we hath disapproved of. Now to support him in that

[12] *Memoirs of Paul Cuffe*, 14, 15.

we both disapprove I think that it is for the want of watchfulness.[14]

Two nieces were entrusted to his care. Although they had good "school learning for girls" Cuffe wished them to continue their studies. Later, when he became the guardian of two grandchildren, he began making arrangements to put them in the New York Yearly Meeting School.

The Westport Friends sold their meeting house in 1813 for $128.72 and erected a new one costing $1198.08. Material costing almost $600, including "nine gallons of cider when raising house—$1.00" was furnished by Captain Cuffe. It is impossible to state just how much if any of this material was furnished gratis but it is safe to say that he carried a heavy responsibility in overseeing the business end of the matter.

[14] Paul Cuffe to John and Jenny Cuffe, September 8, 1808.

CHAPTER II

PROBLEMS OF CITIZENSHIP

"Having no vote or Influence in the Election of those that Tax us yet many of our Colour (as is well known) have Cherfully Entered the field of Battle in the defense of the Common Cause and that (as we conceive) against a similar Exertion of Power (in Regard to taxation) too well known to need a Recital in this place," voicing this sentiment, John and Paul Cuffe and others sent a petition for relief to the General Court, Massachusetts Bay, February 10, 1780. Such requests, however, were not new. At the beginning of the American Revolution there were probably about 7,000 Negroes, slave and free, in Massachusetts. About 1,500 lived in Boston. A petition, signed by Prince Hall and others, praying for the abolition of slavery, was presented to the General Court of Massachusetts Bay in 1777. Another petition dated February 18, 1780, embodies a pathetic and earnest appeal for relief from taxation. It is preserved in the manuscript collection of the Commonwealth of Massachusetts and is signed by John and Paul Cuffe and five others.[10] A copy is with the Cuffe papers. There are two other copies among these papers, both shorter in form, and dated January 22, 1781.

On one of the duplicate petitions in the Cuffe papers there is a notation signed by John Cuffe. "This is the copy," it records, "of the petition which we did deliver unto the honorable Council and House for relief from Taxation in the days of our distress. But we received none."

The petition recites that they were in poor circumstances. When slaves they were deprived of the profits of their labor and of the benefits of inheritance. So distressed were they at this time that only five or six owned a cow. They could not meet the taxes assessed against them. They were aggrieved because they had no vote

[10] *Massachusetts Archives*, Vol. 186, 134–136.

either in local or colonial affairs and nobody had ever heard of one of their number sitting in the Court of the General Assembly. The petitioners most humbly requested the Massachusetts General Court to grant them relief from taxation.

Interest in the Cuffe brothers is now transferred from the State capitol to Bristol County,[11] where these men were indefatigable in their efforts to obtain relief. Late in 1780 a petition was made "To the Honble the Justices of the Court of General Sessions of the peace begun and held at Taunton within and for the County of Bristol." The petitioners ask relief from taxation on the grounds that they are "Indian men and by law not the subjects of Taxation for any Estate Real or personal and Humbly Pray your Honors that as they are assessed jointly a Double Poll Tax and the said Paul is a minor for whom the Said John is not by law answerable or chargeable that the said Poll Taxes aforesaid and also all and regular Taxes aforesaid on their and Each of their Real and personal Estate aforesaid, may be abated to them and they allowed their Reasonable Costs."

The taxes for which complaint was made were for the years 1777 to 1780 inclusive, and amounted to about two hundred pounds. They were heaviest for the years 1779 and 1780. The assessors, then, on December 15, gave Richard Collins, constable of Dartmouth, a warrant for the arrest of the Cuffe brothers. It recites that their taxes were delinquent for

1778:	5	lbs.	17s.	6d.
1779:	9	lbs.	2s.	8d.
	29	lbs.	16s.	10½d.
	29	lbs.	18s.	9d.
1780:	61	lbs.	18s.	4d.
	17	lbs.	7s.	5/25d.
Grand total:	154	lbs.	1s.	1 7/10d.

[11] The quoted documents relating to the question of taxation are in the *Records of the Court of General Sessions*, Taunton, Mass. They were examined for the writer by Professor Arthur Buffinton of Williams College.

The assessors found no estate on which to levy for the taxes. In the name of the Commonwealth of Massachusetts Bay, therefore, they required the "said Richard Collens to take into safe custody the body of the said John and Paul Cuffe and then commit to the common gaol of the said County of Bristol there to remain until they, the said John and Paul Cuffe shall pay and satisfy the above sum with all necessary charges" or be discharged by due process of law. The constable followed the instructions and reported on December 19 that he had placed the Cuffe brothers in the common gaol in Taunton. For this service, including travel for twenty-five "milds," he turned in a bill of twelve shillings, nine pence.

The next step in the legal battle was on the part of the Cuffe brothers. The keeper of the gaol or his underkeeper was directed on the nineteenth of December in the "Name of the Commonwealth of Massachusetts to have the bodies of John and Paul Cuffe said to be Indian men whom you have now in keeping before the Justices of our Inferior Court of Common Pleas now holden at Taunton for said County together with the cause of their and each of their Commitiment and Detention. Hereof fail not and make Return of this writ with your doings therein. Witness Walter Spooner Esqr." Elijah Dean, underkeeper, produced the two men on the same day that he received the writ of habeas corpus.

When the Court of General Sessions of the Peace met on the nineteenth of December it ordered on the petition of John and Paul Cuffe that the assessors of Dartmouth appear at the next term to show cause, wherefore the Prayer of said Petition should not be granted. The order was given to the sheriff of Bristol County on the twenty-ninth of December. The assessors, Benjamin Russell, Richard Kriby, Christopher Gifford, and John Smith were accordingly summoned by Elijah Dean. He served the warrant on the twenty-sixth of February and recorded his fee as twenty-four pence.

Meanwhile, on the twentieth of February the selectmen of Dartmouth were called on to choose an agent to defend the action against the Cuffe brothers. At their annual meeting on the eighth of March the Honorable Walter Spooner, a member of the Massachusetts Constitutional Convention 1780, was chosen in behalf of the town to make answer to the petitioners in question. At the March meeting the case was continued and came up for action at the next meeting of the court.

In the meantime, John and Paul Cuffe made a request to the selectmen of Dartmouth. In the Cuffe papers three such requests are preserved. The one dated the twenty-fourth of April is followed by a notation attesting it a true copy of the request delivered to the selectmen. It asks them to "put a stroak on your next Warrant for calling a town meeting so that it may legally be Laid Before said town By way of voat to know the mine of said town whether all free Negroes and molattoes shall have the same Privileges in this said town of Dartmouth as the white People have Respecting Places of profit choosing of officers and the Like together with all other Privileges in all cases that shall or may happen or be Brought in this said town of Dartmouth or that we have Reliefe granted us Joyntly from Taxation which under our present depressed circumstances and your poor Petitioners as in duty Bound shall ever pay."

The disposition of the case as found in the records is contained in a few sentences. One is dated the eleventh of June and is signed by Richard Collens, constable. It reads as follows:

Then received of John Cuffe eight pounds twelve shillings silver money in full for all John Cuffe and Paul Cuffe Rates until this date and for all my court charges received by me.

Elijah Dean presented his bill for summoning the assessors. It was paid, and the bill with an acknowledgment from Edward Pope is entered in Cuffe's letter book with the tax receipt of the eleventh of June. The other laconic note is from the Records of the Court of General Sessions held at Taunton on June 12. It curtly "ordered that the Petition of Paul Cuffe and John Cuffe and the proceedings thereon be dismissed."

Several writers have commented on the significance of the petitions of the Cuffe brothers and their resistance to the payment of taxes. Practically all of them overestimate the matter. For example, a representative writer says, "This was a day equally honorable to the petitioners and to the legislature; a day in which justice and humanity triumphed over prejudice and oppression; a day which ought to be gratefully remembered by every person of color within the boundaries of Massachusetts, and the names of John and Paul Cuffe, should always be united with its recollection." [13]

There is no documentary proof for statements of this kind. A property qualification for voting fixed by the William and Mary Charter with slight modifications carried down to 1785. Negroes acquired rights and privileges in Massachusetts not by special acts of the General Assembly, but by a judicial act of 1783 based on article one of the Declaration of Rights of the Constitution of 1780.

[13] William Armistead, *Memoir of Paul Cuffe* (London, 1846), 23.

CHAPTER III

THE REDEMPTION OF AFRICA

Early in his life Paul Cuffe became interested in the redemption of Africa. "The travail of my soul," said he, "is that Africa's inhabitants may be favored with reformation." The following letter to James Pemberton not only illustrates Cuffe's style and manifests his spirit but shows the redemption of Africa as the main interest of his life:

WESTPORT 9th mo 14th 1808

Worthy friend

In Reply to thine of the 8-6 mo.

I desire ever to humble myself before my Maker who hath I trust favored me to the notice of my friends. I desire that God will Bless all Our friends who hath been made willing to Rise to our assistance. Without hope of a providential hand we must ever been miserabal.

As to poor me I feel very feebel and all most worn out in hard service and uncapable of doing much for my brethren the African Race but blessed be God I am what I am and all that I can conceive that God pleases to lay upon me to make me an instrument for that service I desire ever to be submissive that his will may be done and I shall not loose sight of the above but endeavor to wright thou again on the subject if thee will wright me if any further information can be given it would be kindly excepted by one who wishes well to all mankind &c.

PAUL CUFFE.

In this cause, however, Paul Cuffe was not struggling alone. The question of ameliorating the condition of the Negro in Africa was, at the opening of the nineteenth century, a matter of general concern. Men with a philanthropic spirit both in Denmark and Sweden had by this time investigated the problem. In France, in addition to individual activity, the society, Les Amis des Noirs, was organized. In England, interest was more pronounced than in any other European country. The African Institution, the Saint George's Bay Company, better known as the Sierra Leone Company, and the British African Colonization Society, directed efforts toward the western coast. The foundation of the Sierra Leone was laid by these societies. This same interest in advancing the civilization of Africa was found among distinguished Americans like Samuel D. Hopkins, pastor of the First Congregational Church in Newport, Rhode Island, Ezra Stiles, sometime president of Yale, and William Thornton, head of the United States Patent Office.[17]

In 1808, when expressions from Cuffe showing his interest in Africa appeared, considerable progress had been made by the English philanthropists. In the first place, they had carried on successful propaganda. They were in touch with the Americans and had the support of the Quakers. In a pamphlet specifically printed to call the attention of Parliament to the "case of their fellow creatures" the Quakers asserted that "Africa, so populous, and so rich in vegetable and mineral productions, instead of affording all the advantages of a well regulated commerce, is scarcely known but as a mart for slaves, and as the source of violent barbarities, perpetuated in order to secure them, by men professing the Christian religion."[18] The leading men in the African Institution, Thomas Clarkson, William Wilberforce, and Granville Sharp, exerted much influence both through personal activity and the agency of the African Institution.

In the second place, the Englishmen, as stated above, had actually established a settlement on the Guinea coast known as Sierra Leone. Many Negroes from London and vicinity, the black American Loyalists, and the Jamaica

[17] For an extended account of these movements see H. N. Sherwood, *Early Negro Deportation Projects*, in Mississippi Valley Historical Review, II, 484 et seq.

[18] *The Case of our Fellow Creatures, the Oppressed Africans, respectfully recommended to the serious Consideration of the Legislature of Great Britain*, London, 1784.

Maroons, settled in Novia Scotia, and the "Willyfoss" Negroes were transported to the Africa coast. The commendable intentions of the promoters of this settlement on the west coast of Africa were conveyed to Cuffe by his Philadelphia friend, James Pemberton, who was in touch with the activities of the African Institution. In September, 1808, he wrote:

> I perceive they are earnestly attentive to pursue the laudable object of promoting the civilization of the Blacks in their own country with a view to draw them off from the wild habits of life to which they have been accustomed, by instructing them in the arts of agriculture, mechanic labor, and domestic industry, by which means they hope to be instrumental in preparing the minds of those uninstructed people gradually to become qualified to receive religious instruction.

Pemberton also called attention to the fact that the leaders of the African Institution were distinguished men and he especially noted that the president was the Duke of Gloucester, a nephew of the King. Moreover, he likened the plan for benefiting the African to the one which the Friends were using to civilize the American Indian. In the concluding paragraph of the letter, Pemberton sounds a personal call to Cuffe:

> Thou wilt be sensible that the undertaking is very important and those concerned to promote it are anxious to receive all the assistance and encouragement they can from the friends of humanity at home and in America. Now if thy concern for the good of the poor untutored people continues and finds thy mind impressed with a sense that any portion of the work is allotted for thee to perform, I hope and trust thou wilt give it thy most serious consideration, and should it ripen to such a degree as to bring thee under an apprehension of religious duty to perform it in such a way as that wisdom which is superior to human may point out, a consultation with thy friends on the occasion may be reasonably useful, tending to thy strength and encouragement.[19]

Already assurance had come from Zachariah Macaulay, Governor of Sierra Leone, that if Cuffe should make a voy-

[19] In the *Cuffe Manuscripts*.

age to Africa he would receive every encouragement from him. As a director of the African Institution he felt that its views would be advanced if any free blacks from America of good conduct and religious principles should be induced to offer their personal assistance. In June, 1810, therefore, Cuffe, as an "ever well wishing Friend," wrote to Friends in Philadelphia that he planned to make a visit to Africa in the fall. He hoped that some solid Friend would feel called on to accompany him as an adviser. In September he laid his plans for the voyage before a large committee of Westport Friends. He was authorized by this committee to pursue his prospects and was given a letter of recommendation.

In this letter his neighbors stated that Cuffe "had lately been received a member of their religious society, that he was highly respected by Friends in Philadelphia, and that he felt a religious concern to assist, as far as in his power, the views of the African Institution. His intention was, provided he met with sufficient encouragement here, to sail from America to Sierra Leone, with a cargo likely to be suitable for the place, and, when there, make such observations as would enable him to judge whether he should do right to encourage some sober families of black people in America to settle among the Africans, and if so, he intended to convey them in his own vessel." They also reported Cuffe as the owner of a vessel and worth five thousand pounds.[20]

The lively interest that Cuffe had had in the people of color at Sierra Leone, his wish that they might become established in the truth, and his desire that they might then do missionary work among the African brethren, influenced him to visit his friends on the Guinea coast. He rented his farm and commended his family to his brother John. The latter wrote his sister Freelove in New York that Paul would be gone for a year, possibly two, and that

[20] *Life of William Allen with Selections from His Correspondence.* (2 vols., Philadelphia, 1847), I, 85, 86.

he went for a "religious visit amongst the inhabitants of that land, our own nation." [21]

When everything was ready the *Traveller* sailed out of Westport for Sierra Leone via Philadelphia. Nine Negroes composed the crew. The story of the voyage from Philadelphia is interestingly told by Cuffe himself in his journal: [22]

1810. 12mo. 4. I called on Friends in Philadelphia. They appointed a time at Arch Street meeting-house, and after a feeling conference, they expressed satisfaction and left me at liberty. Hence it fell under the head of my former advisers, John James and Alexander Wilson, I called on them: John professed that he could not see any other way, better, than to take a load of corn that he had long held, and take it to Portugal or Cadiz. I then had to tell him the said John James, that was not my business; it rather appeared to me that it was not for the profit or gain that I had undertaken this voyage; but I had about four thousand dollars property, and would wish to proceed as far as that would carry me; and it appeared that if this opportunity was neglected, I might never expect to have the opportunity again. John then gave up the prospect of shipping his corn, and he and I left Alexander, and he told me he believed my concern was real, and that he would assist me in fitting out for the voyage and make no charges. I told him It then felt pleasant to me.

1mo. 20th. 19 days out from Philadelphia to Sierra Leone.

Our minds were collected together to wait on the Lord notwithstanding we were on the great deep.

2mo. 2. At three A. M. wind and sea struck us down on our beam ends, washed John Masters overboard, but by the help of some loose rigging he regained the ship again.

2mo. 21st. The dust of Africa lodged on our rigging. We judged that land to be about twenty-five leagues off.

2mo. 24th. At 10 A. M. sounded and got bottom for the first ground that we got on the coast of Africa. Sixty-five fathoms.

3mo. 1st. We came to Sierra Leone road.

[As the directors of the African Institution said, "It must

[21] In *Cuffe Manuscripts.* Dated January 5, 1811.
[22] The *Journal* is in the *Cuffe Manuscripts.*

have been a strange and animating spectacle to see this free and enlightened African entering as an independent trader, with his black crew into that port which was so lately the Nidus of the slave trade."]

3mo. 4th. An invitation was given me this day to dine with the Governor, at whose table an extensive observation took place of the slave trade and the unsuccessfulness of the colony of Sierra Leone.

3mo. 5th. Visited the school of 30 girls, which is a pleasing prospect in Sierra Leone.

3mo. 10th. First day. Attended a Methodist meeting in the forenoon.

3mo. 13th. King Thomas came on board to see me. He was an old man, gray headed, appeared to be sober and grave. I treated him with civility, and made him a present of a bible. a history of Elizabeth Webb, a Quaker, and a book of essays on War: together with several other small pamphlets accompanied with a letter of advise from myself, such as appeared to be good to hand to the King for the use and encouragement of the nations of Africa. He and retinue were thirteen in number. I served him with victuals, but it appeared that there was *rum* wanting, *but none was given.*

3mo. 14. King George from Bullion Shore sent his messenger on board. with a present of three chickens and invited me over to see him.

3mo. 17. This day being the first day of the week we went on shore to the church, and in the afternoon to the new Methodist.

3mo. 18. This day I went to Bullion Shore in order to visit the King George, King of Bullion, who received and treated us very cordially. I presented the King with a bible, a testament, a treatise of Benjamin Holmes, a history of Elizabeth Webb, and an epistle from the yearly meeting, and a history, or called a short history of a long travel from Babel to Bethel.

3mo. 19. Visiting families on Sierra Leone, found many of them without bibles, and others who had bibles with out the living substance of the spirit.

3mo. 28. I breakfasted with the Governor Columbine and after breakfast had conference with him on the subject of the country, and settling in it—to good satisfaction.

3mo. 31. Attended the church. The Mendingo men have the Scriptures in their tongue, viz the old testament, but deny the new testament. They own Mahomet a prophet.

1811. 4mo. 3. Thomas Wainer is much put out, and is exceeding wroth for giving him what I call good advice: but time will make manifest. God alone knows the hearts of men. I desire to have him be my preserver.

CHAPTER IV

IN ENGLAND

When Captain Cuffe sailed from Philadelphia on New Year's Day, 1811, he apparently intended to visit only Sierra Leone. After an examination of the plans then in operation for the civilization of the Africans, doubtless he meant to return to America. However, when there reached him a letter from William Allen with an order in council which Allen and Wilberforce had procured for him, he changed his mind and determined to visit England.[23] He recorded thus this part of the voyage:

1811. 7mo. 12. Arrived safe all well (at Liverpool) after a passage of sixty-two days.[24]

Soon after we got in the dock, two of my men going out of the dock gate, were met by the press-gang and carried to the rendevous. The press gang then came on board my vessel, and let me know that they had two of my men, and overhauled the remainder of the crew, among which they found Aaron Richard, an African that I had taken as an apprentice in Africa to instruct in navigation. They claimed him as a British subject and took him off. At eleven I went to the rendezvous and got the two men first mentioned, but they would not let Aaron off.

7mo. 13. This morning the Ship *Alpha* arrived fifty-two days from New Orleans. All well. My friends Richard Rathbone and Thomas Thompson were very anxious in assisting me to regain Richard . . . They wrote immediately to London for the liberation of Aaron, with a petition to the Board of Admiralty.

7mo. 14. I this day put up with Thomas Thompson, and took a first day meeting with them, and feeling very anxious for Aaron's liberty, I took place in the stage for London. Arrived in London three day morning, six-o-clock, it making thirty-two hours, distance two hundred and eight miles.

7mo. 15. This day passed with the pleasant prospect of passing through a well cultivated and very fertile country. How

[23] *Life of William Allen*, I, 99-105.
[24] The diary is from *Paul Cuffe's Journal* in the *Cuffe Manuscripts*.

often did I feel my mind enlivened with the peaceful desire that this land and people might enjoy a universal and tranquil peace.

7mo. 16. At six this morning arrived in the great city of London. I put up at an inn and took breakfast. At ten-o-clock took a pilot for Plough Court, where I was courteously received by my friend William Allen, who was engaged about the liberation of Aaron.

7mo. 17. This day went to meeting, and in the afternoon Cornelius attended me to see the great church of St. Paul and many other curiosities of London, such as London Bridge, Blackfriars Bridge.

7mo. 18. This day my friend Wm. Allen had a note from Wm. Wilberforce desiring that I should see him at — o-clock.

Wilberforce called for pen, ink and paper and wrote to the Board of Admiralty and sent his man immediately . . .

Wm. Allen and Paul Cuffe then went into the Parliament.

7mo. 19. We went over London Bridge to Lancaster's school, where were taught one thousand scholars by one master. But about eight hundred were then in school. This prospect of the school was the greatest gratification that I met with.

7mo. 20. This afternoon took stage for William Dillwyn's, at whose house I was friendly and cordially received, and took great satisfaction.

7mo. 21. I went and dined with George and Mary Stacey, who were very kind and loving, appeared to live in the truth.

7mo. 22. Spent the fore part of this day in conversing with Wm. Dillwyn on subjects of importance. After dinner Wm. gave me two volumes of Clarkson's work on the slave trade. His wife and two daughters accompanied me to town in their carriages about five miles. At seven this evening Thomas Clarkson arrived.

7mo. 23. Thomas Clarkson sets to for Aaron's liberation. Makes so far, as for certain persons to go with him to the Board of Admiralty, where they found the order had been some days gone, for Aaron's discharge. You may think that it was great consolation to me to think, if God permitted, that I should have the happy opportunity of returning Aaron to his parents and fellow citizens at Sierra Leone.

7mo. 25. Zachariah Macaulay called at Wm. Allen's and had a good conversation. He then invited me to dine with him on the morrow, which was accepted, hoping there my some good come out of it.

7mo. 26. I this day went to Z. Macaulay's where I meet with exceeding kind treatment. He said Macaulay promised to me the continuation of his friendship.

7mo. 27. This morning came to Wm. Allen's from Macaulay's accompanied by Macauley. Thomas Clarkson this day sets off for home, who has been of service and consolation. Thomas is a man of good deportment. My friends this day forwarded a petition to the Privy Council for a license for the *Traveller* to go to Africa, commanded by Paul Cuffe, or some other person.

7mo. 28. In the evening my friend Allen called his family together and we were comforted, and I believe I may say the presence of the precious comforter was felt to be near. In the evening conversation took place between Wm. Allen and P. Cuffe on the most advantageous way of encouragement of the improvement of the Colony of Sierra Leone. I then told Wm. that it appeared that the Colony people wanted help, or encouragement; that I had my mind still impressed that a channel of intercourse should be kept open between America and Sierra Leone, and that my mind was to build a house in Sierra Leone, encouragement might be given of accomodation.

7mo. 30. This morning Cornelius, William and Paul went to see the mint and the works thereof were great and wonderful. I this day took place in the stage for Liverpool at three guineas.

[William Allen records in his diary that he took leave of Cuffe, "in much nearness of spirit; he is certainly a very interesting man."25]

7mo. 31. At six we set forward for Liverpool. The prospect of the fertility of the country was highly gratifying.

8mo. 1. I arrived at Liverpool at nine-o-clock after a passage of thirty-nine hours; took my package to my friend, Thomas Thompson's where I was kindly received.

8mo. 2. I arose much refreshed, and found all well on board, and Aaron Richards had arrived the same afternoon as I did. Saw and had much conversation with many folks, among whom was Stephen Crillett a minister from America. I took breakfast with him at Isaac Hadwins, in whose company, and conversation, I was much comforted, he was to leave Liverpool the next day for the country. My mate and second mate went to dinner with Isaac and he was anxious for more to come along with them. The crew were spoken of in the highest terms for their steadiness, not given

25 *Life of William Allen*, I, 103.

to swearing, but I found to my sorrow that Zachariah had behaved very unbecoming in keeping unbecoming company, and drinking to excess and speaking light of Jesus Christ.

8mo. 3. It felt pleasant to me to hold out that honour without virtue, was not true honor: and also from whence came wars and fightings. I also had to hold out to William and Richard Rathbone that the flesh was imperfect and forewarned, forearmed; and that was not to put too great confidence in me as I was but flesh and blood. For those young men had taken a very early and active part in assisting me in every way and manner not only making their house my home, but stepping forward to give me every aid even petitioning the Board of Admiralty for the relief of Aaron Richards as did also my friend Thomas Thompson afford me every aid, with kind invitation to make his house my home all which I felt easy to accept of. Have this day seen William Bootell the great slave dealer as I have been told, who invited me to his lodgings.

8mo. 4. Attended fore and afternoon meetings—in the former I was favored with the Spirit of Supplication. Capt. Coffin of the Ship *Alpha* and my crew were at the meeting, which was very gratifying to me. Letter from Wm. Allen stating that the license would not be obtained under four or five days.

8mo. 5. A man of color talks of going to Sierra Leone in order to help the colonists. In the afternoon another man proposed going to help in any way that may be helpful, either in printing, school keeping, or by other means. I think here is rather encouragement.

8mo. 6. I this day had further communication with Wm. Thomas, a European, a printer about going to Sierra Leone, who seems to be very anxious and it is concluded to write to London in order to see if it may be encouraged.

8mo. 7. This day took dinner with Wm. and Richard Rathbone in company with Thomas Thompson and William Roscoe, a well engaged man, for the establishing the slave trade, that the ships of war should be commissioned to take all vessels that were found in that trade belonging to whom they would. Also Lord John Russell dined with us.

8mo. 9. I this day took dinner with Captain Bootell and Captain Pane formerly slave dealers, but treated me politely.

8mo. 11. This day all attended meeting, and after meeting the men went home with the Rathbones and took dinner.

8mo. 14. This day I dined with Capt. Brown, Captain of his Majesty's navy ship who was a very civil, goodly man; and his wife and family thoughtful people, on the whole I had a comfortable meal.

8mo. 18. At half past nine in the evening set forward for London accompanied with three very agreeable people.

8mo. 20. At half past five arrived in London, found Wm. Allen and family all well.

8mo. 21. At four-o-clock P. M. I departed from Wm. Allen's after having a comfortable sitting in company of a woman Friend, who appeared to be a chosen vessel unto the Lord, and was a comfort unto us and also a man by the name of Morris Burbeck. Cornelius Hanbury accompanied me to Waltham Stone at Wm. Dillwyn's where we were cordially received. Wm. was very unwell and it appears that his glass is almost run, and his duty faithfully discharged. Much of our time whilst together was taken up for the good, and beneficial improvement of the inhabitants of Africa; for that which might attend for their good, and for the honor and glory of God.

8mo. 22. Half past one this morning I went to meeting with Wm. Dillwyn's family in the coach, where I had a comfortable open meeting, after meeting went home with Wm. Fanster, to dinner. After dinner came Mary Stacey who had good advice delivered it in much love and tenderness.

8mo. 23. This day dined in company with Capt. Eber Clark of and from New Bedford who said he left Peter and Alexander Howard well, and heard nothing but that my family was well. Wm. Rotch mentioned my name in his letter to Wm. Allen and mentioned nothing but my family was well. His letter arrived in good time to do good, and was consolation to me in such a distant land.

8mo. 25. Came from Newington in a carriage with Joseph Bevan. I went to the great meeting where I had pretty clear openings in the forenoon. Took dinner with Wm. Allen's mother and son Joseph, where we were very aggreeably entertained. Came home to Plough Court where we had a good refreshing season in the evening.

8mo. 26. This morning very pleasant; Cornelius Hanbury and I went to the London and West India Docks, which was exceeding gratifying, both to see the shipping, and accomodations in the

Docks, and also the shipping in the river that lay in the tiers as we passed for three miles. They continued to extend as far as I could see; the river is about one-half mile wide. At five-o-clock in the afternoon I dined with Z. Macauley, where I was very agreeably entertained.

8mo. 27. This day met the committee of the African Institution who sat at one P. M. and expressed great satisfaction on the information I gave them, and felt also that I was endeavoring to assist them in maintaining the good cause; with blessing that we may reasonably hope that we may be supported with—to endeavor that the subject may not fall beneath the level where we found it. I made the Duke of Gloucester a present of an African robe, a letter box and a dagger to show that the Africans were capable of mental endowments and so forth.

8mo. 28. This day attended the Grace Street Church meeting. It was comfortable for me to sit with Friends in true humiliation and supplication. And may this be the continuation of our lives through time, that peace may be our lot. [William Allen, writing of the meeting with the Committee of the African Instruction in his diary, says Cuffe "returned very sensible and satisfactory answers" to questions by the Duke of Gloucester and others and that "his simplicity and strong natural good sense made a great impression upon all parties. On the whole it was a most gratifying meeting, and fully answered, and even exceeded all we could have asked." Captain Clarke from New Bedford, Massachusetts, says that he has "known Cuffe from a boy and that a person of greater integrity and honor in business he never met with. I did not give the smallest hint which might call forth this declaration."

In the Seventh report of the directors of the African Institution this meeting is recorded as follows:
African Institution had "the very judicious plan of profiting by the opportunity of inducing Captain Paul Cuffe to settle in Sierra Leone, and carry over with him free blacks of good character and of some property, who might settle in the colony and practice among the natives the mechanical arts, and the cultivation of tropical produce. He and his crew in Great Britain attracted universal respect by the propriety of their deportment, as well as admiration by their singular proficiency in both the science and the practice of navigation. The African board held a meeting, although in vacation time, for the purpose of seeing and confer-

ring with the captain. His royal highness the Duke of Gloucester attended, as he always does, at the Board, and, together with the other Directors, entered fully in to the subjects alike interesting to those distinguished philanthropists, and to their dark-colored but civilized ally."[26] Referring to Cuffe in his diary on this day, William Allen writes: "We had an affecting parting, as it is not very probable that we shall see him any more. He has left a wife and eight children, and a profitable business in which he was engaged, to forward the views of the African Institution, and this, at the risk of his person and property."[27]

8mo. 30. Arrived at Manchester at eight-o-clock.

8mo. 31. David Docknay and Paul Cuffe spent this day in seeing the factories. They have got them to great perfection. They light the darkest room with gas extracted from sea coal. This light far exceeds the candle light; it is more like day light. This air issues out of a small tube and by the blaze of a candle being put to it, it blazes and burns until the gas is stopped. This is done by the turning of the stop that reaches through the pipe. One woman spins one hundred-fifty threads at a time. This afternoon Robert Benson came. John Thorp dined with us this day.

9mo. 1. This day attended meeting, both fore and afternoon. Took dinner at Isaac Crenden's, and then went to see Richard and Martha Routh.

9mo. 2. Took stage for Liverpool arrived at ten. I this day wrote to Wm. Allen and stated the necessity of establishing commerce in Africa and building a vessel in Africa, and if there should be any owner found in London.

9mo. 4. This morning being a pleasant morning Hannah Rathbone's family and myself went to Wm. Roscoes, which was about two miles further. He being a very warm friend for the abolishing the slave trade, many subjects took place between us. He stated the necessity, and propriety of condemning all nations, that might be found in the trade. I likewise was favored to state to him the necessity there was of keeping open a communication between America, Africa and England in order to assist Africa in its civilization and that the two powers to contenance it, even if they were at variance, and to consider it as a neutral path.

[26] *The Seventh Report of the Directors of the African Institution* is in the *Edinburgh Review*, XXI.

[27] *Life of William Allen*, I, 105.

And I could not see wherein the French Goverment may not gain in adopting this neutral path.

9mo. 6. After breakfast went into the blind school and it was wonderful to see the operation of all kinds of work they would go through of spinning, weaving, matting, carpeting, of many colors.

[On this day Cuffe signed a contract with Will Midgley by which the latter was to furnish flannels for shipment on the *Traveller* for Sierra Leone.[28]]

9mo. 17. Took breakfast with my passengers and also with Wm. Rathbone accompanied with a friend belonging to London, where the African conversation took place which was the most expediant method of civilization of Africa.

9mo. 20. At ten-o-clock weighed anchor. . . . A great many attended our departure . . .

11mo. 12. At four P. M. we anchored in Sierra Leone.

[28] In the *Cuffe Manuscripts*.

CHAPTER V

THE RETURN TO AMERICA

Cuffe remained in Sierra Leone for three months. On Sundays he attended the various churches. He made the most of these opportunities to caution the lukewarm and to reprimand closely the unconcerned. On the other days of the week, he explored the country because he wanted to know every advantage this location had for the many settlers he hoped would come from America.

He noted the growing pineapples and was pleased with the Guinea grass so tall that he could just reach the top of it with his umbrella. He found Indian corn and buckwheat growing well. Although he sought diligently he could find no good place to make salt. In his survey of the streams he found two that had fall sufficient for twenty and thirty foot undershot wheels respectively. This pleased him greatly, as the water power made mills possible. On his rounds he distributed many kinds of seeds and silk worm eggs, but few knew what to do with them.

On the eleventh of December he was called to the home of James Reed by the Social Society of Sierra Leone to help draw up a constitution for this organization. Subsequent meetings were necessary to complete the work. When it had been done, the Friendly Society of Sierra Leone was born, beginning to function immediately. A communication from William Allen addressed to John Kizel was presented to the Society. It was duly answered and preparations made for carrying on commercial relations with the London African Institution. The government prohibition on landing rum and tobacco displeased many of the members because it took from them one possibility for lucrative revenues.

In addition to these interests, Cuffe visited the schools and greeted the new missionaries. He was a first class teacher himself and many ambitious Negroes learned the art of navigation from his teachings. Occasionally he took apprentices, and at this time four Africans were indentured to him.

Finally he made arrangements with the Governor for the reception of colonists who might come over from America. They discussed means for civilizing the natives, land grants to the new settlers, and problems of trade for all. When every measure had been taken looking to future relations between England, Sierra Leone, and America, he set sail for his home land.

He was just four days out when Captain James Tildwell of the British sloop of war, *Abrina*, took the *Traveller* back to Sierra Leone. Captain Tildwell did not understand the arrangement by which Captain Cuffe had four indentured servants on board. The matter was immediately brought to the attention of the Governor and Cuffe was permitted to renew his homeward voyage. Cuffe sailed according to the old rhyme—

> If the wind comes before the rain,
> Clear the top sails and hoist them again.
> If the rain comes before the wind,
> Lower the top sails, and take them in.

All went well on sea. But when on April 19, 1812, he reached American waters a grave difficulty beset him. The *Traveller* was bringing to the United States a British cargo. This was contrary to the existing trade laws. What could be done? A pilot boat, the *Daggett*, offered to take him to New Bedford where he could interview the authorities. Moreover, it was an opportunity speedily to reach Westport and see his family. So he left the *Traveller* at sea and took passage on the *Daggett*.

When he returned, Captain John Cahoone in a revenue cutter had condemned the *Traveller* for bringing in a British cargo. There was nothing left for Captain Cuffe to do except to carry his cause to Washington and this he decided to do. Accordingly letters of recommendation were prepared to present the case to the Federal authorities. He engaged the services of John Vase, Amasa Robbins, and others to prepare a petition to the Secretary of War. The Collector of Customs approved the petition. Governor Simeon Martin, Judge Constant Taber, former Congressman, G. C. Champlin, as well as John Coggeshall, I. Vernon, Thomas G. Pitman, and Walter Channing, endorsed his papers.

Armed with these letters of recommendation, he started for Washington. On his way he stopped at Providence where his good friend, William Rotch, Jr., gave him counsel and aid. He put Cuffe in touch with Moses Brown, who brought in the services of Thomas Arnold. They called on the Judge and Attorney-General. All favored Captain Cuffe, and Brown and Arnold signed his general letters of recommendation. While in Providence he made his home with Obadiah Brown and attended fore and afternoon meetings. He stopped off at Philadelphia on the 29th of April, to tell John James his troubles. "In travelling through the country," he wrote, "I perceived that the people seemed to have great knowledge of me."

Arriving in Washington on the first of May, he sought Samuel Hutchinson, who accompanied him to call on President Madison, the Secretary of War, and others to whom he had letters of recommendation. "The Secretary observed to me," wrote the Captain, "that French brandy could not be imported from a British port but observed whether it would be inconvenient to me to have it entered for exportation. I then told him my funds were small, and it would lock up my funds. All people appeared very kindly indeed." The authorities at Washington thought his voyage was innocent and laudable. The *Traveller* and all his property was restored to him without reservation and the government offered its services to him in carrying out his African plans.

On the day following this decision, the Captain started home. "When I took my seat," he wrote, "being the first in, I took the after seat. When the passengers came, in came a blustering powder headed man with stern countenance. 'Come away from that seat.' I was no starter and sat still. He then bustled along and said, 'I want to put my umbrella in the box.' I arose, he then put his umbrella in. He then said, 'You must go out of this for there is a lady coming in.' I entered into no discourse with him, but took my seat; he took his seat beside me but showed much evil contempt. At length the woman and a girl made their appearance. I then arose and invited the woman into the after seat saying we always give way to accomodate the women. We set forward on our journey. On our way at the tavern I was overtaken by Wm. Hunter, member of Congress. He was very free and conversant, which this man above mentioned observed. Before we got to Baltimore he became loving and openly accosted me, 'Captain, take the after seat,' but from the common custom I thanked him, and wished him to keep his seat.

"When I arrived in Baltimore, they utterly refused to take me in at the tavern or to get me a dinner unless I would go back among the servants. This I refused, not as I thought myself better than the servants, but from the nature of the case, thought it not advisable. I found my way to a tavern where I got my dinner. Friend Barnard Gilbert went with me and was friendly. Jesse Talbot, a very worthy friend, had paid every attention to me; by this time I seemingly had friends on every side. I staid at the home of Elisha Tyson, who offered to be a real friend of the people of color."

While in Baltimore the Captain attended Preparation Meeting. He called on a number of his friends, among whom were Daniel Coker and George Collins, teachers of the African school of one hundred and seven children. At a tea where many colored people were present, Cuffe told about his African visit. Plans were made to form a Society to correspond with the London African Institution and the Friendly Society of Sierra Leone.

Cuffe stopped in Philadelphia and New York and renewed old acquaintances, and also made plans for the organization of Societies to communicate with the African Institution in London and the Friendly Society of Sierra Leone. These societies with the one started in Baltimore were centers for the discussion of questions relating to Africa and for commercial undertakings with their African neighbors.

When Cuffe was in New York, his guide introduced him to two Methodist preachers. One said to him, "Do you understand English?" Cuffe replied that there was a part he did not understand, namely, "that many persons who profess being enlightened with the true light, yet had not seen the evil of one brother professor making merchandise of and holding his brother in bondage." The ministers did not clear up the question, and in Cuffe's own words, "We bid each other farewell without any further conversation." He put this same query to the United Society assembled for the Methodist Conference in New York, but it was received with coldness. While it shows Cuffe's zeal in working for the emancipation of slavery, it also gives an index to the state of the popular mind on this subject fifty years before the Civil War.

Elated over the recovery of the *Traveller* and permission to land his cargo, he reached Westport on May 23. He expressed his gratitude to President Madison in the following letter:

I stopped short of my duty in not calling to acknowledge the favor that I received from the seat of Government; for which I desire to be excused. But upon serious reflection, feeling that there is an acknowledgment due unto the ruler of the people—certainly there is greater acknowledgment due unto the Father of all our mercies.

May the blessing of heaven attend thee; may the United States be preserved from the calamities of a war, and be favored to retain her neutrality in peace and happiness.

Another letter equally important went out. It recounted his experiences to William Allen and promised continued interest in all things relating to the uplift of the Negro race. "Paul Cuffe," he wrote in closing, "doth not at present go to Africa, but shall send such characters as confidence may be placed in. At present it is thought that I may be as serviceable towards the promotion of the colony, as though I was to remove. However, as my wife is not willing to go, I do not feel at liberty to urge, but feel in duty bound to escort myself to the uttermost of my ability for the good cause of Africa." [29]

[29] In the *Cuffe Manuscripts.* Dated June 12, 1812.

CHAPTER VI

A QUAKER MISSION

The visit of Captain Cuffe to Africa was a spontaneous movement on his part. He was anxious to contribute to the improvement of his countrymen. His visit to England was a great incentive to the Directors of the African Institution. Both the Duke of Gloucester and William Allen were convinced that the colonists of Sierra Leone needed only a stimulus to their industry and that the Institution could give it without the slightest inconvenience. They regarded Paul Cuffe as a medium for this service—a medium providentially afforded.

One is impressed with the methodical and thorough-going way Cuffe conducted his affairs during the first part of his visit in Sierra Leone. He was soon acquainted both with the land and the people. Just as soon as he obtained information he began its dissemination. A letter was dispatched to America in care of his brother, John Cuffe. The Captain wrote "Hope it may find its way to its destination and obtain its desired effect which will be a consolation to one who wishes well to all mankind both here and hereafter world without end." The following letter dated April 20, 1811, was "The Epistle of the Society of Sierra Leone in Africa,"[30] formed for the further promotion of the Christian religion:

SIERRA LEONE, April 20, 1811.

To the Saints and Faithful Brethren in Christ; grace be unto you and peace from God our Father and the Lord Jesus Christ.

We desire to humble ourselves with that thankful acknowledgment to the Father and Fountain of all our mercies, for the liberty and freedom we enjoy. And our prayer to God is, that our Brethren, who live in distant lands, and are held in bondage, and groan under the galling chain of Slavery, that they may be

[30] *The Cuffe Manuscripts.* Dated June 12, 1812.

..iberated and enjoy the liberty that God has granted unto all his faithful Saints. Dearly beloved Brethren in the Lord, may the power and peace of God rule in all your hearts, for we feel, from an awful experience, the distresses that many of our African Brethren groan under; therefore we feel our minds engaged to desire all the Saints and Professors in Christ, to diligently consider our cause, and to put cause to the Christian Query: whether it is agreeable to the testimony of Jesus Christ, for one Professor to make merchandise of another? We are desirous, that this may be made manifest to all Professors of all Christian denominations, who have not abolished the holding of slaves.

We salute thee, Beloved Brethren, in the Lord, with sincere desire that the works of Regeneration may be more and more experienced. It would be a consolation to us, to hear from the Saints, in distant lands, and we could receive all who are disposed to come unto us with open arms.

Our dearly beloved African Brethren, we also salute you in the love of God, to be obedient unto your masters, with your prayers lifted to God, whom we would recommend you to confide in, who is just as able in these days, to deliver out of the Egyptian bondage: finally brethern, may the power and peace of God rule in all your hearts.

Grace be unto you, and peace from God our Father, and the Lord Jesus Christ, Amen.

JOHN × GORDEN, preacher	GEO. × CLARK
WARWICK × FRANCIS	PETER FRANCIS
JAMES REED	GEORGE CARREL
JOSEPH BROWN	EDWIN × WILLOUGHBY
MOSES × WILKINSON	THOS. × RICHARDS, SEN.
S. JONES	ELI AIKEN
JOHN × ELLIS	JNO. × STEVENSON
ADAM × JONES	JAS. WISE

Two days after he had sent this epistle to his friends in America he wrote a personal note to William Allen in London. He acknowledged the receipt of the license to bring goods to England, called attention to a petition which the inhabitants had presented to Governor Columbine with a request that he lay it before Parliament, and set forth many facts concerning the land and its people. He also announced his intention to keep open a commercial intercourse between America and Sierra Leone in the hope that through such a channel some families might find their way to Africa.[31]

The outline of the petition referred to in his letter to William Allen is inserted as follows:

1st. That encouragement may be given to all our brethern, who may come from the British Colonies or from America, in order to become farmers, or to assist us in the cultivation of our land.

2nd. That encouragement may be given to our foreign brethern who have vessels for the purpose, to establish commerce in Sierra Leone.

3d. That those who may undertake to establish the whale fishery in the colony may be encouraged to persevere in that useful and laudable enterprise.

Cuffe states that several of the most respectable inhabitants signed this petition. From its contents and its date one would conclude that its origin can safely be traced to Cuffe himself. Attention is called to a school for adults and the other schools which accommodate about two hundred and thirty children. In his letter to Allen he gives the names of seven teachers. Mention is made of a Society of Sierra Leone and of the places for public worship. Four meetings are held on Sunday and two on other days. In his letter to Allen the churches are enumerated as follows: two Methodists, one Baptist, and one without denominational designation but in charge of "an old woman, Mila Baxton who keeps at her dwelling house."

A brief paragraph describes poor relief: "An institution," said he, "was formed on the first of the twelfth month last for the relief of the poor and disabled. It is now regularly held on the first second day in every month, at which time proper persons are appointed to take charge of those under the care of the institution. A general meet-

[31] In *Cuffe Manuscripts*. Paul Cuffe to William Allen, April 4, 1811.
A summary of his observations came out in print in 1812. It was called "A Brief Account of the Settlement and Present Situation of the Colony of Sierra Leone in Africa,"[32] and was dedicated to "his friend in New York." It contains an account of the topography of the country and states that the population was 2,518.

[32] Published in New York, 1812.

ing is held once every six months. Everyone can judge of the happy effect of such institutions as these in improving the dispositions and softening the manners of our native brethren."

Five courts are described and attention is called to the supremacy of British law. A short discussion of the native Africans appears, and the letter includes in the "Brief Account" an address "to my scattered brethren and fellow countrymen at Sierra Leone." It closes with these words:

Grace be unto you and peace be multiplied from God the Father, and from the Lord Jesus Christ, who hath begotten a lively hope in remembrance of you; and for which I desire ever to be humbled, world without end, amen.

Dearly beloved friends and fellowcountrymen,

I earnestly recommend to you the propriety of assembling yourselves together for the purpose of worshipping the Lord your God. God is a spirit and they who worship him acceptably must worship him in spirit and in truth; in so doing you will find a living hope which will be as an anchor to the soul and a support under afflictions. In this hope may Ethiopia stretch out her hand unto God. Come my African brethren and fellowcountrymen, let us walk together in the light of the Lord. That pure light which bringeth salvation into the world, hath appeared unto all men to profit withall. I would recommend unto all the saints, and elders and sober people of the colony, that you adopt the mode of meeting together once every month in order to consult with each other for your mutual good. But above all things let your meetings be owed of the Lord, for he hath told us that "Where two or three are gathered together in his name, there will he be in the midst of them." And I recommend that you keep a record of your proceedings at those meetings in order that they be left for the benefit of the young and rising generation. In these meetings let it be your care to promote all good and laudable institutions, and by so doing you will increase both your temporal and spiritual welfare. That the Prince of Peace may be your preserver, is the sincere desire of one who wishes well to all mankind.

The following advice, though detached from the foregoing address, appears to be intended to accompany it:

First. That sobriety and steadfastness, with all faithfulness, be recommended, that so professors may be good examples in all things; doing justly, loving mercy, and walking humbly.

Secondly. That early care be extended towards the youth whilst their minds are young and tender, that so they may be redeemed from the corruptions of the world—such as nature is prone to—not swearing, following bad company and drinking of spiritous liquors. That they may be kept out of idleness, and encouraged to be industrious, for this is good to cultivate the mind, and may you be good examples therein yourselves.

Thirdly. May servants be encouraged to discharge their duties with faithfulness; may they be brought up to industry; may their minds be cultivated for the reception of the good seed, which is promised to all that will seek after it. I want that we should be faithful in all things, that so we may become a people, giving satisfaction to those, who have borne the heat and burden of the day, in liberating us from a state of slavery. I must leave you in the hands of Him who is able to preserve you through all time, and to crown you with that blessing that is prepared for all those who are faithful unto death.

In closing he cites, with approbation, the advice contained in an address to free people of color given in 1796 at Philadelphia before the general convention of abolition societies. They are advised to attend to religion, to get an elementary education, teach their children useful trades, use no spiritous liquors, avoid frolicking and idleness, have marriage legally performed, lay up their earnings, and to be honest and to behave themselves.

An object always dear to Cuffe was the abolition of the slave trade. He thought a commercial intercourse would be conducive to its suppression. For trade in human beings he would offer trade in the legitimate articles of commerce. If such an intercourse could be kept open with cargoes coming and going between Sierra Leone and England and Sierra Leone and America, then "some good sober steady characters may find their way to that country." This would be a laudable method for civilizing Africa, he thought, because the establishment of colonists who would engage in productive enterprises would soon leaven the lump of African idleness and ignorance, and Christians engaged in legitimate business pursuits would inoculate a large area of the African continent.

In order to foster this plan, Cuffe formed while in Sierra Leone in 1812, "The Friendly Society." John Kizell was elected president and monthly meetings were held. It began a business correspondence with the African Institution in London. William Allen ever responsive to Cuffe's "earnest breathings" sent a consignment of goods worth 70 pounds with permission to return the amount in rice, Indian corn, etc. He offered to be their agent in London, and he engaged the services of W. and R. Rathbone of Liverpool in their behalf.

Since the African Institution was not to "engage in commercial speculation" some measure had further to be devised in England to help the Friendly Society dispose of its produce advantageously and promote industry among its members. Therefore, "A Society for the Purpose of Encouraging the Black Settlers at Sierra Leone, and the Natives of Africa generally, in the cultivation of their Soil, by the sale of their Produce" was formed. Some progress was noted for, after four years Cuffe wrote that the Friendly Society was worth 1200 pounds.[33]

Similar movements were going on in America. William Roth of New Bedford on October 10, 1812, wrote William Allen: "Paul Cuffe still continues his concern for his African plan, and has recently petitioned Congress for liberty to send his vessel to Sierra Leone, provided liberty can be obtained from your side. His character stands conspicuously approved as far as it is known, his kind concern for the civilization of Africa, and his devotion of time and money to that object, have greatly strengthened the impression of his real worth and merit; and from some intentions from the President I am led to believe his application will succeed."[34]

[33] On the Friendly Society see *Life of William Allen*, I, 105–116; 139, 140. *History of Prince Le Boo* (Dublin, 1822), 162, 163; *Cuffe Manuscripts*. Paul Cuffe to Samuel J. Mills, August 6, 1816.

[34] *Life of William Allen*, I, 133.

CHAPTER VII

PATHFINDER IN NEGRO COLONIZATION

It was Cuffe's plan to make a trip to Sierra Leone once every year. This would enable him to keep in touch with the colony. He would carry over whatever goods were needed, buy and market the African produce, take desirable emigrants over; withall, he would be a benevolent father to Africa. The Captain himself said, as recorded in *Minutes of Paul Cuffe's Opinions*, 1814: "The most advantageous means of encouragement to be rendered towards civilization of Africa is that the popularity of the colony of Sierra Leone be encouraged; and in order to render them aid and assistance my mind is that some families of good character should be encouraged to remove from America and settle at Sierra Leone in order to become farmers; and to lend them aid in such useful utilities as they are capable of; and in order for this accomodation it appears to me there should be an intercourse kept open between America and Sierra Leone, that, through that channel some people might find their way to Africa; and for their accomodation and reception when arrived I think proper that a house be built that they have some place of refuge or shelter." He thought one thousand pounds might be needed for the beginning of this benevolent purpose.

But there were obstacles in the way. The voyage of the *Traveller* in 1812 was financially unprofitable. The *Alpha* had just returned with a $3000 deficit. A bark that had gone around Cape Horn on a whaling voyage had not returned. It was without insurance and subject to capture by British cruisers. Moreover, the War of 1812 had begun and this seemed an insuperable obstacle.

Already Cuffe had informed William Allen as to his troubles. He had also told him what things urged him to overcome the difficulties in his way. Did not Sierra Leone need a sawmill, a millwright, and a plow? And instead of carrying loads on their heads, how much better would it be if the colonists had a wagon on which to haul the loads. The native Africans, moreover, had been schooled in America and were ready to return. In addition, free blacks in the United States had made application for passage to Sierra Leone. And could not mercantile relations be established between Africa and America in such a way as to supplant the slave trade? There was a possibility, too, of starting the whale fishery on the western coast of Africa.

To achieve these ends was worth a hard struggle. He had overcome difficulties all his life. Surely he could do it again. He would petition Congress for permission to make the voyage and ask William Allen to seek a similar concession from Great Britain. Accordingly a memorial, dated "Westport, 6th month, 1813" was presented to Congress.[35] In it Cuffe asserts that he "could but view the practice of his brethren of the African race in selling their fellow creatures into a state of slavery for life as very inconsistent" with divine principle of equity and justice and that he "conceived it a duty incumbent upon him, as a faithful steward of the mercies he had received, to give a portion of his time and his property in visiting that country, and affording such means as might be in his power to promote the improvement and civilization of the Africans."

He further recites in this memorial that he had visited Sierra Leone to learn about the country and its inhabitants, and that when he was in London, he had the satisfaction to find his recommendations approved by the celebrated philanthropists, the Duke of Gloucester, William Wilberforce, Thomas Clarkson, William Allen, and others. Special provision, moreover, had already been made by

[35] *Annals of Congress*, 13th Congress, 2nd session, I, 861–1863; *National Intelligencer* for January 11, 1814, printed the memorial at the request of its subscribers.

them to carry his plans into effect. One plan was to keep up an "intercourse with the free people of color in the United States in the expectation that persons of reputation would feel sufficiently interested to visit Africa, and endeavor to promote habits of industry, sobriety, and frugality, among the natives of that country." His plans, he continued, had been placed before free blacks in Baltimore and Philadelphia, New York, and Boston. As a result "several families, whose characters promise usefulness, have come to a conclusion, if proper ways could be opened, to go to Africa, in order to give their aid in promoting the objects already adverted to."

In view of these facts, provided Great Britain was willing, Cuffe asked permission to take a ship to Sierra Leone to "transport such persons and families . . . also some articles of provision, together with implements of husbandry, and machinery for some mechanic arts, and to bring back such of the native productions of that country as may be wanted." The trifling commerce, he hoped, would lighten the expense of the voyage.

Congressman Laban Wheaton of Massachusetts presented this memorial to the House of Representatives on January 7, 1814. Four days later the *National Intelligencer* at the request of subscribers published it. The memorial was referred to the Committee on Commerce and Manufacturing by the Speaker of the House.

Interest in Cuffe's request now shifts to the Senate where a measure was passed authorizing the President of the United States to permit Paul Cuffe to depart from the United States with a vessel and cargo for Africa and similarly to return. The House was informed of this action on the twenty-seventh of January and four days later read the Senate bill twice and referred it to the Committee on Commerce and Manufacturing. This committee reported that since the government had been compelled to prohibit the coasting trade, it would be impolitic to relax the provisions on the "application of an individual, for a purpose, which, how benevolently soever conceived, cannot be considered in any other light than as speculative—the efforts heretofore made and directed by the zeal and intelligence of the Sierra Leone Company having failed to accomplish the object designed by its institution."[36]

This report was referred to the Committee of the Whole House and debated on the nineteenth of March. The representatives who wished to grant Cuffe's request agreed that the Senate bill would be an invitation to free blacks to emigrate to Africa. This part of the population they said could well be spared. The opponents of Cuffe's request doubted the expediency of permitting to go out a cargo which must necessarily sail under British license. Such a license would be granted, they argued, only if advantageous to the enemy. The House by a vote of 72 to 65 rejected the Senate measure and Cuffe's request was denied.

He fared little better at the hands of the British Government. Allen carried the request to the ministers and told them that it was the opinion of many that the one thing most needed to help Sierra Leone was to enlist the services of Paul Cuffe. If the Government granted the license, it was hoped that a vessel could be purchased, that Cuffe be made its proprietor, and that it be used to carry African produce to Britain. The ministers, from the Chancellor of the Exchequer on down, were exceedingly kind and were willing to grant the license but could not, owing to the navigation laws, insure the vessel against a seizing officer. Such an officer might consider the boat more valuable than his office. Allen thought such a risk too great either for Cuffe or the African Institution and the request for a license was withdrawn.

Cuffe's spirit would not down. Let Congress turn him down and the British ministers deny his request. There was still one group willing to help him along. This group was the Society of Friends at Westport. Here was fuel

[36] *Annals of Congress*, 13th Congress, 2nd session, I, 1195, 1265.

for the fire of Cuffe's zeal. Ebenezer Baker, clerk of the monthly meeting, on the "16th of the 11th month 1815" records:

> Our friend Paul Cuffe (who is a member of our religious society) informed this meeting that he has a prospect of making a voyage to Africa on business, and in a particular manner, with the laudable view of endeavoring to promote the temporal and civil improvement and comfort of the inhabitants of some parts of that country; which having had our solid deliberation, we feel desirous that he may be enabled to accomplish this object, to the peace of his own mind; and leave him at liberty to pursue his prospect, recommending him to the friendly notice and regard of those amongst whom his lot may be cast.[37]

Just as soon as the war was over Cuffe set sail for Africa. The papers evidently were well supplied with his plans, for a Louisville paper, *The Western Courier*, related that "Capt. Paul Cuffe, a man of color is about to proceed to Africa, with several families to form a settlement there. He will sail in the brig *Traveller*, now at Philadelphia, receiving two families there, afterwards touch at New Bedford and receive the remainder of her company, and then proceed the latter part of October on her voyage."

The *Traveller* cleared from the custom house on the second of December. Two days later Cuffe wrote Allen, "I shall sail through God's permission the first wind after tomorrow." The first wind came the tenth of December. When the *Traveller* finally sailed she carried a cargo of tobacco and soap, candles, naval stores and flour. She had also iron with which to build a sawmill, a wagon, grindstones, nails and glass, and a plow. There were thirty-eight passengers, eighteen heads of families and twenty children.

The Captain himself reported the voyage to the American Colonization Society in this laconic letter:

> Thirty-eight in number went out with me, their expenses were estimated at one hundred dollars per head, but were there a large number they could be carried out for sixty dollars. The expense

[37] *Cuffe Manuscripts.*

of thirty of the above number was born by Paul Cuffe. The others paid for their own passages. In addition to the above expense, I furnished them provisions to the amount of 150 pounds 8s 3d sterling; all this was done without fee or reward—my hope is in a coming day.[38]

The passengers were all common laborers and they wished to cultivate the land. Perry Locke, a Methodist, was licensed to preach. He is an honest man, wrote Cuffe, but "has rather a hard voice for a preacher." Another passenger was Antony Survance, a native of Senegal, who had been sold to the French in St. Domingo. During the revolution he came to Philadelphia. He had learned to read and write and had studied navigation, but Cuffe thought he would never make a mariner on account of seasickness. He paid his passage to Africa and hoped by and by to return to Senegal. He said the black man had two eyes and two ears, the white man has no more. Could he not hear with his ears and see with his eyes. All the passengers were provided with certificates of good character.[39]

The fares paid by the passengers and a contribution from William Rotch of New Bedford amounted to over $1000. Cuffe's expenses consisted of $480 for insurance, $1000 for portage, $703.96 for supplies, and $3000 for passages. His expenses, therefore, exceeded the sources of income by something over $4000.

It was a rough passage and the Captain was troubled with a sick crew. When he reached Sierra Leone on the third of February, the crew was well "for which as well as all other preservations," he wrote, "I desire ever to be truly humbled before the father and fountain of all our mercies." On its arrival at port, the *Traveller* was hailed from a canoe, "What brig is this? where from? what

[38] *Second Annual Report of the American Colonization Society*, 122. *The Western Courier* (Louisville, Kentucky) for October 26, 1815, reported Captain Cuffe's trip.

[39] A memorandum in Cuffe's handwriting and containing the details concerning each passenger is in the *Cuffe Manuscripts*.

cargo?" Cuffe asked to anchor the *Traveller*. But word came from the custom house boat "No Americans permitted to anchor in these waters." It was then near sunset and permission was given to anchor until nine o'clock the following morning. The Governor on the next day allowed Cuffe to anchor in the harbor but could not secure him against seizure by a man-of-war. The *Traveller* remained in the harbor a month and a day enjoying every indulgence and encountering no warship.

The passengers were well received by the Governor and the Friendly Society. They were given a town lot and fifty acres of land. A year's rations for seven families was provided at a cost of 411 pounds 14s 5d. This expense, it seems, was met by the London African Institution. Cuffe thanked his friend William Allen for the "Ardent exercises thee must have had in order to forward the plan." [40]

Cuffe did not succeed so well in the disposition of his cargo. No instructions awaited him from the London African Institution and no arrangements had been made with the British Government. He had, therefore, to pay import duty on the articles he sold; tobacco, soap, candles and naval stores which at first he could not even land. Later, evidently the tobacco at least was landed, because to William Allen was referred a matter in connection with the price of it on which Cuffe and the Friendly Society could not agree. He sold flour at $12 per barrel and purchased camwood at $100 per ton.

As to Cuffe himself, he was well received. He dined with Governor McCarthy and the Chief Justice. William Allen offered him his African quarters during his stay but the Captain declined, for, said he, "I feel myself unworthy to become one of thy family." [41] He went with Governor McCarthy to inspect the schools; he was particularly pleased with the boys' school taught by Thomas

[40] *Cuffe Manuscripts*, Paul Cuffe to William Allen, April 1, 1816.
[41] *Ibid.*

Hurt, a schoolmaster Cuffe himself had brought from England.

He discussed the question of keeping a line of communication open between England and Sierra Leone, advised that an additional place for colonizing be selected, and took an active part in suppressing the slave trade. While he was in Sierra Leone three brigs and four schooners, active in this traffic, were captured. Later he sought to secure from Governor McCarthy the names of the vessels and commanders so that the African Institution or the Abolition Society in Philadelphia could initiate legal proceedings against them.

Every encouragement was given to the Friendly Society. He pointed out to William Allen its prosperity and cautioned him not to make too great advances to it. He was greatly pleased to find it establishing factories at places within the interior. At these points the tribes could secure their own produce. When engaged in enriching the produce of their own country, Cuffe thought that they would be drawn away from the slave trade. Above all things, he pointed out the abuse of the twenty-two license houses which did business with the slave traders. By establishing factories and opening roads from one tribe to another he believed he could render the native chiefs friendly to civilization.

Cuffe kept in touch with everything and everybody. He noted sickness and death; he chronicled the accession of thirteen new colonists to the Baptist church. He also heard complaints. Perry Locke, the licensed Methodist minister, disliked to do jury duty. On receiving the following summons he at once carried it to the Captain:

Mr. Perry Locke. You are hereby summoned and required to appear at the ensuing general session of the peace, which will be held at the court hall in Freetown, on Wednesday, the 10th day of April, at the hour of ten in the afternoon, there to serve as a grand juror; herein fail not, at your peril. W. D. Grant, Sheriff.[42]

[42] *Second Annual Report of the American Colonization Society*, 121, 122.

Cuffe told him that "he complained in America because he was deprived of these privileges; and then he murmured because he was called upon: Go and fill thy seat, do as well as thou canst."[43]

The citizens wished him to begin a settlement at Sherbro, and the African Institution again took occasion to profit by the experience of their "dark colored but civilized ally" who suggested that a house be built on the farm of each settler brought over.

When Cuffe began preparations for the return voyage "it was like a father taking leave of his children." He sailed on April 4th, and after a voyage of fifty-four days reached the United States again. After juggling in his mind the various proposals for ameliorating the condition of "that part of the great family of Africa" in America he concluded: "Nothing: Nothing of much amount can be affected by an individual or private bodies until the government removes the obstruction in the way."[44]

[43] *Second Annual Report of the American Colonization Society*, 121.
[44] *Cuffe Manuscripts*, Paul Cuffe to T. Brine, January 16, 1817.

CHAPTER VIII

AFRO-AMERICAN INTERESTS

Neither voyage to Africa was financially profitable. Cuffe did not make either visit with that end in view. But he was careful to make use of every opportunity to reduce the expense of the trip. An undated item in his letters says property to the value of $1337.15 was landed from the *Traveller* and placed in charge of Thomas Wainer. Blue cloth, cassimere and flannels bought through William and Richard Rathbone of Liverpool were imported when Cuffe made his first voyage to Sierra Leone. Peter and Alexander Howard of New Bedford shared equally with Cuffe in this transaction. The estimated value of the goods was $2300; the profit to each party was $439.93.[45]

Cuffe imported camwood and squills when he returned in 1816, but neither sold well. Abner Gifford made a small sale of camwood in Albany but the bulk of it was sold by Hicks Jenkins and Company of New York. Peleg Howland and Sons and Swift and Barnes, both of Poughkeepsie, purchased some of the camwood.

The *Traveller*, however, was kept busy. In 1816 and 1817 she carried freight along the Atlantic coast and made several voyages to the West Indies. Tuite and Amie, a firm in Port au Prince, was a correspondent of Cuffe. Tuite at one time seems to have lived at Bridgeport and to have established a line of Quaker connections. While Cuffe had business dealings with a number of houses the ones most frequently referred to are Josiah Crodler and Company of Boston, Hicks Jenkins and Company of New York and William Roth, Jr., and Company of New Bedford. At the time of his death Cuffe was constructing salt works at Westport.

Cuffe never allowed his own private business affairs to

[45] Memorandum made by Cuffe in *Cuffe Manuscripts*.

engulf his interests in Sierra Leone. He wrote frequently to the colonists that he took over and he kept in close touch with the Friendly Society. He gave them financial advice, quoted prices, and promised another visit when satisfactory arrangement could be made with either the London African Institution or the British Government. He expressed the wish that an additional port might be selected for a settlement because, from the rumors of insurrection in the South, "many will be glad to find some place where they could send them." [46]

He exhorted the Friendly Society as a whole to "stand fast, grow strong, be respectable, and be active to suppress the slave trade." To its secretary, James Wise, he gave this special message:

"As thou art one of the main spokes in the great wheel in which the Friendly Society are upheld I earnestly instruct thee to stand firm for her support for if she falls and comes to naught, it will be a deadly blow to Africa. I am a well wisher to her prosperity and could I be the means of her firm establishment I think I should consent to be made use of in any way which might be for her advancement. I instruct thee to endeavor that she, the Friendly Society, may not give up her commercial pursuits, for that is the greatest outlet to her national advancement.—I forsee this to be the means of improving both your country and nation." [47]

The African Institutions at Philadelphia and New York were as dear to his heart as the Friendly Society. He kept in close touch with both of them. "I wish these institutions," he said, "to be brought as much under action as possible; by these means the colored people of these large cities would be more awakened than from an individual, and a stranger, and thereby prevailed upon for their own good." [48]

The secretary of the New York African Institution was Peter Williams, Jr., a rector of the St. Phillip's Episcopal Church. Cuffe constantly spurred him on to greater ac-

[46] *Cuffe Manuscripts*, Paul Cuffe to John Kizell, August 14, 1816.
[47] *Ibid.*, Paul Cuffe to James Wise, September 15, 1816.
[48] Quoted in Williams, *Discourse on the Death of Paul Cuffe*.

tivity in the organization. He should write Governor McCarthy of Sierra Leone expressing interest in Cuffe's mission; he should cooperate with the Abolition Society in New York in its efforts to secure information leading to the capture of slave traders; he should open up a correspondence with the Friendly Society.

Cuffe counted on the help of the Institution to break up the slave trade. He expressed to Samuel C. Aikin, of Andover, the view that general manumission could never occur until this trade was really stopped. He reported that in 1815 two hundred sail cleared from Savannah for this traffic. Six vessels had been brought in by the forces in Sierra Leone. If the road could be kept open between Africa and America, it would help the authorities in Sierra Leone. "I believe," he continued, "if there could be mercantile correspondence opened between the African race in America and Africa it would have good tendency to keep open this communication and acquaint them with each other. It would employ their children; and if religious characters wished to visit that country they would obtain a passage." [49] William Allen had asked him again to come to England to help keep communication open between London and Sierra Leone. In harmony with the invitation Rathbone Hodgson Company of Liverpool wrote, "It will give us much pleasure to learn that you are embarking for England."

James Forten seems to have been the leading spirit in the African Institution at Philadelphia. It was no less eager than the sister one in New York to diffuse knowledge about Africa, to help civilize its inhabitants, and to help substitute a beneficial commerce for the slave trade. The Institution had among the members an African Prince, a grandson of King Lurker, who reigned about fifty leagues south of Sierra Leone. He was about eight years old and had been secured by the local Abolition Society in order to educate him. James Forten hoped that his re-

[49] *Cuffe Manuscripts*, Paul Cuffe to Samuel C. Aiken, August 7, 1816.

turn to Africa would serve to open up a correspondence between King Lurker and the Friendly Society which would be very advantageous to the Sierra Leone colony. Forten reported the Institution greatly concerned over the will of Samuel Gist because there was no asylum for the blacks whom he desired to free and whom he finally colonized in Brown County, Ohio.

Neither organization, however, was lively enough to please Cuffe. He feared that their inactivity might cause the mission in Africa to fail. Rather than see the seed planted in Africa perish, he wrote William Allen that he would bestow some further labor; he would come to England if necessary and be used there.

Cuffe had another important purpose in connection with colonization. From the time that he built a schoolhouse at Westport to his death he was interested in the cause of education both in Africa and in America. He said: "I am one of those who rejoice to see good institutions established for the instruction and reformation of our fellow creatures. . . . I approve of the plan for educating young men of color. I think such characters would be useful in Africa." Teachers were sought out for schools in Sierra Leone and passage for them on the *Traveller* was always ready. He contributed to teachers' salaries and was interested in putting children in private boarding schools. Prospect for establishing a school for blacks in Charleston, South Carolina, was laid before Cuffe by Samuel R. Fisher of Philadelphia. The information was a solicitation for advice and financial help.

Naturally, as soon as he returned from Sierra Leone, his correspondence increased. He received many inquiries about that country and to all he gave kind and considerate reply. Dr. Jedekiah Morse of Boston wants to know what offices are held by men of color. There are sheriffs, constables, clerks of court, and jurors; and there is a colored printer. But "Africa calls for men of character to fill stations in the Legislature."

"What does it cost to go to Africa?" asked Thomas Fay, of Providence. "Does there exist any arrangement under the auspices of the African Institution for the payment of passage for those unable to meet this expense?" And the answer comes that it costs about one hundred dollars per person and that there is no arrangement at present with the African Institution. But if you go you must set your face against the slave trade; prepare as do the Irish who come to America.

Peter Williams, Jr., of New York, upon being reminded that there is no time to lose if a mercantile line of business is established between Africa and the United States, makes this inquiry, "Any news from England on colonization? A carpenter here ready to settle in Sierra Leone if his passage paid."

Cuffe wants to know whether James Forten, of Philadelphia, could tell him the cost of a rice mill? Could he refer him to a man who would manage a sawmill; to another who was a good watch repairer? "What are the African news?" asks James Forten. "And can you give me information about Cuffe Johnson who claims he sailed with you twelve years ago and was marked with a mold on his left breast?" Thomas Ash, merchant and employer of Forten, inquires if ebony wood may be obtained on the Gaboon River and reports his intention to make an expedition there.

John James wants Cuffe to visit Philadelphia and clear up unfavorable reports about the Sierra Leone Mission. Several wish to emigrate and they must be saved for Africa. And Cuffe sends to Peter Williams, Jr., of New York for the minutes of Perry Locke and a communication from Governor McCarthy so that he may have documentary evidence to submit to his colored brethren at Philadelphia. "I think it is time," says Cuffe to Forten, "some steps were taken to prevent insurrection."[50]

From Wilmington, Delaware, William Gibbons sends the respect and friendship of his wife and family and asks

[50] *Cuffe Manuscripts*, Paul Cuffe to James Forten, August 14, 1816.

how many Negroes are in Sierra Leone? How far has the colony civilized the natives? What about the moral, religious, civil and political situation?

The colonists who were taken out in 1815 wrote many letters to Cuffe and to their "Dear Friends and Brethren" in America. Friend Gwinn had lost a leg; Samuel Hews and Mrs. Thomas Jarvis were dead. Would Cuffe bring two Bibles when he came over again? Would the American Government purchase a small tract in Sherbro? It is a splendid site for a colony and camwood, palm oil and a little ivory are available there.

And Cuffe writes back: "The camwood is stored in New York, six families in Boston and a considerable number in New York want to go over. They must wait and see how things turn out. There will be no voyage really soon for there is no arrangement made with the London African Institution or the British Government. May Perry Locke get on with his friends in religion. Let George Davis and others meet their financial obligations promptly."

An incident which created no little concern among Cuffe's friends in New Bedford, Philadelphia and New York was the appearance of a colored man who claimed to be a relative of the Captain. He made his appearance in New Bedford late in 1816, where he claimed to be a minister, and the son of Richard Allen. He sat in the pulpit with the local minister and had sittings with the Negroes. Soon he left for Boston with false letters from William Rotch setting forth that he was a brother-in-law of Paul Cuffe and that his home was in New York. He was now using the name Samuel Bailey. He bought nine hundred dollars worth of goods on his credentials and came very near making away with the purchase.

The imposter next appeared in New Bedford, where, on the initiative of William Rotch, he was arrested. Unfortunately, however, he escaped from prison. From New Bedford he made his way to New York where he presented false letters of credit to the extent of $10,000. Here he was brought before the authorities and was requested to leave the State. He went to Albany and was employed by Ira Porter for one month. To disguise himself better he had made a plain suit, Quaker style, and then absconded on one of Porter's fine black horses, worth $200. He rode him to York, introduced himself as Paul Cuffe and found hospitality at the home of Joseph Jessop. Although he attended meeting on the first day, nevertheless suspicions were aroused as to his real self. His conduct and pretentions while at York are further set forth by a contemporary in the following language:

"An African pretending to be the son of the *Celebrated* Paul Cuffe, came here about eight or ten days ago. He was received as Paul Cuffe, in this place, and entertained by members of the Society of Friends. He said he was on his way to Congress, for the purpose of soliciting aid in a project he had on foot, to colonize Sierra Leone, or the *Leone Country,* on the west coast of Africa. He said he had been the first man that put a yoke on a pair of oxen in Sierra Leone.

"He tarried in this place several days, and though he is an artful fellow, he told in the course of his conversation upon the Sierra Leone project some inconsistent stories. He said, for instance, that he would lay a memorial before Congress embracing a view of his Sierra Leone business. One of the Friends advised him to have a sufficient number of copies printed to supply all the members. This, he said, was already done and he had them along with him. On his being pressed to show one of them he could not make it appear that he told a straight story. This gave rise to a suspicion that he was not a *Real* Cuffe, of the Cape Cod breed. He proceeded from this place to Baltimore. Letters were sent from here giving intelligence of the suspiciousness of his character.

"The letters were read to him at Baltimore, upon which he came back to this place to clear up his character. He appears not to have done it to the satisfaction of his friends here, as they took him before a magistrate and had him committed to the care of Robert Wilson. On his examination it appeared that he could neither read nor write, but at the same time exhibited proof of a keeness of intellect seldom met with in persons of his color. The real celebrated Paul Cuffe resides in the State of Massachusetts in the vicinity of Cape Cod at the entrance to Boston Bay."[51]

What was the upshot of the matter is not known but the significance of the affair is well pointed out by the Real Cuffe in a letter to the impostor:

"I think it looks as though thou art arrested from thy labors, and thy words do follow thee. How canst thou, a sinful impostor, call me thy father when I never saw thee to my knowledge. It appears that thou art a scribe, but hath missput the name that thee presumed to assume. It is a great pity that thou who hath been so well treated should make such ill use of it. This I speak to thy shame. The great evil that thou hast embarked upon is not only against me as an individual. It is a national concern. It is a stain to the whole community of the African race. Wilt thou consider, thou imposter, the great number thou hast lifted thy head against, would not it have been good that thou had never been born. Let me tell thee that the manumission of 1,500,000 slaves depends on the faithfulness of the few who have obtained their freedom, yea, it is not only those who are in bondage, but the whole community of the African race, which are according to best accounts 30,000,000. If nothing better can be obtained from thee than the fruit that thou produced, let me intreat thee to petition for a prison for life; Awake thou imposter unto righteousness and pray God to forgive thee, if happily thou may find firgiveness before the door of mercy is closed against thee. Thus thou hast the advise of one who wishes well to all mankind.

PAUL CUFFE.[52]

[51] *Cuffe Manuscripts*, James Forten to Paul Cuffe, January 16, 1817.
[52] *Ibid.*, Paul Cuffe to the Imposter, January 13, 1817.

CHAPTER IX

A Friend in Need

There is no evidence in the Cuffe papers that he was acquainted with the history of the Negro deportation projects in America. It is altogether likely that the one hundred years of individual propaganda, religious and humanitarian exertions, were unknown to him. Means for the dissemination of knowledge were not so well perfected in his day as in ours; the plans for deportation were isolated; not until 1816 did private movements unite with governmental organizations,—facts which further explain why Cuffe knew nothing about the history of the movements to colonize the Negro.

Many of his friends and many persons whose lives were dedicated to Negro emancipation were connected with his plans. But whatever he did appears to have been done wholly on his own initiative. It is the first time, apparently, in the history of colonization that a Negro becomes prominent in the movement. He leads the way in an effort not only to bless the free Negroes, but also to liberate the slaves. It is a constructive effort on the part of the Negro race.

When Cuffe returned from Africa in the early summer of 1816 the cause for which he had given so much time and made so many sacrifices was more prominent than it had ever been in its history. The Union Humane Society, founded in Ohio in 1815 by Benjamin Lundy as an anti-slavery organization, had declared for the removal of the Negro beyond the white man's pale. The Kentucky Colonization Society had petitioned Congress to settle, at public expense, on some unappropriated tract of public land, the Negroes already free and those who might subsequently obtain their freedom. The Virginia Assembly, also, had presented a memorial to Congress praying that the National Government find a place on the North Pacific or African coast for colonizing the free blacks of the State. Finally, the inhabitants of New Jersey petitioned their Legislature to instruct their representatives in Congress to lay before that body at its next meeting as a subject for discussion "the expediency of forming a colony on the coast of Africa, or elsewhere, where such of the people of color as are now free, or may hereafter be set free, may, with their own consent, be removed."[53]

Cuffe returned from Africa about June 1, 1816. The New Jersey meeting was on the sixth of the following November. Final action by the Virginia Assembly was taken on the twenty-first of December of that year. A graduate of Princeton, Robert Finley, then engaged in the Presbyterian ministry and later president of the University of Georgia, participated in the New Jersey meeting. He now took a leading part in the deliberation of a body of men in Washington, D.C., where a national organization was launched for the purpose of deporting to Africa or elsewhere the free blacks of the United States. A preliminary meeting was held on December 21, 1816; the constitution was adopted on December 28, 1816, and on New Year's Day 1817, the officers were elected. This was the beginning of the American Colonization Society.

At this meeting the enthusiasm of Reverend Mr. Finley was boundless. He offered five hundred dollars from his savings to insure the success of the movement, and when some, thinking the plan foolhardy, laughed, he declared, "I know the scheme is from God." The one practical colonizationist, at this time, was Paul Cuffe, and to him Rev. Mr. Finley went for advice and help.

Using for letter paper the blank space of the printed New Jersey petition, Finley wrote Cuffe on December 5 from Washington City. Cuffe was in this way put in touch with Finley's past activities and with his present

[53] For an extended account of the activities mentioned in this paragraph see N. H. Sherwood, *The Formation of the American Colonization Society*, in THE JOURNAL OF NEGRO HISTORY, July, 1917.

exertions. "Many indulge," he wrote, "a hope that could the more virtuous of our own free people of color be removed to the coast of Africa, with their own consent, to carry with them their arts, their industry, and above all, their knowledge of Christianity and the fear of God, great and lasting benefits would arise to the people of *Africa itself*. Knowing that you have been to *Sierra Leone* and must be well acquainted with the state and prospects of the colony, we beg of you such information as you may be able to give on the following heads:

"1. What is the present population of the settlements of Sierra Leone, and what its prospects of happiness and growth?

"2. What is the nature of the soil and what the advantage for settlement on the coast of Africa from Sierra Leone to the equator?

"3. Are there any navigable rivers in the country called Guinea, or any positions where a good harbor might be formed along the coast?

"4. In the region above alluded to, are there any European regular settlements, or does it contain any slave factories?

"5. Whether in your opinion is there any other situation in Africa where the contemplated settlement or settlements could be formed with greater advantage than in the district mentioned above?

"The great desire of those whose minds are impressed with this subject," says Finley, "is to give an opportunity to the free people of color to rise to their proper level and at the same time to provide a powerful means of putting an end to the slave trade, and sending civilization and Christianity to Africa."[54]

Another active member of the group at Washington was Samuel J. Mills, whose devotion to missionary activity is almost unequaled in history. The origin of the American Bible Society, the United Foreign Missionary Society, and the American Board of Commissioners for

[54] *Cuffe Manuscripts*, Robert Finley to Paul Cuffe, December 5, 1816.

Foreign Missions, is attributed to him. Writing to Cuffe, March 17, 1817, Mills said: "Your two voyages to Africa have been of great service in preparing the public mind for an attempt to colonize your colored brethren and probably much is depending on your future assistance as it respects the success of efforts of this kind. I hope you will hold yourself in a state of readiness to aid any great efforts which may hereafter be made." He wanted to know:

1. In what manner would a request from our government for liberty to send free people of color to Sierra Leone be received by the English government?

2. Should the request be granted, would the Americans have equal privileges to trade to the colony?

3. Should an effort be made to explore the west coast of Africa to find a place for a colony, how great a force ought to be employed? Would one vessel be sufficient and what number of men would be required?

4. As a preparatory step to further exertions, would it be best to have an agent go to Africa and to England during the proceeding summer and autumn? Or to either of these places?

5. How should we answer those who say that people of color will not go to Africa if a place is provided?

6. Would those persons who are ready to go to Sierra Leone be ready to aid in establishing a new colony, in another place?

7. What was the expense of carrying out those persons who went to Africa with you, and how was the expense defrayed? Be so good as to add anything you think interesting. I hope you will write to me soon.[55]

Mills supplied Cuffe with the news of the activities at Washington and sent him a pamphlet on colonization. Mills, also, inquired "If the general government were to request you to go out for the purpose of exploring in your own vessel would you engage in this service if offered proper support?" If Cuffe did not go as an agent it was the wish of Mills that he take out another group of colo-

[55] *Cuffe Manuscripts*, Samuel J. Mills to Paul Cuffe, March 12, 1817. See also Richard, *Life of Samuel J. Mills* (Boston, 1906); Spring, *Memoir of Mills* (Boston and New York, 1829); Brown, *Biography of Robert Finley* (Philadelphia, 1857).

nists. "Since you have so generously commended this mighty effort," says Mills, "do not value further sacrifices in order to effect it." The voyage will not only tone up public feeling, it will also give the foundation for an appeal for governmental aid.

To these questions from Finley and Mills Cuffe gave prompt attention. He gave them what facts he had gathered from his two visits to Africa. He wrote with feeling about the slave trade, and raised the question of the desirability of a government vessel making explorations on the west coast of Africa. Small beginnings, he said, had been made in Sierra Leone, but in case there was a general manumission the Cape of Good Hope offered the most desirable place for a colony. Attention was also called to the Congo region. Withal to draw off the colored citizens it seemed best not only to have a colony in Africa but one in America as well. In any event, the slaves should be freed and until they are capable of managing for themselves they might be allowed to work the plantations on a lay.

The work of the African Institution is called to the attention of Finley and Mills and both Peter Williams, Jr., and James Forten are recommended. On returning from his second voyage he states that he received so many applications that he could have taken over the greater part of Boston. He himself is ready to serve in any capacity "although," he continued, "I stand (as it were) in a low place and am not able to see far; but blessed by God who hath created all things and for his own glory they are and were created he is able to make use of instruments in such a way as he pleases and may I be resigned to his holy will." [56]

Both Mills and Finley signed the constitution of the American Colonization Society. Finley was one of the Vice Presidents, and Mills was sent to Africa by the society to make investigations for it. He went via England

[56] Brown, *Finley*, 83.

where he met the colaborers of Cuffe. While in Africa he consulted with the members of the Friendly Society established by Cuffe in 1811. Two of the settlers that Cuffe transported in 1815, Kizell and Martin, acted as interpreters and guides for Mills. In one of Mills' observations he says, "Should a colony be established in this part of Africa, it remains a question whether it should be governed by white men, or whether the people will consider themselves competent to self government in the first instance."

The arguments for and against colonization were considered by Mills and Cuffe. "Whenever the subject of colonization shall be discussed by Congress," says Mills, "some will object that the free people of color will not go to Africa. Again, that it will cost too much to transport them and to afford them the necessary protection. Again it will be said that too many of these people are very useful and are wanted in this country. We should be prepared to meet these objectors as far as possible and trust in God for the success of our efforts."[57]

Mills was right in his anticipation of the argument that the free blacks would not go to Africa. Hardly had the American Colonization Society been formed when, under the auspices of the African Institution at Philadelphia, a meeting estimated at three thousand met at Reverend Richard Allen's church to discuss the question. Many were frightened, for they believed force would be used, particularly in the South, to compel immigration to Africa. James Forten reported none of them favored going to Africa and that they thought the slaveholders wanted to get rid of the free blacks so as to make the slaves themselves more secure. Although Forten was convinced that his brethren would never "become a people until they came out from amongst the white people"[58] he concluded to be silent on the question of deportation for the time being.

When this opposition to the colonization project was

[57] *Cuffe Manuscripts*, Samuel J. Mills to Paul Cuffe, March 12, 1817.
[58] *Ibid.*, James Forten to Paul Cuffe, January 25, 1817.

known to the Society, Finley came to Philadelphia to take charge of the situation. He met the committee to whom the matter was referred and explained to them "the purity of the motives" which actuated many of the leading spirits in the Society. He was so convincing that the committee unanimously decided that "benevolence to them and the land of their fathers guided the movements that were made at Washington."[59] But James Forten showed his confidence in the Captain by writing for his opinion on colonization.

Captain Cuffe had given advice to the men who organized the American Colonization Society, his co-workers in London had been drawn upon, his friends in Sierra Leone had served the agents of the Society in Africa, but his influence did not end with his death. When Bishop Meade was in the South on behalf of the Society he read Cuffe's letters to the free blacks of Savannah. He made use, too, of information obtained from some other Negroes who had been in Sierra Leone and conversed with the emigrants taken over in 1815.

In fact, the Society printed letters from the American Settlers in Africa and disseminated them as propaganda. Perry Locke exhorts his brethren in America to come to the "land of Canaan, abounding in honey and fruits, fish and oysters, wild fowls and wild hogs. The only thing that Africa wants is the knowledge of God—fear not to come, if the Lord will. When you come I hope to be with you and more besides me,—let this be printed if you please."[60]

The testimony of Samuel Wilson was no less convincing. He concludes: "Sir, when I set my foot on the African shore, I had only seven and six pence sterling; now, notwithstanding, all my sickness, I am master of a hundred pounds sterling. I think if I had had something to have begun with, I should have had about four or five thousand."[61]

[59] *Cuffe Manuscripts*, Samuel J. Mills to Paul Cuffe, July 14, 1817.
[60] *Second Annual Report of the American Colonization Society*, 151.
[61] *Ibid.*, 150.

Another letter signed by a number of Cuffe's passengers is directed to the American Negroes in general. It says:

> Be not fearful to come to Africa, which is your country by right. If any of you think it not proper to come, and say it is well with you, you must remember your brethren who are yet in slavery. They must be set free as yourselves. How shall they be set free, if not by your good behavior, and by coming to get a place ready to receive them? Though you are free that is not your country. Africa, not America, is your country and your home. Africa is a good country. You will have no trouble to raise your children when all things are plenty; you will have no want of warm clothing; you will have no need of firewood, for we have it in abundance; and here you will be looked upon like the blessed creatures of the Almighty God, and that bad opinion and contempt which our white brethren harbor, will be quite done away, and the whole of us will become a large and wonderful nation. We will forget all our former troubles when we turn to the land from which our forefathers came. The whole of you will have your own lands and houses; when you cultivate the land, (in which a few horses would be an assistance) you will be supplied with yams, cassada, plantains, fowls, wild hogs, deer, ducks, goats, sheep, cattle, fish in abundance, and many other articles, good running water, large oysters.[62]

Another clever device of the advocates of deportation to make use of the Captain was a dialogue between Absalom Jones on one side and William Penn and Paul Cuffe on the other. The dialogue was printed in *The Union* for June 18, 1818.[63] The scene of the dialogue is in Heaven and the subject is the colonization of the free Negroes in in Africa. Cuffe narrates his connections with the movement and sets forth purposes he had in view. He had hoped by establishing a colony in Africa to draw there gradually all the Negroes in America. In this way slavery would be abolished, Africa would be explored, civilized, and Christianized.

[62] *Second Annual Report of the American Colonization Society*, 152, 153.
[63] See also Brown, *Finley*, note L.

Absalom Jones, opposed to the movement in general, raises objections to it. Why not colonize them on the banks of the Mississippi or the Missouri, he asks. William Penn, a Quaker too, answers the objection by pointing out that the whites are migrating to that section and that were the Negroes to settle there trouble would arise between the two races. The Indians, moreover, would make trouble with the Negroes.

Jones next asks why should the colored people leave America at all? They are happy in America, and more and more is done for their uplift all the time. To this objection Penn replied that prejudice will always keep them down. "Can one imagine," asks he, "that the period will ever arrive in which they will bear any sway in our country, guide our legislative councils, preside in our courts of judicature, or take the lead in the affairs of the republic? Is it possible that the time will ever come in which intermarriages will be sought between their families and those of the most respectable whites? It would be the height of folly to indulge in such an expectation; and until such is the case, they will never occupy the rank or enjoy the privileges of white men; until this is the case, they will ever hold an inferior and subordinate place in society, and be in some degree aliens in their own land." Paul Cuffe had the sensibility and discernment to perceive this state of things, the penetration to discover the early practicable means by which his race could be relieved from their painful sense of inferiority, and the activity to commence the execution of a project to remedy the evil.

Would not deportation stop the manumission of slaves, asks Jones. Penn replies that many southerners are now ready to emancipate their slaves, and that their only handicap is a just provision for them. A colony in Africa would gradually attract to its sphere every slave in America.

At the end of the dialogue Penn and Cuffe convince Jones that the deportation of the free Negroes in America to Africa is a meritorious plan. What the dialogue did for one opponent of the scheme it was hoped that it would do for others.

The experiences of Cuffe were a great asset in the ventures of the colonizationists. In testimony to his services the Board of Managers of the American Colonization Society incorporated the following paragraph in its first annual report:

The managers cannot omit the testimony of Captain Paul Cuffe so well known in Africa, Europe, and America, for his active and large benevolence, and for his zeal and devotedness to the cause of the people of color. The opportunities of Captain Cuffe of forming a correct opinion were superior perhaps to those of any man in America. His judgment was clear and strong, and the warm interest he took in whatever related to the happiness of that class of people is well known. The testimony of such a man is sufficient to out weigh all the unfounded predictions and idle surmises of those opposed to the plan of this society. He had visited twice the coast of Africa, and became well acquainted with the country and its inhabitants. He states that, upon his opinion alone he could have taken to Africa at least two thousand people of color from Boston and its neighborhood. In the death of Paul Cuffe the society has lost a most useful advocate, the people of color a warm and disinterested friend, and society a valuable member. His character alone ought to be sufficient to rescue the people to which he belonged from the unmerited aspersions which have been cast upon them. The plan of the society met with his entire approbation, its success was the subject of his ardent wishes, and the prospect of its usefulness to the native Africans and their decendants in this country was the solace of his declining years, and cheered the last moments of his existence.[64]

[64] *First Annual Report of the American Colonization Society,* 5.

CHAPTER X

THE PALE MESSENGER

The formation of the American Colonization Society stimulated interest in Negro deportation. Both whites and blacks put many inquiries to Cuffe. He was thought of as the prospective first governor of the colony but he did not live to realize this. Near the end of his career his advice to his people was to be quiet and trust in God; be industrious and honest; such conduct is the greatest boon toward liberation. "Experience is the best schoolmaster."

He took advantage of this correspondence to exhort his brethren to improve their morals. To William Harris he wrote: "We must depart from that Monster—I mean intemperance. Examine your selves, your families. Are you clean? If not set about this work immediately. . . . Do not admit him into your houses in any other shape than a mere medicine. I formerly kept him company but for many years I have forsaken him and I find great consolation thereby."

About a year before his death he gave sound financial advice to Edward Cooke. In the postscript of the letter he wrote "My dear Friend Edward Cooke, if I could know that thee had given up the use of strong drink, I should feel rejoiced, and would render thee such aid, that thee could soon become a man of property."

About the same time that he gave this advice, Isaac Gifford received a "Watchword." "By experience," wrote the Captain, "I have ever found when I attended to my business I seldom suffered loss. I have found it to be good to make choice of good companions. I have ever found it not to be profitable for me to sit long after dining and make a tipling habit of wine and other liquors. These very people who adopt those practices when they see a sober, steady man will put business in his way. The surest way to conquer strong drink is to make no use of it. We are born and we must die. Amen.''

He points out to Joel Rogers, chosen to represent the Gayhead people, the fields among his neighbors, ''devasted either by creatures or weeds.'' More frugality is needed. Excessive drink and idleness are very destructive to society. These and similar truths were recommended to Rogers to guide his work for his people. When Cuffe and his wife with some relatives visited there, meeting was held, and ''many lively testimonies borne to the truth of their state and standing.''

The admonitions were in accord with the life of Captain Cuffe. Another lively testimony was given to young men in a meeting in Arch Street, Philadelphia. He said to the young men that ''he was afraid to dignify what he had to say, by calling it a vision, but it appeared to him at a time when he was very low in mind and much cast down, and being very disconsolate, there appeared before him the form of a man, inquiring what ailed him. He said he could not tell. The Form told him the disease was in his heart, and he could show it to him. Upon his expressing submission, the Form took a sharp instrument, separated his heart from his body and laid it before him. He was greatly terrified in viewing it, it being very unclear and contained all kinds of abominable things. The Form said he could never be healed, till he submitted to have his heart cleansed. Then, said he, I fear I never shall be healed. But on the Form asking him, if he was willing to have it cleansed, and he consenting, he took a sharp instrument and separated all that was vile and closed up the heart, replaced it, and healed the wound. Thus he said he felt himself a changed man and a new creature, and then recommended the young men to that Physician who could heal them, although their state was ever so deplorable.

''In the course of his testimony he also related that when he was about twelve years of age he lived upon an island where there was no house but that of his father.

Being one evening near night sent on an errand alone, he became afraid that he should meet with some wild beast that would attack him. He crossed to a fence in order to cut a stick to defend himself; but after cutting it, the thought occurred that he was not on his father's ground, and as he had no right to the stick it was not likely it would serve to defend him. On which he laid it down, near the place he had taken it from and in recrossing the fence laid his hand on a loose piece of wood which was on their own ground resting against the fence. It proved to be a club, which he took up, and went cheerfully on his way."[65]

It was while engaged in activity of this kind that he met "the pale messenger." His health began to fail him early in the spring of 1817. In April, however, he was well enough to attend Quarterly Meeting, but in June he was "on the bed of languishing." An eminent Rhode Island physician was summoned but he could not heal him. He doubtless then realized what he himself expressed in these words to Samuel R. Fisher, February 28, 1817: "May we often call to remembrance that we have no certain containing city here but above all things may we seek one to come whose builder is God that when we put off this body of mortality we may be clothed with the spirit of immortality that we may be prepared and favored to experience that glorious regeneration and friendship of everlasting peace."

On the morning of July 27 the Captain took solemn leave of his family. The hand that had guided the *Traveller* to so many ports was now so enfeebled that it was limp in the grasp of the little grandchildren. He shook hands with all the relations and the immediate members of his own household. As he bade them farewell it was "as broken a time," wrote his brother John, "as wast ever known amongst us." "Not many days hence," he said to his neighbors, "and ye shall see the glory of God; I know that my works are gone to judgment before me but

[65] Memorandum in the *Cuffe Manuscripts*.

it is all well, it is all well." Day by day he kept failing and on first day morning at two o'clock, September 9, the Captain was borne away on the invisible but irresistible tide.[66]

The funeral exercises were held on the following Monday afternoon. In marked solemnity a great concourse of people gathered. After waiting in great silence his friends bore testimony to his work and merit. He was buried in the Friends cemetery at the South Meeting House in Westport, a place of worship formerly known as the Old Meeting House when the Cuffe family worshipped there. "Many of his neighbors and friends," said William Rotch, Jr., "evinced their respect for his memory by attending his funeral (which was conducted agreeably to the usages of the Society of Friends, of which he was a member) and at which several lively testimonies were borne to the truth, that the Almighty Parent has made of one blood all the nations of men, and worketh righteousness, is accepted with him."[67]

The New York African Institution held services for him in October following his death. The funeral sermon was preached in the African Methodist Episcopal Zion Church by Peter Williams, Jr. That trait of character which rendered Cuffe so eminently useful, said the speaker, was "a steady perseverance in laudable undertaking, which overcomes obstacles apparently insurmountable and attains its object, while others fall back in despair."

"Shall I say to you, my African brethren," continued the Reverend Mr. Williams, "go and do likewise? Subjected as we too generally are, to multiplied evils of poverty, made more intolerant by the prejudices which prevail against us, his example is worthy of our imitation. It is only by an honest, industrious, and prudent husbanding of all the means which are placed in our power, that we can hope to rise on the scale of society."[68]

[66] Cf. *Cuffe Manuscripts,* John Cuffe to Freelove Cuffe, September 10, 1817; David Cuffe, Jr., to Freelove Cuffe, July 8, 1817.

[67] Clipping in the *Cuffe Manuscripts.*

[68] Peter Williams, *Discourse on the Death of Paul Cuffe.*

His death was chronicled in many papers with appropriate praise of his life. *Niles Register* noted that all classes of people esteemed his morality, truth and intelligence.[69] *The Columbian Sentinel* praised his charity and particularly his deep interest in his race. "He was concerned not only to set them a good example by his own correct conduct; to admonish and counsel them against the habits to which he found them most prone; but more extensively to promote their welfare."[70] *The Colonization Herald* said, "Captain Cuffe was a man of the strictest integrity, modest yet dignified in his manners, of a feeling and liberal heart, public spirited and well versed in the business of the world."[71]

"In the example of Paul Cuffe," said *The New York Spectator*, "the free people of color in the United States may see the manner in which they may require competency and reputation. It is the beaten path of industry and integrity. Captain Cuffe cultivated his own farm and guided his own ship. He labored with his own hands and kept his own book of accounts. He did not waste his time in idleness, nor his income in extravagance. He was never charged with intrigue in his contracts, neglect in his promises, or fraud in his traffic. . . . His example therefore, is capable of imitation by every free person of color."[72]

One Hundred Years After

Paul Cuffe had some descendants of consequence. Horatio P. Howard, a great-grandson of Captain Cuffe, wrote a short biography of his grandsire and erected a monument in his memory. Ruth Cuffe married Alexander Howard and their son, Shadrack, was the father of Horatio. He was born in New Bedford in 1854, and beginning in 1888 served as a clerk in the Custom House in New York City. Howard died February 20, 1923, leaving consider-

---

[69] *Niles Register*, XIII, 64.
[70] *Cuffe Manuscripts*, Clipping from *Columbian Centinel*, September 17, 1817.
[71] *Ibid.*, Clipping from *The Colonization Herald*.
[72] *Cuffe Manuscripts*, Clipping from *New York Spectator*, October, 1817.

able wealth, $5000 of which he bequeathed to Hampton, and the balance of which he gave to Tuskegee as a fund to establish Captain Paul Cuffe Scholarships.

The monument which Howard erected is of Westerly Rhode Island granite and cost $400. It bears the inscription: "In memory of Captain Cuffe, Patriot, Navigator, Educator, Philanthropist, Friend." It stands five feet high on an elevation in the front part of the church yard and along the principal highway.

The biography is a booklet containing twenty-eight pages and is entitled "A Self-Made Man Captain Paul Cuffe." "By the erection of this lasting Memorial," says Howard, "in honor of the courage, achievements and life work of Capt. Paul Cuffe, a resident of Westport, Massachusetts, for many years, the donor, a great grandson, hopes to awaken and stimulate energy and ambition in the rising generation of Negro youth, that they may profit thereby."

On June 15, 1913, dedication services were held in Central Village, Westport. Rev. Tom A. Sykes, minister of the Westport Society of Friends, presided. The exercises, which were attended by about two hundred people, were opened by a flower brigade of school children led by Horatio P. Howard. Flowers were strewn on the graves of the Captain and his wife. Speeches were made by Rev. Mr. Sykes and Mr. Samuel T. Rex, the designer of the monument. Miss Elizabeth C. Carter read a paper descriptive of the career of Capt. Cuffe. Howard distributed his booklet and showed a compass used by his great-grandfather on his last voyages.

. . . .

The life of Paul Cuffe is noteworthy for several reasons. In the first place, it is a tribute to American democracy. He is an example of an American youth handicapped on every side, but overcoming so well the difficulties which overshadowed him that he won recognition in three continents. There is no place in the world where such achievement is less difficult than America. She offers opportunities for self-recognition unprecedented in the world.

In the next place his life is a tribute to the Quakers. No religious organization has given itself so unreservedly to the uplift of the Negro. This devotion is as old as that which won our political liberties, as deep as the scars on Edith Cavell's heart, and as wide in its reach as the waters of the sea. Cuffe's membership in this religious body and his adherence to its principles gave zest to his zeal for the betterment of his race. His plans grew so comprehensive that they embraced the Negroes of two continents and made calls on his philanthropic spirit for several thousand dollars. In all this he paid a tribute to Quaker ideals and life, and deserves mention with Woolman and Benezet.

The remedy that he believed would relieve the oppression of his race is also noteworthy. To him the withdrawal of the free Negro from the States would remove an obstacle to the emancipation of the slave, and in the course of time wholly stamp out slavery in America. Negroes would be better off by themselves, and those who settled in Africa could help civilize and Christianize that continent. In the meantime the slave trade would disappear.

Negro deportation had been advocated by some of America's most distinguished citizens and soon after Cuffe's death its advocates increased by leaps and bounds. In the early period it was not as futile as it now is and many believed that under governmental support and direction it was in the realm of possibility. When the measure took on its most colossal program in 1817, Cuffe cautioned his brethren to watch its operation for a year or two before taking sides for or against it.

Today Negro colonizationists are few in number. The American Colonization Society itself barely maintains its organization, and only occasionally sends a Negro to Africa. When an individual is sent he usually goes in the capacity of a missionary or teacher. Colonization as a panacea for the amelioration of the Negro race is impracticable. The Negro feels at home in America as much as the white man. Negro uplift must be sought not in deportation but in habits of living exemplified in Captain Cuffe.

There is his industry and thrift. It is a long step from nothing to twenty thousand dollars. And it is a hard step when there is practically no initial footing. But Paul Cuffe did it, and did it because he believed in work. He was always at his task. The dignity of labor he knew and valued. And he knew how to save. He made his money work for him. He stopped the leaks in his business boat. He spent wisely and invested well.

There is his interest in education. The painstaking endeavor and indefatigable effort which belonged to his labor in industry was equally a part of his labor in education. It is difficult for us today with our excellent opportunities for education to realize how meagre they were in Paul Cuffe's day. And if they were meagre for whites a century and one half ago they were all the more so for Negro children. Despite the handicaps he not only mastered the three R's but the principles of navigation as well.

He learned something more valuable than this—the fine art of diffusing knowledge. So dearly did he value education for the youth of his neighborhood that he himself on his own land erected a school building. He made contributions to teachers' salaries. And most of all, he taught the principles of navigation to every young man who offered himself for instruction. Such devotion to a cause grows out of a recognition of its great worth.

There is his interest in religion. He stood for righteousness. No one ever charged him with unfair dealing. His business was clean. He sought the fellowship of the church. He contributed to its needs and gave personal testimony to the power of Christ. Religion was vital in his life; he tried to foster it from Westport to Freetown. He was both a home and a foreign missionary. He knew the value of prayer. He gave advice that was tested first in his own experience.

Overshadowing his industry, his religion, and education stands his optimism. He believed in the victory of righteousness; therefore, he worked for it. He believed in the triumph of truth; therefore, he dedicated himself to it. He realized the mastery of poverty; therefore, he gave pursuit to wealth. He believed in the amelioration of his race; therefore, he consecrated himself to it.

HENRY NOBLE SHERWOOD.

DOCUMENTS

THE WILL OF PAUL CUFFE

Be it remembered, that I, Paul Cuffe of Westport in the County of Bristol and Commonwealth of Massachusetts, yeoman, being at this time (through mercy) in health and of a sound, disposing mind and memory, and considering that it is appointed for all men once to die, I do make and ordain this my last will and testament in the followering manner (viz.)

Imprimis. My will is, and I hearin order, that my just debts and funeral charges together with the expenses of setteling my estate be paid by my executors herein after named, out of my estate.

Item. I give unto my wife Alice Cuffe all my houshould goods except my two desks and book case, and books; I also give her in lieu of her right of dower in my estate, so long as she shall remain my widow, the use and improvement of my now dwelling house and the one half of all my lands, together with one half of the live stock, and all the famely provisions that may be on hand at my decease, and one hundred dollars in money, and all the profits arising from my half of the salt works, that Joseph Tripp & I built together. Should the salt works not be in operation before this will is proved or should not be built, then my will is she should have one hundred dollars annually.

Item. I give unto my daughter in law Lydia Wainer one hundred dollars.

Item. I give unto my daughter Mary Phelpess & to her heirs and assigns forever, the house and lot of land which I bought of Lucy Castino.

Item. I give unto my son Paul Cuffe, and to his oldest male heir forever, the farm that was given to me by my father Cuffe Slocum, and my maple desk, also one half of my wereing appearl, my will further is that five hundred dollars be retained out of my estate, and put to interest in some safe hands, the income of which I order to be used annually for the support of my son Paul Cuffe' family, forever. I also order that one fourth part of the brig

Traveller together with the five hundred dollars, be placed under care and guardianship of my executors, in order that my son Paul and his heirs, might be benefited by it yearly and every year forever, also the one sixth part of the residue be placed under the care & guardianship of my executors for the benefit of Paul & his heirs as above mentioned, forever.

Item. I give unto my son William Cuffe and to his oldest male heir forever, the lot of land which I bought of Ebenezer Eddy called the Allen lot, and one fourth part of the brig Traveller, and my walnut desk and book case standing thereon, and Johnsons Dictionary in two volums, and one half of my weareing appearel, and three hundred dollars in money, to be laid out in building him a dwelling house on the Allen lot.

Item. I give unto my cousin Ruth Cottell fifty dollars. Ruth Howard, Alice Cuffe Jr. and Rhoda Cuffe one half of the brig Traveller, that is to each one of them one eighth part.

Item. I give unto my two grand daughters, namely, Almira Howard and Alice Howard, daughters of my daughters Naomi Howard deceased, fifty dollars to each one, when and as they arive to the age of twenty one years.

Item. I give unto my cousin Ruth Cottell fifty dollars.
Item. I give unto my brother David Cuffe ten dollars.
Item. I give unto my brother Jonathan Cuffe ten dollars.
Item. I give unto my brother John Cuffe ten dollars.
Item. I give unto my sister Freelove Cuffe ten dollars.
Item. I give unto my sister Fear Phelpess ten dollars.

Item. I give unto my three sisters namely Sarah Durfee, Lydia Cuffe and Ruth Weeden, six dollars annually to each one dureing their natural life. Should they or either of them make bad use of the money given them, in such a case I request my executors to pay them in provision or cloathing, and such things that may be for their comfort.

Item. I give unto the monthly meeting or society of friends, called Quakers in Westport, fifty dollars, to be paid over to their treasurer, by my executors, according to direction of the monthly meeting.

Item. My mind and will is that those daughters that are single and unmarried, shall have privelege to live in the house with their mother, and, after their mothers decease, they to have the privelege to live in and occupie the south part of the house, with privelege to the well and in the seller and garden to raise saurce in so long as they remain singel and unmaried.

I give unto my two said sons and four daughters namely Paul, William, Mary, Ruth, Alice and Rhoda all the rest and residue of my estate not hearin otherwise disposed of to be divided between them six equally.

And my will further is, that the one fourth part of the brig Traveller and the one sixth part of the residue, that I have herein given to my son William, I place under the care and guardianship of my executors, to order the use of the same as they shall think best for Williams interest, untill he arives to twenty five years of age. Then if his care and conduct be good, they then are requested to pay the whole over to him together with all the profits ariseing from it.

And my will further is, the balance that may become due to my estate not hearin otherwise disposed of to be divided between or otherway be given up to them.

I further order that all land that I have bought belonging to the estate of Benjmin Cook late of Dartmouth deceased, be returned to the widow and the heirs, they paying what the land cost and interest.

And my will further is that for the payments annually that my executors retain enough of the residue of my estate to put on interest to rais the anual payments mentioned in this way last will.

Lastly. I do constitute and apoint William Rotch Junr. of New Bedford and Daniel Wing of Westport aforesaid executors of this my last will and testament.

In testemony whereof I do hear unto set my hand and seal eighteenth day of the fourth month in the year of our Lord one thousand eight hundred and seventeen 1817.

Paul Cuffe (seal)

Signed, sealed, published and declared by the said Paul Cuffe as and for his last will and testament in the presence of us

EDWARD PHILLIPS
LUTHAN TRIPP
DAVID M. GIFFORD

Oct. 7, 1817, Approved.

From the Records of the Probate Office, Taunton, Mass.

BOOK REVIEWS

Africa and the Discovery of America. Volume II. By LEO WIENER, Professor of Slavic Languages and Literatures at Harvard University. Innes & Sons, Philadelphia, Pa. 1922.

Professor Wiener, in the second volume of his series *Africa and the Discovery of America*, deals exhaustively with the documentary information relating to "the presence in America of cotton, tobacco and shell money, before the discovery of America by Columbus. . . . The accumulative evidence is overwhelmingly in favor of an introduction of the articles under discussion from Africa by European or Negro traders, decades earlier than 1492." (Foreword, p. ix.)

The importance, for the history of Pre-Columbian civilization, of these discoveries cannot be overestimated. Moreover, their significance is not concerned alone with the history of America. They will compel a revision and realignment of historical frontiers in Europe and Africa as well, from a date not later than the first quarter of the fifteenth century. Lastly, "Africa and the Discovery of America" forms, as it were, a sequel to Professor Wiener's *Contributions toward a History of Arabico-Gothic Culture*, enabling the historian to trace the influence of the Arabs as the torch-bearers of civilization. It was they who in the eighth century, through the medium of the Spanish Mozarabs, recreated European culture, and at a later period, through that of the Arabicised Negroes, of whom the West African Mandingoes were the most important, at least almost entirely re-created, if they did not actually create, the civilization of the native American tribes, throughout both continents, and planted, so to speak, in the New World, the seeds of two great modern industries, cotton and tobacco.

Let us then consider, first, what is the bearing of Professor Wiener's work on the history of cotton. Assyria and India were centers of cotton culture at a very early date. The evidence that the Arabs popularized cotton in Africa, in connection with the ceremonial purification of the dead, that is, stuffing the orifices of the body with cotton, is shown by the fact that Arabic *'utb* "cotton," a loan word from Coptic *tbbe* "to purify," has produced the West African "cotton" words, exactly as Arabic *wudu'* "ablution" has given rise, doubtless through Hausa influence, to the "cotton" words of Nigeria. What is particularly important to note, however, is that Arabic *qutn* "cotton" has gone everywhere into the Mandingo dialects, which have, in turn, influenced the native American languages. Thus for example, in South America, the Mandingo *kotondo*, etc., "cotton," derived from Arabic *qutn*, has left derivatives in the Indian languages "from Venezuela south to Peru, and in Central Brazil" (page 80), beside derivatives from Kimbunou *mujinha* "cotton," in eastern Brazil, northward and westward. If we concede the presence of cotton in South America before Columbus, we can only conclude, on the basis of linguistic evidence, that it was introduced either directly or indirectly from Africa. The Aztec word *ychca*, the native Mexican word for "cotton," furnishes no proof that cotton was known to the Mexicans before the coming of the Spaniards, since *ychca* is not originally a specific name, but has reference to any kind of fibre,—of a fluffy character, and came to mean "cotton" only secondarily.

Columbus, however, reported that on Oct. 11, 1492, the Indians of Guanahani brought parrots and cotton thread in balls, to trade for beads and hawks' bills. Either he told the truth, or he did not. If he told the truth, it is still remarkable that the Indians should not only have known of the traders' demand for cotton and parrots, but should also have offered the very articles which Cada Mosto, nearly fifty years earlier, had mentioned as coming from Africa, particularly the cotton, then offered for sale in the Negro markets. Columbus's references to growing cotton are specific in declaring that the cotton grew on trees,—hence it is obvious that he did not see any true cotton growing, but only the false cotton, the product of the tree Bombax Ceiba, used for stuffing mats, but not capable of being spun (page 28). A study of the early records of Mexico is conclusive in the evidence it furnishes to show that cotton never formed part of the tribute due the Mexican emperor, but that the payment of tribute in cotton was "an innovation of the Spaniards, and did not have the sanction of the Aztec tribute" (page 56). Hence we have nothing to indicate that, either in the Indies or in Mexico, the material of which the "cotton clothing" of the natives, mentioned by the Spaniards, was made, was really cotton. If it was cotton, its presence points to contact between America and Africa before Columbus, and the readiness of the natives to offer cotton in exchange for hawks' bills testifies clearly to the extent of trade relations between the two countries.

The contention of archæologists is that cotton culture in Peru may go back to a date as early as 200 A.D. The only criterion for such an assumption rests on the theoretical rate of accumulation of guano deposits, in which mummies, wrapped in cotton, have been found,—calculated at two and one half feet per century. This conclusions is absurd, not only for the stress it lays on the capricious habits of sea-birds, but also for the reason that it fails to take into account the irregularity of the guano deposits, as shown in the Peruvian Government Survey of 1854. No conclusion whatever as to the age of even a single mummy-case can be drawn, owing to certain facts concerning Indian burial customs, recorded by Cieza de Leon in 1553, Ondegardo in 1571, and Cobo, nearly a century later. These travellers state that the Peruvian natives were accustomed to open graves, change the clothes of the dead from time to time, and re-bury them (page 67 ff.). The proof that they told the truth is contained in the report by Baessler, of the X-ray examinations of Peruvian mummy-packs in the Royal Museum at Berlin. One such pack contains "the bones of *four separate individuals,* but of none there were enough to construct even distantly one complete skeleton. Besides, there were some *animal bones* present" (page 71). This disinterment of bodies, and of course the same confusion of the remains, revealed by the X-ray, was practised by the Indians as late as 1621. Nothing then remains to militate against the linguistic testimony so strongly in support of the conclusion that South American cotton culture is of African origin.

Professor Wiener's tentative conclusion that tobacco smoking was of African origin, outlined in his first volume of this series, has been strongly reinforced by a study of the Old-World origin or capnotherapy. "Smoking for medicinal purposes," he says on page 180, "is very old, and goes back at least to Greek medicine. A large number of viscous substances, especially henbane and bitumen, were employed in fumigation, and taken through the mouth, sometimes through the nose, for certain diseases, especially catarrh, toothache and pulmonary troubles. This fumigation took place through a funnel which very much resembles a modern pipe, but by its knot-like end at the bottom of the bowl shows its derivation from the distilling cap of the alchemist's retort.'' The *bitumen* corresponds to the *tubbaq* or *tobbaq* of the Arab doctors, a name applied to several medicinal plants containing a pungent and viscous juice. One of these plants was known in Spain as *tobbaqah*.

Fumigation as a curative measure soon degenerated in Europe into quackery,—the Arab smoke doctor giving place to the itinerant charlatan whose Arabic name lingers in Portuguese *bufarinheiro* ''peddler,'' originally ''smoke vender.'' ''In Africa, medical fumigation spread southward through the Negro country, finding its way to America perhaps a full century before the coming of Columbus. The manner in which smoking was introduced into America is made clear by the history of the Negro *pombeiro*, the African bootlegger in the service of the Portuguese colonists, who taught the natives to drink *pombe*, a kind of intoxicating liquor. This word *pombe* is a corruption of Latin *pulpa*, which through the Spanish *pulpa* has persisted in Mexico as *pulque*, the name of an intoxicant used by the Indians, exactly as Arabic *hashish*, through Spanish *chicha*, has entered Nahuatl, producing the Nahuatl *chichila* ''to ferment, etc.'' The method of preparing the *chicha* in Peru, by masticating grain, is clearly of African origin, since in the Sudan, a kind of drink is made by chewing the fruit of the baobab. The clearest proof, however, that such *pombeiros* reached America in Pre-Columbian days is found in Columbus's reference to the report by the Indians of Hispaniola, that ''*black people* had come thither from the south and south east, with spearheads of *guanin*. Now *guanin* is a Mandingo word; the name of an alloy of 18 parts of gold, 6 of silver and 8 of copper.

The history of shell and bead money, familiar as the wampum of the northern Indians, forms the third part of the present volume, and is perhaps the source of the strongest arguments to show the Pre-Columbian relation of Africa and America. Ultimately, the use of cowry shells for money comes from China, where such shells, called *pei, tze-pei, pei-tze*, had been used from time immemorial. The Chinese name of the cowry, *ho-pei*, probably anciently pronounced something like *ka-par*, is evidently the origin of Sanskrit *kaparda*, Hindustani *kauri* (whence English *cowry*), Dravidian *kavadi* ''cowry.'' ''From the ninth century on, we have many references in the Arabic authors to the cowries in Asia and Africa'' (page 208). It is quite to be expected, then, that in the Negro languages, we should find derivatives of this ultimately Chinese word, descended through the medium of successive borrowings, via Hindustani and Arabic,—that is, Hausa *al-kawara, kawara*, etc., Zanzibar *kauri*, Wolof *korre*, Bambara *kori*, etc., side by side with a group descended from Dravidian *woda* "shell,"—that is Hausa *wori*, Malinke *wuri*, Bambara *wari*.

The substitution of beads for shells, as the development of this primitive form of currency went on, has left its mark likewise in linguistic records. That is to say, we have in Africa a group of words descended ultimately from Chinese *par, pei*, originally meaning "cowry," and secondarily "bead," together with a new group, traceable through an Arabic intermediary stage to Persian *sang* "onyx," the bead-stone par excellence. From the cowry-words have come Benin *cori, kori, koli*, "blue bead," whence *akori*, the "*aggry*" bead of the white traders, Neule *gri* "beads," and Baule *worye* "blue bead," a loan-word from Mandingo *wori*. In Bantu *zimbo*, we have either a Bantu plural of *abuy*, itself a derivative of Maldive *boli, bolli*, which is the Chinese *pei* "cowry," or a direct loan-word, through Arabic or Portuguese influence, of Chinese *tsze-pei* "purple shell." The transference in meaning from "cowry" to "bead" is illustrated in Kaffir *in-tsimbi* "beads." Similarly, the original "bead" words, from Persian *sang* "onyx," have given Zanzibar, Swahili *ushanga* "bead," Kongo *nsanga* "string of blue beads," with a recession of meaning in Kongo *nsungu* "cowry shell."

The transference of African currency to America is shown by two significant facts. First, we have the name. In the Brazilian *caang* "to prove, try," *caangaba* "mould, picture, etc.," is to be seen a form of some African derivative of Persian *sang*, as seen in Zanzibar *ushanga* "bead," Kongo *nsanga* "blue beads," etc., the change of meaning leading to the connotation "mould" being due to the substitution of the European idea of money as a piece of stamped metal, in place of that of bead or shell money. Exactly as the *petun* words for tobacco spread from South to North America along the trade routes, so the words for "money" followed the same course. Jacques Cartier's word *esnogny*, given as the Indian name of shell money,—the shells actually gathered by an African method of fishing for shell-fish with a dead body,—is traceable only to some form of the Brazillian *çaang*, which has also given Gree *soniwaw* "silver," Long Island *sewan* "money." The Chino-African cowry-word, seen in African *abuy*, is preserved in the North American *bi, pi* (plural *peag, peak*) "wampum," side by side with the

Guarani *mboi, poi,* "shell bead." Lest the reader still harbor a lingering doubt of the fact of early trade relations between Brazil and Canada, Professor Wiener shows how Spanish *aguja* "needle" has left derivatives in a large number of Indian languages distant by many hundreds of miles from any Spanish settlement.

Secondly, we have the standard of value. From the earliest times, in China, the purple cowry was more valuable than the white. The same standard prevailed in Africa, and was transferred to the beads when beads were substituted for cowries. Among the Indians, the *blue,* or *dark colored* currency, whether shells or beads, was consistently reckoned as superior in worth to the white. Shell-money was first popularized on Long Island by the Dutch, who, as we are informed, imported cowries and *aggry* beads from the East to sell them to the Guinea-merchants. Moreover, Gov. Bradford has stated that it took the Massachusetts colonists two years to teach the Indians to use shell or bead money. Finally, Professor Wiener concludes that "in the Norman country, . . . the wampum belt, as a precious ornament for European women, had its origin, and was by the Frenchmen transferred to Brazil and Canada" (page 258).

The fifteen full-page illustrations serve well to bring home much of the force of the arguments, even to a casual reader.

PHILLIPS BARRY, A.M., S.T.B.

GROTON, MASSACHUSETTS.

The Negro Press in the United States. By FREDERICK G. DETWEILER. The University of Chicago Press, Chicago, 1922. Pp. 274.

Struck by the number and distribution of Negro magazines and newspapers, many investigators in the social sciences have recently directed their attention to the study of the Negro press. This increased interest resulted largely from the unusual impetus given the Negro press during the World War when it played the part of proclaiming the oppression of the Negroes to the nations pretending to be fighting for democracy when they were actually oppressing their brethren of color at home. And why should not the public be startled when the average Negro periodical, formerly eking out an existence, became extensively circulated almost suddenly and began to wield unusual influence in shaping the policy of an oppressed group ambitious to right its wrongs? These investigators, therefore, desire to know the influences at work in advancing the circulation of these periodicals, the cause of the change of the attitude of the Negroes toward their publications, their literary ability to appreciate them, the areas of their greatest circulation, and the attitude of the white people toward the opinion of this race.

While it is intended as a sort of scientific work treating this field more seriously than Professor Robert T. Kerlin's *The Voice of the Negro,* it leaves the impression that the ground has not been thoroughly covered. In the first place, the author does not show sufficient appreciation of the historic background of the Negro press prior to emancipation. He seems acquainted with such distinguished characters as Samuel Cornish, John B. Russwurm, and the like but inadequately treats or casually passes over the achievements of many others who attained considerable fame in the editorial world. In any work purporting to be a scientific treatment of the Negro press in the United States the field cannot be covered by a chapter of twenty pages as the author in question has undertaken to do. Furthermore, many of the underlying movements such as abolition, colonization, and temperance, which determined the rise and the fall of the Negro editor prior to the Civil War, are not sufficiently discussed and scientifically connected in this work. The book, then, so far as the period prior to the Civil War is concerned, is not a valuable contribution.

The author seemed to know more about the Negro press in freedom. Living nearer to these developments he was doubtless able to obtain many of these facts at first-hand and was able to present them more effectively. He well sets forth the favorite themes of the Negro press and the general make-up of the Negro paper, but does not sufficiently establish causes for this particular trend in this sort of journalism. Taking up the question of the demand for rights, the author explains very clearly what the Negro press has stood for. Then he seemingly goes astray in the discussion of the solution of the race problem, Negro life, Negro poetry, and Negro criticism, which do not peculiarly concern the Negro editor more than others in the various walks of life. Looking at the problem from the outside and through a glass darkly, as almost any white man who has spent little time among Negroes must do, the work is about as thorough as most of such investigators can make it and it should be read by all persons directing attention to the Negro problem.

The Disruption of Virginia. By JAMES C. MCGREGOR. The Macmillan Company, New York, 1922. Pp. 328, price $2.00.

This book was written, according to the author, as an attempt to present an unbiased account of the strange course of events in the history of Virginia from the time of Lincoln's election to the presidency to the time of the admission of West Virginia into the Union. It is, however, more of a polemic than an historical contribution. The author raises this very question himself by his declaration that he has no grudges to satisfy and no patrons to please. "If he seems harsh in his opinions and conclusions regarding the irregular and inexpedient methods employed in cutting off the western counties of Virginia and forming them into a new State," says he, "it is due to the conviction that an unnecessary wrong was committed, a wrong that helped not at all in Lincoln's prosecution of the Civil War." The author is convinced that not only was the act unconstitutional but that it was not desired by more than a small minority of the people of the new State. He believes that the President and Congress, being grateful to the Union men in northwestern Virginia for their loyalty to the Union, rewarded them by giving their consent to the organization of a new State which, nevertheless, was in violation of the principles of the Constitution.

Unlike Professor C. H. Ambler who, in his *Sectionalism in Virginia*, has set forth in detail the differing political interests of the sections of Virginia, this author reduces it to a mere exploit on the basis that the end justified the means. Furthermore, the author differs widely from C. G. Woodson who in an unpublished thesis similarly entitled *The Disruption of Virginia*, presented in 1911 to the Graduate School of Harvard University in partial fulfilment of the requirement for the degree of Doctor of Philosophy, emphasized the economic differences as the underlying causes. Dr. McGregor minimizes such causes by reducing his treatment of the economic situation to a single chapter of ten pages. He then briefly discusses the opening of the breach, the Constitutional Convention of 1829-30 and the growth of sectionalism between that Convention and the Civil War. Approaching the main feature of the work, the author takes up the preliminaries of the Convention of 1861, the various conventions of the northwestern counties out of which evolved the organization of the new State of West Virginia, and finally the question of admission before Congress.

Why such a work could be considered necessary and accepted as a contribution in this particular field when valuable works have already been written upon this subject, is justified by the author on the ground that he has discovered considerable new material which convinces him that the new State movement in West Virginia was unrepresentative of the majority of the people of the northwestern counties but was put through in dictatorial fashion by a militant minority. It is true that some new material has been added to this work, but it hardly convinces well informed historians that the far-reaching and sweeping conclusion of the author are justified by the few additional facts which he has been able to find. Almost a causal study of the history of Virginia shows that the western part of the State became estranged from the eastern because their economic interests were different and the authorities failed to make the improvements necessary to connect these sections and thus unify such interests. By the time of the Civil War the northwestern counties were commercially connected with the North and West and accordingly followed these in that upheaval.

A Comparative Study of the Bantu and Semi-Bantu Languages. Volume II. By SIR HARRY H. JOHNSTON, G.C.M.G., K.C.B., Sc.D. (Cambridge). The Clarendon Press, Oxford, 1922. Pp. 544.

This work is the result of a study of the Bantu languages commenced by the author in 1881 in the Library of the British Museum, and instigated by the project of accompanying the Earl of Mayo on an exploratory expedition in South West Africa, Angola and the countries south and east of the Kunene River. The expedition, according to the author, was extended by him to the upper Congo thanks to the assistance offered by H. M. Stanley. With this large view of Africa his studies were continued with little intermission during the forty years which followed his first introduction into that continent. Even the World War itself was not exactly an interruption but permitted the author to extend the scope of his research by bringing him into closer acquaintance with certain of the western Semi-Bantu languages through the presence in France of contingents of Senegambian troops. The Colonial office, moreover, assisted the work by requesting its officials in British West Africa to examine the Semi-Bantu languages of British Nigeria, South-west Togoland, Sierra Leone and the Gambia. Furthermore, an important discovery of two Bantu languages was made in the southern part of the Anglo-Egyptian province of Bahr-al-ghazal. He is indebted to Mr. Northcote W. Thomas's researches which revealed new and interesting forms of Semi-Bantu speech in the Cross River districts of Southern Nigeria. In the comparison of roots, moreover, the author had considerably more material to draw on than in the case of the first volume. He found also much more information concerning Hōma and Bañgminda through Major Paul Larkin and Captain White. These are the chief features which, he believes, make the second volume a valuable contribution.

In spite of the extensive investigation, however, the author still finds a good deal about which he is not certain. About many of these languages he knows little regarding their structure and grammar. In other words they have been studied merely from the outside. In spite of his extensive travels, moreover, he had so much to do and apparently such a short time in which to accomplish his task that this work, as valuable as it is, can be considered no more than an introductory treatise going a little further into a field inadequately explored. Already he says he finds that he has been reproached for not bringing within the scope of these two volumes a group of languages in the North-east Togoland and Kisi and the Limba tongues of Sierra Leone. Yet although he finds that these have some Bantu features, they were too mixed to justify their treatment here. He found resemblances of the Bantu and Semi-Bantu families elsewhere but not closely enough akin to require their treatment in connection with this work.

Beginning with a treatment of the enumeration and classification of the Bantu and Semi-Bantu languages, the work reviews the languages illustrated in Volume I. Attention is directed to the Bantu in various regions of the continent. The author then discusses the phonetics and phonology of the Bantu and Semi-Bantu languages, prefixes, suffixes, and concords connected with the noun in Bantu and Semi-Bantu, adjectives, pronouns, numerals, adverbs, conjunctions, prepositions, the verbs and verb roots. The maps graphically show the probable origins and lines of migration of the Bantu and Semi-Bantu languages and their distribution in Central and South Africa.

On the whole, the world is indebted to Sir Harry H. Johnston for his enumeration and classification of these tongues, although the work merely marks the beginning of a neglected task. Until some scholar with better opportunities to carry forward this research has produced a more scientific treatise, the works of the author will be referred to as interesting and valuable volumes.

NOTES

On February 20, 1923, there passed away in New York City a Negro of no little distinction in his particular group. This was Horatio P. Howard, the great grandson of Captain Paul Cuffe of African colonization fame. Howard was the grandson of the Captain's daughter Ruth, who married Alexander Howard, and the child of their son Shadrach. Howard was born in New Bedford in 1854 and beginning in 1888 served as a clerk in the Custom House in New York City where he accumulated considerable wealth which, inasmuch as he lived and died a bachelor, he disposed of for philanthropic purposes. He bequeathed $5000 to Hampton and the balance of his estate he gave to Tuskegee as a fund to establish Captain Paul Cuffe scholarships.

Hoping to inculcate an appreciation of the achievements of his great grandfather, he erected to his memory a monument at a cost of $400 dedicated in 1917 with appropriate exercises by the people of both races and made still more impressive by a parade which Howard himself led. On that occasion, moreover, he distributed his interesting biography of the great pioneer in the form of a booklet entitled *A Self-Made Man, Captain Paul Cuffe.*

Henry Allen Wallace, one of the colaborers in unearthing and preserving the records of the Negro, died on the 12th of February. He was the son of Andrew and Martha Wallace and was born in Columbia, South Carolina, about sixty-seven years ago. He was educated in the public schools of Toronto, Canada, the University of Toronto, and Howard University. He began his public life as a clerk in the post office at Columbia, and in the early days of civil service secured, by success in a competitive examination, an appointment as clerk in the War Department in Washington. There he served with an unbroken record for over thirty years, after which he was transferred to the New York office with which he was connected until about eighteen months ago when on account of ill health he was compelled to retire. He afterward made his home with his sister in Chester, Pennsylvania, where he died.

Mr. Wallace was well informed on matters pertaining to the race during the Reconstruction and freely contributed to magazines publishing such material. Furthermore, his assistance was often solicited to correct manuscripts prepared by others who knew less of this drama in our history. His service in connection with finding the names of Negroes who served in southern legislatures and his letters, both of which have appeared from time to time in THE JOURNAL OF NEGRO HISTORY, constitute valuable contributions in this field.

SPRING CONFERENCE

On the 5th and 6th of April there will be held in Baltimore the Spring Conference of the Association for the Study of Negro Life and History. Members of the administrative staff including Professor John R. Hawkins, the Chairman, Mr. S. W. Rutherford, Secretary-Treasurer, and others of the Executive Council, are making extensive preparation for this Conference. The aim will be to bring together teachers and public-spirited citizens with an appreciation of the value of the written record and of research as a factor in correcting error and promoting the truth. The heads of all accredited institutions of learning have been invited to take an active part in this convocation. As it is to be held in Baltimore, near which are located so many of our colleges and universities, it is believed that this Conference will prove to be one of the most successful in the history of the Association.

The program will cover two days and will offer an opportunity for the discussion of every phase of Negro life and history. On Thursday there will be a morning session at 11:00 at Morgan College and an afternoon session there at 3:00 P. M. On the following day the morning session will be held at the Douglass Theatre at 12:00 M. and the afternoon session at the Druid Hill Avenue Y. M. C. A. at 3:00 P. M. The two evening sessions will go to the Bethel A. M. E. Church. In addition to these, special groups of persons cooperating with the Association will hold conferences in the interest of matters peculiar to their needs. Among the speakers will be Professor Kelly Miller, Mr. L. E. James, Mr. Leslie Pinckney Hill, Dr. William Pickens, and Dr. J. O. Spencer.

An effort will be made to arouse interest and to arrange for conducting throughout the country a campaign for collecting facts bearing on the Negro prior to the Civil War and during the Reconstruction period. The field is now being exploited by a staff of investigators of the Association. It is earnestly desired that all persons having documentary knowledge of these phases of Negro History will not only give the Association the advantage of such information, but will attend this Conference to devise plans for a more successful prosecution of this particular work.

Another concern of the Conference will be to stimulate interest in the collection of Negro folklore for which there is offered a prize of $200 for the best collection of tales, riddles, proverbs, sayings and songs, which have been heard in Negro homes. The aim is to study the Negro mind in relation to its environment at various periods in the history of the race and in different parts of the country. The students of a number of institutions of learning are already at work preparing their collections to compete for this prize, and it is hoped that a still larger number will do likewise. This special work is under the supervision of a committee composed of Dr. Elsie Clews Parsons, Assistant Editor of the *Journal of American Folklore*, Dr. Franz Boas, Professor of Anthropology in Columbia University and a member of the Executive Council of the Association, and Dr. Carter G. Woodson, Editor of THE JOURNAL OF NEGRO HISTORY.

THE JOURNAL
OF
NEGRO HISTORY

Vol. VIII., No. 3   July, 1923.

NEGRO SERVITUDE IN THE UNITED STATES*

Servitude Distinguished from Slavery

The first Negroes in the American colonies were called Africans, Blackamores, Moores, Negars, Negers, Negros,

* In the preparation of dissertation the following works were consulted: Ballagh, James Curtis, White Servitude in the Colony of Virginia (J. H. U. Studies, Thirty-first Series, 1913), and History of Slavery in Virginia (J. H. U. Studies, Twenty-fourth Series, 1902); Bassett, John Spencer, History of Slavery in North Carolina (J. H. U. Studies, Seventeenth Series, 1899), and Slavery and Servitude in the Colony of North Carolina (J. H. U. Studies, Fourteenth Series, 1896); Beatty, William Jennings, The Free Negroes in the Carolinas before 1860 (1920); Brackett, J. R., The Negro in Maryland (J. H. U. Studies, Seventh Series, Extra Volume, 1889); Brown, Alexander, The Genesis of the United States, 1605–1616, Two Volumes (1890), and The First Republic in America (1898); Bruce, Philip Alexander, Economic History of Virginia in the Seventeenth Century, Two Volumes (1896); Buckingham, J. S., The Slave States of America (1842); Calendar of Virginia State Papers and Other Manuscripts, 1652–1793, Edited by Wm. P. Palmer, Six Volumes (1875–86); Carroll, Bartholomew Rivers, Historical Collections of South Carolina (1836); Daniels, John, In Freedom's Birth Place, A Study of Boston Negroes (1914); Doyle, J. A., English Colonies in America, Five Volumes (1889); DuBois, W. E. Burghardt, The Suppression of the African Slave-Trade to the United States of America (1896); Eddis, Wm., Letters from America, 1769–77; Hazard, Willis P., Annals of Philadelphia and Pennsylvania in the Olden Time (1879); Henry, Howell Meadows, The Police Control of the Slave in South Carolina (1914); Henning, William Waller, Statutes at Large of Virginia, 1623–1792, Thirteen Volumes (1812); Hotten, J. C., Original Lists of Emigrants, 1600–1700 (1874); Hurd, John C., The Law of Freedom and Bondage in the United

Negroes, and the like.¹ It is highly probable that Negroes were brought to America by some of the early colonists before 1619, for Negroes had been in England since 1553.²

States, Two Volumes (1858-62); Jones, Hugh, *The Present State of Virginia* (1865); *Journal of Negro History*, edited by Carter G. Woodson (The Association for the Study of Negro Life and History); Lauber, Almon Wheeler, *Indian Slavery in Colonial Times Within Present Limits of the United States* (Columbia University Studies, Volume LIV (1913)); Washburn, Emory, *Massachusetts and Its Early History: Slavery as it once prevailed in Massachusetts;* McCormac, E. I., *White Servitude in Maryland 1634-1820* (J. H. U. Studies, Twenty-second Series, 1904); Moore, George H., *Notes on the History of Slavery in Massachusetts* (1866); Work, Monroe N., *Negro Year Book, An Annual Encyclopedia of the Negro;* Neill, E. D., *History of the Virginia Company of London, 1604-24* (1869) and *Virginia Carolorum, 1625-85;* Nell, Wm. C., *Colored Patriots of the American Revolution* (1855); Nieboer, Herman Jeremias, *Slavery as an Industrial Institution* (1900); Palfrey, John Gorham, *History of New England*, Five Volumes (1892); Phillips, Ulrich Bonnell, *American Negro Slavery* (1918); *Records of the Colony of Rhode Island and Providence Plantations in New England*, edited by John Russell Bartlett (1856-65); Rivers, William James, *A Sketch of the History of South Carolina to the Close of the Proprietary Government by the Revolution of 1719* (1856); Russell, John H., *The Free Negro in Virginia 1619-1865* (J. H. U. Studies, Thirty-first Series, 1913); Steiner, (Bernard C., *History of Slavery in Connecticut* (J. H. U. Studies, Series Eleven, 1893); Stevens, William Bacon, *A History of Georgia from its First Discovery by Europeans to the Adoption of the Present Constitution in 1798* (1848); Stroud, George M., *A Sketch of the Laws Relating to Slavery in the Several States of America* (1827); Thwaites, Ruben Gold, *The Colonies, 1492-1750;* Turner, Edward Raymond, *The Negro in Pennsylvania 1693-1861* (1910); *Winthrop's Journal: "History of New England" 1630-1649*, Three Volumes. Edited by James Kendall Hosmer.

¹ Many historians have substituted "slave" for "Negro." Russell, *Free Negroes in Virginia*, p. 16. White servants are also called slaves. Doyle, *History of English Colonies in America*, II, p. 387; Stevens, *History of Georgia*, pp. 289, 294.

² Several years before 1619, Negroes in England were sentenced to work in the colonies. "Two Moorish thieves [negroes] in London were sentenced to work in the American colonies. And they said no, they would rather die at once." Brown adds: "I do not know whether they were sent to Virginia or not." (*The First Republic in America*, p. 219. See also postnote 14.) Again, "I do not know that these negroes were the first brought to the colony of Virginia. I do not remember to have seen any contemporary account which says so. The accounts which we have even of the voyages of the company's ships are very incomplete, and we have scarcely an idea of the private trading voyages which would have been most apt to bring such 'purchas' to Virginia." Pory wrote in September, 1619: " 'In these five months of my continuance here, there have come at one time or another eleven sail of ships

James Otis said: "Our colonial charters made no difference between black and white."[3] Some of such early Negro settlers might have been brought over from Barbadoes or other islands. The English colonists often went to and from the mainland for settlement and trade, and by 1674 Barbadoes was a "flourishing state" with a white population of 50,000 and 100,000 "Negroes and colored."[4] Negroes, along with Spanish explorers, are known to have been in North and South Carolina, Florida, Alabama, New Mexico, and California as early as 1526, 1527, 1540, 1542, and 1537, respectively.[5] However, the first Negroes, thus far known, in the American colonies, were the "twenty negars" introduced at Jamestown, in 1619, by the Dutch frigate.[6]

The first status of these Negroes early imported is of some importance. Although the historians do not always mention the fact, there is nevertheless ample proof of the existence of Negro servitude in most of the American colonies. The servitude did not always precede slavery in every case, nor was it ever firmly established as slavery eventually became. Still it is an interesting fact that Negro servitude frequently preceded and sometimes followed Negro slavery. In colonies where servitude followed slavery, it was due to the fact that these colonies were founded after the change of Negro servitude into slavery was well advanced. Even here, servitude accompanied

into this river.' If he meant that these eleven ships came in after he did, at least three of them are not accounted for in our annals.'' Washburn, *Slavery as it once prevailed in Massachusetts*, pp. 198, 327.

[3] Nell, *Colored Patriots of the American Revolution*, p. 59.

[4] Rivers, *History of South Carolina*, p. 113; Buckingham, *Slave States of America*, I, p. 19.

[5] *The Journal of Negro History*, III, p. 33; Work, *Negro Year Book*, p. 152. "The second settler in Alabama was a Negro."

[6] Ballagh gives an interesting and the most reliable account of this ship and these Negroes. (*History of Slavery in Virginia*, p. 8.) A heated controversy took place over what should be done with the Negroes. "And so the people of her were all disposed of for the year to the use of the company till it could be truly known to whom the right lyeth." Brown, *The First Republic in America*, pp. 359, 369, 391, 325–27.

slavery. In some of the colonies, the question of priority resolves itself into the question of the priority of customary servitude to customary slavery. In this case, however, it is probable that servitude was first, even though slavery was first recognized in law. In certain instances, the records make it certain that servitude preceded slavery. This was the case in Virginia.

Several authorities have shown the extent to which the priority of Negro servitude has been recognized. "At first the African *slave* was looked upon as but an improved variety of indented servant whose term of labor was for life instead of a few years."[7] "As has been mentioned, some Negroes were bound as *slaves* for a term of years only."[8] The Negroes of 1619 and "others brought by early privateers were not reduced to slavery, but to limited servitude, a legalized status of Indian, white, and negro servants, preceding slavery in most, if not all, of the English mainland colonies."[9] "Negro and Indian servitude thus preceded negro and Indian slavery, and together with white servitude in instances continued even after the institution of slavery was fully developed."[10]

Furthermore, there is not the slightest evidence that the colonists were disposed to treat as slaves the first Negroes who landed in the colonies. They had no tradition of slavery in England at that time. "Whatever may have been the intent and hope of the persons in possession of the negroes as regards their ultimate enslavement, no attempt to do so legally seems for a long time to have been made.... for some reasons the notion of enslavement gained ground but slowly, and although conditions surrounding a negro or Indian in possession could easily make him a *defacto* slave, the colonist seems to have preferred to retain him only as a servant. . . ."[11] Servitude, on the other hand, was familiar enough, although not in the form which it

[7] Thwaites, *The Colonies*, p. 98.
[8] Daniels, *In Freedom's Birthplace*, p. 7.
[9] *New International Encyclopedia*, p. 166.
[10] Ballagh, *Hist. of Slavery in Va.*, p. 32.
[11] Ballagh, *Hist. of Slavery in Va.*, p. 31.

eventually assumed in the colonies. The attitude of the colonists, when they first became confronted with the Negro question, was the attitude of Queen Elizabeth and Hawkins when it was proposed to go to Africa to barter for African servants.[12]

It was just as true in the colonial days as now that the attitude which the community takes towards the Negro population is largely determined by their relative numbers. If the Negroes had been numerous in the colonies immediately after 1619, it is reasonable to suppose that their status would have been defined earlier and more sharply than it was. But the numbers were not there.[13] Six years after the introduction of the first Negroes in Virginia, there were but twenty-three in the colony. Meanwhile the white population was about 2500. All through the first half of the century importation of Negroes was of an "occasional nature."[14] Forty years after the first introduction there were but three hundred Negroes in the colony.[15] It was during the last quarter of the seventeenth century that the number of Negroes in Virginia showed a noticeable increase. By 1683 there were three thousand; between 1700 and 1750, the increase was even more noticeable.[16] In Maryland, Negroes were not extensively introduced until the eighteenth century.[17] In 1665 a few slaves were brought to North

[12] Washburn holds that the moral stamina of sturdy people seeking freedom argued against enslavement. *Slavery as it once prevailed in Mass.*, p. 194.

[13] "If twenty negroes came in 1619, as alleged, their increase was very slow, for according to a census of 16th of February, 1624, there were but twenty-two then in the colony." Neill, *Hist. of the Va. Co.*, p. 72.

"When the census was taken in January, 1625, there were only twenty persons of the African race in Virginia. . . ." *Virginia Carolorum*, pp. 15, 16, 22, 33, 40, 59, 225; Brown, *The Genesis of Am.*, II, p. 987.

[14] Ballagh, *History of Slavery in Virginia*, pp. 9–10.

[15] The group brought over in 1638 by Menefie was an unusually large number: "Menefie was now the leading merchant. On April 19, 1638, he entered 3,000 acres of land on account of 60 transports, of whom 23 were, as he asserts, 'negroes, I brought out of England.'" *Virginia Carolorum*, p. 187 note; Ballagh, *White Servitude in the Colony of Virginia*, p. 91 note.

[16] "Intended insurrections of negroes in 1710, 1722, 1730, bear witness to their alarming increase. . . ." *White Servitude in the Colony of Virginia*, p. 92 note.

[17] Brackett, *The Negro in Md.*, p. 38.

Carolina and it was not until 1700 and after that their number reached eight hundred.[18] After their introduction by Sir John Yeamans in 1671 it was not until 1708 that the number of Negroes in South Carolina became a considerable part of the population.[19] In Pennsylvania, as early as 1639, a number of Negroes served a Swedish company. How many there were is not known.[20] In 1644, 1657, 1664 and 1677 several Negroes singly and in groups are known to have been in the region which afterwards became Pennsylvania. In this colony they were spoken of as "numerous" in 1702, but numerous then did not mean so many. Later their number is noticeable.[21] In Massachusetts, from 1638, when the Salem ship, *Desire*, returned from the West Indies with cotton, tobacco, and Negroes, to the close of the seventeenth century the number of Negroes was comparatively small.[22] Josselyn saw Negroes in the colony when he visited it in 1638-39.[23] In 1678, there were 200 in the colony and in 1678 Governor Andros reported that there were but a few. In 1680, Governor Bradstreet said no blacks or slaves had been brought in the colony in the space of fifty years except between forty and fifty one time and two or three now and then. In the nine years from 1698 to 1707, two hundred arrived and in 1735 there were 2,600 in the Province.[24] Immediately after 1619, then, the number of Negroes scattered throughout the colonies was comparatively small. It seems likely that their condition may be described as that of servitude, which at that time universally prevailed, rather than slavery.

[18] Bassett, *Slavery and Servitude in the Col. of N. C.*, pp. 18-20.

[19] Henry, *Police Control of the Slave in S. C.*, p. 3.

[20] Post, p. 262, note 10.

[21] Turner, *The Negro in Penn.*, pp. 1-3.

[22] Moore, *Notes on the History of Slavery in Mass.*, pp. 5, 48; Palfrey, *Hist. of N. E.*, p. 30.

[23] "They have store of children, and are well accommodated with Servants; —— of these some are English, others Negroes: of the English there are can eat till they sweat, and work till they freeze; and of the females they are like Mrs. Wintus paddocks, very tinder fingered in cold weather." *Account of Two Voyages to N. E.*, pp. 28, 139-140.

[24] Moore, *Notes on the Hist. of Slavery in Mass.*, pp. 48-49.

We are likely to think of the status of the early Negroes in America as having been inherited or transplanted. Far from this, the status of the Negro in the early period, like slavery itself, was purely a local development.[25] The status of the early Negroes shows unmistakably that it developed in lines parallel to that of white servitude.[26] The motives which determined the growth of white servitude and Negro slavery are peculiar to the social and economic conditions of the colony of Virginia and its neighbors, whose inhabitants were primarily imported settlers and laborers. White servitude and black servitude were but different aspects of the same institution. As white servitude disappeared, Negro slavery succeeded it.[27]

The reason the early Negroes were not given at once the status of slaves is that there was at this time no legal basis for slavery. The Dutch who settled in New York seem to have defined the status of the Negro slave on the civil law of Holland. In the English colonies it was a local development.[28] Clearly, the ownership in the Negroes was widely recognized and practiced in custom and in law. It is equally clear, however, that white servitude and some form of black servitude existed for a long time side by side with Negro slavery. This recognition of slavery in custom and practice, moreover, makes its appearance near the date of the statutory recognition of slavery by the colonies.[29] Hence, the dates of this statutory recognition

[25] Ballagh, *Hist. of Slavery in Virginia*, pp. 2, 3, 34.

[26] "The main ideas on which servitude was based originated in the early history of Virginia as a purely English colonial development before the other colonies were formed. The system was adopted in them with its outline already defined, requiring only local legislation to give it specific character. . . ." (Ballagh, *White Servitude in the Colony of Virginia*, p. 9.) The status of servitude, customary and legal, similar to that given the Negroes in Virginia is as a rule met with in several of the colonies.

[27] *Post*, p. 254, note 33.

[28] Ballagh, *Hist. of Slavery in Va.*, pp. 28, 29, 34.

[29] White servitude had recognition in statute law by 1630–36 in Massachusetts, by 1643 in Connecticut, by 1647 in Rhode Island, by 1619 in Virginia, by 1637 in Maryland, by 1665 in North Carolina, by 1682 in Pennsylvania, and by 1732 in Georgia. Ballagh, *Hist. of Slavery in Va.*, pp. 36, 37. Russell, *The Free Negro in Va.*, pp. 18, 19, 22, 29.

fix the "upper limit to the period" in which slavery may be said to have had a beginning.[30] In a number of the colonies, not only is absolute ownership in Negroes, hence slavery, conspicuous, by the absence of any records of it, but the priority of Negro servitude and of a free Negro class is established. Ownership in the services but not of the person was characteristic of both whites and Negroes in this early period.[32]

"Prior to 1619 every inhabitant of Virginia was practically a 'servant manipulated in the interest of the company, held in servitude beyond a stipulated term.'" "It was not an uncommon practice in the early period for shipmasters to sell white servants to the planters." By 1619 servitude was already recognized in the law of Virginia.[33]

In this early period the Company, as represented locally by its officials, was the sole controlling and directing power of the colony.[34] The Company was at the outset doubtful about the advantages of bringing in slaves, partly because they were not sure of the value of slave labor, and partly because they feared the Negro would not become a permanent settler and so contribute to the building up and defending the colony. The opposition of the trustees of Georgia to the importation of Negroes was rested on these

[30] Statutory recognition of slavery by the American colonies occurred as follows: Massachusetts, 1641; Connecticut, 1650; Virginia, 1661; Maryland, 1663; New York and New Jersey, 1664; South Carolina, 1682; Pennsylvania and Rhode Island, 1700; North Carolina, 1715; and Georgia, 1755. Prior to these dates the legal status of all subject Negroes was that of servants, and their rights, duties, and disabilities were regulated by legislation the same as, or similar to, that applied to white servants. Ballagh, *Hist. of Servitude in Va.*, pp. 34, 35.

[31] Russell, *The Free Negroes in Va.*, p. 29.

[32] Turner, *The Negro in Penn.*, p. 25; Ballagh, *Hist. of Slavery in Va.*, pp. 30, 31.

[33] Ante, note 30: "It was but natural then that they should be absorbed in a growing system which spread to all the colonies and for nearly a century furnished the chief supply for colonial labor." Ballagh, *White Servitude in the Colony of Va.*, pp. 14, 27, 49. Ballagh, *Hist. of Slavery in Va.*, pp. 32.

[34] The Company secured servants for the colony. Stevens, *History of Ga.*, p. 290; Ballagh, *White Servitude in the Col. of Va.*, p. 15.

grounds.³⁵ Early legislation in order to prohibit the trade in the colonies imposed duties on slaves imported.³⁶ Moreover, it appears that the Company generally held and worked the Negroes, who were purchased, in the interest of the government, frequently distributing them among the officers and planters. This was done, for example, in the island colony, the Bermudas, in Virginia, and in Providence Island.³⁷

Established and universal as white servitude was it not only became the model of Negro servitude but also decidedly influenced its transition to slavery. When Negro servitude passed into slavery, it was white servitude that lent that slavery the mild character which it possessed until the early part of the nineteenth century.³⁸

The earliest authorized effort of England for Negro servants further elucidates this point. In 1562, Sir John Hawkins proposed to take Negroes from Africa and sell them. Queen Elizabeth did not at first approve Hawkins' plan but questioned the justice of it. Hawkins argued that bringing the Africans from a wild and barren

---

³⁵ The Trustees of Georgia held out on account of philanthropic motives. See Du Bois, *Suppression of the Slave Trade*, pp. 7, 8, 26; Declaration of one of the trustees, Stevens, *Hist. of Ga.*, p. 287.

³⁶ Moore, *Notes on the History of Slavery in Mass.*, p. 50. Du Bois, *Suppression of African Slave Trade*, p. 15.

³⁷ In Providence in 1633, "it was recommended that twenty or thirty negroes be introduced for public work, and that they be separated among various families of officers and industrious planters to prevent the formation of plots. Some of these negroes received wages and purchased their freedom, and the length of servitude seems to have been dependent on the time of conversion to Christianity." Lefroy, *The History, of the Bermudaes*, p. 219. Ballagh, *Hist. of Slavery in Va.*, pp 29, 30, notes.

The Dutch dealt with the early Negroes in a similar way. "In practice the heavy duty imposed by the Company seems to have discouraged any large importation. As a natural consequence, too, most of those imported seem to have been in the employment of the Company. Thus we learn that the fort at New Amsterdam was mainly built by negro labor. The Company seems wisely to have made arrangements whereby its slaves should be gradually absorbed in the free population. In 1644 an ordinance was passed emancipating the slaves of the Company after a fixed period of service." Doyle, *Eng. Cols. in Am.*, IV, p. 49.

³⁸ Ballagh, *Hist. of Slavery in Va.*, p. 33.

country would be eminently just and beneficial to the Africans and to the world. He seemed not to have had the purpose of selling the Africans into perpetual servitude: "Hawkins told her, that he considered it as an act of humanity to carry men from a worse condition to a better . . . from a state of wild barbarism to another where they might share the blessings of civil society and Christianity; from poverty, nakedness and want to plenty and felicity. He assured her that in no expedition where he had command should any Africans be carried away without their own free will and consent, except such captives as were taken in war and doomed to death; . . . . Indeed it would appear that Hawkins had no idea of perpetual slavery, but expected that they would be treated as free servants after they had by their labor brought their masters an equivalent for the expenses of their purchase."[39] After this, Hawkins received approval and support from the Queen, and with three ships and crews he went on his trip to Africa.

Upon his arrival he began traffic with the natives. He sought at first to persuade the blacks to go with him, offering them glittering rewards. When the natives did not respond so readily to his entreaty, members of his crew, under the influence of rum, undertook to coerce the Africans.[40] Hawkins sought to dissuade them and reminded the men of his promise to the Queen. They finally succeeded in getting on board a number of Africans and set sail for the Spanish islands where the Africans were to be sold as servants.[41]

The early Negroes of Virginia, moreover, were servants. On the status of "the 1619 Negroes" historians are uncertain, but the popular conception of the situation is undoubtedly erroneous. The Dutch frigate sold the Negroes to the Company which controlled and distributed them. Some of them were clearly retained by the officers while

[39] Carroll, *Hist. Coll.*, I, p. 27.
[40] *Ibid.*, p. 29.
[41] *Ibid.*, p. 29.

others "were put to work upon public lands to support the governor and other officers of the government." There is no evidence that any of these Negroes were made slaves, while evidence that they were servants is abundant.[42]

The statutes of Virginia up to 1661 indicate the existence of Negro servitude rather than that of slavery.[43] In 1630, whites were whipped for fornication with the blacks "before an assembly of *negroes.*" In 1639 and 1640, all persons except *Negroes* were to be provided with arms and ammunition or be fined.[44] Up to that time the acts do not indicate slavery. The act of 1655 refers to Indian slavery.[45] The act of 1659 does not show that Negro slavery existed in the colony, but apparently aims to prevent it.[46] No other acts, in the statutes, throw any light on the status of the Negro before the act of 1661. This acts reads, "In case any English servant shall run away in company with any negroes who are incapable of making satisfaction by addition of time, be it enacted that the English so running away in company with them shall serve for the time of the said negroes absence as they are to do for their own by a former act."[47] The inferences from this act are three: some of

[42] Russell, *The Free Negro in Va.*, pp. 16, 23; Ballagh, *Hist. of Slavery in Va.*, p. 29 notes; Brown, *The First Republic in Am.*, p. 326.

Thomas Jefferson said, "the right to these negroes was common, or, perhaps they lived on a footing with the whites, who, as well as themselves, were under absolute direction of the president." Russell, *The Free Negro in Va.*, p. 24.

[43] *Ibid.*, 23, 24; Ballagh, *History of Slavery in Va.*, 28, 31; Phillips, *Am. Negro Slavery*, p. 75.

[44] Henning, I, pp. 146, 226.

[45] The first time the term "slave" is used in the statutes was in these words: "If the Indians shall bring in any children as gages of their good and quiet intentions to us, . . . that we will not use them as slaves." Henning, I, p. 296.

[46] In Henning, *Statutes* I, p. 540, it is said: "That *if* the said Dutch or other foreigners shall import any negroes, they the said Dutch or others shall, for the tobacco really produced by the sale of the said negro, pay only the impost of two shillings per hogshead, the like being paid by our own nation."

[47] Henning, II, p. 26.

the Negroes in the colony were slaves, others free, and still others servants. The repetition of this act the following year made provision for runaway Negro servants also by a change of statement.[48]

Notwithstanding the statutes, Russel found that in the records of county courts dating from 1632 to 1661 negroes are designated as 'servants,' 'negro servants,' or simply as 'negroes,' but never in the records were the Negroes termed 'slaves'." From the context of the records, moreover, "servant" was distinctly meant and not "slave." Again, according to the census taken in 1624-1625, there were twenty-three persons of the African race in Virginia and they are listed as "servants."[49] In several musters of settlements the names of Negroes appear under the heading, "Servants"; sometimes only "Negro" appears.[50] The General Court in October, 1625, had be-

[48] Russell, *The Free Negro in Va.*, p. 20, note 13.

[49] *Ibid.*, pp. 23, 24; Hotten, *List of Immigrants to Am.*, pp. 202, etc. The "*Lists of the Living and Dead in Virginia*, Feb. 16th, 1623," shows that there were twenty or more Negroes in the Colony; these Negroes are referred to as servants not slaves. *Col. Records of Va.*, p. 37, etc.

[50] "Captain Francis West, His Muster.
****
Servants
****

John Pedro, A Neger, aged 30, in the *Swan*, 1623."
Va. Carolorum, p. 15.
"Muster of Sir George Yeardley, Kt.
****
Servants
****

Thomas Barnett, 16, in the *Elsabeth*, 1620
Theophilus Bereston, in the *Treasuror*, 1614
Negro Men, 3.
Negro Women, 5.
Susan Hall, in the *William* and *Thomas*, 1608
Ibid., p. 16.
"Muster of Capt. William Tucker, Elizabeth City.
****
Servants
****

Antoney, Negro
Isabell, Negro
William, theire child, baptised"

Ibid., p. 40; see a muster also on page 22.

fore it for the first time a question involving the legal status of the Negro in America. A Negro named Brass had been brought to the colony by the captain of a ship. Upon handing down the decision as to what should be done with Brass, since his master had died, the Court "ordered that he should belong to Sir Francis Wyatt, Governor," evidently as servant.[51] Anthony Johnson and Mary, his wife, whose names appeared as servants in the census mentioned above, were, at sometime before 1652, given their freedom from servitude, for in that year they were exempted from payment of taxes by the county court on account of the burning of their home. The order of the court in reference to Johnson and his wife mentioned that "they have been inhabitants in Virginia *above* thirty years." According to this, they had been in the colony at least from 1621 which approaches 1619. It appears that they were among the first Negroes sold at Jamestown. And this, with the understanding that they were not free at first establishes quite well their original status as servants as well as that of the 1619 Negroes and other Negroes in the colony.

The free Negro, Anthony Johnson, in 1653 owned John Castor, another Negro of Northampton County, as his indented servant. In 1655, a Negro was bound to serve George Light for a period of five years.[52] The court record of the discharge of Francis Pryne in 1656 is an example of the discharge certificate of Negro servants:

"I Mrs. Jane Elkonhead . . . have hereunto sett my hand yt ye aforesd Pryne [a negro] shall bee discharged from all hindrance of servitude (his child) or any [thing] yt doth belong to ye sd Pryne his estate.

Jane Elkonhead"[53]

"On the 25 of January, 1624-5, a muster of Mr. Edward Bennett's servants at Wariscoyak was taken, and the number was twelve, two of whom were negroes." *Va. Carolorum*, 225 note. See also Brown, *The Genesis of Am.*, II, 987.

[51] *Virginia Carolorum*, pp. 33, 34; Ballagh, *Hist. of Slavery in Virginia*, p. 30.

[52] Russell, *The Free Negro in Virginia*, pp. 24, 26, 32.

[53] *Ibid.*, pp. 26, 29.

In some cases, as it was with the white servants, Negroes were given written indentures, of which Russell gives several examples. It was an early practice of the colony to allow "head rights," a certain number of acres of land for every servant imported. In 1651 "head rights" were allowed on the importation of a Negro whose name was Richard Johnson. "Only three years later a patent calling for one hundred acres of land was issued to this negro for importing two other persons. Hence, it appears that Richard Johnson came in as a free negro or remained in a condition of servitude for not more than three years."[54] It was a practice also of those who held servants to allow them the privilege of raising hogs and poultry and of tilling a small plot of ground. The court records show that by this means John Geaween, Emanuel Dregis, and Bashasar Farando, as Negro servants, between 1649 and 1652, accumulated property. Again, there are cases illustrating that the Negro servant received "freedom dues" as the white servants at the close of the term of service.[55] Thus the first and early Negroes of Virginia were servants, not slaves. They were not only servants at first, but also servants in general for a period of years.

Negro Servitude and its Priority in other Colonies

Slavery received statutory recognition in the colony of Maryland in 1663, and in North Carolina in 1715. White servitude had long existed in these colonies, receiving statutory recognition in Maryland as early as 1637, and in North Carolina in 1665. Servitude, therefore, had ample time for local definition "before slavery entered upon either its customary or legal devlopment."[1] Ballagh holds that in these colonies, also, Negro servitude historically preceded slavery.[2] In Maryland, particularly, along with Virginia and Massachusetts, the "circumstances sur-

[54] *Ibid.*, pp. 25, 26.
[55] *Ibid.*, pp. 22, 28, 34; Bruce, *Econ. Hist. of Virginia.* II, pp. 52, 53.
[1] Ballagh, pp. 36–37.
[2] *Ibid.*, 32.

rounding the enactments defining slavery'' indicate a natural transition from Negro servitude to slavery. Since servitude existed in these states, it seems probable, from analogy with conditions in other parts of the country, that the early Negroes in these colonies were servants.³

Negro servitude preceded Negro slavery in Massachusetts. This servitude existed legally and underwent a period of development. After the recognition of slavery in 1641, Negro servitude continued along with slavery and in a more pronounced manner.⁴ The early inhabitants of Massachusetts were hostile to the introduction of slavery. This attitude was, perhaps, responsible for the milder form which Negro bondage first assumed, for "the facts of history . . . seem to establish this conclusion, that slavery never was in harmony with the public sentiment of the colony."⁵ The Salem ship, the *Desire*, brought to the Colony, February 26, 1638, "some cotton, tobacco, and negroes." This cargo had been taken on by Mr. Pierce of the *Desire*, at Providence Island, evidently in exchange for fifteen Indian boys and two women, taken as prisoners in the Pequod War.⁶ At this time, it was common to purchase servants from shipmasters and merchants, and so it is not certain that the Negroes brought back by Mr. Pierce were slaves. At Providence, moreover, Negroes had the status of servants.⁷ When Josselyn visited New England in 1638–39, he saw in Boston servants, English and Ne-

---

³ *Ibid.*, 37; Beatty, *The Free Negroes in the Carolinas before 1860*, p. 3.

The children, resulting from the intermixture and intermarriage of the races were likewise servants in these two colonies. Stroud, *Laws Relating to Slavery*, pp. 8–9.

⁴ Servitude was recognized in statute law in this colony by 1630–36. Ballagh, *Hist. of Slavery in Va.*, pp. 32, 33, 36.

⁵ Washburn, *Slavery as It Once Prevailed in Mass.*, p. 193.

⁶ Providence Isle was "an island in the Caribbean, off the Nicaraguan coast. In 1630 Charles I granted it, by a patent similar to that of Massachusetts, to a company of Englishmen, mostly Puritans, who held it till 1641, when the Spaniards captured it." Winthrop's *Journal*, II, pp. 227, 228, 260; Moore, *Notes on the Hist. of Slavery in Mass.*, p. 5.

⁷ Ballagh, *Hist. of Slavery in Va.*, note 2, quoted from *Ca'endar State Papers*, pp. 160, 168, 229.

groes.[8] In 1641, after the adoption of the Body of Liberties, a master of a ship brought two Negroes for sale into slavery, but was compelled by the court to give them up. These Negroes were then sent back to their native country. In 1646, the General Court passed an act "against the heinous and crying sin of man-stealing." In this colony "slaves" testified against white men in court and, for a long time after 1652, served in the militia.[9] Again, beginning with 1700, Judge Sewall and the Quakers started their memorable work against slavery. Charles Sumner said concerning slavery in Massachusetts: "Her few slaves were merely for a term of years, or for life."[10]

The Bond of Liberty, adopted in 1641, evidently made provision for servitude.[11] Negroes were held as servants under this provision. During the entire colonial period until 1791, they were rated as polls, as, for example, in the tax laws, in 1718, which provided that "all Indian, negro and mulatto servants *for a term of years* were to be numbered and rated as Polls, and not as Personal Estate."[12]

Prior to 1700, moreover, Negroes had the status of servants in Pennsylvania. In the region of the Delaware River, which became a part of Pennsylvania, the Dutch had a few Negroes with them in 1636. In 1639, also, a number of Negroes worked under the New Netherlands Company on the South River.[13] It is not definitely known

---

[8] Ante, p. 252, note 23.
[9] Washburn, *Slavery as It Once Prevailed in Mass.*, pp. 208, 215.
[10] Nell, *Colored Patriots in Am. Rev.*, p. 37.
[11] "There shall *never* be *any* Bond Slavery, Villinage, or Captivity among us, *unless* it be lawful Captives taken in just Wars, and such strangers as willingly sell themselves, or are sold to us. And these shall have all the liberties and Christian usages which the law of God, established in Israel concerning such persons, doth morally require. This exempts none from servitude, who shall be judged thereto by authority." *Massachusetts Hist. Coll.*, 28, p. 231; Palfrey, *Hist. of New England*, II, p. 30.
[12] Moore, *Notes on Slavery in Mass.*, pp. 62, 63–64, 248.
[13] "A judgment is obtained, before the authorities at Manhattan, against one Coinclisse, for wounding a soldier at Fort Amsterdam. He is condemned to serve the company along with the blacks, to be sent by the first ship to South River, pay a fine to the fiscal, and damages to the wounded soldier. This seems to be the first intimation of blacks being in this part of the

that these Negroes were servants, although the circumstances indicate that they were. The same is true of the Negroes in the employment of the Dutch during this very early period. Provision was apparently made for their gradual absorption by the free population. As late as 1663, there existed laws which "granted them a qualified form of freedom, working alternate weeks, one for themselves, one for the Company."[14] Among the Swedes, also, in the region of the Delaware, were a number of Negroes. Just after Rising had come to the region as head of the Swedish Company, in 1654, he issued an ordinance that "after a certain period Negroes should be absolutely free." In Penn's charter to the Free Society of Traders, in 1682, there was a provision that if the inhabitants "held blacks they should make them free at the end of fourteen years. . . ." Benjamin Furley, also, vigorously opposed holding Negroes longer than eight years.[15] The Friends of Germantown in 1688, made strong protests against slavery; and in 1693, George Keith declared that the masters should let the Negroes go free after a reasonable term of service.[16] Later on, children of white mothers and slave fathers became servants for a term of years, and the same was true of the children of free Negro mothers and slave fathers.[17]

After 1700, Negro servants were a common and well-recognized class in Pennsylvania. Negroes who were "un-

country. . . . Director Van Twiller having been charged, after Kiet's arrival, with mismanagement. . . . Another witness asserts he had in his custody for Van Twiller, at Fort Hope and Nassau, twenty-four to thirty goats, and that three negroes bought by the director in 1636 were since employed in his private service." Hazard, *Annals of Penn.*, pp. 49-50; Turner, *The Free Negro in Penn.*, p. 1.

It is noteworthy that the Negroes among the Dutch were generally under the supervision of the Company or worked for officers of the Company.

[14] Ante, p. 255, note 37.

[15] "Let no blacks be brought in directly, and if any come out of Virginia, Maryld. (or elsewhere erased) in families that have formerly brought them elsewhere Let them be declared (as in the west jersey constitutions) free at 8 years end." Turner, *The Negro in Penn.*, p. 21, notes 13. 14.

[16] *Ibid.*, p. 66.

[17] *Ibid.*, pp. 24, 25; Stroud, *Laws Relating to Slavery*, pp. 9-10.

able or unwilling to support themselves" were bound by the court for the term of one year.[18] All children of free Negroes were bound out until twenty-one or twenty-four years. Mulatto children "who were not slaves for life" were bound out "until they were twenty-eight years of age." The abolition act of 1780 provided among other things that "all future children of registered slaves should become servants until they were twenty-eight."[19] And again, Negroes manumitted could indenture themselves until twenty-eight.

Negro servants were generally subject to the laws which governed the white servitude; but they were subject further to other laws which gave to the Negro servants a status between that of the white servants and Negro slaves. Negro servants were apprenticed for a longer period than white servants; and such servants were object of a considerable interstate traffic, people from other states selling them into Pennsylvania. They were often apprenticed and generally given some form of freedom dues. So entrenched was Negro servitude here that in 1780 there were probably a greater number of servants in Pennsylvania than slaves.[20]

In Rhode Island Negro servitude preceded and passed into slavery.[21] Although as early as 1652 the practice of buying Negroes for service or slaves for life existed in this colony, this was not sanctioned by law. On the other hand, white servitude was clearly recognized in statute law of 1647.[22] In 1652 the legally established servitude,

[18] Hurd, *The Law of Freedom and Bondage*, I, 290; Turner, *The Free Negro in Penn.*, p. 92.

[19] "On the 1st of March, 1780, before the war of the Revolution was closed, the Assembly of Pensylvania passed an act declaring that negro and mulatto children whose mothers were slaves, and who were born after the passage of the act, should be free, and that slavery as to them should be forever abolished. But it was declared that such children should be held as servants, under the same terms as indentured servants, until the age of twenty-eight, when they should be free. . . ." Watson, *Annals of Philadelphia and Penn. in Olden Times*, pp. 468–469.

[20] *Ibid.*, pp. 93, 94, 98, 101.

[21] Ballagh, *Hist. of Slavery in Va.*, p. 32.

[22] *Ibid.*, p. 36.

as well as the attitude of the colonists, undoubtedly influenced the passing of a law to prohibit slavery and provide for servitude. This law said: "Whereas, there is a common course practiced amongst English men to buy negers, to that end they may have them for service or slaves forever; for the preventinge of such practices among us, let it be ordered, that no blacke mankind or white being forced by covenant bond, or otherwise, to serve any man or his assighness longer than ten yeares, or until they come to bee twentie four yeares of age, if they bee taken in under fourteen, for the time of their cominge within the liberties of this Collinie. And at the end or terme of ten yeares to sett them free, as the manner is with the English servants. And that man that will not let them goe free, or shall sell them away elsewhere, to that end that they may bee enslaved to others for a long time, he or they shall forfeit to the Collonie forty pounds."[23] Although this law was enforced for a time, it soon became a dead letter, for after 1708, when slavery received sanction by statute, buying and selling Negroes was practiced generally.[24]

The first few Negroes in Connecticut were servants along with a few Indian and white servants. It was due, no doubt, to the paucity of the Negroes — there were in 1680 not above thirty in the colony — that they became servants. However, as this number increased, their status became gradually that of slaves by custom. Because of the fear of treachery from the Negro and Indian servants, the General Court, in 1680, ordered that "neither Indian nor negar servants shall be required to train, watch or ward in the Colony."[25] Evidently some of the servants very early had served out their time and had been freed, for by a law, in 1690, "Negro, mulatto, or Indian servants," "suspected persons" and free Negroes who were found wandering could be taken up and brought before a magistrate.[26] An

[23] R. I., *Col. Rec.*, I, p. 243.
[24] Du Bois, *Suppression of the Slave Trade*, p. 34.
[25] Hurd, *Law of Freedom and Bondage*, I, p. 270; Steiner, *Hist. of Slavery in Conn.*, p. 12.
[26] Conn., *Col. Rec.*, XV, p. 40.

act in 1711 made provision for the care of Negro servants and others who came to want after they had served out their time. "An act relating to slaves, and such in particular as shall happen to become servants for life, enacts that all slaves set at liberty by their owners, and all negro, mulatto, and Spanish Indians, who are servants to masters for time, in case they shall come to want after they shall be so set at liberty or the time of their service be expired, they shall be relieved at the cost of their masters." In fact, slavery of the "absolute, rigid kind" never existed to any extent in Connecticut.[27]

THE TRANSITION FROM WHITE SERVITUDE TO SLAVERY

Let us now direct our attention to the change from servitude to slavery. It is well to note here, however, that white servitude did not embrace the chief features of slavery. Nieboer defines a slave as "a man who is the property or possession of another man, and forced to work for him." Again, "slavery is the fact that one man is the property or possession of another."[1] White servitude lacked the final and formal feature of "property," namely complete "possession," and consequently never included either perpetual service or the transmission of servile condition to offspring, although during the first half of its development in the colonies, servitude tended to assume the character of slavery.[2,3]

The servitude that existed up to 1619 underwent change until it finally crystallized into indented servitude. The conditions were not as bad as the testimony of colony servants and observers of the period would indicate, and yet where there were so many references to it the condition evidently obtained.[4] In enlisting new settlers for the colonies, the Company "issued broadsides and pamphlets,

[27] Stroud, *Laws Relating to Slavery*, p. 11, note; Hurd, *Law of Freedom and Bondage*, p. 271.
[1] Nieboer, *Slavery as an Industrial Institution*, p. 42.
[2] Doyle, *Hist. of Eng. Col. in Am.*, p. 385.
[3] Ballagh, *Hist. of Slavery in Va.*, p. 42.
[4] McCormac, *White Servitude in Md.*, pp. 9, 60, 61, 63.

with specious promises, which, however honest its purpose, were certainly never fulfilled."[5] In Virginia in 1613, colonists of 1607 who had served out the term of their original five-year contract were either retained in servitude or granted a tenancy burdened with oppressive and unfair obligations. The changed land policy of 1616 brought upon the colony servants further disadvantages. Before March, 1617, when the men of the Charles City Hundred demanded and were granted their "long desired freedome from that general and common servitude," no freedom had been granted to the colonists. After this until 1619, it was only through "extraordinary payment" that freedom was obtained.[6] Many of these colonists of Virginia, moreover, were retained in servitude until 1624 when the Company dissolved.[7]

Other incidents, growing out of the servant's role, tended to make the condition of servitude more rigid. In order to make the system of labor under the Company successful, Lord Delaware, in 1610, organized the colony into a "labor force under commanders and overseers"; and close watch over the men and their work was accordingly maintained. "The colonists were marched to their daily work in squads and companies under officers, and the severest penalties were prescribed for a breach of discipline or neglect of duty. A persistent neglect of labor was to be punished by galley service from one to two years. Penal servitude was also instituted; for 'petty offences' they worked 'as slaves in irons for a term of years' "; and there

[5] Ballagh, *White Servitude in the Col. of Va.*, p. 15.
[6] *Ibid.*, pp. 19, 31, 24.
[7] "We see, then, that the colonist, while in theory only a Virginia member of the London Company, and entitled to equal rights and privileges with other members or adventurers, was, from the nature of the case, practically debarred from exercising these rights. . . . He was kept by force in the colony, and could have no communication with his friends in England. . . . Under the arbitrary administration of the Company and of its deputy governors he was as absolutely at its disposal as a servant at his master's. His conduct was regulated by corporal punishment or more extreme measures. He could be hired out by the Company to private persons, or by the Governor for his personal advantage." *Ibid.*, p. 26.

were whipping, "hangings, shooting, breaking on the wheel, and even burning alive."[8]

It may be observed from references made to this early servitude that, generally, it was harsh. We read: "Having most of them served the colony six or seven years in that 'general slavery' "; " 'three years slavery' to the colony"; "noe waye better than slavery"; "rather than be reduced to live under like government we desire his Magestie that Commissioners may be sent over with authority to hang us"; and "Sold as a d—— slave."[9] Undoubtedly, these references are not all true; yet, they are not altogether false. At least they indicate that the conditions of this servitude approached slavery.[10] Out of these, informal "slavery" and unsettled conditions of early servitude, indented servitude developed.

As a general rule, every advantage was taken of the servant by the servant-dealers and masters. Opportunity to hold the servant longer than the period allowed by law or to extend his service was not infrequently seized upon, for the laxity of the system and the need of labor in the colonies made this a natural consequence. During the first period of servitude, the term of service in many cases was not prescribed in the indentures; and sometimes servants were brought over without indentures, or with only verbal contracts.[11] Thus trouble about the length of their term of service arose, especially in connection with the servants who did not have indentures. Circumstances indicate that in the interpretation of law and the facts, the master generally triumphed.[12] It was in 1638-39 that Maryland took the first definite step to prevent unfair treatment of servants by their masters. In 1654 it became necessary again

[8] *Ibid.*, p. 23.
[9] Ballagh, *White Servitude in the Col. of Va.*, pp. 23, 24, 25, 43 note.
[10] McCormac, *White Servitude in Md.*, pp. 48, 49.
[11] *Ibid.*, pp. 38, 43; Ballagh, *White Servitude in the Col. of Va.*, pp. 40, 49.
[12] "Where no contract but a verbal one existed there was always room for controversy between master and servant, each trying to prove an agreement that would be to his advantage." *Ibid.*, p. 50.

to pass a law determining the servant's age and length of service. Virginia enacted similar measures in 1643 and 1657. Still, when the servants were ignorant, "which was usually the case," or could not speak the English language, the master took advantage of their shortcomings.[13] Notwithstanding the repeated efforts of the courts and assembly to protect the servant in his relation to the master, the lucrative practice of extending a servant's term, which became customary in the case of Indian and Negro servants, proved a significant factor in the degradation of white servitude.

Under the system of servitude, the conduct of the servant necessarily bore a close relation to the interests of the master. When the servant stole, ran away, "unlawfully assembled" or "plotted," indulged in fornication, spent unusual time in social intercourse, or was secretly married, the master as a rule suffered some loss. And for protection of the master, methods of punishment were resorted to, the character, definiteness, and attendant circumstances of which tended to reduce the servant to the status of a slave.

As the servant had no money with which to pay fines, some other method of punishment had to be used. Corporal punishment of a harsh character appears to have been established. Practiced at first by individuals, it soon became a general custom, and finally found its way into the laws of the colonies. During the period prior to indented servitude, instances of severe whipping of servants are numerous.[14] The first colony law which gave the master the privilege of regulating the servant's conduct in this

[13] "Where the servants were ignorant, which was usually the case, it was to the advantage of the master that there should be no written contract, as there was then a chance of extending the term of service." McCormac, *White Servitude in Md.*, p. 44.

"The Palatines and other German races, who, in the later years formed nearly all of the servant population, knew little of the laws and language and were an easy prey to the abuses of traders and harsh masters. They had been used to very little liberty at home and were slow to assert their rights in America." *Ibid.*, p. 61.

[14] Ante, p. 268.

manner, however, appeared in 1619.[15] Corporal punishment then gradually gained ground and won sanction by the colonial courts. A law in Virginia provided in 1662 "for the erecting of a whipping post in every county" and the General Assembly of this colony, in 1688, reassured the master of his right to whip the servant. All along this right was so much abused[16] that it was restrained in Virginia. In 1705 an act ordered the master not to whip the servant "immoderately"; and to whip a Christian white servant naked, an order from a justice of peace had to be obtained.[17] Several other colonies similarly restrained the right to whip.[18]

Another method of punishment that gradually hardened the conditions of servitude was the addition of time to the term of the servant. This evidently originated in the custom of the Company to prescribe as penalty for offense "service to the colony in public work."[19] This method of punishment was extensively used throughout the colonies. Sometimes the length of additional service was left to the discretion of the master, but this was so abused that the government saw fit to make regulations, which, however, themselves were not free from harshness.[20]

At first the servants undoubtedly enjoyed the right of marriage, but as this proved a source of much inconvenience and loss to the master, since the men servants lost time, stole food and other provisions, and the women servants lost time during pregnancy and in rearing children, laws restricting marriage of servants were enacted in the col-

[15] Henning, *Statutes at Large*, I, pp. 127, 130, 192; Ballagh, *White Servitude in the Col. of Va.*, p. 45.
[16] *Ibid.*, p. 77.
[17] *Ibid.*, pp. 58, 59.
[18] Bassett, *Slavery and Servitude in the Col. of N. C.*, p. 81.
[19] "In this we have the germ of addition of time, a practice which later became the occasion of a very serious abuse of the servants rights by the addition of terms altogether incommensurate with the offenses for which they were imposed." Ballagh, *White Servitude in the Col. of Va.*, p. 45.
[20] Henning, *Statutes at Large*, I, p. 438, II, p. 114, III, pp. 87, 140, 450; Ballagh, *White Servitude in the Col. of Va.*, p. 57.

onies. In Virginia, in 1643, this right was legally restricted. When the servants were secretly married, in some cases the man had to "serve out his or their tyme or tymes with his or their masters — after serve his master a complete year more for such offense committed" while the woman-servant had to double her time of service.[21] In other cases, as in North Carolina, the servants were required to serve one year.[22] Further restriction of the right of marriage appeared in Virginia in 1662. When a woman-servant and a Negro slave were married in Maryland, the woman was, in some instances, reduced to slavery, as she was required to serve her master during the life of her husband.[23] The effect of this law was, in certain instances, to complete practically the transition from servitude to slavery. Children resulting from such marriages were either made slaves for life, or required to serve until they were thirty years of age. Fornication also was made punishable by an addition of time. The woman-servant, who gave birth to illegitimate offspring, received an addition of time of one and a half to two and a half years.[24] When the offspring was by a Negro, mulatto, or Indian, she was required to serve the colony or the master for an additional time of four, five, or seven years. The children in these cases were bound out for thirty-one years.[25] With marriage restricted as it was, the family life of the servants was likely to be dis-

[21] Henning, *Statutes at Large*, p. 257; Ballagh, *White Servitude in the Col. of Va.*, pp. 50–51.

[22] Bassett, *Slavery and Servitude in the Col. of N. C.*, p. 34.

[23] "Instead of preventing such marriages, this law enabled avaricious and unprincipled masters to convert many of their servants to slaves. While this act continued in force, it did more to lower the standard of servitude than any other law passed during the whole period." McCormac, *White Servitude in Md.*, pp. 68–69.

[24] Turner, *The Negro in Penn.*, p. 30; Bassett, *Slavery and Servitude in the Col. of N. C.*, p. 83; Ballagh, *White Servitude in the Col. of Va.*, p. 57.

[25] *Ibid.*, 57; Bassett, *Slavery and Servitude in the Col. of N. C.*, pp. 83–84; Turner, *The Negro in Penn.*, p. 30; McCormac, *White Servitude in Md.*, p. 70.

orderly. Morals of servants were notably loose, and masters sometimes took advantage of their position to corrupt their servants still further.[26]

The servants were also restricted in political affairs. In the earliest period of servitude in the colonies, servants, as "inhabitants," enjoyed with the other "inhabitants" whatever suffrage there was.[27] Later on, however, this rare privilege dwindled to *nil*. For the "first sixteen years of the settlement" in Massachusetts the servants exercised the franchise.[28] In Virginia they voted until 1646 and the freedservant until 1670.[29] In Maryland in 1636, in the first assembly of the colony, only "freemen" seemed to hold sway.[30] Disfranchisement became the rule, however, after the middle of the seventeenth century.[31] The very noticeable scarcity of information on the servant's exercise of the suffrage seems to suggest that as a matter of understanding he did not enjoy the franchise. Evidently there prevailed a certain suspicion concerning not only the servant's ability to use the suffrage, but also his proper use of it; and this attitude was

[26] "If she should be delivered of a child by her master during this period she should be sold by the church wardens for the benefit of the church for one year after the term of service. . . . Here again there was no punishment for the seducing master. It is also evident that the sin of the servant would be an advantage of the master, since he would thereby secure her service for a longer period. We have not the least evidence that such a thing did happen, yet it is possible that a master might for this reason have compassed the sin of his serving-woman." Bassett, *Slavery and Servitude in the Col. of N. C.*, pp. 83-84.

"By the acts giving the master additions of time for the birth of a bastard child to his servant a premium was actually put upon immorality, and there appear to have been masters base enough to take advantage of it." Ballagh, *White Servitude in the Col. of Va.*, p. 79.

The master also encouraged marriage between servants and Negroes. McCormac, *White Servitude in Md.*, p. 68.

[27] Hurd, *Law of Freedom and Bondage*, I, p. 228 note.

[28] *Ibid.*, p. 255.

[29] *Ibid.*, pp. 232, 254; Ballagh, *White Servitude in the Col. of Va.*, p. 93.

[30] Hurd, *Law of Freedom and Bondage*, I, p. 248.

[31] Ballagh, *White Servitude in the Col. of Va.*, p. 90.

also always fairly pronounced toward the recently freed-servant.[32]

The final remedy of the servant, then, was flight. From the beginning of indented servitude, the servants invariably deserted their master's service. While in all cases they did not run away on account of abuses, the practice brought on abuses and other incidents which, during the first part of servitude, became more and more intolerable.

The number of runaways increased as the servants continued coming in. It was comparatively easy for them to escape to the more northern colonies, since the country about them was convenient for hiding and clandestine traveling; and the fugitives themselves, on account of having no physical characteristics distinguishable from those of the other colonists, could not easily be identified.[33] Thus North Carolina became popularly known as the "Refuge of Runaways" and that colony, Maryland, and the Dutch plantations were to fugitive servants what Massachusetts, Ohio, and Canada were later to runaway slaves.[34] The "under-ground railroad," too, had a forerunner in the early period of indentured servitude.[35] Methods of dealing with the runaways necessarily grew more strict, and precautions similar to those of slavery inevitably appeared. "Unlawful assembling," "plotting," and tentative insurrections became a source of apprehension.[36] Then came methods of pursuit, return,

[32] "Thus the liberated servant became an idler, socially corrupt, and often politically dangerous." Doyle, *Eng. Co's. in Am.*, I, p. 387.

"By the temporary disfranchisement of the servant during his term, common after the middle of the 17th century, a serious public danger was avoided. There could be no guarantee, of the judicious exercise of the suffrage with this class who, for the most part, had never enjoyed the privilege before. Their servitude may be regarded as preparing them for a proper appreciation of suffrage when obtained, and the duties of citizenship. . . ." Ballagh, *White Servitude in the Col. of Va.*, p. 90 note.

[33] "To facilitate discovery, habitual runaways had their hair cut 'close around their ears' and 'were branded on the cheek with the letter R.'" Ballagh, *White Servitude in the Col. of Va.*, p. 55 note.

[34] *Ibid.*, pp. 53-54.

[35] McCormac, *White Servitude in Md.*, p. 53.

[36] Ballagh, *White Servitude in the Col. of Va.*, pp. 53, 60.

and punishment of the fugitives. Sometimes the master made the pursuit; at other times the sheriff and his posse did it; and often the constable with a search warrant went in quest of the fugitive. Everyone who traveled was required to have a pass or a certificate of freedom to show his status;[37] and this no doubt afforded the servants a means of using forgery to facilitate their escape to freedom.[38] Again, whenever it was possible, advertisements for runaways were put in the newspapers.[39] During this time, too, there were enacted colonial statutes providing for the return of fugitives by one colony to the other. Colonial governments often accused each other of unduly holding and protecting the runaways.[40]

The greatest abuses in servitude occurred in the punishment of fugitive servants. These abuses, moreover, gradually increased in number and intensified in character.[41] The expense of the servant's capture, return, and loss of time from work, and the desire to prevent running away led to stringent punishment and evident abuses.[42] In Virginia before 1643, some runaways were punished with "additional terms from two to seven years, served in irons, to the public."[43] The act of 1643 in Virginia provided that runaways from their "master's service shall be lyable to make satisfaction by service at the end of their tymes by indenture (vizt.) double the tyme of service soe neglected, and in some cases more if the commissioners . . . find it requisite and convenient."[44] The

[37] *Ibid.*, p. 54; McCormac, *White Servitude in Md.*, p. 54.
[38] *Ibid.*, p. 55.
[39] *Ibid.*, p. 50.
[40] *Ibid.*, pp. 52–53; Bassett, *Slavery and White Servitude in the Col. of N. C.*, p. 79; Ballagh, *White Servitude in the Col. of Va.*, p. 54.
[41] McCormac, *White Servitude in Md.*, p. 54.
[42] "Statute after statute was passed regulating the punishment and providing for the pursuit and recapture of runaways; but although laws became severer and finally made no distinction in treatment of runaway servants and slaves, it was impossible to entirely put a stop to the habit so long as the system itself lasted." *Ibid.*, p. 56; Ballagh, *White Servitude in the Col. of Va.*, pp. 52, 57.
[43] *Ibid.*, p. 57.
[44] *Ibid.*, pp. 57–58; Henning, *Statutes at Large*, II, p. 458.

laws of 1639 and of 1641-42 made running away in Maryland punishable with death, but the proprietor or governor could commute this penalty to servitude of seven years or less.[45] Corporal punishment, too, scathed the fugitives.[46]

Plainly, then, the fugitive servant tended to assimilate the status of the servant to that of the slave and tended to become mere property. The servant could be transferred as property from one person to another, for from the beginning his services were bought and sold. The custom of purchasing and disposing of apprentices and servants was early practiced in Virginia and out of this practice grew the more definite and far-reaching custom of signing the servant's contract. Begun in 1623, it was resented by servants and deprecated by England; and yet with no question of its legality, the selling of servants' time became a common practice.[47] Later on, upon securing the servant in England, the indenture was often made out to the shipmaster or his assigns, and the servant was sold by him to the planters in America. To sell the servants, merchants were sometimes invited on board the ship, where they could look over the human cargo and select those who were desirable. Often it happened that the servants were brought over without indentures. They were made to believe that their lot would be made easy by the master who would buy them.[48] These, too, were sold by the captain to the highest bidder.[49] That the

[45] McCormac, *White Servitude in Md.*, pp. 51-52.
[46] Ballagh, *White Servitude in the Col. of Va.*, p. 59.
[47] "As a result, (my comma) the idea of the contract and of the legal personality of the servant was gradually lost sight of in the disposition to regard him as a chattel and a part of the personal estate of his master, which might be treated and disposed of very much in the same way as the rest of the estate. He became thus rated in inventories of estate, and was disposed of both by will and by deed along with the rest of the property." Ballagh, *White Servitude in the Col. of Va.*, pp. 43, 44.
[48] Eddis, *Letters from Am.*, p. 72.
[49] Example of the advertisement of the arrival of a servantship: "Just Arrived in the Sophia, Alexander Verdeen, Master, from Dublin, Twenty stout, healthy Indented Men Servents Whose Indentures will be disposed of on

servants were dealt with in this way eventually made the indentures as a rule negotiable, and this led to further degradation of the servants' status. The theory that the servant's time was property was tenable as late as 1756 in Virginia, Maryland, and Pennsylvania, for during the war with the French and Indians, when the governments and officers were recruiting the servants of the masters, the masters protested, resisted, and won.[50]

The servant, then, gradually became property, not principally because of a tendency to consider the Negro servant as such, but because of the incidents necessarily arising from the methods which had to be used to make white servitude possible in the colonies. These methods, then, the custom of using them, and finally the tentative legal sanction of them, were fairly well practiced before the Negro's arrival and long before he was considered as chattel.[51]

The Gradual Transition of Negro Servitude into Negro Slavery

The status of the Negro in British America was at first that of a servant. He was not held for life, but set at liberty after a term of service. It was his service, not himself, that was the property or chattel of another, and his offspring was not subject to servitude. Again, he had privileges similar to and in some cases identical with those of the other servants; in many cases the rules which governed other servants governed him as well. In short, the Negro was not the "absolute possession" of another.[1] Moreover, it was some years before he became a slave. Distinctly during this time, his status went

reasonable Terms, by the Captain on board, or the subscribers . . ., etc.'' McCormac, *White Servitude in Md.*, p. 42.

[50] *Ibid.*, pp. 39, 40, 42, 52, 85–89.

[51] Ballagh, *White Servitude in the Col. of Va.*, pp. 31, 33, 68; Ballagh, *Hist. of Slavery in Va.*, pp. 39–40; Russell, *The Free Negro in Va.*, pp. 46–47.

[1] Ante, p. 266.

through a gradual process of transition inevitable in the development of subjection in the colonies.[2]

"Servant" becomes "servant for life" and "perpetual servant" in colonial laws. The progress of extending the Negro servant's term is generally observed in the language of the laws of the colonies. It appears that as the servants went into slavery, "what is termed perpetual was substituted for limited service, while all the predetermined incidents of servitude, except such as referred to ultimate freedom, continued intact." Later the terms "servant for life," "perpetual servant" and "bond servant" were used interchangeably with "slave" and the words "servant" and "slave" and their liabilities were joined in the same enactments.[3] It was some time before the word "slave" was clearly and definitely used, and the servant who became slave lost all the earmarks of a servant.[4]

The practice of holding the servant after the expiration of his term was more characteristic of black servitude than white. As the Negroes increased in numbers, this practice increased. As white servitude declined, the assurance of labor waned. The extension of the Negro's term, then, for a few years longer and eventually to life service appeared a logical as well as a necessary step for the masters to take.[5] Moreover, since the public was

[2] Local conditions and circumstances dictated and directed the form of subjection. For this same reason, both servitude and slavery differed in different sections of the country. Nieboer brings out the local character of subjection when he holds that slavery does not exist as formally among fishing and hunting peoples as among agricultural and that subjection is milder in an open country than in a closed. Nieboer, *Slavery as an Industrial Institution*, p. 55.

[3] Ballagh, *Hist. of Slavery in Va.*, p. 37.

[4] It is not meant that all Negroes became servants and then slaves. Many Negroes became servants and followed the course of servants while others became slaves and remained slaves. At any period, however, during his first three-quarter century at least in the colonies, the most pronounced status of the Negro consisted of a cross-section of a transition from servitude to slavery.

[5] On the significance of the expiration of the white servant's term, Bruce has this to say: "Unless the planter had been careful to make provision against their departure by the importation of other laborers, he was left in a

often led to believe that when at liberty the Negroes were an uncontrollable and probably dangerous element of the population, extension of their terms in servitude gradually gained public approval.[6] Hence, the Negro servant was held whenever the occasion demanded and the opportunity presented itself.

In illustrating the gradual transition into slavery through repeated holding and attempts at holding the Negro servants for life, court cases of Virginia may be taken as typical. Brass, a Negro, whose master, a ship captain, had died, was, upon being threatened with enslavement, assigned by the General Court in 1625 as servant to the governor of the colony instead of as slave to the company of his late master's ship.[7] John Punch, who ran away in company with three white servants, was adjudged by the court, in 1640, to serve his master the "time of his natural life" while the white servants were given four additional years to serve. Anthony Johnson, a Negro to whom attention has already been called, owned a large tract of land on the Eastern Shore. In 1640 he became involved in a suit for holding John Castor, another Negro, seven years overtime. It appears that Castor was set free. Later, however, Johnson brought suit against Robert Parker, a white man, for harboring Castor as if he were a free man; and the court decided that Castor return to his master, Johnson, evidently for service for

helpless position without men to reap his crops or to widen the area of his new grounds. . . . Perhaps in a majority of cases, his object was to obtain laborers whom he might substitute for those whose term were on the point of expiring. It was this constantly recurring necessity which must have been the source of much anxiety and annoyance as well as heavy pecuniary outlay, that led the planters to prefer youths to adults among the imported English agricultural servants, for while their physical strength might have been less, yet the periods for which they were bound extended over a longer time." Bruce, *Econ. Hist. of Va.*, II, pp. 58–59.

[6] Ballagh, *Hist. of Slavery in Va.*, pp. 37–38. "Negro servants were sometimes compelled by threats and browbeating to sign indentures for longer terms after they had served out their original terms." (Russell, *The Free Negro in Va.*, p. 33.) Indian servants, too, were held and reduced to slaves whenever possible. Lauber, *Indian Slavery in Colonial Times*, pp. 196–201.

[7] Ballagh, *Hist. of Slavery in Va.*, pp. 29, 30, 31.

life. Sometime before 1644, a mulatto boy named Emanuel, a servant, was sold "as a slave forever" but later was adjudged by the Assembly "no slave and but to serve as other Christian servants do." In 1673, a servant, who had been unlawfully detained beyond his five-year period, won judgment against his master, George Light; the Negro servant was set free and received his freedom dues from the master.[8] In 1674 Philip Cowan petitioned the governor for freedom on the ground that Charles Lucas kept him three years overtime and then compelled him by threats to sign an indenture for twenty years.[9]

Other indications of holding the Negro servant may be shown. In Pennsylvania, Negro servants were invariably given a longer term of service than the white servants and often held after the expiration of the term;[10] so extensive was the practice of holding these servants that, in 1682 and 1693, laws were enacted against it.[11] In Georgia a road to slavery was paved by extending the servants' terms. Negroes were brought out of North Carolina into Georgia by white servants who, becoming tired of servitude, had these blacks serve out their unexpired terms with the Georgia masters. As this worked well the

[8] Russell, *The Free Negro in Va.*, pp. 32, 31, 32, 33, 34, 38–39.

[9] "Petition of a negro for redress To the Rt. Hon'ble Sir William Berkeley, Knt., Goverr and Cap. Genl of Virga, with the Hon. Councell of State. The Petiti'on of Phillip Corven, a negro, in all humility showeth: That yor petr being a servant to Mrs. Annye Beazley, late of James, City County, widow, deed. The said Mrs. Beazley made her last will and testament in writing, under her hand and seal, bearing date of April, An Dom. 1664, . . . that yor petr by the then name of negro boy Philip, should serve her cousin, . . . the terme of eight yeares . . . and then should enjoy his freedom and be paid three barrels of corne and a sute of clothes." Cowen was sold, it appears, to Lucas who kept him and forced him to sign the long indenture. Palmer, *Calendar of State Papers*, I, p. 10.

Russell correets "Corven" to "Cowan," *The Free Negro in Va.*, p. 34.

[10] "This practice of holding negroes for a longer term than white persons, which lasted for a longer time than had originally been contemplated, since it was allowed to apply to negroes brought into Pennsylvania from other states, bade fair to perpetuate itself and last longer still." Turner, *The Negro in Penn.*, pp. 93, 95, 99–100.

[11] *Ibid.*, 95.

masters lengthened the term of the Negro servants to life.[12] In fact, on account of the reciprocal influence of white servitude and Negro servitude, wherever white servants were taken advantage of and held longer, Negro servants were subjected to harsher treatment and longer extension of term.

The mulatto class in the colonies constituted an element through which transition of Negro servitude into slavery is apparent. As the mulattoes were looked upon as the result of an "abominable mixture" of the races and as representing a troublesome element in society, local laws and colonial statutes were gradually enacted to check and control them.[13] The statutes first aimed at serving as a deterrent upon the women, and hence arose the doctrine of *partus sequitur ventrem*, which imposed the mother's status upon the offspring. However, the first statute to this effect, the act of 1662 in Virginia, was largely enacted because of fornication of Englishmen and Negro women.[14] Statutes enunciating this doctrine were enacted in the other colonies as follows: Maryland, 1663; Massachusetts, 1698; Connecticut and New Jersey, 1704; Pennsylvania and New York, 1706; South Carolina, 1712; Rhode Island, 1728; and North Carolina, 1741.[15] Thus not only Negro mulattoes, that is, the offspring of white men and Negro women, were prevented from becoming servants, but those who were already either freemen or servants were gradually reduced to slavery. To check the growth of the mulatto class, particularly through the intermixture and intermarriage of Negro men and white women, a Virginia law in 1691 provided that the woman be fined, or sold into service for five years, or given five years of

---

[12] Stevens, *Hist. of Ga.*, I, p. 306.

[13] Henning, *Statutes at Large*, pp. 145, 146, 252, 433, 551, 552; *Ibid.*, II, 115; *Ibid.*, III, 87, 453; Ballagh, *Hist. of Slavery in Va.*, p. 57; Turner, *The Negro in Penn.*, pp. 112-113; McCormac, *White Servitude in Md.*, pp. 67-70.

[14] Ballagh, *Hist. of Slavery in Va.*, p. 57; McCormac, *White Servitude in Md.*, p. 67.

[15] Ballagh, *Hist. of Slavery in Va.*, p. 39.

added time, and the mulatto be bound out for thirty years.¹⁶ In Maryland, Pennsylvania, and North Carolina, similar laws were passed.¹⁷ The mulatto, then, in one case was reduced from freeman and servant to slave, and in the other case made a servant for thirty or more years.¹⁸ Thus the debasing of the status of the mulatto helped the transition to slavery.

Just as the fugitive white servant repeatedly gave occasion, through incidents growing out of his capture, return, and deterrence, to lower the status of the servant until it assumed the character of slavery, so the fugitive Negro servant made his lot harder and influenced the extension of his term to perpetuity. The Negro servant, unlike either the Indian or white servant, obviously had little to tempt him to run away from his master; his physical characteristics made detection easy, there was no free Negro population to which he could escape, the unfamiliar country around him held but poor prospects for his making a livelihood more easily than under his master, and the strangeness of his situation undoubtedly had much to do with his acceptance of it. Yet the Negro as a servant did run away. It is very probable that the practice of run-

¹⁶ *Ibid.*, pp. 57–58.

¹⁷ Stroud, *Laws Relating to Slavery*, pp. 8–9; Turner, *The Negro in Penn.*, pp. 24–25, 92; Moore, *Notes on the Hist. of Slavery in Mass.*, p. 54.

¹⁸ The transition is exhibited in another case still more completely. "'This position rendered them especially eligible for gross purposes, both in their intimate contact with the negroes and in their relations to their employers. The law had unwittingly set a premium upon immorality, as the female mulatto not only added an additional term to her period of service, but her offspring was by a law of 1723 in its turn forced to serve the master until the age of thirty-one years. Such mulatto servants, then, were scarcely better off as to prospective freedom than the negro slave. Custom tended to reduce them to a state of slavery. About the middle of the eighteenth century (circa 1765) the practice arose of actually disposing of their persons by sale, both in the colony and without, as slaves. So flagrant was the practice that further legislation was demanded to check the illegal proceeding by appropriate penalties. It would appear that the offenders were those who were entitled to the mulattoes only as servants, but used the power of intimidation or deceit, which could be easily practiced in the case of minor bastards born in their service.'" Ballagh, *Hist. of Slavery in Va.*, pp. 59–60.

ning away to the Indians began when he was a servant.[19] Again, it appears that he ran away not infrequently in company with white servants. In Virginia, in 1640, John Punch, a Negro servant, ran away in company with two white servants. The three were overtaken in Maryland and brought back to Virginia for trial. The court ordered that the white servants' terms be lengthened four years, and that Punch, the Negro servant, "shall serve his master or his assigns for the time of his natural life."[20]

The transition of servitude to slavery, moreover, is distinctly noticed in the change in the conception of property in the service of the Negro to that of property in his person.[21] Like that of the white and Indian servants, the Negro's service through contract, implied and expressed, was owned by the master. This ownership, however, consisted of only the right of the master to the service of the servant. Gradually, as this service necessarily became involved in wills, estates, taxation, and business transactions, the person of the servant instead of his service came more and more to be regarded, both in custom and in law, as property, so that eventually the servant, himself, was considered personal estate. Thus he was "rated in inventories of estates, was transferable both *inter vivos* and by will, descended to the executors and administrators, and was taxable." While he was now a "contractual person," he still retained such incidents of

[19] From the very first, the Indians and Negroes as servants came in contact. Also, there seems to have been a "common bond of union" between Indians and Negroes. Again the colony laws concerning runaway servants generally took care of the Negro and Indian servants in the same act. Russell, *The Free Negro in Va.*, pp. 128–129; Lauber, *Indian Slavery in Colonial Times*, pp. 218, 220–221.

[20] Russell, *The Free Negro in Va.*, pp. 29–30.

[21] "With the change of the status of servitude to the status of slavery, certain of the attributes of the former condition were continued and connected with the latter chief of these, and the fundamental idea on which the change was effected, was the conception of property right which, from the idea of the ownership of an individual's service resting upon contract implied or expressed, came to be that of ownership of an individual's person." Lauber, *Indian Slavery in Colonial Times*, p. 215.

personality as rights of limited protection, personal freedom, and possession of property.[22] As the service of the servant became more and more regarded and treated as a form of property, his personality was completely lost sight of, and his term was extended to the time of his natural life.[23] Easily, then, the Negro servant regarded at first a part of the personal estate came at length to be regarded as a chattel real.

T. R. DAVIS

WALDEN COLLEGE,
   NASHVILLE, TENN.

[22] Ballagh, *Hist. of Slavery in Va.*, pp. 39-40.

[23] Lauber, *Indian Slavery in Colonial Times*, pp. 226, 227, 230; Turner, *The Negro in Penn.*, p. 25. "With the loss of the ultimate right to freedom, the contractual element and the incidents essential to it were swept away, and as the idea of personality was obscured, the conception of property gained force, so that it became an easy matter to add incidents more strictly defining the property right and insuring its protection."

THREE ELEMENTS OF AFRICAN CULTURE

The passion for self expression is one of the most potent factors in social development. No problem of social philosophy yields to a satisfactory solution where the passion for expression is not regarded as a requisite factor. This principle is operative in the life of the individual, the race, and the nation. All human achievements are directly traceable to some inward urge, and evolution, as a theory, is but the universalization of this principle. Civilization, whether in its more perfected stages or whether in its manifestations that are crude and rudimentary, is essentially a measure of human expression. The inward urge that drives mankind onward has a variety of manifestations and the difference in the number of these manifestations is the measure of differences between various civilizations, and between civilization and barbarism or savagery. The impulse that moves the saintly worshipper in St. Peter's to kiss the rosary as he kneels low-bowed and earnest before the high altar is the same that moves the aborigine in Zululand to dance in frenzied ecstacies around his devil-bush. That there are various degrees of self-expression, with a maximum in this nation and age, and a minimum in that, is a fact that is as undeniable as it is obvious; but that there are impulses of cultural possibilities which are lavished upon some races while totally withheld from others is a thesis which finds no sanction in history or archaeology.

Archaeology is the guiding light in which we grope in our attempt to explore the life of ancient man. In Europe and in Asia we have unearthed numerous evidences of pre-historic cultures. There may have been surprise at the antiquity and variety but certainly not at the location, for it was highly probable that the present high civilization of Europe and Asia had risen from the ruins of older ones;

yet it cannot be longer doubted that when archaeology as a searchlight was turned upon Africa there was occasion of surprise when that Dark Land yielded evidences of a civilization that antedated the arrival of the European. It would be just as hard to designate the African cultures as purely Negro as to designate the European cultures as purely Teuton. However, a study of African culture promises richer results when it can be identified with certain Negro tribes or such Negroid tribes as have a large extraction of Negro blood. The findings of archaeology have not only a backward look but also a meaning for the future and especially is this true of African cultures, which not only throw light upon the past of the black man but may also become prophetic of his future. It shall be the purpose of this treatise to analyze the African cultures so as to disclose their essential elements and to compare these elements with their counterparts in European cultures.

Once attention had been directed towards Africa, there arose numerous archaeological expeditions and especially noteworthy were the findings of those from Germany and England, the two European countries which had the most ambitious schemes of colonization. In details there is not always agreement among the various archaeological explorers; but, in the main, there is a unanimity that is marvelous and especially is this true when there is evidenced such keen rivalry that is at bottom doubtless economic.

What are the essential elements of civilization? What are the cultural manifestations which constitute the *sine qua non* of human progress? What is the "irreducible minimum" of civilization? A studied answer must include ethics, art and government, for without any one of these no social order can claim for itself an approach to civilization. The cultures of nations and races must be expressive of these cardinal elements of social expression. In investigating African cultures and their essential elements it is deemed best to dwell at greatest length on the positive aspects of these cultural manifestations. To attempt a negative exposition of the primitive cultures of any people will not reveal any worthwhile criterion of its worth especially when the scope of investigation is limited to three essential elements of culture. If ethics, art and government constitute the irreducible minimum of civilization which is manifested in certain cultural aspects, it is clear at the outset that specialization in ethics, art and government is the measure of a people's advancement.

I. Ethics

Of the African peoples let us consider first their ethics. It can hardly be doubted that it was an important step in man's upward journey when he reached what anthropologists have called "the dawn of mind" but it was no less momentous an event when there was within him the dawn of morality. Morality is the highest defensive weapon which mankind can wield. So important has it become in the struggle for existence that, to man, the highest form of greatness is a moral greatness. That the highest civilizations of history have been grounded in moral strength has become an historical postulate, but what of the races and nations that live beyond their pale? Were the Africans in their crude and primitive surroundings moral beings? Tillinghast and Beauvais would doubtless answer in the negative. The former in his *The Negro in Africa and America* is loud in his criticism of the ethical standards of the African, in fact he seriously doubts the advisability of saying that the tribes of Africa have an awakened moral sense. Frobenius, however, comes forward with an assertion to the contrary, asserting: "I cannot do otherwise than say, that these human creatures are the chastest and most ethically disposed of all the national groups in the world which have become known to me."[1] In justice to the other "national groups" we may say that Frobenius here doubtless overdraws the virtues of

[1] Frobenius, *The Voice of Africa,* 673.

the Yoruban tribes, yet his assertions when taken with ever so much reserve would lead to the conclusion that the Africans have considerable moral sense. Frobenius leaves no doubt that the Yorubans are a mixed people, although certain degrees of mixtures of people are found everywhere; and the fact that they are mixed alone will not vitiate the validity of Yoruban civilization as a phase of African culture. Roscoe in writing of the Baganda tribes has been as careful to impress us with their blackness as Frobenius has been to indicate the Yoruban mixture. He says: "Sex profligacy is open and thought to be no wrong. They thought it no moral wrong to indulge the sex desire."[2] Yet Roscoe further says: "The most stringent care was exercised by the king and chiefs, but it proved inefficient to keep the sexes apart, while horrible punishment meted out to the delinquents when caught seemed to lend zest to the danger incurred."[3] The significant thing in Roscoe's account is not the open sex profligacy but the "stringent care exercised by kings and chiefs" and the "horrible punishment meted out to offenders." After all, there is abundant evidence that even in Baganda there is some ethical standard.

Roscoe continues: "Theft is not common among the people for they were deterred from stealing by fear of punishment which was certain to follow."[4] The very fact that there was fear of punishment is indicative of some conception of social morality. Fear as a preventive of crime is not the most commendable incentive to morality, but it is one that must be employed in all civilizations; for man is first an animal then a moral being. The fear referred to does not prove that the Baganda has the highest type of morality, but it proves that they have a type and this is significant for primitive peoples. The low standard in anything may be prophetic of higher ones which are approachable only by means of the lower ones as stepping

[2] *Baganda, Their Customs and Beliefs*, 10.
[3] *Ibid.*
[4] Roscoe, *Baganda*, 12.

stones. This is true in art, science and religion. The fact that the Bagandas were "hospitable and liberal and that real poverty did not exist"[5] shows the presence of a social consciousness which in many ways evidences a standard of ethics. According to Roscoe the thief was killed on the spot, death for adultery was certain;[6] yet he attempts to maintain his thesis as to their lack of morality in these words: "The moral ideas of the people are crude, it was not wrongdoing but detection that they feared; men were restrained from committing crimes through fear of the power of the gods."[7] It is obvious that "detection" is to be feared only where there are detectives and these are present only when they have been called forth in response to some social demands.

There is still other light to be turned on the ethical status of the African tribes. Bent, more sympathetic towards the natives of Mashonaland, delivers himself thus: "Not only has Khama established his reputation for honesty; but he is supposed to have inoculated his people with the same virtue. I must say that I looked forward with great interest to seeing a man with so wide a reputation for integrity and enlightenment as Khama in South Africa. Somehow one's spirit of skepticism is on the alert on such occasions and especially when a Negro is the case in point; and I candidly admit that I advanced towards Palapwe fully prepared to find Ba Mangwato a rascal and hypocrite and I left his capital after a week's stay there one of his fervent admirers."[8] But Dent adds: "Doubtless on the traversed roads and large centers where they are brought into contact with traders and would-be civilizers of the race, these people become thieves and vagabonds, but in their primitive state the Makalangas are naturally honest, exceedingly courteous in manner."[9]

[5] *Ibid.*, 120.
[6] *Ibid.*, 263.
[7] *Ibid.*, 267.
[8] Bent, *Mashonaland*, 22.
[9] *Ibid.*, 53.

It is plain to the impartial critic that judged by our ethical standards the peoples commended above would fall far short; but this is no less true with the earliest civilization of historic times. Standards not only vary from age to age but from people to people. In arguing to support the thesis that in Africa the lowliest tribes had some ethical standard, it is not necessary to prove that these standards compare favorably or unfavorably with those of modern times. Such is beside the question and with the testimony of the English and German archaeologists before us we are safe in saying that the African tribes had an ethical standard and thus the potentials of a civilization based upon morality. Neither can it be proved that the ethical standards of the tribes of Baganda, Mashonaland and Yoruba are without worth because they differ in so many particulars from our own. Later we shall attempt to show just why there is such disparity between their ethics and ours. Furthermore, it is not necessary to prove that ethical contacts with Europeans affords no basis for the tribesmen but it is reasonable to suppose that the ethics of the African tribes had possibilities the same as the earliest nations of Europe and Asia; and if contacts with Europeans be argued against the proposition that the Africans evolved an ethical standard, the same argument may be used to bedim the glory of our own civilization.

We, therefore, contend that whatever possibilities lie with the people who can evolve an ethical standard surely must lie with the African. It is true that the happy faculty of coordinating ethics with ideals has made nations great and civilizations splendid, and that such faculty evidenced itself in the long-dark continent of Africa. The principle of evolution is just as operative in the world of ethics as in the world of physical sciences. Ethics must grow and outgrown ethics is ethics notwithstanding. The most rabid critic does not deny to Africa ethical origins, but such authorities as Tillinghast and Beauvais would deny their practical worth. These men criticize the standard rather than deny that there are ethical manifestations of culture. Ellwood in his Sociology and Social Problems contends that the regulation of sex relations has been the greatest achievement of man. Granting the truth of this statement, we have evidences that the African made desperate efforts to regulate sex relations both by a kind of public opinion and by punishment; for Roscoe says: "It was looked upon as a great disgrace to a family if a girl was with child prior to marriage."[10] We are certain that there was "marriage" and this itself is an indication that an attempt had been made to regulate the all-important matter of sex. Roscoe further held that "the marriage vow was binding."[11] Both those writers who commended the ethics of the Africans and those who belittled their standard, then, are essentially agreed to the fact of their ethics. Although there were wide variations in the standards of different tribes, we are abundantly justified in assuming that the ethics of the Africans was as susceptible to improvement as our own. The more advanced standards were prophetic of still more advanced ones.

II. Art

What a man admires is an infallible index to his innermost soul. Whether in the adornment of some temple or the crude markings upon primitive pottery, man is ever striving to express himself in his labors. Strange to say that though the passion for self-expression is dominant in human activities, the art of expression is still in its infancy. We may divide human artifacts into two classes, namely, those of utility and those of aestheticism. That the latter has a form of utility we should in no case deny but as to the utility of aesthetics we deem it beside the point here to discuss. When we use the term "art" in this treatise it will have the specific meaning of the attempt on the part of man to express his emotions; or his attempt to satisfy the aesthetic cravings in the soul. That

[10] Roscoe, *The Baganda*, 79.
[11] *Ibid.*

there are such cravings is a fact which is universally conceded. That there are many evidences of such attempts among all civilized lands none will deny. That man's attempts at artistic expression is a criterion of his civilization is an historic fact. There can be no civilization without its concomitants of aesthetics. Man seeks beauty for beauty's sake, and he alone of the animals gives evidence of such propensity to a pronounced degree. In song, upon canvas, and in marble, humanity has poured forth its innermost soul of sentiments inexpressibly sublime. There is no passion, no object that has not at some time inflamed the soul and moved some mortal to the abode of the gods.

What have the explorers in Darkest Africa found to indicate that the Africans loved the beautiful? What have the Africans to show as specimens of fine art? The music of Negro peoples has become proverbial. In so far as song is an expression of aesthetic propensities the African abundantly qualifies as a lover of art. Whether the strength of a Wagner or the melody of a Beethoven; whether the melody of a southern plantation or a concert in Symphony Hall, the principle of the music is the same. The crude instruments of which the explorer tells us are mute testimonials of the African's attempts to express himself in song and music. There were to be found in the Bagandaland, according to Roscoe, drums for dancing and the "royal" drum was elaborately decorated, thus showing a combination of sight and soul appreciation for beauty. He said that the harp and stringed fife were also found in this same tribe. The pottery found in this region was glazed and figures painted thereon indicated beyond doubt artistic design of no mean order. The basketry had various figures worked through the skillful manipulation of the bark fibres. Roscoe asserts that polychrome paintings were much in evidence among the Baganda tribes and their work in ivory corresponded favorably with the same kind of work found in Europe during the Neolithic Age.

Whether fine art was indigenous is not a pertinent question but the significant thing is that Roscoe found these tribes actually giving expression to what seemed to be a well-developed sense of the beautiful.

When Bent reached the ruined city of Zimbabwe, he found the natives playing upon one-stringed instruments with gourds as resonators and he avers that "the sound was plaintive if not sweet."[12] That a mode of dress is primitive is no proof that it lacks taste and a subtle refinement. This is amply illustrated by the striking beauty of Egyptian costumes which now again grace the modern stage. Though four thousand years have elapsed since Egypt basked in the pristine glory that was hers, we have many evidences that what was pretty then is not ugly now. This is no less true of the remnants of those who saw the sun of glory shine upon Mashonaland. In remarking about their apparel Roscoe is positive in the assertion that "their dress evidences taste when not contaminated with a hybrid civilization."[13] Like the Cretans, they displayed artistic tendencies to the extent the simplest tool bore evidences of ornamentation. If such tendency in the Cretans was indicative of the artistic temperament, a similar tendency in the Africans must be similarly interpreted.

According to Roscoe, definite stages are well defined and can be definitely traced in their paintings. At first the themes were things and later they were men and the human body as a design for the artist is clearly portrayed. There was a "breast and furrow" type of painting that marked almost every object with which they had to do. The piano with iron keys was very much like such instruments found in Egypt. The Jews' harp was found in many quarters. There can be no doubt that music had its place in the life of the Mashonaland. But music is a fine art and its value lies largely if not wholly in its appeal to our aesthetic natures. What can be the meaning of such evidences of love of music

---

[12] Bent, *Ruined Cities of Mashonaland*, 18.
[13] *Ibid.*, 37.

among the African tribes? Can it not be interpreted as their response to the appeal of the beautiful?

Of the great defensive walls of Zimbabwe Bent says: "The fort is a marvel with its tortuous and well-guarded approaches; its walls bristling with monoliths and round towers, its temple decorated with tall weird-looking birds, its huge decorated bowls. The only parallel that I have seen were the long avenues of menhirs near Carnac in Brittany. One cannot fail to recognize the vastness and power of this ancient race, their greatness of constructive ingenuity and their strategic skill."[14] Of course, there is evidence that the present inhabitants of those ruined cities were not the tribes that once ruled mightily in these regions. Bent himself holds that such high culture must have come from another people. The very fact that the present population seems so far below the level of culture that once prevailed there is the only evidence upon which Bent predicates his argument that another race than the Negroes were the bearers of this great culture. However, it is hardly probable that the level of culture was foreign to the Negroes who lived in the palmy days of Zimbabwe. There must have been an overlapping of cultures even if we grant that another race produced the culture of this region. It is hardly probable that a dominant race would have wholly abdicated in favor of the natives and it is still less probable that the natives could have dislodged a race so strongly fortified. It is highly probable that the same race of people could have produced the peoples who occupied the level of these two very different cultures. No one supposes that the inhabitants of Athens today are equal to the Greeks of the days of Pericles. Yet they are connected with the same great race.

Aside from the ancient walls and temples reputed to be the products of a genius foreign to the tribes of today, Bent comments favorably upon the art such as is the product of the modern inhabitant. With regard to a beautiful

[14] Bent, *Ruined Cities of Mashonaland*, 113.

bowl he says: "The work displayed in executing these bowls, the careful rounding of edges, the exact execution of the circle, the fine pointed tool marks and the subjects they chose to depict point to a race having been far advanced in artistic skill." Hunting scenes are numerous and in the processions of men, animals are often put in to make for relief, sometimes a bird is introduced for the same effect. It is quite singular that in one of the hunting scenes the sportsman is a Hottentot. Sculptoring was usually done in soapstone and the bird upon the post is a subject which is frequently depicted. The drawings found by Bent in the Mazoe Valley were simple yet beautifully executed. The magnificent hand-made pottery is decorated in patterns of red and black which colors are obtained from hemolite and plumbogo. If we turn with Bent to Mtokoland and see in the Mtoko's kraal the drawings of the Bushmen, "we can trace distinctly three different periods of execution. The first is crude and now faint representation of unknown life; the second is deeper in color and admirably executed and partly on top of this latter are animals of the best period of this art in red and yellow. The third is an inartistic representation of human beings which evidently belongs to a period of decadence and in the execution of this work the colors invariably are red, yellow and black."[15]

What significance has this manifestation of art? What coloring does it give to the cultural development of Africa? It simply means that the African like other peoples enjoys the finer sentiments that make life worth living. Among the writers there is as much unanimity on the question of African art as there is on African ethics. All told, it goes to show that in the essentials of culture the tribes of Africa are not entirely wanting and there are many close parallels between the cultural development in Africa and that in Neolithic Europe. What difference there is is one of degree and not of kind. While Lady Lugard's work savored

[15] *Ibid.,* 292.

more of politics than of archaeology, it cannot be doubted that her vote may be cast on the side of those who contend that the cultural manifestations of the African are pronounced when their background is considered. Though crude and rudimentary, though often hidden beneath brutal superstitions, there is always a cultural norm with brilliant possibilities for social betterment. At best we can be no more than fundamentally right or fundamentally good, and this lends color to the claim of the African to real culture.

III. Government

Much has been said about the feeble government which the African sets up. More has been said of his innate inability in matters of civic importance. The matter of government is important, for it is doubtful if there can be any approach to any civilization worthy of the name without some stable form of government. It is generally conceded that the democratic form of government is the best developed stage of the body politic; but this form even at present is far from realization. While it is a great and inspiring ideal, its presupposition is that people are capable of self-government and in many cases this is a supposition that is not based on fact and cannot be corroborated in practice. If democracy is the highest form, absolute monarchy may be the lowest form. Yet monarchy is a form of government and despite the low esteem in which it is held within recent years, it must be admitted that for ages monarchical government was the guardian and custodian of civilization. It is more necessary to have some government than it is to have good government.

Africa is no exception to this rule. Frobenius goes so far as to say that the government in the Yorubaland was fashioned after a republic.[16] With superior and subordinate officials the Yorubans had the semblance of an orderly government. There was the king with a senate which filled the function of cabinet as well. At the court were coun-

---

[16] Frobenius, *Voice of Africa*, 180.

sellors-at-law and attorneys for the state. Says Frobenius: "Before the advent of Mohammedanism, forms of civilization of equal value and significance must have been operative in the Soudan."[17] "In fact," he continues, "the government was excellent and I was delighted with the simple administration of the law and official summary punishment in Makwa."[18] Of the Great Benin tribes Roth says: "If theft is seldom heard of here, of murder we hear still less.[19] When the Arabs first visited Negroland by the western route in the eighth and ninth centuries of our era, they found the black kings of Ghana in the height of their prosperity. But the black kings of Ghana had long passed into oblivion when Edris, one of the greatest kings of Bornu, was making gunpowder for the musketeers of his army contemporary with Queen Elizabeth."[20]

El Bekri, a Spanish Arab and author of Tarikh-es-Soudan says of Mansa Musa one of the nobles of Ghana: "He was distinguished by his ability and holiness of life. The justice of his administration was such that it still lives."[21] Three hundred years later a Songhay said of him: "As a pious and equitable prince, he was unequalled for virtue and uprightness."[22]

The duration of the Soudanese empires, moreover, will bear comparison with that of others which are better known to fame. Ghana enjoyed an independent existence of about eleven hundred years—that is, a period nearly equivalent to the period of existence of the British Empire from the abolition of the Saxon Heptarchy to the present day. Melle which succeeded Ghana had a shorter national life of about two hundred and fifty years. Songhay counted its kings in regular succession from 700 to 1591—a period which almost equals the life of the Roman

[17] *Ibid.*, 360.
[18] *Ibid.*, 388.
[19] Roth, *Great Benin*, 86.
[20] *Ibid.*, 82.
[21] Roth, *Great Benin*, 128.
[22] *Ibid.*, 129.

Empire from the foundation of the republic before the Christian era to the downfall of the empire in the second half of the fifth century. The duration of Bornu was less reputable.

The civilization represented by these empires was no doubt, if judged by modern standards, exceedingly imperfect. "The principle of freedom, as we understand it, was probably unknown; authority rested upon force of arms; industrial life was based upon slavery; social life was founded on polygamy. Side by side with barbaric splendor there was primeval simplicity. Luxury for the few took the place of comforts for the many. Study was devoted to what seems to us unprofitable ends. Yet the fact that civilization, far in excess of anything which the nations of northern Europe possessed at the earlier period of Soudanese history, existed with stability enough to maintain empire after empire through a known period of about 1500 years in a portion of the world which mysteriously disappeared in the sixteenth century from the comity of modern nations."[23]

Bent holds that "three hundred years before the Portuguese came to this country the natives were ruled over by a chief with the dynastic name of Nonomapata. From the evidence brought forward we are well within the range of probability when we say that in various parts of Africa there has been a very close approach to well-ordered government dating from ancient days. That these governments are non-existent today can not be laid to their discredit nor to their faulty organization. It is a fact that the earth has not produced the government that could very long defy the ravages of time. A journey down the wreckstrewn highway of the ages will reveal the dry bones of a thousand empires and it is not surprising that the humbler states of Africa can be numbered among them. The fact that there are evidences of decadent states in tribal Africa has its parallel in various parts of Europe today."

[23] *Ibid.*, 217.

We have shown that archaeological research has revealed that the darkness in Africa has not been from time immemorial. We have found that the "*quod novi ex Africa*" is obsolete in an archaeological sense. We have brought forward testimony deduced from reliable sources that Africa is not without an historic past. We have further shown that in eastern, central and western Africa the natives not only exhibit now these cultural manifestations, but also there is revealed aboundant evidence of a prehistoric culture that compares favorably with the earlier cultures of Europe. We are candid enough to admit that in standard the cultures of Africa are inferior to our own, but we must also admit that the present high standards in our own ethics, art and government have not always prevailed and that there is a past to these standards which is not always assuring.

There is one question that demands an answer before we have concluded. It is a question that is as reasonable as it is vexatious. Why have not the nations of Africa kept pace with other mightier countries? Why is Africa at present suffering political dissection which would have been impossible had she fully developed the cardinal elements of ethics, art and government? Why is there no help for her dismemberment which constitutes the pity of the age? The answer to these questions is obvious when we shall have considered, first, one of the fundamental propositions in human psychology. The rise of one nation may hinder the rise of the other. It is not improbable that an accentuated civilization in Europe might have retarded civilization in Africa. We do know that the slave trade had a tremendous effect on their fortunes. When once a group makes unusual progress and by its ambition destroys the bridge over which it passed, it cannot be doubted that its ambitions considerably alter the fortunes of others at its mercy. Lady Lugard cannot be gainsaid when she asserts thus with regard to the slave trade: " Through the chaos of these conflicting interests, the practice of slave-raiding, carried on alike by the highest and lowest, ran like the poison of a destructive sore, destroying every possibility of peaceful and prosperous development."[24]

There may be further asked the question why did not Africa rise as did the other peoples and make her exploitation impossible. We are forced to turn from social to natural factors. The geography of Europe is quite different from that of Africa. When wave after wave of migrants left the Iranian plains and turned west and east and south, it is clear that those who turned into Africa had an endless journey before them ere they had to the margin come. Of great mountain ranges there were none. On the monotonous plains of Africa the cultural extensions must have been horizontal. The races that went into Europe were more quickly stayed in their onward march by the coldness of the north. Not only this but they were in the midst of a mountainous country where tribes and peoples could drift into human eddies and there remain out of the current of human activities for ages. Not only might they remain aloof from the busy thoroughfare of migrating myriads but within each eddy there was the possibility of a growth in culture in its simpler aspects. By and by, the culture of one eddy was crossed with the culture of other eddies that had developed in other cultural directions or farther in the same direction. In time there was by reason of the northern limit of Europe a rebound of the population and this was also a rebound of cultures. The various crosses and modification of cultures made it more probable that civilized progress would be accelerated. The culture of Europe was, by reason of the physical geography, a heterogeneous culture, while that of Africa was necessarily homogeneous in view of the geography of that continent.

In support of my contention I refer to Ripley who says: "The remarkable prehistoric civilization of Italy is due to the union of cultures, one from Hallstatt region having

[24] Lugard, *A Tropical Dependency*.

entered from the west via the Danube, the other coming from the southeast by sea being distinctly Mediterranean. From the fusion of these cultures came the Umbrian and Etruscan civilizations." Ripley further contends that the ancient high civilization of Mesopotamia was possible because it was a point of convergence of immigration and invasion. Civilization has always been accentuated at points where cultures could cross.[25] There are few or none such points in Africa; hence the retardation of cultures there. As Lady Lugard said, the slave trade aggravated the cultural disadvantages which grew out of the physical geography of Africa, and because of its monotony of environment there has been little or no cross fertilization of cultures, the indispensable requisite to cultural development.[26]

GORDON BLAINE HANCOCK

[25] Ripley, *Races of Europe.*
[26] Lugard, *A Tropical Dependency.*

METHODISM AND THE NEGRO IN THE UNITED STATES

The first converted Negro Methodist was baptized by John Wesley. November 29, 1758, he wrote in his diary: "I rode to Wandsworth, and baptized two Negroes belonging to Mr. Gilbert, a gentleman lately from Antigua. One of these was deeply convinced of sin; the other is rejoicing in God, her savior, and is the first African Christian I have known. But shall not God, in his own time, have these heathen also for his inheritance?"[1] Eight years later (1766) the first Methodist congregation of five met in the private house of Philip Embury, in New York. One of that number was Betty, a Negro servant girl.

In 1816, fifty years after that first service in New York, the Methodists in the United States numbered 214,235 communicants. Of these 171,931 were white and 42,304, or nearly one-fourth, were Negroes. Two interesting facts are, that of these 42,304 Negro members, 30,000 or nearly three-fourths were in the South, and gathered principally from the slave population.[2]

These figures indicate the faithfulness of early Methodism to the Negro, whether bond or free. These words and spirit of Freeborn Garrettson only illustrate those of Coke, Asbury, and their associates. Under divine guidance, Garrettson had freed his slaves. He says: "I often set apart times to preach to the blacks, . . . and precious moments have I had, while many of their sable faces were bedewed with tears, their withered hands of faith stretched out, and their precious souls made white in the blood of the Lamb."[3]

[1] The fact that John Wesley organized a Sunday-school in Savannah, Ga., in 1736, is recorded on a bronze tablet seen near the entrance of the Protestant Episcopal Cathedral in Savannah.
[2] *Minutes of the Methodist Conference.*
[3] Matlack, *Slavery and Methodism,* 29. Coke's *Journal,* 12, 13-14.

In 1786 Asbury organized the first Sunday School in the United States in the house of David Crenshaw, Maryland.[4] Both Negro and white youth attended. One of the first converts in that school was a Negro, John Charleston, who afterwards became a noted preacher.[5] Four years later the Conference provided for Sunday Schools for white and black children, with text books and volunteer teachers; and all ministers were directed to use diligence in gathering the sons and daughters of Ham into societies, and administer among them full discipline of the church. In 1800 the ordination of Negroes was authorized. Where the colored membership was large, and it was desired, especially in the cities and larger towns, separate services and churches were provided. The policy of the church, as to the association of the races in worship, is indicated by the following from the report of the Board of Missions in South Carolina, in 1832: "As a general rule for our circuits and stations, we deem it best to include the colored people in the same pastoral charge with the whites, and to preach to both classes in one congregation, as our practice has been. The gospel is the same to all men, and to enjoy its privileges in common promotes good-will."[6] There were many eminently successful Negro local preachers, whose services were very acceptable to white congregations. During these first fifty years all the Negro societies or classes were under the direct care of white churches and pastors.

At the close of the first half century of Methodism in America what is known as African Methodism had its beginning. Difficulties arose as to church seating and pastoral service, and in New York there was dissatisfaction concerning proposed legislation on church property. The outcome was a distinct and successful movement in

[4] One celebrated Negro, known as "Black Harry," was Bishop Asbury's travelling companion. When for any reason the Bishop could not fill an appointment the people were pleased to hear him. Matlack, *Methodism*, 29.

[5] *Minutes of the Methodist Conference, 1832.*

[6] *Ibid.*

favor of separate Negro Methodist denominations. At Wilmington, Delaware, in 1813, the Union American Methodist Episcopal Church was organized. In 1815 the African Methodist Episcopal Church had its beginning in Philadelphia and five years later the African Methodist Episcopal Zion Church was organized in New York. The conviction underlying these separate Negro denominations is, that there is less opportunity for friction on account of race prejudice, whether among whites or blacks, and freer and better opportunities for the development of self-help and racial capabilities.[7]

The organization of African Methodism, independent of white control or association, in the North, was the most striking event previous to 1844, when the white Methodist hosts, North and South, were to be divided. In the South the chief event of interest, outside of faithful work of itinerants in preaching to the slave population in connection with regular pastorates, was the successful founding of plantation missions. Thus far the converts had been chiefly among the more favored or house-servant class. Beyond these were vast multitudes, probably four-fifths of the two million slaves of that day, where intellectual and moral paganism reigned. Philanthropists, both in and outside of the various churches, saw and recognized the necessity of some movement beyond the regular church work, to carry the blessings of Christian civilization into the gloom of this darker Africa in America. Methodists led in this important work.

The plan adopted was to send missionaries to the plantations, to be supported by the planters themselves, who were friendly to the work. Doctor (afterwards Bishop) Capers was the apostle of this forward movement. The importance of these efforts of this churchman are attested on a modest stone over the grave of the Bishop, at Columbia, South Carolina, by these words, " Founder of Missions to the Slaves." Under his guidance heroic itinerants

[7] Arnett, *Budget;* Woodson, *History of the Negro Church,* chapter IV.

were found to brave the dangers of disease and bodily discomfort, and go into the swamps and plantation cabins on a mission as holy as that which sent Cox to Africa and Carey to India. Not a few of them died as martyrs, but the places of those who fell were quickly filled. Volunteers would arise in the annual conferences and say to the Bishops, "Here are we, send us." This language is one of a sample of all: "We court no publicity; we seek no gain; we dread no sickness in going after the souls of these blacks for whom Christ died. If we may save some of them from going down to the pit, and succeed in pointing their steps to the heavenly city, all will be well."[8]

The greatest success was in South Carolina, where, in 1839, at the end of ten years, seventeen missionaries were employed. There were 97 appointments, embracing 234 plantations and 6,556 church members, to whom preaching and the sacraments were regularly given. They had also under regular catechetical instruction 25,025 Negro children.

In 1844, when the division of American Methodism became inevitable, these plantation missions were in the full tide of success. They were maintained and rejoiced in by the whole Methodist Episcopal Church. Their chief support, however, came from Methodists and other friends in the South. In the year mentioned there were 68 missions in nine of the Southern States, with 80 missionaries and 22,063 members. In that year, white southern conferences paid $22,379.25 to this work. It is estimated that the conferences in the South gave for this cause $200,000 during fifteen years, up to 1844.[9]

The "Brother in Black," however, brought the republic an irrepressible conflict, ending in frightful civil war. So, too, it must be said, that in Methodism, for nearly a century Negro slavery was the occasion of discussion and legislation, and at last of division, which Calhoun considered the beginning of the dismemberment of the Union.

[8] Wightman, *Life of William Capers*, 295-296.
[9] *Minutes of the Methodist Conference, 1844*.

Methodism grew with the colonies, and at the close of the American Revolution had 84 preachers and 15,000 members in its societies. It was the first organized American church that officially gave its benediction, through Washington, to the young republic. Its spirit and itinerant system kept its organizations on the front wave of every movement of population. Its mission was salvation to rich and poor alike, regardless of race. Its only test of membership was "a sincere desire to flee from the wrath to come." Peoples of every station in life, bond and free, educated and illiterate, rich and poor, political friends and antagonists, were alike attracted by the impassioned appeals of her apostolic missionaries. Her form of government brought into annual and quadrennial conferences all questions of polity or principle involved in administration. Other churches might relegate important questions of discipline to individual societies; Methodism could not. Every important matter must be settled by a majority vote of representatives of the whole church.

On doctrines there were no divisions. Not so as to questions relating to African slavery. As to the abstract right and wrong of that institution, for many years there was but little division among Methodists. Later some in the South talked of the "divine institution," and occasionally a Northern man claimed that a Christian might buy and sell slaves without sin. The legislation of the church, however, was clear and explicit to this effect: "Slavery is contrary to the laws of God and man, and wrong and hurtful to society." All buying and selling of slaves, then, was forbidden.[10] Gradually the irrepressible conflict began in the church. The Northern section more and more taught that slavery was wrong, and could in no way be excused or tolerated by the church of Christ, without partaking of its sin. The South held that slavery was a civil institution, approved by the word of God, and that the church was not responsible for its existence or

[10] *Minutes of the Methodist Conference, 1784;* McTyeire, *History of Methodism,* 28.

its abuses. The duty of the church in its relation to slavery was taught to be loyalty to civil government, as represented by national and State laws, and to give the gospel as far as possible to both master and slave.

For more than half a century the largest growth of the church had been in the Southern States, and Southern views as to slavery modified legislation in relation to that institution. On the other hand, with the development of the West and Northwest, the balance of legislative influence shifted northward until in the historic General Conference of 1844, Bishop Andrews of Georgia, having become related to slavery by marriage, was requested by a vote of 111 to 69 "to desist from the exercise of his episcopal office so long as this impediment remained."[11] Then followed the inevitable division, and the organization of the Methodist Episcopal Church, South. Only seventeen years later the Civil War began and Southern Methodist hosts gave their sympathies, prayers, votes, money and sons to the Army of Gray; while Methodists in the North, to quote the words of Lincoln, "sent more prayers to heaven and soldiers to the field" for the Army in Blue, than any other Christian church. Thus may people of God of like faith have diverse consciences and differ, first, in sentiment and policies, then in conviction and duty, and at last prayerfully face each other at the cannon's mouth in deadly combat.

The years from 1844 to 1846 were indeed momentous in the history of the American Methodism in its relation to the Negro. That little company of five in New York in seventy-eight years had in 1845 come to be a multitude of 1,139,583 communicants, whose presence and spiritual energy were felt in every community of the republic, North, South, East and West. Of that membership, 150,120 were Negroes, chiefly in the South, and mostly gathered from among the slave population. But now there was to be division, the North to be more and more anti-slavery and the South to be more and more pro-slavery.

[11] *Minutes of the Methodist Conference, 1844.*

Then followed three Methodist divisions as related to the Negro: First, the African organizations already mentioned, with their chief strength in the Eastern States; and second, the Methodist Episcopal Church, South, with a total membership of 447,961 in 1846. Of these 118,904 were Negro slaves with few exceptions This church occupied all the territory of the Southern States exclusively, except along the border. Methodists in Maryland, Virginia, Delaware and the District of Columbia, including the Baltimore and part of the Philadelphia Annual Conferences, and also many members along the border farther west, did not join in the Southern movement. In the third place, then, there remained in the Methodist Episcopal Church still (1846) a total membership of 644,558. Of these 30,516 were Negroes, of whom about 20,000 were slaves.

The following twenty years were crowded with far-reaching events in church and state, as affecting the Negro. Each of the three divisions of Methodism had its place according to its convictions during that twenty years of agitation and war. The distinctly Negro organizations in the North, while having slaves in their own communions, were, of course, anti-slavery in principle, and sought in every way to advance the cause of abolitionism. Outside of Maryland and Delaware they had no churches in the South, except one in New Orleans and one in Louisville. A church organized in Charleston was driven out, after an attempted Negro insurrection. Permission was given by the mayor of St. Louis to one of its ministers to preach in that city, but the permit was afterwards recalled on learning the sentiments of his church.[12]

During this period of twenty years the Methodist Episcopal Church had wonderful growth throughout the North and West in membership, church buildings, publishing interests, educational institutions, and in social and moral power. Her entire membership rose from 644,294 to 1,032,184. Her Negro membership, however, steadily de-

[12] Tanner, *African Methodism*, 72.

clined. In 1846 it numbered, as we have seen, 30,516, while in 1865 at the close of the Civil War there were only 18,139. Shut away from the large Negro populations of the South, and confronted with aggressive African Methodism among the smaller Negro population in the North calling for separation from the whites in ecclesiastical organization and government, the field of operation of the Methodist Episcopal Church was necessarily proscribed among Africa's sons and daughters. She was, however, faithful to her trust and retained her Negro membership in church and conference relations, and, as the years went by, became more and more permeated with sentiments of antagonism to slavery, both as related to the church and the nation.

To this branch of Methodism, moreover, belongs the honor of establishing the first Methodist institution of higher learning for the education of colored people. In 1855 the Cincinnati Annual Conference appointed the Rev. John F. Wright as agent "to take incipient steps for a college for colored people." In two years Wilberforce University, near Xenia, Ohio, was established, with fifty-two acres of land and large and commodious buildings. The next year the Visiting Committee of the Conference reported the school in a flourishing condition, and said: "The examinations showed conclusively that the minds of the present class of students are capable of a very high degree of cultivation." Under the presidency of Rev. R. S. Rust the school was successful until financial embarrassment compelled suspension in 1863. One reason given was the War, and the consequent difficulty of obtaining funds from the South. From the beginning, the friendly co-operation of the African Methodist Episcopal Church was encouraged and received. Fortunately the leaders of that denomination were able to assume the indebtedness which was a nominal sum as compared with the value of the property. The lands and buildings were transferred with the good wishes and prayers of the Methodist Episcopal Church, ministry, and people, and Wilberforce University became, and continues to be, the chief educational center of African Methodism in the United States.[13]

Freed from all embarrassments from connectional relations with abolition sentiment the Methodist Episcopal Church, South, prospered in its way. Her territory was rapidly extending westward and southwestward, population and wealth were increasing, and slavery being embedded in the national and state constitutions, pro-slavery sentiment prevailed without question. Her total membership from 1846 to 1861 advanced from 449,654 to 703,295. This was, in fifteen years, an increase of 162,749. Dividing this increase by races, we find that among white people the growth was from 330,710 in 1846 to 493,459 in 1861, being an increase of 162,749. During the same period the Negro membership went from 118,904 to 209,836, being an increase of 90,932. Efforts to increase the slave membership in connection with the regular charges were continued with encouraging results, and the plantation mission work among the slaves was prosecuted with gratifying success. The largest figures were reached in 1861, when there were 329 Negro missions throughout the South, with 327 missionaries and 66,559 members. It is estimated that the Methodist Episcopal Church, South, from 1844 to 1864, when freedom came, expended $1,800,000 in plantation work among the slaves.[14]

The sudden emancipation of almost 4,000,000 Negro slaves meant new and tremendous responsibilities for the loyal and philanthropic people of the Northern States. The churches and benevolent organizations of the South had all shared largely in the demoralization caused by the Civil War, and were without financial resources. Neither was it reasonable to expect that the Southern people would do for free Negroes what they had done for them when

[13] *Special Report of the U. S. Commissioner of Education*, 1871, pp. 372-373.
[14] *Minutes of the Methodist Conference.*

slaves, much less enter upon the absolutely necessary missionary movement, to prepare the newly enfranchised for the responsibilities incident to freedom.

For more than half a century, outside of what the general and State governments have done or attempted to do, the tide of philanthropic and Christian aid for the Negro has gone Southward, and will continue as long as needed. How many million dollars have been expended by churches, educational boards and individual philanthropists has not been computed. Neither has anyone attempted to measure the results of the work of the many consecrated men and women, who have given and are still giving their lives for the uplift of the Negro race since emancipation. The results are manifest. Already the advance of this people since freedom in morality, intellectual development and economic success has no parallel, in the same time, in the history of any other race.

The Methodist Episcopal Church and the two large branches of African Methodism were in the fore-front of this movement from the beginning. The African Methodist Episcopal Church had at first its chief increase in the South along the Atlantic Coast, especially in South Carolina and Florida. Bishop Arnett, the statistician of that denomination, estimates that 75,000 of the Negro membership of the Methodist Episcopal Church, South, transferred ther church relations to that denomination. The African Zion Church as a factor in the South had its beginning in North Carolina and Alabama. It is estimated that at least 25,000 of the Southern Negro members united with this branch. Both of these sections of African Methodism have continued to prosecute their work of evangelization and education throughout the South, as well as the North, and continue powerful factors in the evangelistic forces of American Methodism as related to the Negro. In 1921–22 the membership of the African Methodist Episcopal Church was 550,776; and that of the African M. E. Zion Church was 412,328.[15]

[15] The A. M. E. Church has Wilberforce University, Xenia, Ohio, with

The policy of the Methodist Episcopal Church, South, toward the Negro Freedmen took definite form in 1866. At the General Conference held that year at New Orleans, provision was made for the organization of its remaining Negro membership into " separate congregations and districts, and annual conferences." If the colored people should desire, and two or more Negro annual conferences be formed, a separate ecclesiastical autonomy would be granted. The reasons for the organization of this new separate Negro Methodism are given in its Book of Discipline over the signature of its first four Bishops. They say that the Southern Methodist Conference " found that, by revolution and the fortunes of war, a change had taken place in our political and social relations, which made it necessary that a like change should also be made in our ecclesiastical relations." The result was that, in 1871, the Colored Methodist Episcopal Church of America was organized to be composed exclusively of Negroes, and officered entirely by members of this race. Here we have the beginning of a third large section of African Methodism. The new organization started with 80,000 members made up of nearly all who still remained in the Methodist Episcopal Church, South.

It would be very interesting to speculate as to the probable results, could the Methodist Episcopal Church, South, have continued its work among the Freedmen, which it had for years carried forward with such excellent results among the slaves. But it is no part of this paper to criticize or philosophize. This branch of Methodism, second in numbers and influence in the nation, with all but 30,000 of its

enrollment of 1,070 and an annual income of $145,000. This church has ten other schools with an enrollment of 4,448, several of which have college classes. The total annual income of all these schools is $309,820.00. There are also theological classes at several centers with total enrollment of 156.

The A. M. E. Z. Church has seven schools with an attendance of 2,128 and an annual income of $43,331.00. The leading school of this church is Livingstone College in North Carolina, with an attendance of 504 students and an annual income of $13,633.

members in the South, now has 2,239,151 members, a few of whom are Negroes.

Commencing with 1883, the Methodist Episcopal Church, South, took definite and forward steps for the education of the Negro. A Board of Trustees was appointed in co-operation with the Colored Methodist Episcopal Church. In 1884, Paine Institute was founded at Augusta, Georgia, and contributions of over $90,000 have been contributed to that school. Lane College, Jackson, Tennessee, has also been aided. The Colored Methodist Episcopal Church has seven schools with an enrollment of 2,509 and an annual income of $113,830. Fifty-seven students of theology are taught in two schools and college courses are offered in several of their institutions.

We have yet to speak of the work of the Methodist Episcopal Church. When freedom came, as we have seen, this church had (1864) 18,139 Negro members principally in Maryland, Delaware and adjacent territory. The Negro membership in this branch of Methodism now (1923) in the United States is 385,444.

As the way opened during and following the Civil War to reach the masses of the South both white and Negro, the Methodist Episcopal Church extended its work of reorganization southward among both races. Her Bishops and other church officials organized missions and conferences and opened up schools. Each benevolent society of the church aided financially. The support of pastors was supplemented by the Missionary Society; the Board of Church Extension aided in building houses of worship; the Sunday School Union and Tract Society gave their co-operation, and the Freedmen's Aid and the Southern Educational Society, now the Board of Education for Negroes, and the Woman's Home Missionary Society developed the educational work. In 1864, the Negro work in Maryland, Delaware and adjacent territories was organized into the Washington and Delaware Annual Conferences. In the other border States where the Negro membership was small, the preachers with their congregations were admitted into white conferences. With unwavering and magnificent purpose for over half a century, with fraternity and co-operation for all other churches in the same field, and impelled by a conviction of duty to needy millions irrespective of race, this branch of Methodism has gone forward with its work of education and evangelization irrespective of race. The results have been very remarkable. The white membership has grown on what was slave territory from 87,804 in 1860 to 475,641 in 1922; while the Negro membership in the same territory has increased from 18,139 in 1864 to 370,477 in 1922.

Following the wishes of both races the policy of separate conferences, churches and schools has been carried out in the South. There are several strong Negro churches in white conferences in the North. The New Conference elected Dr. W. H. Brooks, one of its Negro pastors, a delegate to the General Conference in 1920. The Methodist Episcopal Church has thirty-seven annual conferences in the Southern States with properties in parsonages, churches, schools of different grades, hospitals, and the like valued at $63,495,130.00. In 1856 the property of this church of all kinds in the same territory was less than $2,000,000. Seventeen of these conferences include the work among white people, and nineteen, the work among Negroes; and each group of conferences covers the Southern States from Delaware to Texas.

The twenty annual conferences in the South among Negroes have properties in parsonages and churches valued at $19,767,430. There are also thirty-two Negro institutions of learning in these twenty conferences with enrollment of 8,868 and lands with buildings and equipment valued at $6,522,642. The outstanding professional and collegiate institutions for Negroes are Gammon Theological Seminary, Atlanta, Meharry Medical College, Nashville, and colleges in several of the principal cities of the South. The total church properties named above, in Negro Methodist Conferences of the Methodist Episcopal Church on former slave territory, is $25,218,230.00. These conferences raised $1,500,000 during three years from 1870 to 1872 for general church work at home and in foreign fields outside of pastoral and other local church expenses.[16]

There is no separation on account of race in annual conferences, churches or schools in the Methodist Episcopal Church, except as desired and requested by those interested. As the result of many petitions and extended discussions the General Conference, which met in 1876, in Baltimore, passed a law that the annual conferences in the Southern States which had both Negro and white members could separate, provided each group voted in favor of it. Under this action with few exceptions the division was made, where desired. The same law prevails in reference to churches and schools. The nineteen Negro conferences have ninety-two delegates in the General Conference, the law-making body for the whole church. These delegates have representation in all legislation. One or more Negro ministers or laymen are on each of the general boards of the church — publication, education, missions — home and foreign, Epworth League, and the like. Nearly a score of able and effective Negro men and women are official representatives of the general church boards in their work among the Negro conferences.

Six Negroes have been elected bishops in the Methodist Episcopal Church. Four were missionary bishops, with full episcopal authority on the continent of Africa. Of these Bishop Scott remains and is on the retired list. In their fields these bishops were not subordinate but co-

[16] Gammon Theological Seminary, Atlanta, Ga., has seven professors, 142 students, buildings and equipment $145,000 and an endowment of $500,000. Meharry Medical College, Nashville, Tenn., ranks A among medical colleges in the United States, has 43 teachers, 646 students, $350,000 in grounds and equipment and $560,000 in endowments and has graduated two thirds or more of the Negro physicians, dentists and pharmacists in the United States. Eleven colleges under the Board of Education for Negroes has 248 teachers; an enrollment of 4,326. Only a small proportion are below the eighth grade in scholarship.

ordinate with general superintendents. Their episcopal work was of the same type as that of William Taylor, James Thoburn, Oldham, Warne, and Hartzell, white missionary bishops in Africa and India.

The General Conference in 1920 elected Robert E. Jones and Matthew W. Clair general superintendents. The former has his episcopal residence in New Orleans and the latter in Liberia. They preside in turn at the semiannual conferences of the Board of Bishops and will preside at the General Conference in 1924.

The great mass of Negro Christians in the United States will continue to prefer churches made up of their own race. This is natural and on the whole the best for many reasons. On the other hand, the door of every church of Christ should be open for all. At present in twenty-nine white Protestant churches in the United States with a total membership of over 4,000,000, there are 579,690 Negro members. Nearly three-fourths of that membership are in the Methodist Episcopal Church.

The total Negro Methodist Church membership in the United States is 1,756,714. Of that number 1,330,409 are in the African Methodist Episcopal, the African Methodist Episcopal Zion and the Colored Methodist Episcopal Churches; 385,444 in the Methodist Episcopal Church and 41,961 in seven smaller African bodies. If we multiply the total membership by $2\frac{1}{2}$ we have 4,557,117, which represents, approximately, the enrolled membership and constituency of Negro Methodism in the United States.

JOSEPH C. HARTZELL.

NOTES ON THE SLAVE IN NOUVELLE-FRANCE

The French Canadian historian, François-Xavier Garneau, in his *Histoire du Canada*, says: "Nous croyons devoir citer ici une résolution qui honore le gouvernement français: c'est celle qu'il avait prise de ne pas encourager l'introduction des esclaves en Canada, cette colonie que Louis XIV préférait à toutes les autres à cause du caractère belliqueux de ses habitants; cette colonie qu'il voulait former à l'image de la France, couvrir d'une brave noblesse et d'une population vraiment nationale, catholique, française sans mélange de races. En 1688, il fut proposé d'y avoir des nègres pour faire la culture. Le ministère répondit qu'il craignait qu'ils n'y périssent par le changement de climat et que le projet ne fût inutile. Cela anéantit pour ainsi dire une entreprise qui aurait frappé notre société d'une grande et terrible plaie. Il est vrai que dans le siècle suivant, on étendit à la Louisiane le code noir des Antilles; il est vrai qu'il y eut ici des ordonnances sur la servitude: néanmoins l'esclavage ne régnait point en Canada: à peine y voyait-on quelques esclaves lors de la conquête. Cet événement en accrut un peu le nombre un instant; ils disparurent ensuite tout à fait."[1]

In another place speaking of the proposal of Denonville, the Governor, and De Champigny, the Intendant, at Quebec, in 1688 to introduce Negro slaves by reason of the scarcity and dearness of domestic and agricultural labor, and the refusal in 1689 of the minister to permit, Garneau says: "C'était assez pour faire échouer une entreprise, qu'aurait greffé sur notre société grande et terrible plaie paralyse la force d'une portion considerable de l'Union

---

[1] Quoted by the Archivist of Quebec in the work cited (infra) at p. 109, from F. X. Garneau, *Histoire du Canada*, 4th Ed., Vol. II, p. 167. See note 2 for translation.

Américaine, l'esclavage, cette plaie inconnue sous notre ciel du Nord."[2]

This language has been considered by some—rather heedlessly be it said—to indicate that Garneau thought that Negro slavery did not exist in French Canada, but a careful examination of his actual words will show that he denied only the prevalence " l'esclavage ne régnait point en Canada," not the existence. Slavery was not so widespread in Canada as to become a curse, " a great and terrible plague," " paralyzing energy."

[2] F. X. Garneau, *Histoire du Canada*, 1st Ed., Vol. II, p. 447. Andrew Bell, *History of Canada*, Montreal, 1862 (translated from Garneau's work). Vol. I, p. 440, treats the statement of Garneau somewhat slightingly. His translation reads: "In 1689, it was proposed to introduce Negroes to the colony. The French ministry thought the climate unsuitable for such an immigration and the project was given up. Thus did Canada happily escape the terrible curse of Negro Slavery." Bell's note, pp. 440, 441, shows that he understood what the facts actually were.

The translation of the two passages follows:

"We think we should mention here a determination which is honorable to the French Government. It is the resolve not to encourage the introduction of slaves into Canada, the colony which Louis XIV preferred to all the others by reason of the warlike character of its inhabitants—the colony which he wished to make in the image of France, to fill with a brave noblesse and a population truly national, Catholic, French, without an admixture of foreign races. In 1688, it was proposed to have Negroes there as farm laborers: the minister replied that he feared that they would die there by the change of climate, and that the project would be futile. That, so to speak, destroyed forever an enterprise which would have struck our society with a great and terrible plague. It is true that in the succeeding century, the *Code Noir* of the Antilles was extended into Louisiana, it is true that there were ordinances as to slavery there; but, nevertheless, slavery did not prevail in Canada. There were scarcely any slaves at the time of the conquest. That event increased the number of them a little; they later disappeared entirely."

"That was sufficient to wreck a scheme which would have engrafted in our society that great and terrible plague which paralyzes the energies of so considerable a part of the American Union, slavery, that plague unknown under our northern sky."

It will be seen that Garneau does not say or suggest that slavery was entirely unknown in French Canada, but only that it did not "reign" (ne régnait point), *i.e.*, was not prevalent; that while there were a few sporadic cases, the disease was not endemic, and it did not become a plague.

For the proposal of 1688-9, see my *The Slave in Canada*, pp. 1, 2 and notes (JOURNAL OF NEGRO HISTORY, Vol. V, No. 3, July 1920, and published separately by The Association for the Study of Negro Life and History, Washington, 1920).

If there were any doubt as to the existence of Negro (and other) slavery in Canada before the British Conquest, it would be dispelled by the document printed in the latest Report of the Archivist of the Province of Quebec.[3] These are Notarial Acts (Actes notariés) preserved in the Archives at Quebec and are of undoubted authenticity; they range from September 13, 1737 to August 15, 1795, the first 14 being before the capture of Quebec in 1759, the last 3 after that event.

The first document is the sale of a Negro[4] called Nicolas by Joseph de la Tesserie, S. de la Chevrotière, ship-captain, to François Vederique of Quebec, ship-captain, for 300 livres.[5] The Negro was about 30 years of age and the Act was passed before midday, September 13, 1757.

The fourth, September 25, 1743, evidences a sale of five

[3] *Rapport de L'Archiviste de la Province de Québec pour 1921-1922* . . . L.—A. Proulx Imprimeur de Sa Majeste le Roi /1922: large 8 vo., pp. 452. This Report is well printed on good paper, with excellent arrangement and faultless proof reading; both in form and in matter it is a credit to the able and learned Archivist, M. Pierre-Georges Roy, Litt.D., F. R. S. Can., and to the Government of Quebec. To anyone with a knowledge of French, the publications of this Department are of inestimable value on the early history of that part of Canada.

[4] "Le nommé Nicolas, neigre de nation" was present with vendor and purchaser before the Notaries, Boisseau and Barolet, in the office of the latter at Quebec. The Vendor says that he had acquired the Negro from Sieur de St. Ignace de Vinceclotte.

[5] From the official Report of General James Murray, Governor of Quebec, to the Home Government June 5, 1762, it appears that he considered the livre worth 2 shillings sterling, about 48 cents.

General Murray's Report will be found in Drs. Shortt and Doughty's *Documents relating to the Constitutional History of Canada, 1759-1791,* Ottawa, 1918 (2d. Edit.), pp. 47-81. It is, however, quite clear that the ovaluation is too high. The livre was the old French monetary unit which was displaced by the franc. In the first ordinance passed by the civil government at Quebec, the ordinance of September 14, 1764, the value of a French crown or six livre piece was fixed at 6/8, making the livre 13 1/3 pence sterling (about 26 cents). The Ordinance of March 29, 1777, 17 George 3, c. IX, made the "french crown or piece of six livres *tournois*" worth 5/6; and the same value was assigned to it in Upper Canada by the Act (1796) 36 George 3, c. I, s. 1 (U. C.)—the livre was worth not far from 20 cents of our present money. This was the livre tournois. The livre of Paris was also in use until 1667 and was worth a quarter more than the livre tournois.

Negro slaves, two men and three women and girls⁶ then in the house of "la dame Cachelièvre," the vendor being Charles Réaume, merchant of l'Isle Jésus near Montreal, the purchaser Louis Cureux dit Saint-Germain, for 3000 livres.

The seventh, January 27, 1748, is the sale of a Negro[7] slave called Robert, 26 to 27 years of age, by Damelle Marie-Anne Guérin, widow of Nicolas Jacquin Philibert, merchant of Quebec, to Pierre Gautier, sieur de la Veranderie, for 400 livres in cash or bills payable by the Treasurer of the Navy having currency in the country as money—the Negro to be delivered on the first demand " avec seulement les hardes qu'il se trouvera avoir lors de la livraison et trois chemises."[8]

The eighth, June 6, 1749, evidences the sale by Amable-Jean-Joseph Came, Esquire, sieur de St. Aigne, officer in the troops in Quebec (a detachment from the troops of L'Isle Royale), to Claude Pécaudy, Esquire, sieur de Contrecoeur, Captain of the troops (a detachment of the Navy) in garrison at Montreal, of a Negro woman, Louison, about 17 years old, for 1000 livres.

The tenth, May 26, 1751, gives us the sale by Jacques Damien of Quebec to Louis Dunière, Jr., of a Negro, Jean Monsaige "pour le servir en qualité d'esclave," for 500 livres. But as "le dit nègre paraissant absent du jour d'hier soir, pour par le dit . . . Denière disposer du dit nègre comme chose à luy appartenant le prenant le

---

[6] "Cinq neigres esclaves dont deux hommes et trois femmes et filles"—names and ages not given; but the slaves are identified by the statement that the purchaser had seen them "chez la dame Cachelièvre." The witnesses were Louis Lambert and Nicolas Bellevue of Quebec and the Notary was Pinguet. The vendor, Réaume, signed but the purchaser St. Germain did not, "ayant déclaré ne sçavoir écrire ni signer."

[7] "Negre esclave"—the spelling vacillates between "neigre," "negre," and "nègre." I have not found the first form in French literature; the word comes from the mediaeval "Niger." See Du Cange, sub voc. The word no doubt had the usual variations; modern French has only the last form, i.e., nègre. My French Canadian friends cannot help me as to the spelling; but they tell me of a French Canadian saying "Un plan de negre" meaning "Un plan qui n'a ni queue ni tête," but this is probably only jealousy.

[8] "With only the clothes he stands in at the time of delivery and three shirts." "Shirt" has no gender in French.

dit . . . Dunière sur ses risques, périls et fortune, sans que le dit . . . Dunière puisse tenir à aucune'' and it is expressly provided ''le dit . . . Damiens sic cède, quitte et transporte au dit . . . Duniere sans aucune garantie le dit nègre pour par le dit . . . Dunière en disposer ainsy qu'il avisera.'' What a tragedy lies underneath these words![9]

The thirteenth, May 4, 1757, is a sale by Estienne Dassier, formerly Captain in the Navy, then living ''en sa maison, rue de Buade,'' Quebec, to Ignace-François Delzenne, merchant-goldsmith, living ''en sa maison, rue de la Montagne,'' of a Negro, Pierre, about 18 years of age, whom the purchaser had had in his house since the previous November. The Negro is sold for 1192 livres, 600 in cash, 592 in a fortnight, whatever happens to the Negro who is now to be at the risk of Delzenne, the purchaser. The purchaser as security hypothecates all his property movable and immovable. He also expresses his knowledge of and satisfaction with the condition of the Negro.[10] On July 1, 1757, Dassier acknowledges payment of the 592 livres.

These are all sales of Negros during the French regime; there are two instances of sales of Mulattoes in this period, but there are five of the sale of Indian slaves, Panis (fem. Panise).[11]

[9] Dunière receives the right to dispose of the Negro, Jean Monsaige, as his own property, but Damien does not undertake delivery: The slave being absent since the previous evening (perhaps like Eliza knowing of a proposed sale), Dunière takes all the risk of obtaining him without recourse to anyone in case of failure; and Damien sells him without any warranty. This and the fifth are the only instances, until the seventeenth, of a Negro having a family name. The notaries are Barolet and Panet.

[10] The purchaser undertakes all risks, the price remains payable in any event. ''Laquelle somme demeure acquise au d. s. Dassier par convention expresse quelque evenement qui puisse arriver au d. neigre d'en cy-devant aux risques et perils du d. s. Delzenne.''

[11] As to Panis, Panise, see *The Slave in Canada*, p. 2 and note 4. The name Pani or Panis, anglicized into Pawnee, was used generally in Canada as synonymous with ''Indian Slave'' because the slaves were usually taken from the Pawnee tribe. It is held by some that the Panis were a tribe wholly distinct from the tribe known among the English as Pawnees, *e.g.*, Drake's *History of the Indians of North America*.

The second act, September 14, 1737, is the sale by Hugues Jacques Péan, Seigneur of Livaudière, Chevalier of the Military Order of St. Louis, Town Major of Quebec, to Joseph Chavigny de la Chevrotière, captain and proprietor of the ship *Marie-Anne* then in the roads of Quebec, of an Indian girl Thérèse of the Renarde Nation, about thirteen or fourteen, and not baptized.[12] The purchaser had seen her, admitted her soundness in life and limb (le connait pour être saine et n'être estropiée en aucune façon) and paid 350 livres for her. The vendor was to keep the "sauvagesse" until the departure of the purchaser, not later than the end of the coming month, but not to guarantee against accident, sickness or death, binding himself only to treat her humanely and as he had been doing.

The third, October 1, 1737, gives the sale by Augustin Bailly, Cadet in the troops of the marine residing ordinarily at Saint-Michel in the Parish of Saint-Anne de Varennes, to Joseph de Chavigny de la Chevrotiètre, Sieur de la Tesserie,[13] Captain in the Navy, of an Indian (male) of the Patoqua Nation, age not given, bought by Bailly on the ninth of May preceding from Jean-Baptiste Normandin dit Beausoleil according to a contract passed before Loyseau, Notary at Montreal. The price was 350 livres, 250

[12] We are told, Littré, *Dictionnaire de la Langue Française*, 4to, Paris, 1869, *Sub voc*. Nègre: "Louis XIII se fit une peine extrême de la loi qui rendait esclaves les nègres de ses colonies; mais quand on lui eut bien mis dans l'esprit que c'était la voie la plus sûre pour les convertir, il y consentit." (Montesquieu Esp. des Lois, XV, 4) "Louis XIII was much troubled concerning the law which made slaves of the Negroes in his Colonies; but when he had become impressed with the view that that was the surest way to convert them, he consented to the law,"—the ever recurring excuse for the violation of natural right.

There was much discussion whether it was lawful to hold a fellow Christian in slavery; and it was a distinct advantage that a slave was not baptized. In 1781, the Legislature of the Province of Prince Edward Island passed an Act, 21 George 3, c. 15, expressly declaring that baptism of slaves should not exempt them from bondage. The notaries in the present case were Pinguet and Boisseau and the act was passed in the latter's office.

[13] The purchaser here is the vendor Joseph de la Tesserie, Sieur de la Chevrotière, of the first transaction—he is also the purchaser in No. 9 *post*.

in money and 100 paid with two barrels (barriques) of molasses.[14]

The ninth is the sale, September 27, 1749, by Jean-Baptiste Auger, merchant of Montreal but then in Quebec, to Joseph Chavigny, Sieur de la Tesserie, of an Indian girl (une panise) of about 22 years of age named and called Joseph for baptism, price 400 livres, Island money,[15] which the purchaser promises and agrees to send to be invested in pepper (?) and coffee for the account and at the risk of the vendor, Auger, by the first ship leaving Martinique for Canada, the pepper (?) and coffee to be addressed by the purchaser, de la Tesserie, to Voyer, a merchant at Quebec for the account of Auger. De la Tesserie hypothecates all his goods as security. The eleventh, November 4, 1751, is the sale by Jacques-François Daguille, merchant, of Montreal but then in Quebec, to Mathieu-Theodoze de Vitre, Captain in the Navy, of an Indian girl (une panise) about ten or eleven, called Fanchon but not yet baptized,[16] price 400 livres cash.

The twelfth, September 8, 1753, sale by Marie-Josephe Morisseaux, wife and agent of Gilles Strouds of Quebec, then at Nontagamion, to Louis Philippe Boutton, Captain of the Snow,[17] *Picard,* of an Indian girl (une sauvagesse panise de nation nommée Catiche) of about twenty years of age, price 700 livres payable on delivery, "with her clothes and linen as they all are."

The fifth, December 27, 1744, is a contract by Jean-Baptiste Vallée of Quebec, rue de Sault-au-Matelot, the owner of a Negro, commonly called Louis Lepage, whom

[14] The notaries were Pinguet and Boisseau and the act was passed in the latter's office.

[15] "Argent des Iles," West-Indian currency to be invested in Martinique. The notaries were Barolet and Panet and the act was passed in the latter's office.

[16] See note 12 supra: The notaries were Barolet and Panet and the act was passed in the latter's office.

[17] French "senaut," English "snow," a sort of vessel with two masts. The notaries were Sanguinet and Du Laurent; the act was passed in the latter's office.

Vallée certifies as belonging to him, and to be faithful and well-behaved. Vallée hires him to François de Chalet, Inspector General of the Compagnie des Indes to serve him as a sailor for the whole remaining term of de Chalet's tenure of the Ports of Cataraqui (Katarakouye, i.e., now Kingston, Ontario) and Niagara (on the east side of the river). The Negro is to serve as a sailor on the boats of the ports. Vallée undertakes to send him from Quebec on the first demand of de Chalet to serve him and his representative in all legitimate and proper ways, not to depart without written leave, etc. The amount to be paid to Vallée was 25 livres per month, de Chalet in addition to furnish the sailor a jug (pot) of brandy and a pound of tobacco a month, and for his food, two pounds of bread and half a pound of pork a day.[18]

The sixth act is a petition, April 27, 1747, to the Lieutenant Civil and Criminal of Quebec by Louis Parent, merchant of Quebec, asking him to direct Lamorille, Sr., and Jugon who had by judgment, April 25, 1747, been named as arbitrators, for the valuation of a Negro, named Neptune, part of the estate of the late Sieur de Beauvais, that they should proceed with their valuation — Chaussegros de Léry to be present if he wished, but if not, the two to proceed without him. A direction was given by Boucault to meet at his place the next day at 2 P. M. and a certificate by Vallet, the bailiff (huissier) to the Superior Council at Quebec, is filed that he had served Chaussegros de Léry, La Morille, Sr., and Jugon.

The first instance here recorded of sale of a slave after the Conquest by the British was November 14, 1778. This, the fourteenth document copied, evidences a sale by George Hipps, merchant butcher, living in his house, rue Sainte-Anne in Upper Town, Quebec, to the Honorable Hector-Theophile Cramahé, Lieutenant-Governor of Quebec, of a mulatto slave called Isabella or Bell about fifteen years

---

[18] The notary was Barolet who signed the act as did Vallée, De Chalet, and two witnesses, Charles Prieur, Perruquier, and Jean Liquart, merchant.

old.[19] She had been already received in Crahamé's house, and he declared himself satisfied with her. She had been the property of Captain Thomas Venture who had sold her at auction to Hipps. The price paid by Cramahé was £50 Quebec money, equal to 200 Spanish piastres; and Hipps acknowledged payment in gold and silver. Cramahé undertakes to feed, lodge, entertain, and treat the slave humanely.

The next, the fifteenth, April 20, 1779, is the sale of the same mulatto girl, Isabella or Bell, by Cramahé to Peter Napier, Captain in the Navy, then living at Quebec, with her clothes and linen for 45 livres, Quebec or Halifax money. Napier undertakes to treat the slave humanely.[20]

The sixteenth, August 15, 1795, is the first written in English, all the preceding being in French. It is dated August 15, 1795 and is sale by Mr. Dennis Dayly of Quebec, tavern-keeper, to John Young, Esquire, of the same place, merchant, of "a certain Negroe boy or lad called Rubin" for £70 Halifax currency. Dayly had bought the

[19] "L'esclave et mulatre nommée Isabella ou Bell, fille, âgée d'environ quinze ans, avec les hardes et linges à son usage." She is to obey her new master and render him faithful service. The price is expressed as "cinquante livres monnaye du cours actuel de Quebec, égale à deux cents piastres d'Espagne"—Fifty pounds Quebec currency equal to two hundred Spanish dollars. The word "livre" was in English times used for "pound." The pound in Quebec or Halifax currency was in practice about nine-tenths the value of the pound sterling.

The Ordinance of September 14, 1764, made one British shilling equal to 1s. 4d. Quebec currency, *i.e.*, the Quebec shilling was ¾ of an English shilling; the Ordinance of May 15, 1765, confirmed their valuation, making 18 British half-pence and 36 British farthings one Quebec shilling, but the Ordinance of March 29, 1777, made the British shilling only 1/1 and the British crown 5/6.

"The Seville, Mexico and Pillar Dollar" was by the Quebec Ordinance of December 14, 1764, made equal to 6/ of Quebec currency or 4/6 sterling; the Ordinance of March 29, 1777, equates "the Spanish Dollar" to 5/ Quebec currency (which was then substantially nine-tenths the value of sterling), *i.e.*, 4/6 sterling; the Upper Canadian Act of 1796 equated "the Spanish milled dollar" to 5/ Provincial currency or 4/6 sterling.

The notaries in the case were Berthelot Dartigny and A. Panet, Jr.; the act was passed in Cramahé's house, rue St-Louis."

[20] The same notaries appeared and the act was passed in the same place.

boy from John Cobham, of Quebec, September 6, 1786.[21]

The last, the seventeenth, is the most pleasant of all to record. John Young appeared, June 8, 1797, before Charles Stewart and A. Dumas, Notaries Public, in the former's office with the lad Rubin, and declared that he bought him from Mr. Dennis Dayly, August 15, 1795. He, as an encouragement to honesty and assiduity in Rubin, declared in the presence of the Notary, Charles Stewart, that if Rubin would faithfully serve him for seven years, he would give him his full and free liberty, and in the meantime would maintain and clothe him suitably and give him two and sixpence a month pocket money, but if he got drunk or absented himself from his service or neglected his master's business, he would forfeit all right to freedom. This was explained to Rubin, "who accepted with gratitude the generous offer." All parties, including the Notaries, signed the act, Rubin Young by his mark, so that the slave by good conduct and refraining from drunkenness would achieve his freedom, June 8, 1804.

I have discovered certain Court proceedings copied in the Canadian Archives at Ottawa,[22] which have not been made public in any way and which are of great interest in this connection. A short historical note will enable my readers to understand the proceedings more clearly.

After the Conquest of Canada, 1759–60, for a few years the country was under military rule. The three Districts of French times, Quebec, Montreal, and Three Rivers, were retained, each with its Governor or Lieutenant Governor. To administer justice, the officers of militia in each Parish, generally speaking, were constituted courts of first instance with an appeal to a council of the superior officers

---

[21] The notaries are A. Dumas and Charles Stewart; the act was passed in the latter's office.

[22] See the latest Report of the Archives of Canada.

The Ordinance of General James Murray establishing Military Courts in Quebec and its vicinity will be found printed in Shortt and Doughty's *Documents relating to the Constitution of Canada*, pp. 42, 44. General Gage's Ordinance established them in the District of Montreal will be found in the publication of the Archives of Canada. *Le Règne Militaire*.

in the British Army in the city, this court having also original jurisdiction.

On July 20, 1762, a council sat, as of original jurisdiction, composed of Lieut. Col. Beckwith, Captains Falconer, Suby, Dunbar and Osbourne, to hear the plea of a poor Negro called André against a prominent merchant of Montreal, Gershon Levy. The proceedings, recorded in French, are somewhat hard to decipher after a hundred and sixty years have elapsed but well repay the labor of examination.

André asked to be accorded his liberty, claiming that Levy had bought him of one Best, but that Best had the right to his services for only four years which had now expired. Levy appeared and claimed that André could not prove his allegation, but that he (Levy) had bought him from Best in good faith and without any knowledge of the alleged limitation of the right to his services. Of course, Best could sell only the right he had and it became a simple question of fact. The court heard the parties, ordered André to remain with his alleged master until he had proved by witnesses or by certificate that he "had been bound to the said Best for four years only, after the expiry of which time he was to have his liberty."

The following year, April 20, 1763, the council sat again to hear the case. Lieut. Col. Beckwith again presided, and Captains Fraser, Dunbar, Suby and Davius sat with him. The parties were again heard and witnesses were called by André; but they were "not sufficient"— and "the Council ordered that the Decree of July 20, last, shall be executed according to its tenor; and in consequence, that the said Negro André remain in the possession of the said Levy until he has produced other evidence or has proved by baptismal extract or the official certificate of a magistrate of the place where he was born that he was free at the moment of his birth."[23] Although these

---

[23] It is to be observed that it was considered that *prima facie* the Negro was a slave. The same rule was applied in many states (Cobb, *Law of Negro Slavery*, pp. 253 sqq.), unless the alleged slave had been in the enjoyment of

courts continued until the coming into force of purely civil administration of justice, September 17, 1764, I do not find that André made another attempt to secure his liberation from the service of Le Sieur Gershon Levy, negotiant.

I am indebted to my friend, Mr. R. W. McLachlan, F. R. S. C., of the Archives of the District of Montreal, for a memorandum of the following sales of which a record exists in Montreal:

1784, December 16, James McGill of Montreal for and in the name of Thomas Curry of L'Assomption in the Province of Quebec, sold to Solomon Levy of Montreal, merchant, for £100 Quebec currency, a Negro man Caesar and a Negro woman, Flora.

1785, February 20, Hugh McAdam of Saratoga sends by his friend John Brown to James Morrison of Montreal, merchant, "a Negro woman named Sarah" to sell. "She will not drink and so far as I have seen, she is honest."[24]

1785, March 9, Morrison sells Sarah to Charles Le Pailleur, Clerk of the Court of Common Pleas, for £36.

1785, January 11, John Hammond of Saratoga, farmer,

freedom; but Chief Justice Strange of Nova Scotia and his successor Salter Sampson Blowers by throwing the onus upon the master did much toward the abolition of slavery in that province. See *The Slave in Canada*, pp. 105-108.

[24] I here copy the letter, *verbatim et literatum*, a delightful literary effort.

SARATOGA 20 Feby 1785.

Dr Sir,
    I send by John Brown a Negro woman Named Sarah my Right & Lawful property—which you will Pleas Dispose of with the advis of your friends.—I have Wrote Mr Thomson on the same subjet—she has no fault to my knolage She will not Drink and so fare as I have seen she is honest—many many upertunitys she has had to have shown her Dishonesty had she been so in Clined . . . I am sory to give you the troble—She cost me sixty five pounds should not Liek to sell her under.— Should you not be able to get Cash you may sell her for furrs of any Kind you think will sutt our market and send them down by the Return sladges; any trobl you my be at shall Pay for these.

        I am Dr. Sir. Your
          as hurede frind &c:
            HUGH MCADAM

Mr. Morrison
   mercht. Montreal.

As to a subsequent disposition of Sarah, see sale of June 6, 1789.

sold to Paul l'Archeveque dit La Promenade, gentleman, a mulatto boy called Dick, 6 years old, for £30 Quebec currency.[25]

1785, April 26, sale by William Ward of Newfane, County of Windham, State of Vermont, to P. William Campbell in open market at Montreal of three Negroes, Tobi (aged 26), Sarah (aged 21) and child for $425. These had been bought with another Negro, Joseph, a year older than Sarah, from Elijah Cady of Kinderhook, County of Albany, State of New York, for £250.[26]

1789, June 6, James Morrison who had sold Sarah for

---

[25] It is possibly the same mulatto boy, Dick, the subject of the following Bill of Sale:

THUSBERRY octrs 19. 1785.

Know all men By these presents that I William Gillchres in the County of Rutland and State of Vermount, Yoeman for and in consideration of twenty pound Law Money to you in hand paid by Joseph Barrey of Richmond in the County of Cheshier in State of New Hampshier yeo man whereof I acknoledg the receipt and barggained and sold one molate Boy six years old naimed Dick to him the said Joseph Barney and his heirs for ever, to have and to hold the said molater boy, I said William Gillchres who for myself and my heirs promise for ever to warrant socuro and defend said promise against the lawful claims or demand of any person or persons in which I have set my hand, hereunto, and seal this nineteenth day of October one thousand seven hundred and eighty-six, in the eleventh year of endipendency.

(Signed) WILLIAM GILLCHRES

Signed, sealed
in the presence of us
   (Signed) ELISHA FULLAN
      LUCY YEOMANS
      On the back of this document were written thus the following words:
        Novemer ye 15, 1786
           Recevd the contents of
        the within bill by me
          Joseph Barrey
     29 Nover   1786. .
     Witness) Martin McEvoy
     present)
     John Carven
         Gillchress
          Bill of Morlato
           Boy nd. Dick Gun

[26] I assume New York Currency, in which case the pound was 20 York shillings or $2.50.

McAdam to Charles Le Pailleur, bought her for himself and sold her to Joseph Anderson of Montreal, gentleman, for £40.[27] The purchase from Le Pailleur is evidenced in French; it was for £36.

1790, December 23, Guillaume Labart, Seigneur, living at Terrebonne, sold to Andrew Todd, merchant of Montreal, a young panis called Jack, about 14 years of age, for £25.

1792, August 10, "Joshuah Stiles, late of Litsfield in the county of Birkshire, Massachusetts, at present in Montreal," sold to Daniel Carberry of Montreal, hair-dresser, a Negro boy named Kitts, aged 15 years, for the sum of one hundred and fifty dollars each of the value of five shillings Halifax currency.

1793, July 11, Jean Rigot, master hair-dresser, living on Boulevard St. Antoine, sold a mulatto slave boy, Pierre, aged 16, to Sir Charles Chaboille, merchant of the Upper Country (*i.e.*, Niagara, Detroit, Michillimackinac), for $200 Spanish, each worth s.5 Halifax currency. Rigot had raised the boy from infancy (l'ayant élevé de bas age).

1793, July 27, William Byrne, formerly captain in the King's Royal Regiment of New York, in a letter of May 29, 1793, having promised his adopted son, Phillip Byrne, on his marriage to Mary Josephine Chêne, daughter of Charles Chêne of Detroit, to give him a Negro boy, Tanno, aged 16, and a Negro woman, Rose, aged 28, carried out his promise by Deed of Gift, July 27, 1793, but he stipulates for "half the young ones"!!

1795, December 15, François Dumoulin, merchant of the Parish of Ste. Anne, Island of Montreal, sells to Meyer Michaels, merchant of Montreal, a mulatto named Prince, aged about 18, for £50.

1796, November 22, John Turner, Sr., merchant, sold to John Brooks, a Negro man named Joegho, aged 36, for £100, Quebec currency, and a Negro woman, Rose, aged 25, for £50.

1797, August 25, Thomas Blaney (attorney for Jervis

---

[27] 1787, January 10, George Brown and Sarah a Negress were married by Cave—it was probably the same Sarah.

George Turner, a soldier in the 2d Batt. Royal Canadian Volunteers) and Mary Blaney, his wife, sold to Thomas John Sullivan, tavernkeeper, a Negro man named Manuel, aged about 33, for £36.[28]

1781, August 9, sale per inventory of the estate of the late Naethan Hume, "one pany boy, Patrick, sold to McCormick for £32."

Perhaps this paper may well close with the following:

1781, October 31, a Negro, named York Thomas, a freeman, indentured himself for three years to Phillip Peter Nassingh, a Lieutenant in his Majesty's 2d Battalion, New York, for and in consideration, the said Nassingh to provide the said servant with meat, drink, washing, lodging, and apparel, both linen and woolens, and all other necessaries, in sickness and in health, mete and convenient for such a servant, during the term of three years and at the expiration of the said term, shall give the said York Thomas, one new suit of apparel, above his then clothing, and £6 Halifax currency.   WILLIAM RENWICK RIDDELL

OSGOODE HALL,
  Toronto, Dec. 23, 1922

[28] While this was in fact and in law a sale, the transaction was far more than a mere transfer of property: The Notary John Abraham Gray has the Notarial Act No. 74 which shows that Manuel, the negro man voluntarily engaged as servant, to Thomas Sullivan, under the usual conditions of servitude, for five years, at the end of which term, the said Manuel, if he should faithfully carry out his said engagement was to be emancipated and set at liberty according to due form of law, otherwise he was to remain the property of the said Sullivan.

A Notarial Act now in the possession of the Historical Society, Chicago, dated at Montreal, August 15, 1731, passed before the Notary Charles Benoit et St. Désiez, evidences the sale by Louis Chappeau to Sieur Pierre Guy, merchant, both of Montreal, of an Indian lad of the Patoka nation, aged about 10 or 12 years, for 200 livres paid in beaver and other skins. See *Report of Canadian Archives*, 1905, vol. 1, lxix.

It may be of interest to note that on pp. 476, 477 of the same report is copied a memorial (October 29, 1768) of the inhabitants and merchants of Louisiana in which they complain, *inter alia*, of D'Ulloa the Spanish Governor of Louisiana (1766-8) forbidding "the importation of negroes to the colony under the pretext that this competition would hurt an English merchant of Jamaica who had sent a vessel to D'Ulloa to confirm the contract for the importation of slaves. In creating this monopoly, he had robbed his new subjects of the means of procuring slaves cheaply...."

DOCUMENTS

Banishment of the People of Colour from Cincinnati

Prof. T. G. Steward of Wilberforce University directs attention to the following from *The Friend* which carries an important document bearing on the Free Negroes of Ohio:

In the course of the present year, a law of this state has been brought into view, by the trustees of Cincinnati township, requiring people of colour to give bond and security not to become chargeable to the public, and for their good behaviour—also imposing a fine on those who may employ them. This law was passed upwards of twenty years ago, and I believe has remained inoperative, or nearly so, to the present year. In order that the effects and bearing of the law may be correctly understood, I subjoin the proclamation or notice by the trustees.

To the Public

The undersigned, trustees and overseers of the poor, of the township of Cincinnati hereby give notice, that the duties required of them, by the act of the general assembly of Ohio, entitled *An Act to Regulate Black and Mulatto Persons,* and the act amendatory thereto, will be rigidly enforced, and all black and mulatto persons, now residents of said Cincinnati township, and who emigrated to, and settled within the township of Cincinnati, without complying with the requisitions of the first section of the amended act, aforesaid, are informed, that unless they enter into bonds as the said act directs, within thirty days from this date, they may expect at the expiration of that time, the law to be rigidly enforced.

And the undersigned would further insert herein, for the information of the citizens of Cincinnati township, the third section of the amendatory act aforesaid, as follows: That if any person being a resident of this state, shall employ, harbour, or conceal any such negro or mulatto person aforesaid, contrary to the provision of the first section of this act, any person so offending, shall forfeit and pay for such an offence, any sum not exceeding one hundred dollars, one half to the informer, and the other half for the use of the poor of the township, in which such person may reside, to be recovered by action of debt before any court having competent jurisdiction, and moreover to be liable for the maintenance and support of such negro or mulatto, provided he, she, or they shall become unable to support themselves. The co-operation of the public is expected in carrying these laws into full effect.

WILLIAM MILLS,
BENJAMIN HOPKINS,
GEORGE LEE,
Trustees of Cincinnati Township.

COMMENT

When this proclamation was issued, there were upwards of 2,000 people of colour, residing in this city, and nearly all obnoxious to the operations of the law; many of them had resided here for a considerable time, and were comfortably situated—they became unsettled and deprived of employment by this act of banishment and proscription, and much suffering and distress ensued. They deputed two of their number to select and provide a place for them to remove to, who procured a tract of land in Canada. In the meantime some of them commenced making preparations to leave the country, and as the time was very short which the trustees allowed them, they had to incur great losses in disposing of their property, selling for twenty dollars, what cost one hundred dollars. When the thirty days expired, and it was ascertained all did not, or could not comply with the requisitions of the trustees, mobs assailed them at different times, stoning their houses and destroying their property; in the progress of these disgraceful transactions one white man was killed and others wounded.

It is thought about five hundred have gone to Canada, many of these with means exceedingly limited to provide necessaries in a wilderness country, and encounter the rigours of a northern winter; one of their agents, a coloured man, informed me of an instance where twenty-eight persons had set out with a sum not exceeding twenty-five dollars. I confess my mind has been impressed with fearful apprehensions that they will greatly suffer or perish with hunger and cold! Some of them view this act of banishment with so much horror, they have told me the white people had better take them out in the commons and shoot them down, than send them to Canada to perish with hunger and cold!

The Friend, Nov. 28, 1829.

First Protest Against Slavery in the United States

Prof. Steward invites attention also to the following extract from *The Friend* published in Philadelphia April 1831, said to be the first document against slavery published in this country:

"At a General Court held at Warwick the 16th. of May 1657.

"Whereas there is a common course practiced among Englishmen, to buy negroes to that end that they may have them for service or as slaves forever; for the the preventing of such practices among us, let it be ordered, that no black mankind or white being, shall be forced by covenant, bond or otherwise, to serve any man or his assigns longer than ten years, or until they come to be twenty-four years of age, if they be taken in under fourteen, from the time of their coming within the liberties of this Colony—at the end or term of ten years to set them free as the manner is with the English servants. And that man that will not let them go free, or shall sell them away elsewhere, to that end they may be enslaved to others for a longer time, he or they shall forfeit to the Colony forty pounds."

The court that enacted this law was composed as follows: John Smith, President; Thomas Olney, General Assistant, from Providence; Samuel Gorton from Warwick; John Green, General Recorder; Randal Holden, Treasurer; Hugh Bewett, General Sergeant.

The Friend, April, 1831.

A Negro Pioneer in the West

Mr. Monroe N. Work invites attention to the fact that in an issue of December 23d, 1920, the *Advertiser Journal* of Kent, Washington, ran the following story:

"The best and largest yield of wheat ever exhibited," grown in western Washington. It sounds like a real estate folder. And yet at the World's Centennial Exposition held in Philadelphia in 1876, W. O. Bush, son of George Bush, one of the first settlers on Puget Sound, won the gold premium for wheat he grew on Bush Prairie, just south of Olympia; to this day the wheat is preserved in the Smithsonian Institute.

This record of great wheat yield is a part of the history of one of the families that came to the Northwest and had that quality that made them successful here. George Bush was the first colored man to come to this part of the country, the forerunner of the large number of useful citizens of his race who have followed with the increasing population. He was born in Pennsylvania in 1814, and with his wife from Tennessee started west in 1844.

Before coming west with his family, Bush had made a trip to this country with a number of companions, coming north along the coast from the Mexican border and suffering from the innumerable hardships of the trail, hunger and Indians. He must have liked the prospects, for it was only a short time later that we find him again headed in this direction in company with a number of other hardy pioneers.

The character that made him face the privations of immigration ingratiated him with his companions. There was an unwritten law in Oregon at that time that no colored people should be allowed to settle in that territory. When the group of which Bush was a member approached the Columbia river country and learned of the rule it was decided that if any one attempted to molest Bush all of the members of the company would fight to protect him.

The practice in Oregon was to whip the colored man and if he left after the whipping it was all right and nothing further was done, but if he did not take advantage of the opportunity to escape he was whipped again and again until he either left or died.

There is not any record of an attempt being made to molest Bush, who, with his companions, stayed at the Dalles for several months and later at Washougal at the mouth of the Cowlitz. The following year—1845—they came on to Puget Sound and settled at the head of Budds Inlet at the falls of the DesChutes and founded the town of New Market, now Tumwater.

Those who made up this party were Michael T. Simmons, James McAllister, David Kindred, Gabriel Jones and Bush. The latter decided not to settle right in Tumwater and went back onto the prairie land about four miles and took up a donation claim of 640 acres. It was on that claim that the prize wheat was grown by his oldest son thirty-two years later. There on that claim Bush died in 1863, while the great war for the freedom of his race was being waged. His widow followed him two years later.

Of their six sons, the state has heard a great deal. The eldest, W. O. Bush, was born before the couple left Missouri on their way west, and got the hard training of the pioneer. He took to farming and that he worked the prairie land where his father had settled for all it was worth is shown by the crop he took to Philadelphia. The soil of that section is a black sandy loam on a gravel base. The soil is not too thick in some parts and has a tendency to drain, particularly during the hot, dry summer.

Shorly after the formation of the state Bush was elected a member of the legislature and served two terms during 1890 and 1892. His record in the law-making body was an honorable one and that he was highly respected by the people of Thurston county was shown when they sent him to the Chicago World's Fair in 1893 to look after the county's agricultural exhibit.

Concerning the Origin of Wilberforce

While at Tuskegee Institute in 1914 Mrs. Emma Castleman Bowles, who has since died, related this account of the origin of Wilberforce. This story does not agree with the account given in Bishop D. A. Payne's *African Methodist Episcopal Church* (423 ff.). The value of the document lies mainly in the light which it throws upon the relations between wealthy slaveholders and their children of slave women. There must be much truth in the narrative, for Payne's sketch says that in 1859-60 a majority of the 207 students enrolled " are the natural children of Southern and Southwestern planters." The *Special Report of the United States Commissioner of Education*, published in 1871 (372-373), supports this statement. Mrs. Bowles' story follows:

Mrs. Emma Castleman Bowles said her father was Stephen S. Castleman, a slave holder who lived on the Yazoo River, about 150 miles from Vicksburg. He owned the Ashland plantation. She was born June 3, 1845. Her mother was a half sister of her father's wife. When Castleman married, her mother was sent to wait on her mistress. Castleman lived with both women. Castleman had two children by his wife and five by his concubine. He hired a white woman to teach Emma. This woman was paid $500 a year. Mrs. Bowles said she was not taught anything, not even to read. She spent her time playing with her half-brother and riding a pony which her father had bought for her.

In March 1858, Castleman sent his daughter Emma to Cincinnati by his brother-in-law, her half uncle, O. Leroy Ross. Here, she was emancipated and acknowledged as Castleman's daughter. Ross then brought her to Wilberforce and placed her in school.

Tawawa Springs was a summer resort for Southern slave holders. The Springs were medicinal. The Hotel Tawawa had 350 rooms, extensive grounds, elaborate water works for fountains, etc. There were several cottages on either side of the hotel. Slave holders would bring their families and slaves and live either in the hotel or in the cottages. A law was passed in Ohio forbidding the bringing of slaves into the State. Then white help and free Negro servants were used. The place declined financially and was finally sold for debt. Several planters banded together bought the place and turned it into a school for their illegitimate children by Negro women. Stephen S. Castleman was one of these men. Mrs. Bowles said this was done about 1856 or 1857.[2]

There were about nine teachers, all Yankees. The first principal was Rev. M. P. Gaddis. Richard Rust was the first President. The students, with a few exceptions, were children of slave holders.

Money was deposited in Cincinnati banks for the use of the children. President Rust was given power to draw on banks as the children needed money.

The following were named as among the slave owners who brought their children to the school. A planter named Mosley from Warren, Miss., brought seven children by three different mothers and freed them. Senator Hemphill of Virginia brought two daughters and emancipated them. A planter by the name of Smith brought eight children from Mississippi with their mother about 1859. He had a slave man and woman to wait on them. He was arrested and made to emancipate them. He bought a large tract of land for them. A brick house he built was later owned by Colonel Charles Young. The woman had lived with Smith under compulsion, and as soon as she was emancipated would have nothing more to do with him. Mrs. Bowles said that she went to school with these children and often visited the family. She had seen the mother strip herself to the waist and show how her back had been mutilated to make her submit to her master's wishes. A man named Piper came and brought 10 children and their mother. She was jet black. After the war he married her and settled in Darke County, Ohio.

[2] The school began in 1855.

General T. C. McMackin, a hotel owner of Vicksburg, Mississippi, was appointed by Castleman as his daughter's guardian. She said that she got in a fight with another school girl and was put on bread and water. She wrote her father. He had McMackin come to Wilberforce and adjust the matter. Her father, and she said the fathers generally, lavished money on their children. She had a box that held fifty silver dollars. This her father kept full of silver dollars for her to buy candy with.

Abolition was preached constantly in the school. She came to hate slavery. She had seen great cruelties inflicted on her mother and other slaves. Her mother took up with a slave man. Emma was a child, sleeping in the room. Many a night her father would come and curse the slave and compel him to leave the cabin. Then he would whip him and her mother. Whipping was on bare back from 39 to 300 lashes. Slave stripped naked and hands and feet tied to stakes driven into the ground. Stocks were also used. The lash and the stocks were both used on her mother's slave husband. They were put in the stocks at night and whipped night and morning.

Mrs. Bowles was courted in school by a class-mate, named George W. Harding, whose father was a large slave holder in Tennessee. President Rust tried to break it up. He wrote her father. Castleman wrote his daughter that he did not send her North to waste her time with a nigger. If she did not stop he would come and get her, cow hide her and bring her home and put her in the cotton field. She replied that "if her mother was good enough for him to sleep with, that a nigger was good enough for her to marry." She married Harding March 5, 1862. He had received considerable wealth from his father. When they married he had $55,000,[3] and later inherited $80,000 from his mother.

The war stopped communications with the South. As soon as the war closed, Castleman wrote to find out about his daughter and learned that she was married and the mother of two children. He wrote to her to come home and leave her niggers. If she didn't she would not get any of his property. She wrote him that he had beaten her mother and made her bear five children out of wedlock and that she would not forsake her husband and her lawfully born children.

[3] Harding squandered his property and died a pauper. Mrs. Harding then married another student of Wilberforce, A. J. Bowles.

COMMUNICATIONS

Mr. John W. Cromwell has addressed the Editor the following letter which may interest persons directing their attention to the record of the Negro in West Virginia:

Dear Sir:

While reading your *Negro Education in West Virginia* I was reminded of my acquaintances in that State, and I thought of the striking contrast between the West Virginia of 1877 and that of 1923.

On invitation of Prof. Brackett, President of Storer College, I attended a Teachers' Institute and Educational Convention, held at Harper's Ferry, in 1877. There I first saw a gathering of young teachers, vigorous and alert, none more chivalric in bearing than the central figure in the person of John R. Clifford, at that time Principal of the Grammar School at Martinsburg. To me it was quite a contrast from dealing with the civil service of the Treasury Department at Washington on the one hand, and my experience with the young men there a few years before as I had beheld them in central Pennsylvania.

The bearing of the men was more than matched by the excellence of the women. Outstanding at the time was a young woman whom I could not at first determine whether I should rate her as a young pupil in one of the classes or one of the faculty. I soon found that she was a student teacher, also an elocutionist of grace, skill and power. So impressed was I that Storer College thenceforth was a regular place of visit during commencement season, and I soon found myself on its trustee board.

During one of these commencements, Frederick Douglass was booked to speak on John Brown; but Andrew Hunter, the prosecuting attorney who convicted John Brown, came to Harper's Ferry, and declared that Frederick Douglass should not speak in Jefferson county, where Brown was convicted and hung. He also said: "If Douglass dares to come here, I'll meet him, denounce him, and crush him!" Douglass came; so did Hunter. At the proper time, Douglass was escorted to the rostrum, and without invitation

Hunter followed and took a seat close to Douglass, the master of American orators, who spoke as I never heard him before; and when through started to his seat. Hunter interrupted him, arose, and advanced toward Douglass with outstretched hand and exclaimed: "Let us shake hands," and while so doing, said: "Were Robert E. Lee here, he would shake the other," and pausing a few seconds, with all the power of his nature he said: "Let us go on!" to which Douglass replied: "IN UNION TOGETHER!" And everybody on the campus shouted—making the occasion one of dramatic as well as historic interest.

As editor of *The People's Advocate*, of Washington, D. C., the incident was sketched in bold and striking outlines for the country, and was read eagerly. It also forms an incident of one of the chapters of The *"Life and Times" of Frederick Douglass*.

In 1882, the Knights of Wise Men, with headquarters at Nashville, Tennessee, held their convention at Atlanta, Georgia. Thither went such representatives of the day as William J. Simmons, of Kentucky; Frances L. Cardozo, of Washington, D. C.; Bishop Henry M. Turner, of Georgia; Richard Gleaves, of South Carolina; John R. Lynch, of Mississippi; Robert Peel Brooks, of Virginia; Prof. J. C. Corbin, of Arkansas, and many other distinguished men interested in the order.

John R. Clifford, of Martinsburg, West Virginia, was one of the party and a most distinguished orator was he, whose masterly oration delivered in the State Capital of Georgia, with Governor Colquitt, and other state officials, was a fitting setting for the presentation of a beautiful gold-headed cane, with the convention's and his initials carved on it. Robert Peel Brooks was chosen by the delegates to present the gift.

The career of Mr. Clifford for twenty years' work as a teacher, brought him to the forefront, and he was appointed by three different W. Va. State Superintendents to hold and conduct Teachers' Institutes. Mr. Clifford holds a life-time teacher's certificate in honor of this distinguished service. He was the first colored man in West Virginia to be admitted to the bar in the early eighties. He became editor of the *Pioneeer Press* in 1882 at Martinsburg, and ran it regularly for thirty-six years, being honored with the deanship of Negro journalism a short time before the *Pioneer Press* ceased to exist.

Mr. Clifford, single-handed and alone, filed charges against Prof. N. C. Brackett, head of Storer College, killed and wiped out

Brackett's drawn color line, that barred colored people from going there as had been their privilege. He was the only colored editor in West Virginia who was a member of the State Editorial Association for twenty years, and was chosen the last year as its historian.

While defending a client sometime ago, a United States Commissioner and Mr. Clifford got into a controversy over some witnesses he wanted summoned, and it was kept up until the Commissioner demanded that he stop and go on, or he would put Clifford in jail. Undaunted he continued and gave the Commissioner to understand that just as long as he refused to summon the witnesses, he would contend for it; whereupon the Commissioner had him put in jail, where he remained for an hour and twenty-two minutes. Getting out he asked for his client, who had been tried and jailed. He was brought back. Clifford went his bond, sent him home, preferred charges against T. T. Lemen, United States Commissioner, and W. D. Brown, United States Marshal. Clifford went to the Department of Justice in Washington, D. C., proved his charges and had both put out of office and his client was set free.

He was appointed, by Senator B. K. Bruce and Frederick Douglass, Commissioner for the state of West Virginia to the New Orleans Exposition. He was elected three times President of the National Independent Political League, was chosen Principal of the Manassas Industrial School, where he and Frederick Douglass spoke on the occasion of his inauguration. He resigned because of his contention for better water.

He was the first man to impanel a colored jury in the state of West Virginia, and for so doing, was knocked down in the court room three times with deadly weights, causing the blood to run down into his shoes. When knocked down the third time, U. S. G. Pitzer, a Republican (?) prosecuting attoney, sprang on him, but with apparent superhuman skill and force, Clifford turned him at a time when there was not a soul in the court room (everybody having run out) but Pitzer & Clifford, with the latter on top, and had not Stephen Elam rushed in and pulled Clifford off of Pitzer and carried him out, death might have been the result,—Elam is still living. Later Pitzer was nominated for the Legislature, and Clifford canvassed Berkeley County on his bicycle exhibiting his bloody shirt (which he still has) and the day before the election Clifford spoke in the band-stand in the Public Square for an hour and thirty minutes, waving his bloody shirt and the following day Pitzer was defeated by 1336 votes.

He is a 33° Mason and a Past Grand Master of W. Va.; member of the American Negro Academy, and helped to shoot off the shackles from four million slaves and cement this Union on the bloody battle fields during the war of the sixties and holds an honorable discharge in proof of it.

He gives credit to the late Hon. John J. Healy of Chicago, Ill., for his early education thru the public schools of Chicago. He attended and graduated from Storer College 1875, and holds an honorary diploma from Shaw University.

JOHN W. CROMWELL.

Mr. Monroe N. Work, who has spent some time establishing the official roster of Negroes who served in State conventions and legislatures, has turned over for publication the following letters giving the record of Peter G. Morgan, a prominent citizen of Virginia:

MR. MONROE N. WORK,
    Editor *Negro Year Book*,
        Tuskegee Institute, Ala.

My dear Mr. Work:

I am extremely sorry that many pressing duties have prevented me from letting you have the information asked for in your letter under date of September 1st, bearing upon the late Peter George Morgan of Petersburg, Virginia.

I gathered from the information in possession of his sons, that he, (Peter G. Morgan) was in his day one of the most prominent colored men in the city of Petersburg. He was a carpenter by trade and followed said trade for a number of years. Later he acquired the knowledge of shoe making and became a first class shoemaker, which trade he also followed for a number of years before the Civil War. He was twice sold as a slave, and he purchased himself at $1,500 and completed the payment on the fourth of July, 1854 at the White Sulphur Springs, his master being part owner of the Springs at that time. Later on he purchased his wife, paying $1,500 for her and two small children in 1858, thereby himself becoming a slave holder. He removed to Petersburg in

1863 and continued to work at his trade as shoemaker. Meanwhile he made use of every possible opportunity to increase his knowledge of books, although he had no opportunity to attend any school. In this way he became a fairly well educated man, certainly ahead of many at that time, and at the close of the Civil War was able to train his own children and the children of his neighbors. He served in the Constitutional Convention of the State of Virginia in 1867, this latter date was given me this week by a gentleman in Richmond, who served as page in the Legislature of Virginia fifty years ago. I am enclosing a clipping which was passed into my hands a few weeks ago, which contains some of the names of those who served in this particular convention.[1]

It has occurred to me that the Rev. Dr. Bragg, of Baltimore, Maryland also served as page some time, later and perhaps he would be able to assist me in supplying correct data, provided errors are made in the dates in this correspondence.

Mr. Morgan served in the Legislature of Virginia two terms, 1869-1871, and 1871-1872.

Now, my dear Mr. Work if additional information is desired, bearing upon the late Peter George Morgan, please do not hesitate to command my services, and I shall be very glad to do my best to assist you.

With kind regards and best wishes, believe me,

Very sincerely yours,

Signed: JAMES S. RUSSELL,

Principal.

[1] COPY OF CLIPPING FROM UNDESIGNATED PAPER AS MENTIONED IN ABOVE LETTER.

The Radical State Convention, which was in session in Richmond on Thursday, elected the following State Executive Committee, with Ex-Governor H. H. Wells as chairman: First district—Rufus S. Jones, Isaac Morton and Robert Norton. Second district—R. S. Greene, Peter G. Morgan and H. H. Bowden. Third district—Wm. C. Wickham, J. M. Humphreys and Langdon Boyd. Fourth district—Geo. W. Finney, John T. Hamletter and Ross Hamilton. Fifth district—Thos. J. Jackson, Alexander Rives and I. F. Wilson. Sixth district—John F. Lewis, Thos. H. Hargest and John R. Popham. Eighth district—W. B. Downey, John M. Thatcher and J. B. Sener. Ninth district—R. W. Hughes, G. G. Goodell and John W. Woest.

COMMUNICATIONS

ST. PAUL NORMAL AND INDUSTRIAL SCHOOL
LAWRENCEVILLE, VIRGINIA,
October 23, 1920.

MR. MONROE N. WORK,
　Tuskegee Institute,
　　Alabama.

My dear Mr. Work:

Your very kind letter of the 18th instant has been received and contents carefully noted. I have delayed replying to your letter that I might secure definite information from the Register of the General Assembly of Virginia. My letter to you contained information from the memory of my brother-in-law and another aged gentleman, with whom I conferred regarding the information you had asked me to supply. I have just secured first hand information which contains practically the same information as given in my letter, still it comes with authority. You will note please the slight correction to be made in reference to the years he served in the Legislature of Virginia.

You have my full permission to use the matter in any way you see fit, making the slight correction in the dates the Hon. Peter G. Morgan served in the Legislature.

With kind regards and best wishes, believe me,
　　　　　　Sincerely yours,
　　　　　　Signed: JAMES S. RUSSELL,
　　　　　　　　Principal.

COMMONWEALTH OF VIRGINIA
GOVERNOR'S OFFICE
RICHMOND

October 22, 1920.

DR. JAMES S. RUSSELL, Archdeacon,
　St. Paul Normal and Industrial School,
　　Lawrenceville, Virginia.

My dear Dr. Russell:

The Register of the General Assembly of Virginia, on p. 409, carries the information that Peter G. Morgan of Petersburg, was a member of the Convention of 1867–1868; was a member of the

House of Delegates of Virginia at the session of 1869-70, and in 1870-71.

I hope that this is the information you desire.

Yours very truly,

Signed: LeRoy Hodges,

Aide to the Governor.

The Education of the Negro

Captain A. B. Spingarn has supplied the following valuable information given in these extracts from the laws of the State of New York:

May 10th, 1923.

Dr. Carter G. Woodson,
    Journal of Negro History,
        1216 You Street, N. W.,
        Washington, D. C.

My dear Dr. Woodson:

The following extracts from the Session Laws of the State of New York for 1826 and 1832 may be of interest. I did not see mention of the latter one in your invaluable, *The Education of the Negro Prior to 1861.*

"Chap. 145 of Laws of 1826.

An Act *to provide for the colored Persons who are occupants of Lots in New Stockbridge.* Passed April 11, 1826.

1. Be *it enacted by the People of the State of New York, represented in Senate and Assembly,* That it shall and may be lawful for the commissioners of the land-office to cause letters patent to be issued to the persons respectively, who have been reported by the appraisers of lands in New Stockbridge, as colored persons, for the lots set to their names as occupants, in the same manner as grants of land are authorized to be made to those who have been so reported, as white persons persons settled on said land: *Provided* . . ."

"CHAP. 136 of Laws of 1832.

AN ACT *to constitute the coloured children of Rochester a separate school.* Passes April 14, 1832.

The People of the State of New York, represented in Senate and Assembly, do enact as follows:

1. The commissioners of common schools of the towns of Gates and Brighton, in the county of Monroe, or a majority of them, may in their discretion cause the children of colour of the village of Rochester to be taught in one or more separate schools.

2. The commissioners of common schools of the towns of Gates and Brighton, shall discharge the duties of trustees of such school, and shall apportion thereto a distributive share of the moneys for the support of common schools."

Very sincerely yours,
ARTHUR B. SPINGARN.

BOOK REVIEWS

Piney Woods and Its Story. By LAURENCE C. JONES, Principal of the Piney Woods Country Life School, with an introduction by S. S. McClure. (New York and Chicago: Fleming H. Revell Company. Pp. 154. Price $1.50 net.)

This is a story of a Negro brought up and educated in a more favorable environment than most of the members of his race but, nevertheless, imbued with the spirit of social uplift of those of his group unfavorably circumstanced. With this vision he cast his lot in Mississippi, where he toiled against odds in the establishment and development of a school which is today an important factor in the progress of the Negroes of Mississippi.

This volume had a forerunner in a shorter story *Up Through Difficulties*. As the influence of the school extended, however, and a larger number of friends became interested in his efforts, there arose such a demand for a brief statement of the history of this institution that it was necessary to meet this with a publication in this handy form. Coming then from the heart of a man who has given his life as a sacrifice for the advancement of his oppressed people, the story has been well received by the friends of education in general, and especially by those who appreciate the arduous labors of that class of pioneers so nobly represented by the author.

And well might such a story be extensively read; for, as S. S. McClure has said in the introduction, it is a story "of Negro education, intelligence and sensitiveness, who turned his back upon everything that usually makes life worth living for people of his kind and went, without money or influence, or even an invitation, among the poorest and most ignorant of his race, for the sole purpose of helping them in every way within his power." As it has been said, it is persuasively and sincerely told. It is therefore, to quote further from Mr. McClure, "a valuable human document; a paragraph in a vital chapter of American history."

Briefly told, the story describes in detail the beginnings of the educator, his early school days, the development of his school in the midst of "Pine Knots" under the "Blue Sky," its "Log Cabin" stage, the more hopeful circumstances later attained, and its widening influence. In the chapter entitled the "Message of Hope" there is an unusually interesting account of how once during the World War the author was misunderstood by certain white persons who, from the outside, heard him at a revival urging the Negroes to battle against sin, ignorance, superstition, and poverty. Understanding some but not all of the words used by the speaker, the eavesdroppers reported him as stirring up the Negroes in the South to fight the whites. A mob was easily formed in keeping with the custom of the country, and the author was speedily picked up and thrown upon a pile of wood, when guns were cocked and primed to shoot him down before he was to be offered up. Thereupon, however, one of the mob demanded that he make a speech, by which he so convincingly disabused their minds of any such sinister intention of stirring up an insurrection among the Negroes that he was finally released and befriended rather than lynched.

The Book of American Negro Poetry. By JAMES WELDON JOHNSON. (New York: Harcourt, Brace and Company. 1922. Pp. 217.)

A review of a book of poetry is out of place in an historical magazine unless, like the volume before us, it has an historical significance. It cannot be gainsaid that the poetry of a race passing through the ordeal of slavery, and later struggling for social and political recognition, must constitute a long chapter in its history. In fact, one can easily study the development of the mind of a thinking class from epoch to epoch by reading and appreciating its verse. It is fortunate that Mr. James Weldon Johnson has thus given the public this opportunity to study a representative number of the talented tenth of the Negro race.

The poems themselves do not concern us here to the extent of showing in detail their bearing on the history of the Negro. The student of history, however, will find much valuable information in the interesting preface of the author covering the first forty-seven pages of the volume. The biographical index of authors in the appendix, moreover, presents in a condensed form sketches of the lives of thirty-one useful and all but famous members of the Negro race. Much of this information about those who have not been in the public eye a long time is entirely new, appearing here in print for the first time.

The aim of the author is to show the greatness of the Negro

as measured by his literature and art. He believes that the status of the Negro in the United States is more a question of national mental attitude toward the race than of actual conditions. "And nothing," says he, "will do more to change that mental attitude and raise his status than a demonstration of intellectual parity by the Negro through the production of literature and art."

In the effort to show "the emotional endowment, the originality and artistic conception and power of creating" possessed by the Negro, the author has begun with the Uncle Remus stories, the spirituals, the dance, the folks songs and syncopated music. He then presents the achievements of the Negro in pure literature, mentioning the works of Jupiter Hammon, George M. Horton, Frances E. Harper, James M. Bell and Albery A. Whitman. A large portion of this introduction given to the early writers is devoted to a discussion of Dunbar. He then introduces a number of poets of our own day, whose works constitute the verse herein presented. Among these are William Stanley Braithwaite, Claude McKay, Fenton Johnson, Jessie Fauset, Georgia Douglass Johnson, Annie Spencer, John W. Holloway, James Edwin Campbell, Daniel Webster Davis, R. C. Jamison, James S. Cotter, Jr., Alex Rogers, James D. Carrothers, Leslie Pinckney Hill, and W. E. B. DuBois.

The McKinley and Roosevelt Administrations, 1897-1909. By JAMES FORD RHODES, LL.D., D.Litt. (New York: The Macmillan Company, 1922. Pp. 418.)

Fortunately Mr. Rhodes does not make the mistake of designating this as a volume continuing his history of the United States from 1850 to 1877. Like the volume recently written to treat the period from Hayes to McKinley, this one does not show the serious treatment characteristic of the earlier work of Mr. Rhodes. The author makes no introduction but enters upon the discussion of the political events which he considers as having constituted the most important facts of history during this period. In this volume Mr. Rhodes is largely concerned with the rise and fall of political chieftains, who have attained high offices in the services of the nation or with the record of those who have championed principles which have not been acceptable to the American people. The most valuable facts of the book are the bits of first-hand information which he obtained by personal contact with the statesmen of the time. From this volume, however, one gets very little more general information than he would from an observer who has closely followed the various presidential campaigns. Furthermore, there is not much discussion of the social and economic questions which have engaged the attention of the American people because of their bearing on shaping the destinies of the nation. As a narrative for ready information of men and measures of this period it is interesting, but judged from the point of view of modern historiography, the book cannot be seriously considered as a very valuable work on American history. When one has finished reading the volume he will find his mind filled with what men have done and what they have failed to accomplish, but he will not easily grasp the meaning of the forces which during the last generation have given trend to present-day developments in the United States.

Students of Negro history will wonder what mention the author has made of the rôle which the race played during this period. In any expectation of this sort they will find themselves disappointed. With the exception of references to the Booker Washington dinner at the White House, the Brownsville Affair, and the Roosevelt attitude on Negro suffrage, the race does not figure in this history. It is interesting to note Rhodes's statement to the effect (230) that Roosevelt said to him that he made a mistake in inviting Booker T. Washington to dine at the White House. With the usual bias of the author, it is not surprising that he justifies the dismissal of the Negro soldiers charged with participating in the riot at Brownsville (340). After reading this volume, one who has not lived in this country would be surprised to come here and learn that we have such a large group of citizens about whom so much was said and to whom so much was meted out during this stormy period.

The Journal of John Woolman. Edited from the Original Manuscripts, with a Biographical Introduction, by AMELIA MOTT GUMMERE. (New York: The Macmillan Company. 1922. Pp. 643.)

From the time of the first publication of the *Journal* of this unusual man in 1774, he has been known to the world as one of its greatest characters because of his wonderful spirituality and deep interest in all members of the human family regardless of race or condition. It is decidedly fitting then that this valuable record should be reprinted and be made accessible to a larger number who will find it an inspiration to those engaged in reform and valuable in throwing light on heroism in the past.

The author, however, has another reason for the new edition of this *Journal,* inasmuch as there are many editions of the *Journal* proper, and a multitude of publications in which Woolman's *Essays* and appreciations of him appear. The reason is that the descendants of Woolman "have recently made accessible by presenting to learned institutions, which are glad to guard them, the manuscripts of the *Journal* and of most of his *Essays* as well as letters, marriage certificates of the family and other documents."

The work is arranged in chapters presenting his immigrant ancestry, his youth and education, his marriage, his participation in the slavery discussion, his Indian journey, his experiences as schoolmaster, his final tours, and his death. The book is well printed and neatly bound. It contains thirty-three interesting illustrations which decidedly enhance the value of the book. Among these should be noted the portrait of John Woolman, his birthplace, his home, important pages from his manuscripts, and his grave.

Chapter IV, which deals with the endeavors of John Woolman to emancipate and elevate the Negro race, will be of unusual help to students of Negro history. Around Woolman and his coworkers, beginning in 1760, centered the effort toward the liberation of the race, which engaged the attention of the Friends, especially during the struggle for the rights of man. Carrying the doctrine of natural rights to its logical conclusion, Woolman was among the first to insist that Negroes had a natural right to be free both in body and mind. To this end, therefore, he bore testimony against slavery wherever he traveled in this country and abroad; and down to the close of his career he lived up to the conviction that all men are born equal before God "Who hath made of one blood all nations that dwell upon the face of the earth."

NOTES

Miss A. H. Smith, who during the last seven years has served the Association as Office Manager and Assistant to the Secretary-treasurer, has recently retired from the service. The Association is immeasurably indebted to Miss Smith for the faithful service which she has rendered the cause, and it will be difficult to fill her position. Although offered opportunities for earning a larger stipend elsewhere, she remained with the Association because of her interest in the work which it has been prosecuting. The Association wishes her well and earnestly hopes that she may be welcomed in some other field of usefulness.

The American Catholic Historical Society has announced a prize of $100 offered by this society for the best historical essay on the subject "Catholic Missionary Work Among the Colored People of the United States (1776–1866)." The prize money has been donated by the Most Rev. Sebastian Messmer, Archbishop of Milwaukee.

All persons who are interested in the welfare and progress of the Negroes of the United States are eligible to compete for the prize under the conditions specified by the Society. The conditions are:

The subject must be treated within the years specified (1776–1866). Although the history of Catholic missionary activity among the colored people of this country during the colonial period is not barred, the essays shall be judged upon their value for the years 1776–1866.

The essays shall be typewritten on one side of the page only, and shall not be less than 4,000 words and may not exceed 8,000 words.

All essays entered for the prize must be received by the Secretary of the American Catholic Historical Society, 715 Spruce Street, Philadelphia, not later than December 1, 1923.

Each essay shall be signed with a motto and accompanied with a sealed envelope marked on the outside with the same motto and enclosing the writer's name and address.

The committee appointed to act as judges for the competition is composed of: the Rev. Peter Guilday of the Catholic University of America, Washington, D. C., Chairman; Dr. Lawrence Flick, of Philadelphia; Thomas F. Meehan, associate-editor of "America," New York; Dr. T. W. Turner, of Howard University, Washington, D. C.; and the Rev. Joseph Butsch, S. S. J., of St. Joseph's Seminary, Baltimore.

An arrangement has been made whereby contestants seeking guidance in research work in the preparation of the essay can obtain aid by writing to the chairman of the committee of judges.

The Oxford University Press has published a history of *The Partition and Colonization of Africa*, by Sir Charles Lucas. This work includes the territorial rearrangement resulting from the recent war.

Through *East and West*, London, S. B. de Burgh Edwardes has published *The History of Mauritius, 1507–1914*. A Mauritian himself, he has had every opportunity to write a readable and interesting volume.

The History of the Conquest of Egypt, North Africa, and Spain, by Ibn Abd Al-Hakam, is now being published through the Yale University Press in its Oriental Series. This work is the earliest account of Mohammedan conquests extant. It is edited from manuscripts in London, Paris and Leyden, by Professor Charles C. Torrey.

Herbert Jenkins, London, has brought out *The Mad Mullah of Somaliland*, by Douglas J. Jardine, an officer of the British administration in Somaliland from 1916 to 1921.

The Royal Chronicle of Abyssinia, an extract translated from the Ethiopic Chronicle in the British Museum by H. Weld Blundell, has been published by the Cambridge University Press.

PROCEEDINGS OF THE SPRING CONFERENCE OF THE ASSOCIATION FOR THE STUDY OF NEGRO LIFE AND HISTORY HELD IN BALTIMORE, APRIL 5TH AND 6TH, 1923

The conference enjoyed the welcome and hospitality of Morgan College where the morning and afternoon sessions were held on the 5th, and of the Baltimore Public School System, the Druid Hill Avenue Branch of the Young Men's Christian Association, and the Bethel A. M. E. Church, which provided for the day sessions of the second day and for both evening sessions. The success of the meeting was due in a large measure to the cordial reception given the Association by Dr. J. O. Spencer, the president of Morgan College, and by Dr. Pezavia O'Connell and Dean L. M. McCoy. Mr. Mason A. Hawkins, Dr. Frederick Douglass, Dr. A. L. Gaines, and Mr. S. S. Booker willingly cooperated in the same way with respect to the meetings in the city.

The first session was held at Morgan College on Thursday at 11 A. M. Dr. Pezavia O'Connell, who presided, delivered an able address impressing upon the students of the institution the importance of the work undertaken by the Association. He was then followed by the officers of the Association, who outlined in detail the history, the purposes, and the achievements of the organization. Other remarks were later made by Miss Georgine Kelly Smith, who proved to be a very effective speaker in directing attention to certain neglected aspects of Negro life.

At 3 o'clock in the afternoon, the officers of the Association assembled with the faculty of Morgan College in a joint meeting to acquaint the instructors with the plans and procedure of the Association and to secure their cooperation in the extension of this work through some local organization which may direct its attention to the collection of Negro folklore and to the preservation of the records of the Negroes in Maryland. Much interest was aroused and steps were taken to effect such an organization.

The first evening session was held at 8 o'clock on the same day at Bethel A. M. E. Church in the city of Baltimore. On this occasion the Spring Conference was welcomed to the city by Mr. Mason A. Hawkins, the principal of the Colored High School, who briefly discussed the importance of the work and the opportunity which it afforded Baltimore for becoming better informed as to what is being done for the uplift of the race through this scientific effort. The response to this address was made by President G. A. Edwards of Kittrell College. He made a favorable impression upon the audience by directing attention to the importance of securing the cooperation of a large number of persons with an intelligent interest in the race. He emphasized the fact that such a significant task should not be neglected and left to the sacrifices of the few persons of vision who, without adequate support, may unduly toil in the prosecution of this task and thus fail to succeed because of bearing a burden which should be shared by all.

The principal addresses of the evening were delivered by Dr. J. O. Spencer, Dr. C. G. Woodson and Dean Kelly Miller. Dr. Spencer discussed the subject "Thinking Straight on the Color Line." He deprecated the lack of information on the Negro and showed how, in the midst of ignorance as to the actual achievements of the race, persons have learned to hate men of color because they are not acquainted with them. To remedy the situation, then, there must be a universal interest in the study of Negro life and history. Dr. Woodson sketched in brief the record of the Negro from time immemorial, mentioning the important contributions of the race to civilization and the necessity for the study of this record to inspire the race with a hope of greater achievement and to disabuse the mind of the white man of the idea of racial superiority. Dean Kelly Miller spoke on the worthwhile qualities of the Negro. His aim was to show that every race has in it certain elements which are peculiar to that group, thus giving it in this respect a chance to make a contribution which can come from no other source. He, therefore, emphasized the importance of encouraging the best in all races and giving to each every possible opportunity for development. Among the exceptional qualities which he ascribed to the Negro are patience, meekness, the gift of music, the sense of art, response to religion, and brotherly love.

The first session of the second day was held at 1 o'clock P. M., at the Douglass Theatre. This occasion was that of an assembly of the members of the Association, together with the students and faculty of the Baltimore Colored High School and other members of the local teaching corps. The important address was delivered by Professor John R. Hawkins, president of the organization. The purpose of this discourse was to outline in the simplest and most effective way possible the necessity for children knowing more about themselves and about their ancestors. The speaker endeavored to show how the achievements of the Negro have been omitted from the textbooks studied by the youth in the public schools so as to impress the Negro with the superiority of other races and the so-called inferiority of their own. These students were urged, therefore, to avail themselves of the opportunity to become acquainted with this neglected aspect of history through supplementary reading in the home, in clubs, and in literary circles. How this would stimulate the mind of the youth and inspire them to greater achievement through knowledge of the distinguished service of others of their race in the past, was eloquently emphasized by the speaker. Some remarks were made by President G. A. Edwards of Kittrell College and Dr. C. G. Woodson.

At 3 o'clock P. M. the Spring Conference assembled at the Druid Hill Avenue Branch of the Y. M. C. A. The purpose of this meeting was to discuss Negro history from the various points view of the teacher, the minister, the editor, and the professional man. The discussion was opened by Mr. L. S. James, principal of the Maryland Normal and Industrial School, with a brief survey of the situation in Maryland with respect to the development of the Negro schools and especially in the matter of teaching Negro history. His very informing address was well received. Then, appeared Mr. G. Smith Wormley of the Myrtilla Miner Normal School, Washington, D. C. He presented Negro history from the point of view of the teacher. He treated the matter pedagogically, setting forth the purpose of the teaching of history and at the same time urging upon his hearers the necessity for teaching the leading facts of Negro history by correlating them with the topics of history as it is now offered in the schools. His illuminating discourse made a favorable impression and evoked discussions from various persons.

Among those prompted to speak were Mrs. N. F. Mossell of Philadelphia, who spoke of history from the point of view of the child, showing how necessary it is to supply the young people with elementary reading matter, serving as a stepping stone to the teaching of the more difficult phases of the record of the Negro. Dr. George F. Bragg explained how the minister is concerned with the history of the Negro and briefly summarized the important contributions of Negro ministers not only to the history of the race, but to the preservation of its records. Mrs. Ella Spencer Murray expressed her interest in the work and outlined how each one might aid the movement by soliciting members and subscribers throughout the country, especially among white persons who may be neutral or indifferent as to what the Negro has achieved.

Mr. S. W. Rutherford, the Secretary-Treasurer of the Association, delivered a short address to point out how by organized effort, with courage and concentration, the movement may be further promoted and the work expanded throughout the country by cooperating with the Director who should and must have the support of all interested in the Negro. Bishop John Hurst then mentioned briefly the necessity for more publicity, and expressed his interest in securing a fund adequate to the employment of a staff to popularize the work and increase the income of the Association. Dr. Thomas E. Brown, of Morgan College, delivered a short address emphasizing the necessity for a more scientific study of the records and directing attention to the undeveloped possibilities of the race which cry for the attention of those scholars with the necessary training to treat the records of this group scientifically.

The session closed with an address by Ex-Congressman Thomas E. Miller of South Carolina. He proved to be an attractive figure at the sessions of the Association, being a man well advanced in years, one who served in local offices during the Reconstruction and finally reached Congress. He restricted his remarks to the discussion of the free Negro prior to the Civil War, the class to which he himself belonged. He asserted that many free Negroes were never known. Because of the fear of disclosing their status, many of them were recorded as slaves. In the same way, some of their important achievements were kept in secret for the reason that freedom of conduct in their case was proscribed by public opinion. Furthermore, he stated that they were often misunderstood because they are reported as having hated the slaves. He then explained the relations of the free Negro to the whites and to the slaves, bringing out how they were subjected to punishment for associating with the bondmen, and, therefore, became estranged from them by the processes of safeguarded instruction in the caste system of the South.

At the second evening session at the Bethel A. M. E. Church, two important addresses were delivered. The first one, "Hints on Race History from an Old Book" by Prof. Leslie P. Hill, proved to be unusually instructive. This discourse was based upon Abbé Grégoire's *Litterature des Nègres*, intended to emphasize the unusual achievements of the Negroes as a proof that because of their superior intellect they were entitled to freedom. Mr. Hill directed very little attention to the characters well known in this country, restricting his remarks largely to those who rose to prominence in European countries where their records have never been studied to the extent of impressing the historians of this country.

Then appeared Dr. William Pickens, the Field Secretary for the National Association for the Advancement of Colored People, who delivered a very enthusiastic address on "Negro History in the Public Schools." Dr. Pickens showed not only how uninformed the white people are as to the record of the Negro, but that the race itself knows very little of what it has achieved. He briefly mentioned a number of instances connected with the local history of Maryland, of which the people themselves living on the very soil on which these events took place, knew nothing. He then adversely criticized the attitude of the public school systems toward the teaching of Negro history and urged his hearers to take seriously the question of memorializing and influencing educational authorities to incorporate into their courses of study textbooks on Negro history setting forth the truth as it is. He urged, moreover, that in the meantime while such a battle is being waged to reach this end, the Negroes themselves should through clubs and literary circles make a systematic study of such works.

THE JOURNAL OF NEGRO HISTORY

Vol. VIII., No. 4   October, 1923.

ABRAM HANNIBAL, THE FAVORITE OF PETER THE GREAT

Abram Hannibal, more commonly known as the "Negro of Peter the Great," or "Peter's Negro" was one of the quaintest figures in the Russian history of eighteenth century. From slavery to mastership and riches his peculiar fate led him. He began his life under yoke in Africa but died a general and wealthy landlord of the frozen North, leaving his children and grandchildren to be prominent in the politics and literature of Russia.

The name of "Peter's Negro," no doubt, belongs to history; but comparatively little is known of him, many important details of his biography being still incomplete and unascertained. Outside of the Russian sources there were Hannibal's own memoirs, written in French, but not long before his death Abram burned them. About the beginning of nineteenth century there appeared Hannibal's biography in German, written by a certain Helbig (*Russische Gunstlinge*), but hardly anything trustworthy could be learned from this work. As far as we know, nothing was ever published of "Peter's Negro" in English. Even the Russian sources are mainly official records and dry documents, not of a great historical value, if of any. The best information about Hannibal may be obtained from the unfinished novel *The Negro of Peter the Great* (1827) and other works by Pushkin, Hannibal's great-grandson, the famous writer and founder of the modern school of nineteenth century literature in Russia.

Some of later historians doubt many of the assertions of Pushkin, holding that, great as the poet was, he nevertheless was subject to the common human weakness of exaggerating one's forefathers' merits. The important facts of his career, however, have been learned. In the year 1705, as for many years before and after, thousands of Negroes were made prisoners and brought from the interior to the coasts of the dark continent to be shipped to the slave markets of America and Asia. Among others there was a little boy, barely eight years of age, whom Arabs, his masters, called Ibrahim. He was sold to the Turks and, the same year, brought to Constantinople. His fate could be easily guessed. He was wanted for a slave in a rich Turkish home, or perhaps an overseer in a harem. He became the latter after being brutally handled.

But at that time Savva Ragusinsky, a Russian nobleman, after a short stay in Turkey was preparing to leave for his home country. He wanted to bring a present of some kind to his Czar Peter, the stern reformer of Russia, afterwards called "the Great." Ragusinsky knew the Czar's love for curious objects and thought nothing better than two live black boys could win him Peter's favor. The Czar had at his court many servants of different races, brought to St. Petersburg from all over the world, but only a few Negroes were among them.

Ragusinsky bought or, according to some documents, simply stole several Negro boys, who only a few months before were brought to the slave-shacks of Sultan Selim II. One of these, who started on a long trip to their new Northern home, was the little Ibrahim. The Czar liked the rare present and almost from the beginning distinguished Ibrahim from other slaves. The boy was unusually bright for his age. He quickly picked up the Russian language and alphabet, and before long began to feel that the court of St. Petersburg was his home. Peter kept Ibrahim in his apartments, and Ibrahim accompanied the Czar in latter's journeys through Russia and foreign countries, not as a servant but rather as one of the family. When because of the war of Russia with Sweden, Peter had to be constantly with his army, Ibrahim shared with his friend-master all the dangers and privations of bivouac-life.

In 1707, while in Vilno, Ibrahim was christened in Orthodox faith. His father-in-Christ was the Czar himself, who was assisted in this task by the Polish queen, the wife of King Augustus. The little Negro was given a new name of Peter, but he cried and refused to answer it, preferring his old Arab name. The Russians, however, could not get used to the strange Oriental sound and called him Abram instead of Ibrahim. His surname—Hannibal—was given to him by the Czar in memory of the famous Carthaginian.

In 1716 Peter went on his second tour of Western Europe with Hannibal as usual accompanying him. Among other countries they visited France, and here Hannibal was left to begin his studies more seriously. Hannibal, then 19 years old, showed fair capacity for mathematics and physics. Supplied by the Czar with money and other means of assistance, he entered a military engineering academy in Paris, where he remained for about 2 years. He joined the French army afterwards, which was then engaged in the war against Spain, and participated in many battles. He proved to be an able engineer and a good commander. In one of the battles—"an underground combat," as it is related in an eighteenth century document—Hannibal was wounded in the head, but not dangerously, and was brought back to Paris.

Hannibal stayed in Paris till 1723, communicating with the Czar by letters which are preserved in St. Petersburg state archives. Hannibal complained in them that the Russian treasury and Peter himself almost completely forgot about him, compelling him to live in great poverty on the verge of starvation. If he could obtain no allowance, Hannibal wrote, he would have to walk from Paris to Moscow, begging alms on the way.

Pushkin, however, asserts that his great-grandfather while in Paris was well provided for by Peter with money and had an unlimited opportunity to mingle in the French society circles. His appearance aroused curiosity; his wits, education and war record respect. His black curls with a bandage over them—his wound did not heal completely for a long time—could be frequently seen amid white wigs of the French aristocrats. He was well received in the best salons of Paris, being everywhere known as "le nègre du Czar." The Duke of Orleans, who as a regent ruled over France at that time, favored Hannibal with his attention and when in 1723 Peter asked Abram to come back to Russia, the regent tried to persuade Hannibal to remain in France, promising him a brilliant military and court career. Although the Czar permitted Hannibal to take his own choice between France and Russia, the young man decided to return to St. Petersburg.

Thus, contradicting Hannibal's complaining letters, Pushkin describes his great-grandfather's sojourn in Paris. He evidently based his testimony on the family accounts, which as almost any such narratives contain perhaps more fiction than history. But, on the other hand, the historians, who contradict Pushkin, have no other proof of their infallibility than these Paris letters of Hannibal.

Reliable information concerning Hannibal after his return to Russia, however, is not so scarce. Immediately upon his arrival in St. Petersburg, Hannibal was appointed an officer in the Preobrajensky Guard-regiment. He became an "engineer-lieutenant" in the "Bombardir-company," of which the Czar himself was the captain. But another crisis was reached when, according to Pushkin, it appeared about that time that Hannibal was a son of a Negro king, and his elder brother came from Africa to St. Petersburg with an offer of a rich ransom for Hannibal.

He met with no success, as Hannibal himself did not want to return to the village on the banks of Niger.

The situation did not seem so favorable for Hannibal, moreover, when in 1725 Peter the Great died. Menshikov, former pie-peddler and life-long favorite of the late Czar, elevated himself to the position of sole adviser to Peter's widow, Catherine I. He alone virtually ruled Russia for several years. When Catherine I died and young Peter II sat on the throne, Menshikov wanted the boy Emperor to marry his younger daughter. He feared, however, his numerous enemies at the court, among whom he counted Hannibal, the young Czar's instructor in mathematics. Consequently Hannibal was exiled to Siberia in 1727. Officially he was neither arrested nor deprived of his rank and property. He was sent to the borders of China with orders to "transfer from the town of Selenginsk into another location" and to "take an exact measure of the Great Chinese Wall." Menshikov evidently thought that the severe Siberian frosts would sooner or later kill the young African. But Hannibal being strong and healthy and accustomed from childhood to cold climate withstood the hardships of the Siberian wilderness.

In 1729 he fled from Selenginsk but was arrested before he could reach Europe. His papers and valuables taken from him, Hannibal was brought to Tomsk, a city in Western Siberia. There for some time he was kept as a prisoner, although his salary as an officer was still paid. In January of 1730 he was freed but not permitted to leave Siberia. He was appointed to serve in the Tomsk garrison as a major.

Soon afterwards St. Petersburg was the scene of a new coup-d'etat. Anna, a niece of Peter the Great, was summoned to the Russian throne. Counts Dolgorukov became the most powerful persons at the court. New hopes were aroused in Hannibal, as the Dolgorukovs were his friends, since the time he and they lived in France. Hannibal without asking or waiting for permission left Tomsk, but when some time after he arrived in St. Petersburg he learned that Dolgorukovs lost their influence as suddenly as they won it, that they were arrested, and after all their estates had been confiscated, were exiled to Siberia. Great dangers threatened Hannibal as a Dolgorukovs' friend. Biron, erstwhile a stable man but now adviser and lover of Anna, sought Hannibal's life. Field-marshal Minich, commander-in-chief of the Russian army, however, saved Hannibal by granting him a commission to inspect fortifications in Lifland. In a little village near Reval, then, Hannibal lived in obscurity for 10 years, fearing every day the arrival of a messenger from St. Petersburg with an order for his arrest.

Before his coming to Lifland, Hannibal married the beautiful daughter of a Greek captain by the name of Dioper. Almost from the first day of their marriage he began to suspect her infidelity. The birth of a white baby-girl proved his suspicions and justified their divorce. The Russian court sent Hannibal's wife to a convent, and Hannibal married Christina-Regina Von-Sheberg, a Lifland German woman. She gave birth to five sons, all of whom were mulattoes. His first wife's white daughter he kept in his home, gave her a good education and a considerable dowry, but never permitted her to come before his eyes.

In November of 1741 Elisabeth, a daughter of Peter the Great, was proclaimed the Empress of Russia. She immediately returned from exile all former favorites of her father. Among these was Hannibal, on whom she showered various honours. He was given the post of commandant of city of Reval. About ten villages with several thousands of white slaves were presented to him as his personal property. He was decorated with medals and ribbons and asked to come to St. Petersburg. He preferred, however, to stay on his newly acquired estates.

Other important tasks awaited him. In 1752 he was commissioned to fix the Russo-Swedish boundary line. In 1756 he was one of the members of the Ladoga Canal Commission and also of the Commission for the Inspection of the Russian Forts. In 1762, with a rank of general in chief, he retired from public service, being then an old man. His services were remembered at the court for a long time after, however, for once Catherine II asked him to compose a plan of St. Petersburg-Moscow Canal.

During his last years he was frequented by spells of sudden fear, the consequence of his old sufferings. He was especially afraid of the sound of a bell, imagining that his persecutors were coming again. Under one of these spells, as we mentioned above, he destroyed his memoirs not long before he died in 1782 in his eighty-fifth year.

He did not want his sons to join the army or be at the court, fearing they might be involved there in dangerous intrigue. Ivan, his elder son, joined the army against his will, and only after he won fame as a brilliant victor over the Turks could he on his knees receive his aged father's forgiveness. Ivan Hannibal distinguished himself not only as a strategist but as a man of a great personal valor as well. He participated in the Russian naval expedition to Greece and captured Navarin, a Turkish fort, in 1770. He was the hero of the Chesma battle. Returning to Russia in 1779 he founded the city of Kherson in the Ukraine, of which he was appointed a governor. Later Ivan Hannibal quarreled with Count Potemkin, lover of Catherine the Great and ruler of Southern Russia. The Empress defended Hannibal and decorated him, but he left the service and went to live in one of his numerous estates. There in 1801 he died.

His brother Ossip (Joseph) was a naval officer in the Black Sea Fleet and for several years navigated the Mediterranean. Of other sons of Abram Hannibal very little is known. Ossip's daughter Nadejda, a Creole of striking beauty, married Pushkin, of an ancient Russian noble family. In 1799 a son was born to them and named Alexander, who later won fame as the greatest poet of Russia. He was killed in 1837, while duelling with a diplomat over the honor of Pushkin's wife, who was not worth her great husband's noble love.

While all the works of Pushkin could be bound together in one volume, thousands of books have been written on him and on what he created. Numerous monuments are erected in his honor all over Russia; special magazines entirely dedicated to him are published; and in famous paintings by distinguished Russian artists are pictured different periods of Pushkin's short life. When you look at these paintings, black curls, olive skin and thick lips speak to you of Pushkin's race. He himself was proud of it, all but worshipping his great-grandfather in many of his verses.

ALBERT PARRY

THE MOVEMENT OF NEGROES FROM THE EAST TO THE GULF STATES FROM 1830 TO 1850

The migration of Negroes to the Gulf States, during the years 1830 to 1850, was from the point of view of the Negroes themselves wholly involuntary. The blacks, being at that time preponderately slave, accompanied their masters to new homes in the South and Southwest or constituted the traffic of the domestic slave trade. Explanation of their migration must be sought, therefore, not in any unrest that may have been manifested by the Negroes, but rather in the causes that underlay the movement of the masters to new homes, and that enabled the domestic slave trade to become a profitable enterprise.

This migration, which in some ways assumed a peculiar aspect, bears a definite relation to three general circumstances. In the first place, there was a comparative decline in the productiveness of the seaboard border slave States. In the second, the accessibility to the new lands and practically virgin soils of Alabama, Mississippi, and Louisiana invited the migration of innumerable planters from the border States to this new region. Finally, the rapidly increasing demand of the planters of the Gulf region for slave labor with which to cultivate cotton and other native products tremendously stimulated the domestic slave trade.

Although the seaboard border States, led by Virginia, sent south the bulk of the slaves, it must not be thought that the migration was alone from these States. In fact, as early as 1840,[1] not only Virginia, Maryland, the District of Columbia, and Delaware, but also North Carolina became slave-exporting areas. Later, too, when the impoverishment of her lands made impossible the further extension

[1] Hammond, *The Cotton Industry*, I, 53 (cited from *Slavery and the Internal Slave Trade*, 12).

of cotton culture, South Carolina joined with these other States and Georgia in exporting slaves to Alabama, Mississippi, Louisiana, and, after 1845, to Texas.

The decline in the productiveness of some of the seaboard border slave States has been ascribed to various causes. The failure to rotate crops and the lack of proper and sufficient fertilizer necessary to prevent an impoverishment of the soil some hold to be primary causes. The almost complete dependence upon unskilled, unintelligent slave labor, the conviction prevalent everywhere in slave territory that such labor made that of white men dishonorable, together with the failure to develop fully the manufacturing facilities at hand, have been also generally advanced to explain the decline, particularly, of Maryland and Virginia.

The chief agricultural staple of these States was tobacco. The characteristic soil of the region—a sandy loam—while warm and stimulating was easily exhausted,[2] especially when the planters had improper and inefficient fertilizer, traceable in some measure to a numerical deficiency of live stock, and the incessant culture of tobacco, without crop rotation. The price of tobacco, moreover, was throughout the years from 1818 to 1840 exceedingly low and, at the same time, the newer States of Kentucky, Tennessee, and Missouri, as well as the Carolinas and Georgia, were producing large quantities of tobacco. The net result in Virginia and Maryland, therefore, was to make the culture of the plant exceedingly unprofitable.[3] It is held that the soil-exhausting character of tobacco culture, together with the falling prices of the plant, constituted the dominant factors in the decrease in value of agricultural lands of Virginia from $206,000,000 in 1816 to $80,000,000 in 1829.[4]

[2] Emerson, *Geographical Influences in American Slavery*, 18 (Bulletin, Amer. Geographical Society, xliii).

[3] Collins, *The Domestic Slave Trade*, 23 (cited from Hunt's *Merchants' Magazine*, vi, 473).

[4] *Ibid.*, 26.

If the impoverishment of the land through tobacco culture was one factor in the declining productivity of Virginia and Maryland, the almost complete use of unskilled Negro slave labor, particularly in the former State, was decidedly another. Not only was slave labor costly, in that the non-producers, as well as the constant workers, had to be provided for, but also because of the overwhelming ignorance and inertia of such labor. "The grand secret of the difference between free labor and slave labor," wrote a former Virginia resident to the *New York Times*, "is that the latter is without intelligence and without motive."[5] A large tobacco planter of Virginia adds to this his testimony that the slave's incapacity to perform duties complex in nature, or requiring the least intelligence, precluded the cultivation there of the finer grades of tobacco.[6] While, therefore, the Negro slave was tractable and capable of hard work, he was, without strict supervision, a most unproductive worker. The universal employment of the slave despite his ignorance and inertia doubtless furnishes one clue to the failure of Virginia to exploit, in a reasonable degree, her manufacturing resources.[7]

This costly failure has been ascribed also to the reluctance of white labor to perform any duties to which slaves might be assigned. Slave owners and white laborers held in mutual repugnance the employment of white men at such tasks. According to Olmsted,[8] slave owners have held that the poor whites would refuse to do such work if possible, and, if compelled to submit, would do only so much as they found absolutely necessary. Under all circumstances they do such work reluctantly and "will not bear driving." "They cannot be worked to advantage with the slaves, and it is inconvenient to look after them, if you work them separately."

The natural consequence of the policy thus pursued by

[5] Olmsted, *Cotton Kingdom*, II; App. C, 382.
[6] *Ibid.*, 89.
[7] *Ibid.*, 365 (cited from the *Lynchburg Virginian*, date not given).
[8] *Ibid.*

Virginia was, despite the fact of her early command over greater wealth and a larger population than the other States, to force her to descend, in part, from her former high estate.[9] A comparison of values of the agricultural lands of Virginia and Pennsylvania, in 1850, shows those of the latter, although of smaller acreage, to have a larger sale value an acre and a larger total value. A similar comparison between Virginia and New Jersey gives the same result.

That the conditions stated as obtaining in 1850 had long existed there seems to be no lack of evidence. Thomas Marshall made, in the Virginia legislature of 1831-'32, searching and detailed statements of the declining wealth and productivity of the State.[10] Such conditions as he pictured made plain that the planters of Virginia must either improve their lands by rehabilitating the soil, acquiring better farming implements, and improving their plow animals,[11] or migrate to the more promising lands elsewhere, or sell their slaves. The records show that by some planters one or another of these methods was adopted. Moreover, Maryland, a sister State of Virginia, because of the exhaustion of her soil by tobacco culture, found essential to her relief the same procedure.[12] With reference to Maryland, the census of 1840 shows an actual decrease over that of 1830 in the slave population[13] of the commonwealth.

To what parts, then, did these slaves go? The theatre of the largest expansion of slavery[14] was the "Western Cotton Belt," the section which shall be herein considered, comprehending parts of Alabama, Mississippi, Louisiana, and Eastern Texas. The chief distinction between the soils of these States constituting the Atlantic Coastal Plain from Virginia to South Carolina and those of the "Western Cotton Belt" is the occurrence of extensive limestone belts

[9] *Ibid.*, II, 364-5, 367, 369, 303-4; I, 11, 35. See also App. A2, *Census of 1850.*
[10] Ambler, *Sectionalism in Virginia*, 193.
[11] Phillips, *American Negro Slavery*, 185.
[12] De Bow's *Review*, x, 654.
[13] *Compendium, Seventh Census*, 1850, 84.
[14] Emerson, *op. cit.*, 118.

in the latter. "The soils in these limestone belts are largely residual, calcareous and usually have a humus content, which gives the soil its black color"[15]—hence the name "Black Belt." The soils of these belts contain much clay and require careful preparation, but they are durable and extremely fertile. Moreover, an excellent water navigation[16] extending well into the region constituted an additional factor in the extension of the cotton culture and of Negro slavery into this territory.

According to Phillips,[17] the lands of the "Western Cotton Belt," most preferred in the early period, lay in two main areas, the soils of both of which were more lasting and fertile than those in the interior of the Atlantic States. "One of these areas formed a crescent across south-central Alabama, with its western horn reaching up the Tombigbee River into northeastern Mississippi." The soil of this area was of black loose loam. Everywhere it was thickly matted with grass and weeds, except where there was visible "limestone on the hill crests and prodigious cane brakes in the valleys." This tract known locally as the prairies or "Black Belt" was smaller than the other which extended along the Mississippi, on both sides, from northern Tennessee and Arkansas to the mouth of the Red River. This tract contained broad alluvial bottoms, as well as occasional hill districts of rich loam, the latter being especially noticeable around Natchez and Vicksburg. The broadest expanse of these bottoms, the Yazoo-Mississippi Delta, received but few migrants prior to the middle "thirties." The planters seem to have settled first in the bottoms, while the other choice lands were competed for by the large and smaller planters, as well as the poor farmers.

These lands were not only, by soil and climate, ideally suited to the production of cotton, but they were reasonably cheap in price. As late as 1849 there was much uncultivated, though fertile agricultural land in each of the cotton-

[15] *Ibid.*, 171.
[16] *Ibid.*, 118.
[17] Phillips, *op. cit.*, 173.

growing States. At that time the total acreage and the area in use in several of the Gulf States were listed as follows:[18]

State	Total No. of Acres	Acres Owned
Alabama	32,462,080	15,911,520
Louisiana	29,715,840	6,263,822
Mississippi	30,174,080	15,811,650

There was under these circumstances small wonder that there migrated planters from the worn-out lands of the seaboard slave States, including the less fertile districts of Georgia,[19] and parts of Kentucky and Tennessee. In the absence of statistics giving the exact number of slaves migrating thus with their owners, the estimates of contemporaries and of later writers may be serviceable. *The Virginia (Wheeling) Times* said [20] that intelligent men of that day estimated the number of slaves exported from Virginia, during the year 1836, to be 120,000, of whom two-thirds (80,000) were carried south by their masters. The *Quarterly Anti-Slavery Magazine* (vol. ii, 411, July, 1837) gives the *Natchez Courier* as the authority for the estimate that during 1836 as many as 250,000 slaves, some of whom were accompanied by their masters, were transported from the older slave States to Alabama, Mississippi, Louisiana, and Arkansas.[21] P. A. Morse, of Louisiana, writing in 1857, says that "the augmentation of slaves within the cotton States was caused mostly by the migration of slave owners." On the basis of sources accessible to him, Morse estimated that three-fifths of the slaves removed from the border States to the farther South, from 1820 to 1850, migrated with their masters.[22] Accepting the "three-fifths estimate" of Morse, Collins has made deductions which indicate that approximately 15,900 slaves went south annually with their masters during the decade from 1830 to

---

[18] De Bow, *op. cit.*, vii, 166.
[19] Hammond, *op. cit.*, I, 53.
[20] Collins, *op. cit.*, 52.
[21] *Ibid.*, 52.
[22] *Ibid.*, 62.

1840; while during the next decade the annual migration was about 9,000.[23]

One of these migrant planters,[24] who, in 1835, left his tidewater estate in Gloucester County, Virginia, was Colonel Thomas S. Dabney. Prompted by the necessities of his family to seek more favorable soil, he sought land in Alabama, Louisiana, and Mississippi, finally settling in the one last mentioned. Colonel Dabney carried with him more than two hundred slaves, established himself on a plantation of four thousand acres, and each year contrived, by clearances, to put under cultivation an additional hundred acres. Planters of this type, with large numbers of slaves and sufficient funds to extend their holdings, tended to concentrate both slaves and lands in a few hands.

If the demand for new lands brought great numbers of slaves southward during the years from 1830 to 1850, there were also at work forces which caused many other slaves to be exported in the domestic slave traffic. The extension of the cotton culture in the more southern States, the increased exportation of cotton, the advancing profits therefrom, the development of large sugar plantations in Louisiana, and the decreased average working life of the slave created among the planters of this region an extraordinary demand for slave labor. At the same time such seaboard States as raised tobacco were suffering from a depression in the tobacco markets. The African slave trade, moreover, had been legally suppressed, thus rendering the seaboard and other border slave States the sole legal source of supply for the slave labor required by the lower South.

The income of some of the plantations on these fresh lands was immense.[25] It was considered not uncommon for a planter in Mississippi or Louisiana to receive an income of thirty thousand dollars annually. Extremely prosperous planters, it is said, took in from $80,000 to $120,000 in a single year. The enormous profits arising from such

[23] *Ibid.*, 64, 65.
[24] Phillips, *op. cit.*, 179, 180.
[25] Collins, *op. cit.*, 27.

investments in the face of the unusual demand for slaves enabled prices of bondmen to rise inordinately high. Thus it was that a prime field hand, a Negro between the ages of twenty and thirty years, could command a price varying from five hundred to twelve hundred dollars,[26] and, in some cases, fourteen hundred dollars or more. In fact, slave traders rapidly grew rich from the traffic. One is reported as having earned thirty thousand dollars in a few months, while Franklin and Armfield, members of a firm with headquarters in Alexandria, are said to have earned more than thirty-three thousand dollars in a single year.[27]

The effect of the growing demand for labor, reflected in the high prices being offered for slaves, tended to concentrate the interest of the Virginia planter on his slaves, as it had been hitherto concentrated on tobacco.[28] Prompt and efficient methods were devised whereby Negroes were made ready for the market.[29] Olmsted was informed by a slave-holder that in the States of Maryland, Virginia, North Carolina, Kentucky, Tennessee, and Missouri, as much attention was paid to the breeding and growth of Negroes as had been hitherto given to the breeding of horses and mules.[30]

As to the precise number of slaves exported in response to the high prices paid for them, there seems to be no conclusive evidence. Resort must be had, therefore, to estimates of contemporaries and later writers. *The New Orleans Advertiser* of January 21, 1830, says: "Arrivals by sea and river within a few days have added fearfully to the number of slaves brought to the market for sale. New Orleans is the complete mart for the trade—and the Mississippi is becoming a common highway for the traffic."[31] In the summer of 1831, moreover, New Orleans reported,

[26] Collins, *op. cit.*, 28.
[27] *Ibid.* (cited from Mary Tremain, *Slavery in District of Columbia*, 50).
[28] Olmsted, *Seaboard Slave States*, I, 278-279.
[29] *Ibid.*, I, 280-281.
[30] Olmsted, *Cotton Kingdom*, II, note, 58.
[31] Collins, *op. cit.*, 46, 47 (from the *African Repository*, V, 381).

in one week, the arrival of 381 slaves, nearly all of whom were from Virginia.[32]

Not all of the exportations of slaves were by sea as is attested by records of Sir Charles Lyell, Basil Hall, and Josiah Henson.[32a] At a later period, Featherstonhaugh tells of an overland expedition of slaves to the South. Of this coffle of slaves he says:[33] "Just as we reached New River, in the early grey of the morning, we came up with a singular spectacle, the most striking one of the kind I have ever witnessed. It was a camp of Negro slave-drivers, just packing up to start; they had about three hundred slaves with them, who had bivouacked the preceding night in chains in the woods; these they were conducting to Natchez, upon the Mississippi River, to work upon the sugar plantations in Louisiana. It resembled one of those coffles of slaves spoken of by Mungo Park, except that they had a caravan of nine waggons and single-horse carriages, for the purpose of conducting the white people, and any of the blacks that should fall lame, to which they were now putting their horses to pursue their march. The female slaves were, some of them, sitting on logs of wood, whilst others were standing, and a great many little black children were warming themselves at the fires of the bivouac. In front of them all and prepared for the march stood, in double file, about two hundred male slaves, manacled and chained to one another."

In the year 1831 there set in a reaction[34] against the importation of slaves into the Gulf States as a result of fear from troubles like Nat Turner's insurrection. Louisiana in 1831, and Alabama and Mississippi in 1832, passed laws prohibiting the importation of slaves into those States. The Alabama law was repealed in December, 1832, that of Louisiana in 1834, and that of Mississippi in 1846. More-

---

[32] *Ibid.*, 47 (from *Niles Register*, Nov. 26, 1831).

[32a] Basil Hall, *Travels in North America*, III, 128, 129; Sir Charles Lyell, *A Second Visit to the United States*, II, 35; Henson, *Uncle Tom's Story of his Life*, 53.

[33] Featherstonhaugh (G. W.), *Travels in America*, 36.

[34] Collins, *op. cit.*, 128, 130, 132-3.

over, there is no evidence to show that these laws really checked importations. The fright engendered by the slave insurrection in Virginia was not sufficient to triumph over the practical demands for such labor. Collins holds that during the years from 1832 to 1836 the largest migration of Negroes to the South and the Southwest occurred.[35]

Since cotton was the prime factor in effecting the prosperity of the Southwest, and its extension of culture and advance in price dictated largely the demand for slaves, the number of slaves yearly exported may bear some relation to the price of cotton. After 1835, the price of cotton declined.[36] This, together with the panic of 1837, caused a falling-off in the domestic slave trade, except in 1843, and the low price of cotton which continued until 1846 and hindered the revival[37] of the traffic in men. In 1843, however, five thousand slaves were sold in Washington as compared with two thousand in the previous year. These increased sales were doubtless in some measure due to the decline in the price of tobacco,[38] and the renewed activity of the sugar industry, incident to a new duty on that product.[39] For the whole decade from 1840 to 1850, however, a decrease in the slave traffic is shown by the fact that the per cent of increase in the slave population in the cotton States was barely half as great as during the previous decade.[40]

Some time after 1845, however, the demand for slaves seems to have exceeded the supply. A writer in the *Richmond Examiner* of 1849 is quoted as having said: "It being a well accustomed fact that Virginia and Maryland will not be able to supply the great demand for Negroes which will be wanted in the South this Fall and Spring, we would advise all who are compelled to dispose of them in this

---

[35] Collins, *op. cit.*, 54, 55 (cited from Hammond, *The Cotton Industry*, App. I).

[36] De Bow's *Review*, xxiii, 475.

[37] Hammond, *op. cit.*, App. I.

[38] Collins, *op. cit.*, 54 (from De Bow, *Ind. Resources*, iii, 349).

[39] *Ibid.*, 54 (De Bow, *Ind. Resources*, iii, 275).

[40] De Bow's *Review*, xxiii, 477.

market to defer selling until the sales of the present crop of cotton can be realized, as the price then must be very high for two reasons: first, the ravages of the cholera; and secondly, the high price of cotton."[41]

Three important events seem to have stimulated the slave trade during this period. First, there came the admission of Texas as a State in December, 1845; second, the increase in the price of cotton from 1845; and, third, the discovery of gold in California. The first of these opened to development a vast cotton country, which could be legally supplied with slave labor only through the domestic trade. The second event, the rise in the price of cotton, gave a new impetus to the production of cotton, and the California gold rush infused new life into all avenues of trade.[42] During this period and the decade following, Collins says that because of the great demand for slaves the price of them increased one hundred per cent; yet no evidence of a large increase in the traffic is shown.[43]

TABLE No. 1   TOTAL COTTON CROP IN BALES:[44]

1833	1,070,000
1837	1,081,000
1840	2,178,000
1843	2,379,000
1849	2,727,000

PRODUCTION OF COTTON BY STATES—(POUNDS):[45]

TABLE No. 2	1826	1833	1834
Virginia	25,000,000	13,000,000	10,000,000
North Carolina	18,000,000	10,000,000	9,000,000
Louisiana	38,000,000	55,000,000	62,000,000
Alabama	45,000,000	65,000,000	85,000,000
Mississippi	30,000,000	70,000,000	85,000,000

The statistics of cotton production and prices further elucidate this question. Table No. 1 shows a continuous

[41] *Richmond Examiner*, 1849.
[42] Collins, *op. cit.*, 54, 55 (from Hammond, *Cotton Industry*, App. I).
[43] *Ibid.*, 56. (*Key to Uncle Tom's Cabin*, 149; De Bow's *Review*, xxvi, 649).
[44] *Compendium, Seventh Census*, 1850, 191.
[45] De Bow's *Review*, xxiii, 477

increase in the production of cotton during the successive periods considered. Table No. 2 depicts the declining significance of Virginia and North Carolina as cotton-producing States and the shift of the lead of cotton production to the Gulf States. Table No. 3 shows the total production

COTTON PRODUCTION IN POUNDS: [46]

TABLE NO. 3
1839	790,479,275
1849	987,637,200

of cotton in the years considered and is significant, in that it emphasizes the important cotton-producing areas. During these years Alabama, Mississippi, Louisiana, and Georgia, together, produced more than two-thirds of the total cotton crop.[47] Table No. 4 is self-explanatory, while Table

AVERAGE PRICE A POUND OF COTTON IN FIVE-YEAR PERIODS: [48]

TABLE NO. 4
1830–1835	10.9 cents
1835–1840	14.4 cents
1840–1845	8.1 cents
1845–1850	7.3 cents

No. 5 shows the yearly fluctuations of the average price of

AVERAGE PRICE A POUND OF COTTON: [49]

TABLE NO. 5
1835	16.8 cents
1836	16.8 cents
1840	8.6 cents
1841	10.2 cents
1842	8.1 cents
1843	6.1 cents
1844	8.1 cents
1845	6.0 cents
1846	7.9 cents
1847	10.1 cents
1848	7.6 cents
1849	6.5 cents

cotton after 1840. In the years 1835 and 1836, the price

[46] Collins, op. cit., 32 (Statistics of Agr., 42, Census of 1890).
[47] Compendium, Seventh Census, 1850, 191.
[48] Ibid., 191.
[49] Collins, op. cit., 32.

is high relative to the later years in the two decades, and, assuming the continued demand for cotton, should have stimulated the domestic slave traffic by effecting a large demand for slaves at high prices. The lowest price is reached in 1845, followed by a rise till 1847, and then a decline in 1848 and 1849. That the demand for slaves was not at this time abated must be traceable to the fact that not more than three-fifths [50] of the slaves in the Cotton States were engaged in the production of cotton, while other occupations, notably sugar-production in Louisiana, demanded an increased quota.

The statistics of slave population are designed to show the increases of that type both in the States of Alabama, Louisiana, and Mississippi, and in selected areas within these States. In 1850, the civil subdivisions, as counties or parishes, which possessed the greatest density of slave population in Texas, as well as in the other States named, were located in those areas of the most fertile soil for producing cotton or cane. This concentration is but an evi-

SLAVE POPULATION IN THE GULF STATES: [51]

Table No. 6	1830	1840	1850
Alabama	117,549	253,532	342,844
Louisiana	109,588	168,452	244,809
Mississippi	65,659	195,211	309,878
Texas	......	......	58,161

PER CENT. SLAVE INCREASE BY DECADES: [52]

Table No. 7	1830–1840	1840–1850
Alabama	115.68	35.22
Louisiana	53.70	45.32
Mississippi	197.31	58.74
Texas	......	......

dence of the influence of these factors in calling forth the slave migration to the Southwest.

[50] De Bow's *Review*, xxiii, 477.
[51] *Compendium, Seventh Census*, 1850, 191, 84.
[52] De Bow's *Review*, xxiii, 477.

CONCENTRATION OF MIGRATION UPON SELECTED AREAS: ALABAMA:[53]

Table No. 8

Counties	1830	1840	1850
Barbour	....	5,548	10,780
Chambers	....	7,141	11,158
Dallas	7,160	17,208	22,258
Greene	7,420	16,431	22,127
Loundes	....	12,569	14,649
Macon	....	5,850	15,596
Madison	14,091	13,265	14,326
Marengo	2,987	11,902	20,693
Montgomery	6,450	15,486	19,427
Perry	4,331	10,343	13,917
Pickens	1,630	7,764	10,534
Russell	....	7,266	11,111
Sumter	....	15,920	14,831
Wilcox	4,070	8,292	11,835

CONCENTRATION OF MIGRATION UPON SELECTED AREAS (continued): MISSISSIPPI:[54]

Table No. 9

Counties	1830	1840	1850
Adams	9,649	8,740	14,395
Claiborne	6,174	7,743	11,450
Hinds	3,197	13,375	16,625
Jefferson	6,702	9,176	10,493
Lowndes	1,066	8,771	12,993
Madison	2,167	11,533	13,843
Marshall	....	8,250	15,417
Monroe	940	6,460	11,717
Noxubee	....	7,157	11,323
Warren	4,183	10,493	12,096
Wilkinson	7,877	10,894	13,260
Yazoo	2,470	7,237	10,349

The average increase of slave population in the States considered was 103.30 per cent for the decade from 1830 to 1840, while that of the next decade was less than half so great, being 51.41 per cent.[55] These percentages, though both significant, cannot be explained wholly in terms of Negro migration. If the estimate of the increase in slave population by births over deaths be for each decade twenty-

[53] *Census of 1830*, 98–101; *Census of 1840, Compendium*, 54; *Census of 1850*, 421.

[54] *Census of 1830*, 102–3; *Census of 1840, Compendium*; *Census of 1850*, 497.

[55] De Bow's *Review*, xxiii, 476.

CONCENTRATION OF MIGRATION UPON SELECTED AREAS (concluded):
LOUISIANA[56] (concluded):

TABLE No. 10

Parishes	1830	1840	1850
Ascension	2,813	4,553	7,266
Feliciana, E.	3,652	7,571	9,514
Feliciana, W.	6,345	8,755	10,666
Iberville	4,509	5,887	8,606
Madison	.....	3,923	7,353
Natchitoches	3,570	6,651	7,881
Orleans	16,603	23,448	18,068
Point Coupee	4,210	5,430	7,811
Rapides	5,321	10,511	11,340
St. James	5,027	5,711	7,751
St. Landry	5,057	7,129	10,871
St. Mary's	4,304	6,286	9,850
Tensas	.....	.....	8,138

TEXAS:[57]

TABLE No. 11

Counties	1850
Austin	1,549
Bowie	1,641
Brazoria	3,507
Cass	1,902
Cherokee	1,283
Fayette	1,016
Fort Bend	1,554
Grimes	1,680
Harrison	6,213
Lamar	1,085
Matagorda	1,208
Nacogdoches	1,404
Nueces	1,193
Red River	1,406
Rusk	2,136
San Augustine	1,561
Walker	1,301
Washington	2,817
Wharton	1,242

eight per cent,[58] and if from 1830 to 1840 forty thousand and from 1840 to 1850 fifty thousand foreign Negroes were imported[59] into the country as slaves, the number migrat-

[56] *Census of 1830*, 104-107; *Census of 1840, Compendium; Census of 1850*, 473.
[57] *Census of 1850*, 503-4.
[58] *Ibid.*, 476.
[59] Collins, *op. cit.*, 64, 65.

ing from the more Northern States was materially smaller than at first appears to be the case. Phillips says that from 1815-1860, the volume of the slave trade by sea alone averaged from two thousand to five thousand [60] annually; but Dew, in 1832, estimated that six thousand slaves were annually exported from Virginia.[61] Collins, moreover, has made most elaborate calculations in this matter.[62] Accepting the estimate of Morse that three-fifths of the slaves who went south during the period from 1820 to 1850 migrated with their masters, Collins has deduced that the average annual export of Negroes for sale, during the decade from 1830 to 1840, was 10,600; and of the next decade, 6,000. On the basis of the principle underlying this calculation, it would follow that approximately 15,900 slaves migrated south with their masters during the earlier decade; while 9,000 went annually in this way during the decade from 1840 to 1850. Finally, if this principle of calculation be accepted, and the facts upon which it is based be well founded, approximately 26,500 Negroes found their way annually to the cotton and contiguous territory during the period from 1830 to 1840; while from 1840 to 1850 the annual number was 15,000.

What were some effects of this vast migration of Negro slaves to the Gulf States? The mere concentration of a large slave population in this region gains significance when it is considered in its numerical relation to the whites. Throughout the two decades from 1830 to 1850, there was a progressive increase in the white population here, and yet, in 1850, the whites in Alabama exceeded the slaves by less than one hundred thousand. In Louisiana the excess was 11,000; while in Mississippi the slaves were in the majority by some 14,000.[63] This situation was fraught with great possibilities. Would the slaves undertake a

[60] Phillips, *op. cit.*, 195.
[61] Hammond, *op. cit.*, I, 53 (from Dew in the *Pro-Slavery Argument*, 399).
[62] Collins, *op. cit.*, 64, 65.
[63] *Compendium, Seventh Census*, 1850, 63.

servile insurrection? To this dangerous aspect much thought was given, and thorough precautions were taken to protect the whites against such an upheaval. The immediate effect of this movement of the slaves to the Gulf Regions, however, was the final commitment of that section to a regime of slavery and the unification of a solid South based on interests peculiar to that section.

Although the emancipation of the blacks as a result of the Civil War has made possible the movement of not a few Negroes away from the Gulf Region, they still form a substantial portion of the population. They supply as in former days the bulk of the cotton hands. Many live in ignorance and in poverty, disfranchised and subjected to the economic exploitation of the ruling classes. They have therefore been a potent force in the creation of a social problem, the solution of which seems not yet to be found, except it appears in the present migration of these Negroes to industrial centers in the North.

A. A. TAYLOR

NEGROES IN DOMESTIC SERVICE IN THE UNITED STATES *

Introduction

The term *Domestic Service* as used in this study will include those persons performing household duties for pay. In early colonial history indentured servants performed household duties without pay. They were usually imported convicts, assigned to labor for a term on some estate, receiving only their living and stipulated benefits at the termination of their service.[1] In modern use the word "servant" denotes a domestic or menial helper and implies little or no discretionary power and responsibility in the mode of performing duty.[2]

In this discussion of Negroes in domestic service in the United States the facts presented disclose the part Negroes have had in the changes and developments of domestic service in the United States during the past thirty years.[3] They also show to some extent the relation of Negro domestic

---

* This thesis was submitted in 1923 in partial fulfillment of the requirements for the degree of Master of Arts in the Faculty of Political Science of Columbia University.

[1] Bruce, *Economic History of Virginia in the 17th Century*, Vol. I, p. 573.

[2] *Century Dictionary and Cyclopedia*.

[3] The following works were found helpful in preparing this dissertation: W. A. Crossland, *Industrial Conditions Among Negroes in St. Louis* (Studies in Social Economics, Washington Univ., Vol. I, No. 1, St. Louis, 1914); Isabel Eaton, *Special Report on Domestic Service* in THE PHILADELPHIA NEGRO by W. E. B. DuBois (Philadelphia, 1899); George E. Haynes, *The Negro at Work in New York City* (New York, 1912); Frances A. Kellor, *Out of Work;* Knickerbocker Press (New York, 1904); W. I. King, *Employment, Hours and Earnings in the United States, 1920-1922;* Asa E. Martin, *Our Negro Population* (Kansas City, 1913); *Monthly Labor Review* (U. S. Bureau of Labor Statistics, 1919-1920); Ruth Reed, *The Negro Women of Gainsville, Georgia* (1921—A Master's Essay—Phelps Stokes Fund Scholarship); *Report of U. S. Industrial Commission, Domestic Service,* Vol. XIV; I. M. Rubinow, *Depth and Breadth of the Servant Problem* (McClures Magazine, Vol. 34, 1909-1910); Lucy M. Salmon, *Domestic Service* (New York, 1901).

workers to white workers and to some of the larger problems in this field of employment.

The primary data used here were gathered in three ways. First, the writer was a dollar-a-year worker of the Woman in Industry Service, United States Department of Labor, in 1919; and while visiting cities in this work obtained from employment agencies some data on domestic service. Secondly, as domestice service Employment Secretary, United States Employment Service, Washington, District of Columbia, from January 1920 to May 1922, the writer kept careful record of pertinent facts with a view to further study and analysis of this information at a later time.

Three different record cards were used at this office. One was for the employer with name, address, telephone number, kind of help desired, work to be done, whether to "sleep in" or "sleep out," afternoons off, breakfast and dinner hour, size of family, wages, etc. Another card was kept for the employee with name, address, birthplace, age, marital condition, number of dependents, grade at leaving school, kind of work desired, minimum wages applicant would accept, names of three recent former employers and their addresses. On the back of this card were written the name of the employer engaging the worker, the date, and kind of work. There was also a card of introduction for the applicant which the employer mailed back to the office.

A personal canvass of eleven employment agencies in New York City and one in Brooklyn was also made in 1923. The records of only two of these agencies were used, because more time could not be given to securing material in this way.

In the third place, in 1923 a general schedule asking questions relating to number, sex, age, marital condition, turnover, efficiency, wages, hours, specific occupations, living conditions and health was sent by mail to employment secretaries in twelve cities North, South, East, and West, with whom contacts had been established through acquaintances and friends. Responses were received from ten of these cities with data for 1,771 domestic and personal service workers.

I. NUMBER AND SEX OF NEGROES IN DOMESTIC AND PERSONAL SERVICE

Because of the difficulties inherent in the classification of occupations the United States Census Bureau has classified all domestic and personal service occupations in one group. It has not been possible, therefore, to ascertain the exact number of workers engaged exclusively in domestic service. For example, the domestic and personal service classification includes indiscriminately barbers, hairdressers, manicurists, midwives, hotel keepers, policemen, cooks, servants, waiters, bootblacks, and the like.

Fifty years ago there were in the United States 2,311,820 persons ten years of age and over engaged in domestic and personal service, 42.1 per cent of whom were males and 57.9 per cent females. During the succeeding thirty years there was an average increase for males and females combined of 108,961 a year. So that in 1900, persons ten years of age and over engaged in domestic and personal service numbered 5,580,657. As far as distinction from domestic service occupations can be made, the number engaged in personal service has continued to increase since 1900. By contrast, during the decade from 1900 to 1910 and from 1910 to 1920 there was a rather steady decline in the number of those engaged in domestic service. However, the two groups of domestic and personal service occupations combined showed that the number ten years of age and over by 1910 had decreased 1,808,098, and by 1920 had further decreased 367,667. Males constituted 6.4 per cent of the decrease from 1910 to 1920 and females 93.6 per cent. The number of children from 10 to 15 years of age engaged in domestic and personal service in 1910 were 112,171. In 1920 the number had decreased to 54,006.

The trend of the number of Negroes in domestic and personal service occupations compared with the general trend of the total number is indicative of the relation of Negroes and Caucasians in these occupations. We may, therefore, discuss the number and sex of Negroes ten years of age and over engaged in these occupations.

In 1900 there were in the United States 1,317,859 Negroes ten years of age and over gainfully employed in domestic and personal service: 681,926 females and 635,933 males. In 1910 the number of females had increased to 861,497 and the males had decreased to 496,100. In 1890 the total number of Negroes ten years of age and over gainfully employed in domestic and personal service constituted 20.7 per cent of the total number so employed and held third place among all nationalities so employed. Negro men held first place among men thus employed and constituted 40.8 per cent of the total number of male domestic workers.[4] This proportion does not take into account the fact that there were about eight white persons to one Negro in the total population. At that time one in every 5.6 Negroes ten years of age and over gainfully employed was in domestic and personal service. In 1900 Negro women domestic workers occupied second place in point of numbers among the total number and outnumbered the Negro male domestic workers 3 to 1, while the white female domestic workers outnumbered the white male domestic workers about 7 to 1.

The census figures dealing with servants and waiters for 1910 and 1920 in five Southern States where Negroes perform practically all of the domestic service and in five Northern States where conditions are quite different indicate the similarity in the trend of the numbers for both races in domestic service. Although the number of waiters increased by 40,693 between 1910 and 1920, the number of other domestic servants so decreased that we have the following figures for waiters and other domestic workers.

[4] *Report of the U. S. Industrial Commission*, Vol. XIV. DOMESTIC SERVICE, p. 745.

Servants and Waiters 10 years of age and over, in selected States, 1901–1920

TABLE I State	1910		1920	
	Male	Female	Male	Female
Georgia	8,719	38,165	7,752	38,165
N. Carolina	5,553	28,555	4,855	21,321
Louisiana	7,112	30,982	6,761	28,306
Maryland	8,125	32,292	6,859	26,305
Virginia	9,535	42,797	3,144	33,781
Massachusetts	16,969	71,853	16,574	51,941
Ohio	11,695	64,408	15,170	50,232
Minnesota	6,581	37,207	6,134	26,939
Pennsylvania	24,103	134,374	22,173	98,798
New York	63,395	198,970	69,869	151,455

The figures show a decided decrease of domestic servants in both Southern and Northern States between 1910 and 1920, except male servants in Ohio and New York and female servants in Georgia.

The increase in male servants in Ohio and New York may be accounted for by the large increase of waiters in those States. There is no apparent explanation for the lack of change in the figures of female domestic workers in Georgia. It may be said, however, that Georgia has not suffered an actual decrease in its Negro population during the past ten years as have Mississippi, with a 7.4 per cent decrease, Kentucky with a 9.8 per cent decrease, Louisiana with a 1.8 per cent decrease, Alabama with 0.8 per cent decrease, Delaware with a 2.7 per cent decrease, and Tennessee with a 4.5 per cent decrease. This decrease in the Southern States has been due to the migration of Negroes to Northern industrial centers.

For example, the Negro population of Chicago increased from 44,103 in 1910 to 109,456 in 1920; that of New York City increased from 91,709 to 152,467. The number of Negroes in domestic and personal service in these and other Northern industrial centers has increased during the past ten years because the Negroes who have migrated North could enter domestic and personal service more easily than they could other fields of employment.

Since the total number of Negroes in domestic service

has decreased while the total Negro population has increased, the question arises as to why the number of domestic and personal service workers has not kept pace with the growth of the Negro population. In twenty years between 1890 and 1910 Negroes in the United States gainfully employed increased about 65 per cent in agriculture, about 66.6 per cent in trade and transportation, about 129.5 per cent in manufacturing and mechanical pursuits, and about 65.3 per cent in domestic and personal service.

The Census of 1920 shows that of the gainfully employed 4,824,151 Negroes ten years of age and over, 45.2 per cent were in agriculture, forestry, and animal husbandry; 22.1 per cent were in domestic and personal service; 18.4 per cent were in manufacturing and mechanical pursuits; 9.4 per cent were in trade and transportation; 1.7 per cent were in professional service; 0.8 per cent were in clerical occupations; 1.0 per cent were in public service; and 1.5 per cent were engaged in the extraction of minerals. This increase in occupations other than agriculture and domestic and personal service is largely due to conditions incident to the World War. Because of the 3 per cent immigration restriction, Negroes are being attracted to the North in large numbers and are entering industrial pursuits. For several years at least, this movement will most probably continue.

II. Age and Marital Condition of Negroes in Domestic and Personal Service

In 1900, 53.4 per cent of all the women sixteen years of age and over engaged in domestic and personal service were from 16 to 24 years of age. Of the Negro women 16 years of age and over engaged in domestic and personal service, 35.1 per cent, or more than one-third, were between the ages of 16 and 24. The percentage in the other age groups of the total number of women 16 years of age and over engaged in domestic and personal service decreased by classes. That of Negro women 16 years of age and over engaged in domestic and personal service decreased by classes until those 55 years of age and over constituted only 9.6 per cent of the total number of Negro women so employed. The modal age of Negro male domestic workers like that of white male domestic workers was from 25 to 44 years. The age distribution of domestic and personal service workers for 1920 is about the same as that for 1900. Because of the incompleteness of the age data obtained from the general schedule sent to employment agencies, they were not used for this study. The average ages of the 9,976 male and female Negro domestic and personal service workers of Washington, D. C., were: 30.5 years for the males and 28.1 years for the females.

In 1900, among Negro women the percentage of breadwinners did not show such a marked decline after marriage as among white women. Of the Negro female breadwinners 32.5 per cent were married, while only 9.0 per cent of the female breadwinners of all the races were married. The percentage of married Negro male domestic and personal service workers is higher than that of married female workers, while the number of widowed and divorced is three and one-half times as great among female as among male domestic and personal service workers. In 1920, 29.4 per cent of all the female domestic and personal service workers 15 years of age and over were married, while 70.6 per cent were classed as single, widowed, divorced, and unknown.

The significance of age grouping and marital condition of Negro domestic workers in their relation to employers is borne out by the testimony of experienced employment agents in New York City, Philadelphia, Baltimore, Washington, D. C., Chicago, and Detroit. Women domestic workers between the ages of 20 and 25 are the most sought after by employers. Those between 25 and 35 years of age are next in favor. All of the agents testified to the unpopularity of the young girl domestic worker. She is employed principally because of the tight domestic labor market. Employers apparently feel that a majority of the women beyond the ages of 45 and 50 have become too set in their ways, somewhat cranky, and largely unable to do general housework. The most frequent objections of employers to young girl domestic workers are: They are untrained and inexperienced; they are unwilling to sleep in; they are saucy; and their interest in men company causes them to neglect their work.

The older Negro women in domestic service, realizing that with their advancing years their possibilities for employment become less, often hesitate and even fail to give their correct ages when applying at employment agencies for positions. For example, a New York City agency registered a woman who gave her age as 34, but whose written references, yellowed with age, showed that she had worked for different members in one family for fifty years. Frequently an older woman registrant when asked her age hesitates and ends by saying "just say 'settled woman.'"

In addition to the age situation of Negroes engaged in domestic service, the marital condition of female domestic workers furnishes a perplexing problem for both their employers and themselves. The testimony of employment agents relative to employers' most commonly registered objections to hiring married women for domestic service is: Married women take away food for the support of their families; married women have so many responsibilities and problems in their own homes they oftener than not go out to work with a weary body and a disturbed mind; married women find it difficult to live and sleep on employers' premises.

Besides these problems there is apparently a still more perplexing one for the Negro domestic workers with children of their own or other dependents, namely, how to provide proper care and protection for their dependents while they are away from home at work, especially if the hours are long. Day nurseries are often mentioned as a possible solution for this particular problem, but they exist for Negroes in very few cities of the South. Even in the District of Columbia with a population of servants and waiters—servants largely Negroes—totaling 21,444, there is not one day nursery for Negro children. The other alternative is to get some elderly woman to take care of a child. The usual charge made by such a woman for a limited number of hours during the day is from $5 to $6 a week, the mother furnishing food for the child. With these two items and carfare deducted from a mother's weekly wage of $9 there is little left for other necessities.

The problem of dependents manifests itself also among widowed and divorced Negro women engaged in domestic service. The U. S. Employment Office, Washington, D. C., registered 9,774 Negro women 15 years of age and over for domestic service from January, 1920, to May, 1922. Of this number 5,124 were single, 2,579 were married, 2,071 were widowed or divorced. Of the widowed or divorced 2,056 had from 1 to 5 dependents; 79 had from 6 to 10 dependents. Although no record was made of the number of breadwinners in each of these families, many of these widows expressed their weight of responsibilities by referring to the high cost of living when their children had no one to look to for support but themselves.

Divorced domestic workers and also unmarried mothers constitute marital groups that are not all together negligible. Three of the divorced women sent from the Washington office had the added problem of finding their husbands at their respective places of employment after absences of 5, 2, and 2 years respectively. Among the 5,124 single registered at the Washington office there were reported 9 unmarried mothers.

In the District of Columbia there is a Training School for delinquent Negro girls, a large number of whom go into domestic service when they are paroled. They are better trained than the average domestic employee, but since the Training School requires them to keep their young babies with them, it is difficult to place them in homes. If they take a room and attempt to do day work they have the difficult problem of getting someone to take care of their children.

The marital condition of 471 new applicants for domestic positions in Indianapolis, Indiana, for 1922, is given in the following table:

Showing marital condition of 471 women seeking work as domestic servants—
TABLE II   *Indianapolis, Ind., 1922*

Widows	63
Separated from husbands	50
Married and living with husbands	238
Divorced	34
Single	85
Unmarried mothers	1

The large proportion of married persons in the table may be accounted for, in part, by the fact that 51 per cent of the total number had recently come into Indianapolis from the adjoining States of Kentucky and Tennessee.

III. Turnover, Training, and Efficiency of Negro Domestic and Personal Service Workers

The increase of 13,738,354, or 14.9 per cent, in the total population of the United States during the last decade, and a decrease of 367,667 in the domestic and personal service occupations population increases the possibilities of turnover. In 1890, the average tenure of service of a domestic worker in the United States was less than one and one-half years.[5] Ten years later the average length of service of a Negro domestic worker in the seventh ward of Philadelphia was five years less than one month.[6] Many of these workers perhaps had been for a long time in the older families of Philadelphia. Figures for a three-year period, from 1906 to 1908, show that the modal period of service of the New York Negro domestic worker was at that time from six to eleven months.[7] In 1914, among 104 unskilled Ne-

[5] Salmon, Lucy M., *Domestic Service*, p. 109.
[6] Eaton, Isabel, *Special Report on Domestic Service* in THE PHILADELPHIA NEGRO, by W. E. B. DuBois, Philadelphia, 1889, p. 480.
[7] Haynes, George E., *The Negro at Work in New York City*, New York, 1918, p. 85.

gro workers of St. Louis—cooks, laundresses, porters, chambermaids, waiters, scrubwomen, manual laborers, and the like—the greatest frequency for length of service among the men was from one to three months, and among the women from three to six months.[8] Six years later the largest proportion of Negro domestic workers of Gainesville, Georgia, showed a disposition to remain in one position less than three months, while the next largest proportion remained in one position from three to six months.[9]

Some concrete illustrations of the frequency of turnover may be referred to as further evidence. Nearly two hundred different women were sent out from the Springfield, Massachusetts, office for day work in 1915. Two years later over 500 different workers were sent out from that office, about 200 of whom were Negro women. Of these 167 white women and 124 Negro women were placed with employers less than ten times in 1917; 2 white and 4 Negro women were sent out from 41 to 50 times; 3 white and 1 Negro woman were placed fifty times during 1917. In 1918, the Springfield office reported as having filled 4,000 places with 1,000 women.[10]

In 1920 the United States Employment Office, Washington, D. C., placed 1,488 different women for day work, all of whom were Negroes except one. Of these, 458, after being given permanent positions for every day in the week, were referred again not over twelve times; 23 of them were sent out over fifty times, and 5 of them over one hundred times during the year. General housework was so unpopular during that year that few would take it. Although the turnover in day work was greater than that in any other specific employment handled by the domestic service section of that office, the 164 cooks remained in one position on an average of about three months.

There was, however, in the District of Columbia during

[8] Crossland, W. A., *Industrial Conditions among Negroes in St. Louis*, St. Louis, 1914, p. 30.

[9] Reed, Ruth, *The Negro Women of Gainesville, Georgia*, 1921, p. 25.

[10] *Massachusetts Bureau of Statistics, Springfield Report*, 1915-1918.

the fall and winter of 1920 a decrease in the rate and volume of turnover for Negro day workers and hotel workers consequent upon the minimum wage law which became effective for hotels and restaurants in the spring of 1920. Many Negro women displaced in the hotels turned to day work. For this reason added to the normal increase during the first half of 1921, the number of day workers increased to 3,115. White workers did not have to apply for day work because they could secure positions in hotels and restaurants.

During an unemployment period which extended over the latter half of 1921 and the first half of 1922, when so many men were thrown out of work, the day workers increased to 4,615. There were more day workers than there were positions for them. Consequently the turnover in day work decidedly decreased, but it increased in general housework. Many who could not get a sufficient number of days' work to make ends meet were forced to turn to general housework.

The difficulty of keeping an accurate record of the turnover in general housework makes the value of figures on turnover in general housework seem very questionable. However, the length of service of 1,000 general houseworkers sent out from the Washington office for the latter half of 1921 and the first few months of 1922 gives a fairly accurate picture of the situation at that time.

Length of Service of 1,000 General Houseworkers, Washington, D. C., 1921-22
TABLE III

317 remained in one position 1 week or less.
582 remained in one position from one to three months.
101 remained in one position 4 months and over.

Some of the conditions of the turnover at that time are illustrated by typical cases. One employer advertised for a general houseworker without laundry, with the privilege of going at night, and with hours off. Eleven domestic workers answered the advertisement in person, and no two met at the house at the same time. The employer engaged every one of them, to return to work the next morning. Every one of them gave assurance of being there, but not one of them came. Another employer with only two in family, very desirous of securing a general houseworker, called up six different employment agencies, each of which sent her a worker. Among the number there was one man. The employer put every one of them to work, each in a different room, with the idea of choosing the two best ones at the end of the day and engaging them for permanent work—thus assuring herself of securing one worker. She managed her plan, as she thought, very successfully, but the next morning she did not have a single worker.

Employers' statements on reference blanks, and reports from employment agencies indicate that the reasons generally given by domestic workers for leaving positions are that they wish a change, or the hours are too long, or the work is too hard, or the employer is too particular, or they have no time off. Time off for domestic employees is no doubt greatly limited. Negro domestic workers, however, proverbially take Christmas Day and the Fourth of July off, giving such various excuses for their absence as death in the family, automobile accidents, and the like. Just after these two holidays, large employment agencies handling Negro help are for the most part swamped with applicants.

To some extent turnover in domestic service is linked up with lack of training and efficiency of domestic workers. Because of their great need of domestic help, employers frequently engage persons who are so utterly untrained that they cannot be retained. There is a tendency on the part of employers to propose to a domestic worker that each take the other on a week's trial. Domestic workers are inclined to refuse such offers on the ground that they are looking for permanent employment. This suggestion of trying out domestic workers leads logically to the question of training and efficiency in domestic service.

Training of White Domestic and Personal Service Workers

Some facts relative to the special opportunities for the training of white household workers in England and in the United States may throw some light on the problem of efficiency. In England, following the World War and under the ministry of reconstruction, there was created a women's advisory committee to study the domestic service problem. Each of the four sub-committees appointed made a report. Among the advisory committee's final recommendations for getting the work of the nation's homes done satisfactorily and reducing waste, were technical training for domestic help and fixed standards of qualifications for them. This committee reported that in 1914 there were only ten domestic service schools in England and Wales, and four of these were in the London area. During the year of 1922 courses of three months' duration were given at some technical institutions in England in all branches of household work and management. This training enabled women to take the better posts in daily or residential work. Training in cooking and catering could be had at any technical college for three or more months as required.

To help meet the serious unemployment situation the Central Committee on Women's Training and Employment in cooperation with the Ministry of Labor set up homecraft training centers in districts where unemployment was most noticeable. At these centers a course of training was given for about three months, such as would enable women to take posts in domestic service at the end of the course. These classes were most successful. By August, 1922, about 10,000 women had received the training and the courses were still continued. These courses were given to women and girls between the ages of 16 and 35 upon their signing an agreement to be punctual in attendance, to do their best in making the classes successful, and stating their willingness to enter domestic service after receiving their training.

In the United States, in 1900, there were more illiterate

persons in domestic and personal service than in any other field of employment except agriculture. The number of agricultural colleges in the different States for the purpose of developing improved farming and farmers has increased since that time, and the Federal Government farm demonstration agents are actually teaching the citizens on the plantations where they live and work. Facilities for the training of domestic help, however, have received little attention from State or Federal Government, and private enterprise in this field has been very limited.

Just twenty years ago the Home Economics Committee of the Association of Collegiate Alumnae of the United States, through the inspiration of Mrs. Alice Freeman Palmer and Mrs. Ellen H. Richards, undertook an experiment for studying at first hand the problems of household labor. Among the disabilities in domestic service regarded as fundamental causes of the disfavor in which it was held, was the low grade of intelligence and skill available among domestic service workers. This household aid company committee opened a training center and applied educational tests to its candidates and undertook to give a course of six weeks' training to each aid before she was sent out to work. The number of aids taking the training was small. Mainly because of a lack of funds, however, the experiment was given up after a trial of two years. Prior to that time the civic club of Philadelphia attempted to standardize the work and wages of domestic workers in that city.

Nearly twenty years later, a committee on household assistants was organized in New York City by the United States Employment Service. The committee succeeded in planning a household occupations course to be given at the Washington Irving High School, and made efforts to advertise the course; but since no one registered for it the committee concluded that the matter would have to be taken up and pushed by employers before it could succeed.[11]

Some of these efforts, however, have met with a meas-

[11] U. S. Department of Labor, *Monthly Labor Review*, Aug., 1919, p. 206.

ure of success. The Bureau of Household Occupations of the Housewives' League of Providence, R. I., organized in November, 1918, has conducted very successful training classes for domestic workers. No meals or lodging are to be furnished the household attendants of the Bureau. The Bureau of Occupations under the auspices of the Housewives' League of Hartford, Connecticut, has given its training courses through the generosity of some of its members. One member taught cooking, another taught waiting table, another laundry work. Classes were taught in the homes of some of the members with much success.

Training of Negro Domestic Workers

Available data shows that opportunities for the special training of Negro domestic workers have been even less than those for white domestic workers. During the latter quarter of the 19th century Mrs. L. J. Coppin, of Philadelphia, maintained a small home for the training of the Negro domestic workers of Philadelphia. In the comparatively few social settlements for Negroes there is meagre opportunity for training in domestic service. The Domestic Efficiency Association of Baltimore, Maryland, an organization of employers, has announced its plans for opening a training school for white and Negro domestic workers. This Association maintained in 1921 and 1922 a training school for Negro domestic help, in which special lessons could be given or general training for one month or more. A rate of $5 a week for board, lodging, and training was charged. If an applicant had no money the Domestic Efficiency Association advanced it on her signing an agreement to secure her position through the Association when ready for it, and to repay the debt out of her wages at the rate of at least $2.50 a week.

The domestic science training given in the public schools may be a small factor in the efficiency of Negro domestic workers, but most of the permanent domestic workers do not go beyond the fifth grade in school and thus do not go far enough to get an appreciable amount of domestic science training. Negro workers who go through the high or normal schools do not enter permanently into domestic service. This statement is based on the data indicated by the permanent occupations of 606 Negro graduates of the Sumner High School, St. Louis, Missouri, of 305 graduates of Miner Normal School, Washington, in the District of Columbia, of 15 graduates of the Gainesville, Georgia, public schools 1917–1919;[12] and on data for students applying at the Washington, in the District of Columbia, and the Indianapolis Employment Agencies. Tables IV and V below set forth these facts.

Occupations of 606 Negro High School Graduates, Sumner High School, St. Louis, Mo., 1895–1911 [13]

TABLE IV

Occupation	Number
Those engaged in, or prepared for, teaching	288
Entered college	49
Clerical work	43
Postoffice clerks	30
Entered business	4
Mechanics	17
Women at home or married	120
Miscellaneous	32
Unknown	23

Although Tables IV and V direct one's attention to the limited fields of employment for Negro high school graduates, especially so since clerical and mechanical work, business and professional service, must be engaged in almost wholly among Negroes, yet few if any of the 911 graduates have entered domestic service. The young women graduates of the Gainesville, Georgia, schools 1917–19, with the exception of three, entered higher institutions of learning.

In Washington, in the District of Columbia, during the academic year 1920–22 there were among the 9,976 applicants for domestic work, 17 male and 159 female students who had attended or were attending high school; 75 female

[12] Reed, Ruth, *op. cit.*, p. 44.
[13] Crossland, William A., *op. cit.*, p. 93.

normal school students; 13 male and 126 female college students. Also in Indianapolis, in 1922, 73 female high school students and 12 female college students applied for domestic service. These large numbers of high school, normal school, and college students seek domestic service mainly for after-school hours, Saturdays, Sundays, summer months, and temporarily for earning money to continue their education, or until they can find other employment.

Occupations of 305 Negro Graduates of Miner Normal School, Washington, D. C., 1913–1922

TABLE V

Occupation	Number
Teaching in Washington, D. C.:	
Elementary	207
Kindergarten	50
Domestic Science	4
Domestic Art	3
Manual Arts	1
Drawing	1
Music	1
Ungraded	1
Teaching in Maryland	8
Teaching in Virginia	2
Teaching in North Carolina	1
Teaching in South Carolina	1
Teaching in New York	1
Substitute teachers in Washington, D. C.	2
Students	5
Government Service	7
Housekeepers	5
Printers	1
Private Music Teachers	1
Physicians	1
Insurance	1
Y. W. C. A.	1

Table VI shows the grades on leaving school of 8,147 Negro domestic workers—men and women—of the Washington, D. C., office; and Table VII shows grades on leaving school of 471 Negro domestic workers, not separated by sex, of an Indianapolis Employment Office conducted by Flanner House in that city. Each of these workers was personally interviewed by the agent at each respective office. The reported grade of each on leaving school was placed on an application card which was filed for reference. The application cards were filled out solely on the testimony of the applicants. The agent in the Washington office handling the women did not ordinarily register men except as man and wife applied at the same time, or a woman sent her husband to the agent, or a special employer asked the agent to select male help, or teachers in the Negro schools sent boys and men who were in search of work. Therefore, the number of men from the Washington office for whom grades are given is comparatively small.

In examining Tables VI and VII below one must take into consideration several factors. In the first place, 81.2 per cent of the Washington applicants and 73.9 per cent of the Indianapolis applicants were born in the South where the standard is not so high as in the North; and many of these applicants attended school in the rural districts of the South where the schools were not standardized, and only a few schools had any domestic science instruction. Then, too, a large proportion of them left school some years ago when all of the grades or groups of a school were taught by one teacher in one room.

Those persons who could not read or write seemed to feel their illiteracy very keenly. Many of them offered excuses by saying that the "white folks raised" them; or their parents died and they had to help the other children; or they were "sickly," and the like. Those who had never been to school but could read and write a little were listed as being in the first grade. One applicant said that she had never been through any grade but she could read and write and go anywhere in the city she wished to go. Another one, an elderly woman, expressed her regrets because she never had a chance to go to school, but she had learned to read and write so that she could sign her name instead of simply "touching the pen" when she was transacting her business.

Grades on Leaving School of 7,975 Female and 172 Male Negro Domestic Workers from the U. S. Employment Service, Washington, D. C., 1920–1922

TABLE VI

	Male	Female
Illiterate	8	418
1st Grade	5	244
2d Grade	7	436
3d Grade	9	842
4th Grade	17	1,073
5th Grade	31	1,417
6th Grade	28	1,237
7th Grade	25	998
8th Grade	42	1,310

Grades on Leaving School of 387 Negro Domestic Workers, Irrespective of Sex, Indianapolis, Ind., 1922

TABLE VII

Illiterate	1st Gr.	2d Gr.	3d Gr.	4th Gr.	5th Gr.	6th Gr.	7th Gr.	8th Gr.
21	7	11	22	44	63	51	47	120

The figures show that of a total of 7,975 female applicants for domestic work in Washington, D. C., 4,430, or 55.5 per cent, had received school training in the sixth grade or below; leaving only 29.9 per cent who had seventh or eighth grade training. Of the 387 applicants for domestic service in Indianapolis, 168, or 43.3 per cent, had received school training up to the fifth grade or below; and 219, or 56.7 per cent, had been to the sixth grade or below, leaving 43.3 per cent who had been in the seventh or eighth grade. The larger proportions of those from higher grades in Indianapolis may be accounted for by the lesser opportunity in other occupations as compared with Washington, and by the smaller number of applicants involved. In short, domestic service as a regular occupation does not attract and hold Negro workers of the higher grades of educational training and intelligence.

In order to understand exactly what is meant by saying that consideration of certain factors must be taken into account in any attempt to formulate some idea of the educational status of the rank and file domestic worker reckoned by his grade when he left school, some letters, typical of the educational equipment among the 9,774 domestic workers (applicants), should be read. These letters were written to the agent in the Washington, D. C., office by 5th grade domestic workers.[14]

Many of these domestic workers also showed their lack of training by their inability to figure out their weekly wages at the rate of $40, 45, or $50 per month. Such inability often caused them to feel and say that their employers were "cheaters." To a considerable number of them, $40 a month meant $10 a week, and vice versa; $45 a month meant $11.25 a week, and $50 a month meant $12.50 a week. They generally secured their pay twice a month— the first and the fifteenth. However, such an arrangement did not seem to clarify matters, since they thought of four weeks as making a month.

Then comes the question of the efficiency of Negro domestic workers. In Philadelphia, Baltimore, Detroit, Indianapolis, and Washington, D. C., agents find that employers of domestic labor, like other employers, do not like

---

[14] THREE SAMPLE LETTERS OF THE 5TH GRADE DOMESTIC WORKERS OF WASHINGTON, D. C.

Miss X (The agent)

Dear Friend i am sorry to any that i am confind to bed this week but hope to see you again some day i taken sick last friday but i full fill that other place all right but could not go out saturday.

Daisy

Daer Mrs. X (The agent) daer Madam can you get my husban are job in are lunch room cafe boarding or apt. house he is are well exspierence sheref cook we both would like are job together if could get me are dash (dish) wash place please maggie.

Letter from Bell Jones

Dear Mrs. X (the agent) i am writing you a fue lines to let you here from me i am the lady you got me a home with Mrs. Jones at Smithburg, Md I have a little boy with me you know by the name of Bell Jones i dont want to stay up here much longer and i want you to get me a good home down in Washington for me and my little boy with some good white people with no children and a room in the house for me and my little boy my little boy is a mighty good little boy he is not noisy i want to leave sept. 4 i am tired of this place because there is no cullard people up here they are all white i have not been off the lot since i have been out here please get me a good home dont let it be out of town.

Yours Bell Jones

to write down their grievances, but many of them do make complaints to the agents over the telephone about the inefficiency of domestic help. Agents in Detroit and Indianapolis state that Negro domestic workers from the South—many of them from the farms and untrained, unaccustomed to Northern methods of domestic work—find it difficult to give satisfaction. The consensus of opinion of eleven white and Negro agents in New York City was that with respect to efficiency there are three distinct types of domestic workers in New York City. In the first place, comes the West Indian, who is unaccustomed to domestic work, and therefore unable to convince himself that he is on that plane. He makes a more or less inefficient domestic worker. Then there is the New York Negro who has difficulty in adjusting himself to domestic duties. The southern Negro, however, a decidedly different sort of laborer, makes a more efficient domestic worker than either of the other two types.

Opinions elsewhere also vary. There was a migration of Negro women domestic workers from Georgia to Springfield, Massachusetts, in 1916–1917. Many of these women were very satisfactory employees and compared favorably with northern born Negro women domestic workers of that locality, according to the *11th Annual Report of the Massachusetts Bureau of Statistics*. In the United States Employment Office, Washington, D. C., where all sorts and conditions of domestic workers were handled, reports from employers on the efficiency of the new workers from the South indicated that they were unaccustomed to modern methods of housework and were less efficient than northern born workers.

In any attempt to rate the efficiency of Negro domestic workers by verbal testimonials and written references from their employers or by wages received or length of service period of the workers, due consideration must be given to factors beyond the workers' control. Some of these factors are differences in the standards of efficiency in the many homes and the temperament of employers together with the attitude of some employers toward Negroes generally. For example, occasionally, a former employer, in sympathy with the struggles of Negroes and not wishing to hinder an unsatisfactory worker from securing another position, writes for her a letter of recommendation. Sometimes another employer, because of misunderstanding of some sort between her and the worker, refuses to give any reference whatever.

In 1890, 57 per cent of 1,005 housekeepers representing the whole United States found more or less difficulty in securing efficient help. This probably was an underestimate of the true condition.[15] In 1901, out of 1,106 domestic workers from all sections of the United States, 34 per cent were rated excellent; 37.4 per cent good; 24.8 per cent fair; 3.8 per cent poor. Although these figures indicate that 96.2 per cent of the total were between excellent and fair, the Commission's report in summing up the matter states that according to the testimony of employers of domestic labor and of employment agents, the character of the service rendered by domestic laborers is in a large proportion of cases unsatisfactory. It further states that the quality of men's work is about the same as that of women's work.[16]

In New York City, employment agencies send reference blanks to former employers of domestic workers to be filled out and returned.[17] These references are kept on file as a

[15] Salmon, Lucy M., *Domestic Service*, p. 124.
[16] U. S. Industrial Commission Report, *op. cit.*, p. 751.
[17] THREE SAMPLE REFERENCES FOR DOMESTIC WORKERS, NEW YORK CITY

Winchester Ave., Bronx, N. Y.   July 14, 1921.

    To Whom it may Concern:

        Doris X has been in my employ and performed her duties satisfactory. She is honest and capable.

                                                               Signed ——

    The following person had two reference blanks containing the same questions filled out by her former employers. She had been a child's nurse in the first position and nurse-maid in the second.

record of the domestic worker's capability, sobriety and honesty. From 1906 to 1909 efficiency ratings taken from such blanks for 902 Negro domestic and personal service workers were as follows: 25.6 per cent very capable; 10.2 per cent fairly capable; 2.2 per cent inefficient, and 2.0 per cent not stated.[18] One employment agency in this city made 304 placements of Negro women domestic workers during January, 1923. According to those workers' references from their former employers 93.3 per cent were capable or fairly capable and honest. This high degree of efficiency among domestic workers from this one office is due probably to the fact that this office with its limited staff of secretaries makes no attempt to handle the evidently inexperienced workers. The other employment agencies in New York and Brooklyn visited in 1923 spoke favorably of the quality of service rendered by domestic workers in these cities, according to their reports from employers.

Opinions of employers are not conclusive evidence of the efficiency or inefficiency of workers, but they throw considerable light upon the question. Written references are more or less held in disfavor by the Washington, D. C., employers of domestic labor because they feel that domestic workers sometimes write their own references. This is true to a limited extent. Many of the workers come from small towns and rural sections where the employers of domestic labor do not use elegant stationery, the best Eng-

First Blank. January 27, 1923.		*Second Blank.* Jan. 30, 1923.
Is she honest?	Exceptionally so	Yes
Is she temperate?	Yes	Yes
Is she neat?	Yes	Yes
What of her disposition?	Best I have ever seen	Wonderful
Does she thoroughly understand her work?	Yes	Yes
Why did she leave?	Presumably to be near her husband	Because she was tired of permanence and had a chance to go to the states with our friend

Remarks—Her services with our family for five years have always been most satisfactory.

[18] Haynes, George E., *op. cit.*, p. 87.

lish, and the most correct spelling in writing references for domestic workers who leave for the cities. Such references do domestic workers coming to Washington, D. C., more harm than good.

However, domestic workers are more and more seeking written references on leaving their places of employment because they are beginning to realize that such are generally required by employers. Often a former employer has moved away from the city, is in Europe, or has died, when the domestic worker needs most to refer to her. A prospective employer usually doubts that such an excuse, if given, is true. Of course, some workers do try to take advantage in this way, but most of them are not so unwise.

Types of written and oral testimonials of employers of domestic labor in Washington, D. C., are also informing.[19]

[19] FIVE SAMPLE REFERENCES FOR DOMESTIC WORKERS AND ONE LETTER FROM AN EMPLOYER, WASHINGTON, D. C.

Woodford Land, Va.

Lillie worked for me for a long time and she is a nice worker and a fine cook and she worked for Mrs. —— three years going on four, and she got married there with them and she worked for Mrs. —— and she nursed Mrs. ——'s three children.

From Mrs. ——

The following reference is for Fannie B.—who, evidently half crazy, changed her name after registering at the Washington office because she said she had so many "Enemons" (enemies).

To Whom in May Concern:

This is to certify that Fannie B has been a trustworthy maid. As to her honesty none come no better. She is very capable and in general very satisfactory.

Mrs. ——

To Whom it May Concern:

This is to say that Sarah — has been in my employ 8 months and that she is a good cook, tries hard to please, and has been nice always to the children.

She has been honest and reliable and likes to try new or fancy dishes.

Signed——Mrs. E. M.

(The foregoing Mrs. E. M.'s name and telephone number were given to another lady who had interviewed Sarah relative to offering her a position, Mrs. E. M. told the second lady that Sarah once stole things but she had had a

In cases where three or more employers testified to the efficiency or inefficiency of a worker, the word "efficient," "inefficient," or "poor" was written across the bottom of his application card. The following table in some measure represents in detail the character of service reported to the United States Employment Service, Domestic Section.

Summary of Testimonials of Former Employers of 9,976 Wage Earners Engaged in Domestic Personal Service, Washington, D. C., January 1920–May 1922

TABLE VIII	Efficient		Fairly Efficient		Inefficient	
	No.	Per ct.	No.	Per ct.	No.	Per ct.
Male	90	44.6	94	46.5	11	19.4
Female	3,008	30.8	4,543	46.5	1,892	.05
Total	3,098	37.7	4,637	46.5	1,903	9.7

No Report

	No.	Per Cent.
Male	7	.03
Female	331	.03
Total	338	.03

good lesson so she thought she would not steal any more. She also said that Sarah was none too clean, and that she gave the girl the above reference because she thought she had improved greatly.)

Sarah Jackson held a domestic worker's certificate bearing the golden seal of a Washington, D. C., Federation of Women's Club.

The X Federation of Women's Clubs awards this certificate to Sarah Jackson for 13 years faithful service in the employ of ——

Signed,
Mrs. —— President,
Mrs. —— Chairman Home Economics Dept.

Robert and wife, each about 40 years of age, bring this written reference from a southern town:

This is to certify that I have known "Shine" and his wife for about a year, during which time he has been running a shoe shine establishment in this town. "Shine" is a steady, alert, energetic boy and I feel sure he will please his employer in the work in which he is given a trial.

Signed, H. C. L.

(Letter to the Employment Agent from an Employer.)

My dear Mrs. X.

I fear you think I am very hard to please but having had a butler for 38

In this table 44.6 per cent of the males as over against 30.8 per cent of the females are reported as being efficient, while 19.4 per cent of the females and only 0.05 per cent of the males are listed as inefficient. This should not lead to the conclusion that the male Negro domestic workers of Washington, D. C., were more efficient than the female Negro domestic workers of that city, since the 202 male domestic workers do not represent the rank and file. They represent men of family responsibilities, and students working their way through high school and college. Both of these groups had a more or less definite responsibility and aim in doing domestic work and therefore were more willing, at least for a time, to accommodate themselves to conditions obtaining in it. The office received no report concerning .03 per cent of the workers. Occasionally both employer and employee were so well pleased with each other that neither was heard from unless the office in its follow-up work discovered the happy situation.

The opinion of employers that 19.4 per cent of 9,773 Negro female domestic workers of Washington, D. C., were reported inefficient does not, without other data, justify this as a scientific conclusion. Some typical examples of their inefficiency are interesting.[20] The inefficiency is due

---

years, since dead, a maid and a cook 32 years, since married, it cannot seem that I am, when I once get the right one.

The last girl you sent me Anna by name disliked very much being directed or being spoken to. I am giving her up for she has a most violent temper, the most impertinent person I have ever seen. In a way I am sorry for her. None of us think she is all there. Will you try again for me?

[20] TYPICAL EXAMPLES OF INEFFICIENCY AMONG WASHINGTON, D. C., DOMESTIC APPLICANTS

(1) A day worker—laundress—not knowing how to cut off the current and unscrew the wringer on an electric washing machine, when a garment wrapped around the cogs, ruined the cogs by trying to cut the garment from between them.

(2) A day worker—one of the best laundresses—hurrying to finish her work placed her hands on a revolving electric machine tub, both arms were carried beneath the tub and had not the current been speedily cut, her arms would have been crushed. As it was the tubs had to be cut in order to extricate her arms. After that she was afraid to use an electric washing machine.

in large measure to pure ignorance which for the most part is the sequel to lack of opportunity and training. For example, the older type cook, who cannot read and write, finds it difficult, if not impossible, to carry all the different modern salad and dessert combinations in her memory and cannot supplement her instructions by the use of literature on domestic science.

Employment agencies in Chicago in 1923, moreover, have hardly told the whole truth in giving the following figures on the efficiency of 200 female domestic workers and 200 male domestic workers: *Women*, satisfactory 175, or 87.5 per cent; unsatisfactory 10, or 5.0 per cent; neither satisfactory nor wholly unsatisfactory 15, or 7.5 per cent. *Men*, satisfactory 125, or 62.5 per cent; unsatisfactory 45, or 22.5 per cent; neither 30, or 15 per cent.

Efficient domestic workers apparently regret that they are in an occupational group representing such a high degree of ignorance and inefficiency. They sometimes take

(3) To ask at the office in a group of from 200 to 250 women for a first class laundress—one who knew how to fold the clothes just so after they were ironed as well as wash them out according to rule—and not find one who felt that she could do the work properly was a common occurrence.

(4) A young woman sent out to do general housework and cooking cut the bone out of a 3½ pound sirloin steak which she fried up into such bits that it was not recognized by her employer. When she was questioned about it, she said "that is every bit of that steak. You did not expect me to cook bone and all, did you?"

(5) A young girl sent out to do general housework and cooking when questioned by her employer about the kinds of dessert she could make, said she sure could make jello but was not so good at making other desserts.

(6) The rank and file of general houseworkers looked upon making salad dressing and salads as an art belonging to fine cooks. Many said they had never tried to make bread of any kind.

(7) An elderly cook who had been at the business for 50 years wished cooking and cooking only. Her price was $75 per month. That's what she "ingenally" got. When she was asked if she could read or write she said she could not. She had never been to school a day in her life, but she realized that cooking is tedious work. "Everything I does, I does by my head; its all brain work, you see I has a good 'cal to remember," said she. However, she felt confident that she could cook anything that was put before her to cook.

(8) A young woman sent out to do cleaning left the print of her hand greasy with furniture oil in a freshly papered wall.

pride in saying that they have never worked for poor people. Such a class of workers is represented by a Washington, D. C., domestic worker who gave as her former employers Mrs. John Hays Hammond, Mrs. Arthur Glasgow, Senator Beveridge, Senator Guggenheim, and President Wilson. She took pride in the fact that she could even show anyone a piece of the president's wedding cake.

Honesty in domestic service is so closely associated with efficiency that practically no reference for a domestic worker is complete without some statement about this qualification. In 1890 Miss Salmon raised a serious question with regard to the honesty of Negro domestic workers in the South. Her question was based on answers received from schedules sent to employers of that section.[21] In 1901, 92.6 per cent of 583 domestic labor employers representing the whole United States testified that their employees were honest and responsible. Most employment bureaus were also agreed upon the general honesty of domestic workers.[22] In 1899 the Philadelphia Negro domestic worker of the Seventh Ward was described as purloining food left from the table but as having the balance in his favor in regard to honesty.[23] In 1906 opinions of former employers of 902 Negro wage-earners in domestic and personal service in New York City were that 91.3 per cent were honest; 7.1 per cent were either honest or fairly so; 0.6 per cent were dishonest, and no statement was given for 1.0 per cent.[24]

Out of 9,638 Negro domestic workers reported upon for Washington, D. C., between the years of 1920–1922, only .2 per cent were rated by their former employers with assurance as being dishonest; 90.4 per cent were listed as being honest. There were various answers for the 9.4 per cent. Some did not remain long enough to have judgment passed upon them. Others were in a doubtful class but with no

[21] Salmon, Lucy M., *op. cit.*, p. 123.
[22] *Industrial Commission Report*, *op. cit.*, p. 1901.
[23] Eaton, Isabel, *op. cit.*, p. 486.
[24] Haynes, G. E., *op. cit.*, p. 87.

proof against them, and the like. This low percentage of dishonesty eliminates the tradition of taking food except in seven cases. The seven cases of food taking are included because they were directly reported and regarded by the employers as dishonest. Some employers, according to their own statement of the case, do not regard taking food left from the table as stealing, although such is against the will of the employer. According to the southern tradition of a low wage and taking food to piece it out, domestic workers are still virtually expected to follow this custom.

200 women and 200 men domestic workers of Chicago have the following record for honesty: *Women,* honest, 199, or 99.5 per cent; dishonest, 1, or 0.5 per cent; *men,* honest, 197, or 98.5 per cent; dishonest, 3, or 1.5 per cent.

Employment agents in other leading cities already mentioned have very little complaint against the honesty of Negro domestic workers except in the matter of taking food. Their explanation of the psychology of such dishonesty is as given above.

IV. WAGES, HOURS, AND SPECIFIC OCCUPATIONS

While wages and efficiency are in some degree related in domestic service, there is the custom of paying the "going wage" for specific occupations, irrespective of efficiency. Wages vary, of course, in different sections of the country and in different localities. Occasionally attempts are made to grade such laborers. One employment bureau, in Indianapolis, for example, divides its day workers into grades A and B with respective wages of 30 cents and 25 cents an hour for each grade.

Two other questions current in the problem of wages in domestic service, both of which seem to be slowly lending themselves to adjustment, are the payment of weekly wages instead of bi-weekly or monthly wages, and equal pay for equal work irrespective of whether a man or a woman, a Negro or a white employee, does the work. Bi-monthly payment in domestic service has come to be the custom due largely to the convenience of the employer, and to the possibility of weekly wages increasing the turnover. A domestic worker often leaves unceremoniously as soon as he gets his first pay. However, workers claim that the custom of bi-weekly or monthly pay inconveniences them since they cannot arrange to pay their rent, or purchase clothing and other necessities on that basis.

The question of equal pay for Negro domestic workers does not enter the domestic service wage problem of the South because Negroes pre-empt this field in that section. Although the scarcity of domestic labor seems to be settling this matter in other sections of the country, it still persists in some measure. Twenty-five years ago Miss Eaton discovered that Negro butlers on Rittenhouse Square, Philadelphia, received on an average $36.90 a month, while white butlers were getting from $40 to $45 a month.[25]

In the fall of 1921, during the period of labor depression, eleven of the Washington, D. C., clubs and expensive boarding houses attempted to make a change from Negro to white chambermaid-waitresses at an increase of $10 a month for each worker. The four clubs that succeeded in making the change discharged their white chambermaid-waitresses after one week each and re-employed Negroes at the old wage of $35 a month. One of the successful employers felt that, inasmuch as the white servants were no more satisfactory than the Negro workers, she had just as well keep the Negroes and pay them less.

When the minimum wage law for women and minors of Washington, D. C., recently declared unconstitutional by the United States Supreme Court, went into effect, practically all of the hotels and restaurants in that city immediately discharged Negro workers and took on white ones. Some of the managers told the agent at the United States Employment Bureau that they were making the change because white servants were more efficient than Negro workers. Other managers, some of whom had used Negro

---

[25] Eaton, Isabel, *op. cit.*, p. 449.

labor for more than fifteen years, simply said that $16.50 a week was too much to pay Negroes, and, therefore, wished white workers instead. The few hotels and restaurants that retained Negroes as a rule put them on a much shorter working week than 48 hours, thus reducing their pay.

Boarding houses and institutions such as private schools, sanatoria, and the like, that offer excuses and fail to pay workers should be mentioned in this connection. The manager of one such boarding house in Washington, D. C., was sued by a worker who won her case because other unpaid laborers testified against the manager. The superintendent of a small private school in that city—also among such paymasters—had repeatedly been reported to the Minimum Wage Board which forced her to pay the Negro women day workers. After a few months of such experience she changed her help and began to employ men, over whom the Minimum Wage Board had no jurisdiction.

The wages of Negro domestic workers today are considerably higher than they were in past decades, as is shown by a comparison of figures in past periods for the Continental United States and for selected cities with figures in 1920–1923. For the twenty-five years prior to the World War there had been only a slight wage increase in domestic and personal service. During the World War there was a considerable increase in wages for both male and female domestic workers, the increase for the latter being larger than that for the former. Since the World War wages for such workers have fallen to some extent but not anywhere near the pre-war level.

The following tables, with one exception, show the wage changes at different ten-year periods over a range of 30 years. In Table IX the figures from the Boston Employment Bureau illustrate the fact that the average weekly wages for female domestic workers of Boston were decidedly higher than elsewhere in the country. This table also makes clear the fact that wages for men were considerably higher than those for women.

Average Daily and Weekly Wages in Selected Domestic Service Occupations, 1889-1890 [26]

TABLE IX

Occupation	Weekly Wages for the United States	Weekly Wages for Boston, Mass.
Women		
Cooks	$3.72	$4.45
Cooks and laundresses	3.39	
Chambermaids	3.39	3.86
Waitresses	3.19	3.7
Second girls	3.16	3.7
Chambermaids and waitresses	3.10	
Parlor maids		3
General servants	2.91	3
Men		
Coachmen	$7.84	
Coachmen and gardeners	6.54	
Butlers	6.11	
Cooks	6.08	
	Daily Wages	
Women		
Laundresses	.82	
Seamstresses	1.01	
Men		
Gardeners	1.33	
Chore-men	.87	

Table X below gives average wages for selected domestic service occupations in the United States for a decade

Average Weekly Wages for Selected Domestic Service Occupations in the United States, 1900 [27]

TABLE X

Occupation	Average Weekly Wage
Women	
General houseworkers	$3.28
Cooks	3.95
Waitresses	3.43
Other specialists	3.54
Men	
For all domestic service occupations	6.03
Women	
For all domestic service occupations	3.51

later than the figures of Table IX. The slight variation in the figures of Table X from those of Table IX may be

[26] Salmon, Lucy, *Domestic Service*, p. 90.

due to probable error incident to the collection of the data or to some other factor. The indications of these two tables, however, with ten years intervening between the compilation of the data, are that wages probably had changed very little, if any.

In comparison with the two preceding tables, Table XI below gives wages for domestic service in Philadelphia for about the same period. The weekly wages range higher than for the country as a whole. The lower wages in the southern border and middle sections of the United States have reduced the average for the country below that for this eastern city in which also special conditions may have operated to bring such wages above the general level.

Average Weekly Wages of Negro Domestic Workers of Philadelphia, 1896-1897 [27]

TABLE XI

Occupation	Average Weekly Wage
Women	
General worker	$3.24
Janitress	4.06
Chambermaid-laundress	3.58
Cook-laundress	4.00
Laundress	4.04
Lady's maid	3.63
Chambermaid and waitress	3.17
Waitress	3.31
Women	
Chambermaid	3.17
Child's nurse	3.35
Errand girl	2.00
Cook	4.02
Men	
General worker	5.38
Valet	8.00
Cook	6.17
Waiter	6.14
Coachman	8.58
Butler	8.24
Bellboy	2.61

Table XII which follows is drawn from *The Negro at Work in New York City,* and shows the modal wage groups

[27] Eaton, Isabel, *op. cit.,* pp. 447–449.

for specific occupations in domestic and personal service, New York City, 1906-1909. Although data for New York City are not typical of the entire country, these are the only available figures for this period, and they may indicate the trend of wages in domestic personal service in that section. In comparison with the preceding Table of Wages in Philadelphia, the increase in wages in New York City may be due to differences of conditions in the two cities rather than to any general increase or decrease in wages.

Modal Wage Groups for Selected Occupations, 1906-1909 [28]

[28] Haynes, George E., op. cit., p. 81.

TABLE XII

Occupation	Range of Model Wage
Female	
Switchboard operator	$4.00–4.99
Chambermaid	4.00–4.99
Chambermaid-cook	5.00–5.99
Chambermaid-laundress	5.00–5.99
Chambermaid-waitress	4.00–4.99
Kitchenmaid	4.00–4.99
Cook	5.00–5.99
Cook and general worker	5.00–5.99
Cook-waitress	4.00–4.99
Cook-laundress	5.00–5.99
Errand girl	Less than 4.00
General houseworker	4.00–4.99
Laundress	4.00–4.99
Lady's maid	4.00–4.99
Parlor maid	4.90–4.99
Nurse	Less than 3.00
Pantry girl	4.00–4.99
Waitress	4.00–4.99
Dishwasher	4.00–4.99
Male	
Bellman	Less than 4.00
Butler-cook	5.00–5.99
Waiter	5.00–5.99
Butler	5.00–5.99
Coachman	5.00–5.99
Cook	5.00–5.99
Elevator operator	5.00–5.99
Furnaceman	5.00–5.99
Gardener	4.00–4.99
Hallman and doorman	4.00–4.99
Houseman	5.00–5.99
Janitor	5.00–5.99

The last decade embraces the World War when wages in domestic and personal service were at their maximum. The following tables for selected cities present graphically the increase in wages for male and female domestic workers and the slight increase in wages of females over that of males. These tables also show how wages vary in different sections of the country. Although these figures are for 1920, and the first quarter of 1921, the decline in wages generally did not begin until the fourth quarter of 1920, and it was not so pronounced in domestic and personal service as in many other occupational groups, and was scarcely appreciable in domestic service until the middle of 1921.

Tables XIII, XIV, XV, XVI, and XVII indicate that although wages in domestic and personal service among Negroes have fallen somewhat, they are still far above those of pre-war times. They also show that since the War there has been considerable decline in rates paid men for day work in New York City and Washington, D. C., but very little decrease in the rates for women day workers in either of the two cities.

Any analysis of these tables must take into consideration that female day workers in the cities included in the tables receive their carfare and at least one meal; cooks, general houseworkers, waiters and waitresses, housemen, mothers' helpers, some kitchen help, part-time workers and nurses receive their meals and, in many instances, their quarters.

In this table wages for clerical workers, factory workers, laborers, truckers, butchers, etc., are given in comparison with the wages of domestic and personal service workers. For example: a stenographer receives $18 a week, while a cook receives from $18 to $25 a week and board; a factory girl receives from 25 cents to 30 cents an hour, while a day worker in domestic service receives $22 a week, and a cook receives $25 a week and board.

Weekly Wages of 118 Negro Men in Domestic Service by Specified Occupations, New York City, 1920-1921 [29]

TABLE XIII

Occupations	Number Employed		Weekly Wages
Cleaners	3		$ .50 per hour
	5		3.00 per day
Cooks	2		15.00–17.99
	3		18.00–19.99
	3		25.00 or more
Dishwashers	2		10.00–12.99
	4		13.00–14.99 and meals
	1		15.00–17.99
	11		18.00–21.99
	1		26.00
Doormen	1		38.50 and meals
	3	(monthly)	40.00–79.00
Elevator operators (apt. house)	1	under	10.00
	1		10.00–12.99
	11		15.00–17.99
	1		18.00–21.99
Elevator and switchboard operators	6		14.00
	6		17.00
	1		18.00
Firemen (apt. house)	1		3.00 per day
	1		20.00–24.99
	1		20.00 and board
	1		30.00
Janitors (apt. house)	1	(monthly)	20.00 and apartment
	1	(monthly)	30.00 and keep
	1	(monthly)	40.00 and keep
	1	(monthly)	60.00 and keep
Assistant janitors (apt. house)	1		10.00–12.99
	1		15.00 and room
Porters-apartment houses	1		16.00
	6		18.00–20.99
Waiters	3	under	10.00
	18	(exclusive of tips)	15.00–17.99
	6		18.00–20.99
	7		10.00–11.99

[29] Haynes, George E., *unpublished data.*

Range of Weekly Wages of 754 Negro Women in Domestic and Personal Service, Specified by Occupations, New York City, 1920–1921 [30]

TABLE XIV

Occupations	Number Employed	Wages
General houseworkers	5	under $ 9.00
	706	10.00–18.00
Chambermaids	1	under 9.00
Chambermaids-waitresses	7	12.00–18.00
Cooks	6	15.00–21.00
Kitchen helpers	8	12.00–17.00
	2	under 9.00
Mothers' helpers and Nurses	9	10.00–15.00
Nurses (practical)	3	15.00–21.00
Waitresses	5	12.00–14.00

Range of Daily and Weekly Wages of 1,565 Male and Female Negro Domestic and Personal Service Workers, Washington, D. C., 1920

TABLE XV

Occupations	Number Employed	Daily Wages	Weekly Wages
Male			
Butlers	7		12.00–15.00
Chauffeurs	3		14.00–15.00
Chauffeur-butler	13		14.00–15.00
Elevator operator	6		9.00–10.00
Janitors and housemen	34		10.00–12.00
Cooks	21		18.00–20.00
Furnace and yardman	10		7.00– 8.00
Waiters	11		9.00–10.00
Dishwashers	12		9.00–12.00
Day workers	6	4.00	
Female			
General houseworkers	49		10.00–12.00
Cooks	83		10.00–20.00
Maids	86		9.00–10.00
Waitresses	112		9.00–10.00
Personal maids	5		10.00–12.00
Kitchen maids	40		8.00– 9.00
Mothers helpers	75		5.00– 7.00
Pantry maids	62		10.00–12.00
Permanent laundresses	3		12.00–14.00
Cook-laundresses	81		10.00–12.00
Chambermaid-waitresses	240		9.00–10.00
Janitress	7		9.00–10.00
Elevator operator	82		8.00– 9.00
Parlor maids	21		9.00–10.00
Day workers	362	2.50–3.00	
Nurse maid	91		8.00– 9.00
Part-time workers	51		6.00– 7.00

[30] Haynes, George E., *unpublished data.*

Weekly Wages of 200 Male and 200 Female Negro Domestic Workers of Chicago by Occupations, 1923

TABLE XVI

Occupations	Number Enrolled		Weekly Wages
Male			
Factory	15		22.00
Waiter	8		15.00 and board
Bus Boys	6		10.00 and board
Elevator	1		14.00
Cook	10		25.00 and board
Cleaning	11	(per hour)	.50
Wringer	2		20.00
Fireman	2		24.00
Shoe shiners	3	(per day)	2.00 and tips
Butchers	6	(per hour)	.47 and up
Houseman	4	(per month)	70.00 room and board
Dishwasher	43		17.00 and board
Porter	10		20.00–25.00
Trucker	25		22.00
Laborers	54	(per hour)	.45–.60

Average Daily and Weekly Wage of Negro Domestic Workers by Occupation for Selected Cities, 1923

TABLE XVII

	Average Wage by Occupation							
	Day Workers	General House Workers	Cooks	Maids	Waitresses	Part-time Workers	Mothers' Helpers	Child Nurses
New York	$3.80	$13.85	$16.50	$13.00	$7 and tips	$8.00	$11.00	$11.00
Philadelphia	2.75	12.50	13.50	9.50	7 and tips	7.50	8.25	8.25
Baltimore	2.75	9.50	11.00	8.50	7 and tips	6.00	5.50	6.00
Washington, D. C.	2.00	9.25	10.75	8.50	8 and tips	7.50	8.00	8.00
Detroit	3.35	9.50	11.00	9.00	7 and tips	9.50	9.50	10.00
Indianapolis	2.25	10.00	13.50	9.00	7 and tips		8.00	13.50
Boston	3.00	12.00	12.50	10.50	10.50			
Los Angeles	3.80		15.00	11.50	8.00			
Montgomery	1.75	7.00		6.50				
Nashville	1.75	7.00		6.50				

Male	Day laborers	Chauffeurs	Cooks	Janitors	Dishwashers	Bell men	Waiters	Porters	Elevator operators
New York	$3.00	$25.00	$20.00	$ 9.50	$12.00	$ 9.50	$10.00	$15.00	15.00
Boston	4.00	25.00	22.50	20.00	12.00	13.50	12.00	15.00	15.00
Philadelphia	3.80	25.00	20.00	15.00	9.50	6.50	7.00	15.00	15.00
Baltimore	3.50	18.00	21.00	15.00	9.50	7.87	9.30	15.00	9.30–15.00

The table above shows that wages in the specified occupations in different sections of the country, for the most part, do not vary very much. Wages for males are given for only four cities because the wages for males in the other cities mentioned, with two exceptions, are about the same as in these four cities. In addition to money wages received for day work, women get their carfare and often one or two meals, while men receive only the money wages. Elevator operators in Baltimore hotels are paid from $40 to $50 a month instead of $15 a week as in apartment houses because more tips are given in hotels.

Although in consideration of the present rate of wages the total annual wage paid for domestic and personal service in the homes of the United States must be large, there seems to be no available data on this point. However, an estimate has been made of the total quarterly wages for 1920 and 1921 and the first quarter of 1922 paid domestic and personal service employees in the hotels and similar institutions of Continental United States. The range of quarterly wages in such institutions for 1920 was 666 to 700 millions of dollars; for 1921, 660 to 678 millions of dollars; and for 1922, 643 millions of dollars. The maximum cyclical decline in the wages of such workers for that period of time was 8.15 per cent.

Even though seven other groups of occupations had a smaller percentage cyclical decline in wages following the war than public domestic and personal service and twelve other groups of occupations had a larger cyclical decline, the average earnings an hour for each domestic and personal service worker are less than that for any other occupation or industry except agriculture. The average earnings in cents an hour for each employee in domestic and personal service were for the first quarter of 1920, 34 cents; for the first quarter of 1921, 34 cents; and for the first quarter of 1922, 33 cents.[31]

[31] King, W. I., *Employment, Hours and Earnings in the United States, 1920-1922*, Chap. V, pp. 5, 19; Chap. IV, p. 3.

Hours of Negro Domestic Workers

Although during the past thirty years there has been considerable advance made in the matter of hours for domestic and personal service workers, the change in this particular has not kept pace throughout the United States with the increase in wages in domestic and personal service occupations. Thirty years ago 38 per cent of 1,434 female domestic employees from all sections of the United States were actually working ten hours a day, 6 per cent of them were working eleven hours a day, 31 per cent were working twelve hours or more a day, and 25 per cent of them were working less than ten hours a day.[32]

In recent years the hours and wages of female domestic and personal service workers in several states of the union have been standardized by the enactment of state minimum wage laws. Utah, which has an eight hour day and a 48 hour week for female workers generally, lists any regular employer of female labor under those occupations covered by law. This would include domestic service for women. The minimum wage rate in this State for experienced women is $1.25 per day. Wisconsin, which has a ten hour day and a 55 hour week for females and minors, includes under its minimum wage law every person in receipt of, or entitled to, any compensation for labor performed for any employer. Domestic workers must be included in this number. Colorado includes under its minimum wage law any occupation which embraces "any and every vocation, trade, pursuit and industry." Since domestic service is a pursuit or vocation, it must come under the minimum wage law of Colorado. The state of Washington has an eight hour day and a 56 hour week and a wage of $18 a week and $3 a day for females engaged in public housekeeping, but not for private domestic workers. North Dakota publicly excludes domestic service and agriculture from its occupations or industries covered by the minimum wage law. Although the other seven State minimum wage laws do not

---

[32] Salmon, Lucy M., *op. cit.*

openly exclude domestic service, it is not included as yet among occupations and industries. Two attempts were recently made in California to secure through legislation a ten hour day for domestic workers. The first bill was defeated. The second bill passed both houses but received a pocket veto.[33] In States where there is no minimum wage legislation the working hours for day workers and part-time workers are standardized on an eight hour basis.

The extensive use of day workers came into popularity largely through necessity during the World War. At that time such a large proportion of the permanent domestic employees found openings in other lines of work that housewives supplemented their own labor by hiring day workers. The large demand for such workers gave them the leverage of establishing for themselves an eight hour day and a wage commensurate with that in many lines of industry. Day workers have retained since the World War both the eight hour day and the advanced wages.

The part-time workers, too, have definite hours. Many of them do cooking and general housework but for only specified hours. Some of them work four or five hours or less in the mornings, especially when the work is largely cleaning. Not a few of them begin in the afternoon and do general housework and prepare dinner and serve it. But the hours are fixed hours. Some part-time workers have a regular place of employment for mornings and another such place for afternoons. Their hours are definite and their wages are thus very good. Frequently the part-time worker has every Sunday off.

The hours for the other domestic service workers generally do not seem to be so well standardized as yet. Three Washington, D. C., employers wished their general houseworkers to come on duty at seven o'clock in the morning, with the promise that the workers could leave when they finished. Although 75.3 per cent of one thousand domestic workers, exclusive of day workers and part-time

[33] *Monthly Labor Review*, U. S. Bureau of Labor Statistics, August, 1920, p. 212.

workers, in the private families and boarding houses of Washington, D. C., were on duty ten hours or over, this would show that the three employers mentioned above were not typical. Three other employers in the same mentioned city maintained an eight hour day for their help by having an extra worker prepare the dinners and serve them.

Apparently no attempt has been made to compare the hours of the private domestic and personal service workers with those of the workers in other industries. An estimate made of the full-time hours a week during 1920 and 1921 for the average employee in all enterprises of whatever size in the Continental United States discloses the fact that the average full-time hours a week for public domestic and personal service workers were from 56.6 to 57.1, while the average for workers in all industries including domestic and personal service was 50.3 to 51.3 hours a week. In New York City, according to employment agents, the practice of an eight to nine hour day for domestic workers generally obtains.

Specific Occupations of Negro Domestic Workers

The chief employment of the day workers in more than three-fourths of the States is laundry work and cleaning. It is significant that in twenty-one States for which the 1920 advanced occupational census sheets have been obtained, where the Negro population is negligible, there is no principal occupation given as that of launderer and laundress "not in laundries." In all of the States for which there are reports given in the cities of those States where the Negro population is large there is such a principal occupation. However, this occupation in spite of the increased popularity of day work during the World War is decreasing in numbers as the following table will indicate. Whether this decrease is due to the "wet wash" laundry system and to the increased facilities in hand laundries we have no data to prove.

Table XVIII given below represents the States so far

as the 1920 census reports go, which have the principal occupation of launderer and laundress "not in laundries." In all of the States except Vermont, the Negro population is quite appreciable. Just why Vermont is not among the 21 States which have a negligible Negro population and no such principal occupation accessible data did not disclose. The reason why the 21 States have no such principal occupation is probably due to the fact that laundry work is so laborious that white domestic workers are averse to it, and those able to have the work done send it to a steam laundry.

The Number of Launderers and Laundresses in 14 States in 1910–1920

Table XVIII State	Male		Female	
	1910	1920	1910	1920
Louisiana	406	389	23,051	17,034
Georgia	832	667	44,710	36,775
No. Carolina	387	296	23,192	15,185
Florida	394	342	14,844	16,552
Dist. of Columbia	121	93	7,920	6,095
Maryland	448	253	16,189	12,418
Delaware	20	26	1,665	1,110
Indiana	300	245	10,130	7,238
Vermont	34	21	1,256	684
Kansas	210	163	4,814	3,760
New Jersey	452	322	11,171	7,626
New Mexico	71	51	1,678	1,299
Oklahoma	154	124	5,349	4,350
West Virginia	140	84	3,923	2,505

A general houseworker has come to be thought of by the public as a maid of all work, and sometimes she is; but in many homes she is relieved of doing the laundry work. In some cities general housework does not always include cooking. For example, in New York City and Brooklyn it may not include cooking unless specified by the terms cooking and general housework. In New York and some other cities men have been tried as general workers.

According to employment agencies, butlers are not used in such large numbers as they were before the World War. During the war it was difficult to secure them because men were needed for war work. Since then wages have been such that employers have largely used chambermaid-waitresses or chauffeur-butlers instead of regular butlers. Among the 779 Negro men in domestic and personal service (New York City, 1921, Table XI), there is not one butler. This does not mean that there are no Negro butlers in New York City, but it indicates their scarcity and shows that employers living in apartment houses can do without them. Negro cooks, however, are yet an important factor in the domestic and personal service groups.

There are still Negro personal maids who make provision for the special comfort and well being of their employers as well as do their little mending, and the like. And there are Negro pantry maids whose first duty it is to make salads. Chambermaid-waitresses and parlor maids to do such as to answer the door bell are also still used. The tendency, however, is in the direction of having but the one general maid, together with a laundress to come in by the day. Mothers' helpers or young girls to assist in all the work of the house and with the children are also being employed quite extensively, and at less wages than would be paid to an older general houseworker.

These different occupations for the most part call for different types of workers. A butler or a chambermaid-waitress who is tall and comely may have access to a larger number and to better places than one who is short. Especially is this true of cooks for apartment or for a general houseworker where there are stairs to climb. These are much more frequently chosen from among the medium-sized women than from the stout women. The reason for the latter choice is apparent. In the case of the butler or chambermaid-waitress, the basis of choice is apparently appearance and custom.

V. Living Conditions, Health, Social Life, Organizations of Negro Domestic Workers, and Their Relation to Employment Agencies

Living conditions here refer only to those on employers' premises. The general living conditions of Negro domestic workers in different parts of the country, or even in different localities of the same section, vary so widely that the subject cannot be treated here. For example, in the South laundresses for the most part take bundle wash to their small homes, and do large "washes" there. Such a situation makes it difficult for southern Negro laundresses to live comfortably and healthfully. Laundresses in the North are relieved of this problem by going to the homes of employers, but, on the other hand, are affected by the excessive rents and the overcrowding in their own homes.

Living conditions on employers' premises for domestic workers vary to some extent in different homes of the same city but to a larger extent in the different sections of the country and in different cities of the same section. In Montgomery, Alabama, for example, out of two hundred Negro female domestic workers interviewed, 54 or about 27 per cent were living in a two-room detached frame house on the rear of the employers' premises. The remaining 73 per cent did not "sleep in" or live on their employers' premises. In Philadelphia, living conditions on employers' premises are reported as being good. They consist, in the main, of a third floor room. Very few basement rooms are offered as living quarters for domestic workers in that city. In Indianapolis, about 50 per cent of those working by the week among the 471 domestic workers go home nights. Living conditions for those "sleeping in" are fair as a rule. Some have basement rooms but a majority of them have rooms either on the third floor or in the attic or over a garage. A small percentage of the homes have a bath room for the maid.

Employment agencies in Boston, New York City, Brooklyn, Philadelphia, Detroit, Chicago, and Los Angeles give favorable reports on the living conditions of domestic workers who "sleep in." While the reports from Baltimore are not as conclusively favorable as for the above-named cities, one fact stands out prominently, namely: that in the main, only apartment houses in that city offer basement rooms as living quarters for domestic workers. Employment agencies in all of the cities mentioned state that there are far more calls for workers to "sleep in" than there are workers who are willing to do so.

Out of 500 domestic workers in Washington, D. C., selected at random from 3,000 permanent employees for the year 1921-22, about 64.1 per cent were requested to "sleep in." Out of an equal number of employers requesting workers to "sleep in," selected in the same manner, about 83 per cent provided basement rooms as sleeping quarters for such workers; about 10 per cent either provided first floor or third floor rooms—some of them with baths; about 7 per cent either offered attics or they failed to furnish a statement as to the location of the rooms. Occasionally an employer would like to have the worker "sleep in" but because of having only a basement room to offer, she would forego her wish in the interest of the health of the employee. Two of the workers sent out from this office were partially incapacitated by the poor living and working conditions. One of the problems, however, involved in housing domestic employees is the frequency of the turnover which necessarily brings in different kinds of workers, varying in degrees of personal cleanliness and health.

Closely connected with the living conditions, too, are the working conditions of domestic employees. In fact, one of the strains of such service often is the lack of break between the place of work and of living, which makes for resulting monotony and much loneliness. Much of a domestic worker's life is spent in the kitchen, in the laundry or on the premises of his employer. The only available accurate data on this point have come from Indianapolis, Ind. This was secured in response to a questionnaire sent to the employers who were patrons of the employment office at Flanner House. The following table gives a summary of the replies as to the appliances employers had in their homes for use of Negro domestic workers.

Replies from 523 Employers Showing the Appliances in the Homes for Doing Laundry Work, in Indianapolis, Ind., April, 1922

TABLE XVIII

		Per Cent
Number having electric machines	249	47.6
Number having water power machines	2	.4
Number having hand power machines	5	.9
Number not having machines of any kind	267	51.1
		100.0
Number having electric irons	479	91.6
Number having gas irons	5	.9
Number having mangles—ironing machine	31	5.9
Number having stationary tubs	202	38.6
Number having driers	3	.6

According to this record about 48.9 per cent of the 523 employers had washing machines of some kind and about 51.1 per cent had none at all; about 38.6 per cent had installed stationary tubs and 0.6 per cent had driers. To one who is conversant with the old way of doing laundry work with heavy portable wooden tubs, and with the lighter weight zinc tubs, into which water was lifted for washing and from which it was lifted after washing, and then placed upon either a dry goods box or a wash bench of uncertain height, this table shows marvelous improvement in working conditions of Negro laundresses in Indianapolis and indicates unusual possibilities there and elsewhere. However, unless there were, in each of the homes having washing machines, a stationary tub, or a rubber tube for draining the water out of the washing machine, there still would be that lifting of water, and possibly undue exertion because of the uncertain height of the portable tub. The principle of having the tub set at the right height involves relief from straining the back, an important item in relation to good health. There were about 98.4 per cent of the 523 employers who had either electric or gas irons or mangles. Such appliances facilitate ironing as well as enable a laundress to do better work. Washing machines and mangles make it possible to do the bed linen at home instead of sending it to a steam laundry. Driers are particularly serviceable in winter when drying out of doors is difficult as well being hard on the laundress because of the cold weather.

The employment agency that sent out the questionnaire congratulated the employers on the marked improvement made in appliances for laundering, and added that like improvements will in time be made in the type and conditions of work rooms in which laundresses must labor.

The Health of Negro Domestic Workers

Although the health of domestic workers is an extremely important matter because of the nature of their work and the homes into which they go, and because their support depends so largely upon their physical ability to work, no records apparently are kept by the various employment agencies relative to the health of the workers. In 1899 out of 152 male and 395 female domestic workers in Philadelphia, 80 per cent of the men had not been ill during the year, and 74 per cent of the women had not been ill during the year. This per cent of good health excluded colds. The most prevalent disabilities among them were: consumption, lagrippe, quinsy, sore throat, rheumatism, neuralgia, chills and fever, and dyspepsia.[34] That there is much opportunity for danger from infection incident to the ill-health of domestic workers cannot be denied.[35]

Very careful note was taken for one week in March, 1922, of the health of women domestic workers reporting at the United States Employment Agency, Washington, D. C. It was not a typical week because of the fact that it followed an epidemic of lagrippe. However, out of 1,043 domestic workers, only 325 or about 31 per cent had not been ill during that winter and had no complaint whatever. Lagrippe, surgical operations, indigestion, heart trouble, weak back, and neuralgia were the illnesses of which they most commonly complained.

There were among the number above, five evident cases of mental disturbance, one of which was taken to St. Elizabeth's Hospital for observation and treatment. Another

---
[34] Eaton, Isabel, *op. cit.*, p. 495.
[35] Reed, Ruth, *op. cit.*, p. 35.

from the number had been discharged from the same hospital after treatment for mental trouble. This fact was not known by the Agency until an officer from the hospital visited the woman at her place of work to see how she was getting along. Three cases that were suspected of having tuberculosis were referred as waitresses at different times to a public hospital, at some risk of course to the reputation of the office, largely to see what the reaction of the nurse in charge would be. In each case the nurse reported that she could not use such a person about the food. Yet such persons were taken into some of the most desirable homes in Washington as household employees.

Social Life of Negro Domestic Workers

The social life of the older domestic Negro workers centers largely in their church and secret order society connections. From 1916 to 1920 seven out of every eleven Negroes in the United States were enrolled in churches. Many of them are willing to accept a place at a much lower wage than another if it gives them their Sundays off so that they may attend their churches.

It is important then to see the scope of such organizations in Negro city life. Kansas City, Missouri, with a Negro population in 1910 of 23,566, had 19 Negro churches and 16 Negro missions in 1913, with a total membership of 7,156. In this city there were 135 different lodges, or households (women's chapters), with a total membership of 8,055, 4,226 men and 3,829 women. The average initiation fee in the men's orders was $11.50 and in the women's $4.51 with additional monthly dues of 50 cents and 25 cents respectively. Endowment insurance policies of these lodges for which there is an annual fee from $2 to $4 are for the most part optional. These 8,055 members pay into their lodges annually $55,411.40. Their property in Kansas City is valued at $46,100. Each of the 135 orders has sick benefits ranging from $2.50 to $4.50 a week and all of them, with

[36] Haynes, George E., *unpublished data*, 1921.

one exception, pay burial expenses in case of death.[37] In Harlem, New York, with a Negro population of about 90,000 in 1920 there are 25 Negro churches and about 16 missions. There are in this densely populated section six moving picture theatres which cater largely to Negro patronage.[38] Gainesville, Georgia, with a Negro population in 1910 of 1,629 had a Negro church membership of 1,023. Five of the Negro lodges in that city admit women, some of whom are members of several lodges.[39] In the lodges composed as they are very largely of the masses of the Negro people with a few of the more intelligent leaders as officers, there are many possibilities for improving the efficiency of the domestic workers.

Just what is the social life of the younger Negro domestic workers, many of whom are away from their own families, is a question. Of the 471 Negro domestic workers registered at the Indianapolis office, about 44.5 per cent were rooming and only about 2.3 per cent were living with parents or relatives. As possible attractions for such workers there are the moving picture and low vaudeville theatres, usually located in Negro neighborhoods, the pool and billiard rooms, cabarets and questionable dance halls.

Dr. Rubinow says that of 2,300 domestic white workers, a large majority of whom were under 30 years of age, interviewed by the Michigan Bureau of Labor, only 51 belonged to fraternal societies of any kind. Of 230 questioned by the Domestic Relation Reform League, 20 belonged to clubs and 15 to classes of some kind, and 118 entertained no men callers. A domestic worker, he says, not only loses caste among other groups of workers, but she loses at the hands of her employers even her family name. She lives a life of loneliness, "in a family but not of it." [40]

[37] Martin, Asa E., *Our Negro Population*, Kansas City, 1913, pp. 180, 143.

[38] Haynes, Geo. E., *unpublished data*, 1921.

[39] Reed, Ruth, *op. cit.*, p. 51.

[40] Rubinow, I. M., *Depth and Breadth of the Servant Problem, McClure's Magazine*, Vol. 34, p. 576, 1909–1910.

Organization of Domestic Workers

In order to show concretely what domestic workers themselves have attempted to do to improve their conditions, some discussion of their organizations as an expression of that attempt is in place here. It is not certain how many of these organizations are still active nor how many have Negro members. Some of them have such members, no doubt. However, three of them are composed entirely of Negroes.

In Los Angeles, California, the "Progressive Household Club" with a membership of 75 domestic workers is still active. This club was organized primarily for the purpose of furnishing a cheerful and welcome home for a domestic worker taking a rest or not employed for a time. It has a self-supporting home which will accommodate twenty-five girls. Their recreational and educational features are not startling, as the secretary writes, but they enable the girls to pass some cheerful hours out of their "humdrum" lives. This club was among the 15 other domestic workers' clubs organized in 1919 and 1920. In 1919 a Domestic Workers' Alliance with a membership of over 200, affiliated with the Hotel Waitresses under the American Federation of Labor, was granted a charter. During that year, the secretary of Hotel and Restaurant Employees of the International Alliance and International League of America reported that this organization had established a domestic workers' union in each of the following cities: Mobile, Alabama; Fort Worth, Texas; and Lawton, Oklahoma. A union of domestic workers was also organized in Tulsa, Oklahoma, in 1919. The following March a charter was granted to a domestic workers' union in Richmond, Virginia.[41] In 1920 there were 10 unions of domestic workers affiliated with the American Federation of Labor. These unions were located in the following cities: Los Angeles and San Diego, California; Brunswick, Georgia;

[41] *Monthly Labor Review*, U. S. Bureau of Labor Statistics, Aug., 1919, p. 212, May, 1920, p. 116.

Chicago and Glencoe, Illinois; New Orleans, Louisiana; Beaver Valley, Pennsylvania; Denison, Harrisburg, and Houston, Texas. The New Orleans Union, a Negro organization, was composed of about 200 members. All of these organizations have now ceased to be affiliated with the American Federation of Labor. There is, however, one union of domestic workers in Arecibo, Porto Rico, affiliated with the American Federation of Labor.

Relation of Negro Domestic Service to Employment Agencies

In view of the volume and extent of turn-over in domestic service, employment agencies, especially in the North, East, and West, have a close relationship to both employers and workers. A person in need of domestic help secures it either by advertising in the help wanted section of the newspapers, by applying to one or more employment agencies, by means of inquiries among friends and acquaintances who may have been a former employer of some available laborer, by accepting some one who may by chance apply in person or by hiring a former worker.

In some of the southern cities where there is no local employment agency, domestic workers are secured in all other of the above-mentioned ways. For example, this condition prevails in Montgomery, Alabama. Although the United States Employment Service, the Department of Labor, and the Municipal Employment offices of Birmingham and Mobile, Alabama, are co-operating, there is no State license applying to local employment agencies except those soliciting laborers to go outside of the State, according to a recent statement from the Alabama Tax Commission. A like condition exists in the State of Louisiana. Georgia, however, issues licenses to employment agencies for domestic positions. In this State as in some others, there is no law regulating the fee which an agency may charge either employer or employee for service rendered. Neither Ohio, Pennsylvania, California, nor Maryland, and several other States have such a fee regulated by law. However, in Pennsylvania, every employment agent must file with the commissioner for his approval a schedule of fees, proposed to be charged for any service rendered to employer or employee, and these may be changed only with the approval of the commissioner. Every employment agent in this State is required to give a receipt to any applicant for any money which the applicant pays him; and if an applicant fails through no fault of his to secure a position to which he is referred, the entire amount paid by such a person to the agent is to be refunded. Such a law obtains in some other States.

In Baltimore there are 50 employment agencies, mainly of a domestic nature. The usual fee charged an employer, though not regulated by law, is $2. An agency ordinarily agrees to supply an employer with help for at least 30 days without additional cost.

New York State issued in 1918, 674 licenses to employment agencies engaged in various kinds of employment business. In 1919, 719 employment agency licenses were issued; in 1920, 728 and in 1921, 788. The law stipulates that the fees charged domestic work applicants by employment agencies shall not in any case exceed ten per cent of the first month's wages. If a domestic worker does not accept a position to which he is referred or fails to obtain employment, the full amount which he paid the agency is to be refunded after three days allowed for obtaining facts. If an employee fails to remain one week in a position, the agency is required to furnish the employer with a new employee, or return 3.6 of the fee paid in by the employer, provided the employer notifies the agency within thirty days of the failure of the worker to accept the position or of the employee's discharge for cause. If the employee is discharged within one week without his fault, another position is furnished him or 3.5 of the fee returned.

Employment agencies in New York State must also give receipts for money paid them. Day workers receiving a rate of $3.60 to $4.00 per day each pay an initial fee of 50 cents to the agency furnishing them with work. Employers of domestic labor pay the agency for one month's service a flat rate of from $6 to $10 for general houseworkers and from $3 to $5 for part-time workers. For a temporary laborer, employers pay a fee of $1 and for a day worker they pay a fee of 50 cents. For commercial and industrial placements an employee pays to the agency 5 per cent of her first month's wage, but no charge is made for the employer furnishing the work.

The laws of Massachusetts regulating employment agencies of a domestic nature are almost similar to those of New York State, the difference in the main being in the size of the fees. In Massachusetts an intelligence office keeper is entitled to receive from an applicant, employer or employee, a fee of 25 per cent of the first week's wages; and in case of day work a fee of 10 per cent of a day's pay. The Michigan domestic employment agency fees for employee and employer are about the same as that for New York State.

In the District of Columbia, a domestic employment agency is entitled to receive in advance from an employer $2 for each employee for at least 30 days service, and from an applicant for work $1. One-half of this fee is to be returned on demand if such applicant does not have a fair opportunity of employment within 15 days from date of payment. When an applicant actually receives employment at a wage of $25 a month or more he pays the agency an additional $1. However, it is a common practice among Washington employment agencies to have applicants pay $2 in advance of securing a place for work. In the light of the total amount of money paid in wages of domestic and personal service, especially with such a heavy turnover, the fees paid to employment agencies by both employers and employees evidently amount to quite a considerable sum.

Thirty years ago Miss Salmon in her study of domestic

service pointed out, not only the exorbitant fees charged by employment agencies, but the vice and crime nurtured by them.[42] In 1915 investigations of Miss Kellor in Baltimore, Philadelphia, New York, Boston and other cities brought out some more striking facts. In Philadelphia 84 per cent of the employment agencies were in private residences and 3 per cent of them were in business buildings. In New York 85 per cent of these agencies were conducted in very close contact with the families of the agents. In Chicago 81 per cent of them were in buildings occupied by families. In Boston 73 per cent of the agencies were in business buildings and only 27 per cent were in residences. The poor business methods of many private intelligence offices, surrounded by gambling dens, fortune tellers, palmists and midwives, and their frauds are insignificant as compared with their conscious, deliberate immorality. Miss Kellor says that many Negro intelligence offices are hopelessly immoral but that some city authorities often argue that since they do not affect the whites there is no reason for disturbing them.[43]

The Third Biennial Report of the Department of Labor and Industry of Maine for the year 1915–1916 contains a warning against employment agencies collecting fees in excess of the law. This report recommends that the important economic task of employment be taken out of the hands of the agents and placed under management of the State. A similar note was voiced by one of the committees of President Harding's conference on unemployment.

The large experience with both municipal and State offices and with the United States Employment Service has given unmistakable evidence that the recruiting and placement of labor is a public necessity and a general benefit to the whole community. It can therefore well become a matter conducted under public supervision and at public expense. Domestic service, especially in large cities and particularly because of the absence of organization and

[42] Salmon, Lucy M., *op. cit.*, p. 115.
[43] Kellor, Frances A., *Out of Work*, pp. 197, 222, 225, 229.

group connection of the workers, is especially in need of such public direction.

Summary and Conclusions

From 1870 to 1900 there was an increase in the total number of persons engaged in domestic and personal service in the United States. Since that time there has been a steady decrease in the number so engaged. Although Negroes have followed the general trend of increase and decline, in proportion to their population, they furnish a larger percentage of domestic workers than any other group in the United States, the female workers outnumbering the male.

The fact is also evident that Negroes are gradually entering trade and transportation and manufacturing and mechanical pursuits. With the existing conditions following the World War, and the present restriction on immigration, the opportunities in these fields of labor are enlarging and domestic and personal service workers are, therefore, correspondingly decreasing.

The ranks of the domestic service workers are being recruited to some appreciable extent from the younger Negro women, between the ages of 16 and 24 years. The very young women and the old women are not the most sought after by employers because of their inexperience on the one hand, and on the other, their inability to do domestic work. The problems of married women in domestic service are increasing because of their family responsibilities and cares which make demands upon their earnings and energy.

The domestic labor turnover has increased the past thirty years. During and since the World War, it has been so greatly accentuated that the modal period of service is from 3 to 6 months. The length of the period of service will perhaps become still shorter because of the increasing opportunities in trade and transportation and in manufacturing and mechanical pursuits.

Provision for the training of domestic workers generally has been meager, and in the case of Negro domestic workers it has been less than that for them as a group. Since the World War greater attempts have been made to extend training to domestic workers both in England and the United States, the government in each of these countries taking a small part in this extension of education. Training especially for Negro domestic workers has been undertaken. Employment agencies under government supervision, with the co-operation of domestic service employers, offer possibilities for such training and for the standardization of private household work. However, Negroes with any appreciable degree of intelligence are not entering domestic service as a permanent employment. This field in the United States is being left largely to the untrained and inefficient.

During the twenty years preceding the World War, very little advance was made in the wages of domestic workers, but during the war their wages increased about 150 per cent. Since the war, according to Dr. King, while the decline in public domestic service wages has not been as great as that in many other fields of employment, the average earnings an hour in money wages of public domestic service workers are still below those in a majority of the industries. Although there has been an increase in wages of domestic service workers, their working hours are longer than those of any other group of laborers.

In some cities living conditions on employers' premises for domestic workers are good, in others there is need of great improvement along this line. However, with the increasing disinclination on the part of the domestic workers to "sleep in" and the slowly growing public interest in standardizing house work, this problem will in time be solved. There has been much improvement in the working conditions of domestic employees, but there is still need of much more.

The indications are that little attention is paid to the

health and the social life of domestic workers. This neglect, especially of the health of domestic workers, is no doubt fraught with dangerous consequences, not only for themselves but for the homes and welfare of the nation.

That the social life of the older Negro domestic workers is supplied at least to some extent in their churches is proved by the fact that about seven out of every eleven Negroes in the United States are enrolled as members of churches. Their interest in secret orders is also shown by the number of members and the money spent in such organizations. As social attractions for the younger domestic employees, there are such places as dance halls, moving pictures, pool and billiard rooms, and the like. The social stigma attached to domestic service bars young domestic workers from many of the entertainments of real value and benefit.

Domestic workers in ten or more cities of the United States have attempted to better their conditions by means of organized effort. The organization in California is rendering real service to its members through its home. With the present large percentage of domestic workers who are rooming in the various cities, and the conditions obtaining in many rooming houses connected with employment agencies, there is urgent need of establishing clubs or homes for domestic workers.

Many private employment agencies in their relation to the homes of the United States act as brokers. The fees charged both the employer and the employee are generally exorbitant. The service rendered by them is on the whole poor. The harm inflicted upon society by many of them is irreparable. Public control of employment agencies has great possibilities for social betterment.

ELIZABETH ROSS HAYNES

DOCUMENTS

Documents and Comments on Benefit of Clergy as Applied to Slaves

The following transcripts from the records of the Superior Court of Richmond County, North Carolina, illustrate the application of benefit of clergy to slaves charged with and found guilty of crimes punishable with death.*

Fall Term 1828

State
vs   } Burglary
George (A Slave)

Pleads "Not Guilty"
The following
Jury empaneled therein
(Viz) (1) Cyrus Bennet

(2) Alen Shaw   (3) Try McFarland
(4) Wade LeGrand   (5) George Wright
(6) James Covington   (7) William Crowson
(8) Thos. B. Blewett   (9) Israel Watkins
(10) Risdon Nichols   (11) Lenard Webb
(12) Hampton Covington—

Who find the Prisoner "not Guilty" of Burglary in manner and Form as charged in the Bill of Ind't'm't But guilty of Grand Larceny . . .

The Prisoner appeared at the Bar and being asked by the Court If he had any thing to say why Sentence of Death should not be pronounced against him, Answered by Council praying the benefit of his Clergy. Which was allowed him by the Court & adjudged that he receive *THIRTY NINE* lashes on his Bare Back & stand committed till his Master enter into recognisance of $200 for his good behavior for the Space of Twelve months & pay cost of Prosecution. . . . Sentence to be Carried into effect on Tomorrow at 4 Oclock P. M.

---

* These documents were collected by Prof. Wm. K. Boyd, of Trinity College, Durham, North Carolina.

Fall Term 1828

State   Pleads "Not Guilty"
vs   No. 19   The following Jury
Dennis (a Slave)   Burglary   empanelled & sworn
                                               (1) James Meacham

(2) George Wright   (3) John Gibson
(4) Silas Jones   (5) Lemuel Chance
(6) Wilie Chance   (7) Thomas Bostick
(8) Ananias Graham   (9) James LeGrand
(10) Elias Pate   (11) Hugh McLean

(12) George Hunesucker . . . Who find the Dfd't not guilty of the Burglary as charged in the Bill of Indtmt; but guilty of Grand Larceny . . .

The prisoner appeared at the Bar and being asked by the Court If he had any thing to say why sentence of death should not be pronounced against him; replied by his Council, praying the Benefit of his Clergy; which was allowed; and the prisoner Dennis, to be taken to the Whipping Post and receive Thirty nine lashes on his Bare Back. Sentence to be carried into effect at 4 O'clock P. M. on Saturday.

Spring Term 1832

                                                      1. Alexander Shaw
State
vs   No. 19   The following Jury
Harry (a Slave)   Burglary   empanelled & sworn—viz.

(2) Cyrus Bennet   (3) Try McFarland
(4) George Wright   (5) Silas Jones
(6) John Gibson   (7) Barton C. Everett
(8) William Everett   (9) Jno McAlister
(10) William Strickland (11) Francis T. Leak

(12) Peter H. Cole Who find the Dfdt guilty in manner and form as charged in the Bill of Indictment.

The Prisoner appearing at the Bar, being asked by the Court if he had any thing to say why sentence of Death should not be heaped against him, replied through his Council praying the Benefit of his Clergy. . . . Which was allowed . . . and he was sentenced to be carried to the whipping Post and there to receive Twenty Lashes on his bare Back. . . . Sentence to be carried into effect at 4 Oclock this afternoon.

Investigation of the law pertaining to benefit of clergy

in the slave-holding States reveals the following facts. It existed for a longer or shorter time in Delaware, Maryland, Virginia, the Carolinas, Georgia, Alabama, Mississippi, Kentucky, Arkansas, and Missouri. Slaves were admitted to benefit of clergy in Virginia in 1732, and although the privilege was abolished as it applied to free persons in 1796, it remained legal for slaves until 1848. Likewise Kentucky withdrew the privilege from whites in 1798 but did not deny it to slaves until 1852. Alabama admitted slaves to benefit of clergy in 1805, but in 1807 all laws, customs and usages relating to Benefit of Clergy were abolished. Slaves were admitted to the privilege in North Carolina in 1816, and it was not denied them until benefit of clergy was abolished in 1854. In the other slave-holding States slaves were not admitted to benefit of clergy by statute but a law of Maryland of 1751 which imposed the death penalty on slaves without benefit of clergy implies that the privilege prevailed there through custom. Benefit of clergy was abolished in Maryland in 1809, in Georgia in 1817, in Mississippi in 1822, in Arkansas in 1838, in Delaware in 1852, in Missouri in 1845, and in South Carolina some time during the reconstruction period.

An interesting feature of benefit of clergy was its relation to the amelioration of the criminal law. In this respect there is a parallel between English and American practice. The English statute of 1706 (5 Anne 6) provided that "if any person shall be convicted of any such felony, for which he ought to have had the benefit of his clergy, if this act had not been made, and shall pray to have the benefit of this act, he shall not be required to read, but without reading, shall be allowed, taken and reputed to be, and punished as, a clerk convict, which shall be as effectual to all intents and purposes, and be as advantageous to him, as if he had read as a clerk; anything in this act, or any other law or statute, to the contrary notwithstanding." Thus benefit of clergy was extended to all classes in England.

A few years later Delaware adopted the principle of the English statute: "that if any person convicted of any such felony as is hereby made capital, for which he ought by the laws of Great Britain to have the benefit of clergy, and shall pray to have the benefit of this act; he shall not be required to read, but without any reading shall be allowed, taken and reputed, and punished as a clerk convict," etc. Likewise Virginia in 1732 adopted the application of benefit of clergy as laid down in the statute of Anne: "and if any person be convicted of a felony, for which he ought to have the benefit of clergy, and shall pray to have the benefit of this act, he shall not be required to read, but without any reading, shall be allowed, taken, and reputed to be, and punished as a clerk convict; which shall be as effectual, to all intents and purposes, and as advantageous to him as if he had read as a clerk; and any other law or statute, to the contrary notwithstanding." Thus, in the language of Pike, "a relic of extreme barbarism" became "the first step towards a modification of the previous laws which deprived a man of his life by a brutal mode of execution for a very petty transaction." (*A History of Crime in England*, II, 281.)

Another parallel between English and American experience was in the abolition of benefit of clergy. In Virginia and Kentucky it was denied to free persons when servitude in a penitentiary was substituted for most of the older penalties for felonies. These states anticipated the policy of England, for benefit of clergy was not there abolished and service in workhouses substituted for existing penalties until 1827. The Virginia policy adopted in 1796 was due to some extent to the example of Pennsylvania which revised its penal system in 1786. The abolition of benefit of clergy in most of the other Southern States was contemporaneous with revisions of the criminal codes.

But given a penal system in which imprisonment was the principal feature, it was not advantageous to the slaveowner or to the State to give prison sentences to slaves.

And here the ghost of benefit of clergy would not down. In place of imprisonment the slave was usually corporally punished. In the language of the Alabama statute of 1807, "when any negro or mulatto whatsoever shall be convicted of any offense not punishable with death by this act, . . . he or she shall be burnt in the hand by the sheriff in open court or suffer such other corporal punishment as the court shall think fit to inflict." Likewise Mississippi in 1822 enacted that "if any negro or mulatto slave was convicted of felony not punishable with death, such negro or mulatto should be burnt in the hand and suffer such other corporal punishment as the court should think fit to inflict, except when he or she shall be convicted of a second offense of the same nature, in which case such negro or mulatto slave shall suffer death." Most interesting are the laws of two States in which benefit of clergy was not provided for. According to the Black Code of Louisiana when slaves were charged with crimes punishable with death or hard labor for life, the jury might at its discretion commute the death penalty and inflict a lesser punishment. In Florida a slave guilty of crime punishable with death might at the discretion of the court suffer instead a whipping not exceeding thirty-nine lashes, have his ears nailed to a post and stand one hour, and be burned in the hand.

In the light of the documents quoted and the statutes cited the statement so frequently made that benefit of clergy disappeared in America at the time of the Revolution, and the dictum of an Indiana judge that "it is unknown to our laws" (I Blackford 63), can not be taken at their face value.

WM. K. BOYD

TRINITY COLLEGE,
DURHAM, N. C.

COMMUNICATIONS

The following from Mr. A. P. Vrede of Paramaribo, Surinam, Dutch Guiana, South America, will be informing and interesting to persons interested in missions as a factor in the uplift of the race:

CORNELIUS WINST BLYD
The First Negro Presbyter in Surinam

PARAMARIBO, Feb. 5, 1923.

Dear Sir:

Likewise as in 1861 the Freedman Association sprang up for aid for the enlightenment of the freed blacks on American soil, so in the epoch from 1738 to 1818 did the missionaries of the Evangelical Brother's Union take upon their shoulders the burden of the enslaved blacks on Surinam. Then, too, their way was not always paved with roses. No they had to face the same mockery, the same martyrdom. They were jailed, despised because for the slaves to remain in their ignorance was favorable to the filling of their "masters" purses.

Let us go back to the year 1850 to see what had been happening on one of the plantations situated on the beach of the Matapica. On these plantations, there we found the administrator, Mr. Rouse, in charge of the plantation administration, busy in making arrangements for transportation of the properties of the plantation, nicknamed by the slaves, "Domiri," to upper Surinam, to the plantation St. Barbara. Among the properties over which Mr. Rouse's superintendenceship extended, we found among living stock a slave family, Father Dami, his wife bearing the name of Ma Jetty, but better known by the name of Ma Jetty of Domiri, so called because her birth-place is Domiri. Father Dami and Jetty had two daughters, the one called Christina and the other, known in slave registration by name of Wilhelmina. So it was on a windy morning of the dry season, that we found this little family. They, too, were occupied with the removal of the plantation properties. It was a busy day. The rays of the sun pierced the backs of the slaves. Their bodies glimmered in their going to and fro as rubbed black-ebony wood furniture.

When the work was over, we left Domiri with its slave caravan for St. Barbara. St. Barbara as aforesaid situated on the upper Surinam the main-stream of the colony Surinam. Entering Mr. Rouse's new dominion from the rear we found the slaves uncommonly active, so different from that they had displayed for a time ago at Domiri.—They were jolly about the coming emancipation days. As we were wandering along the slaves' cabin-rows, it was then July 19, 1860, we heard a baby cry. Turning our heads toward where the voice had been coming from, we detected that it came from the cabin inhabited by the family headed by Father Dami. We walked into, found that Wilhelmina, Dami's daughter, had added to her family a male member. There he lay down sprawling on the floor in pieces of rag clothes used for his bed and pillow. But this child will grow up to become a distinguished man among his people, a shepherd to watch over his flock. Winst, or Profit, the administrator, Mr. Rouse, called him. One would try to solve that puzzle of nomenclature in those days. But we know and understand it now better. It was the time when the administrator was expecting to get for every slave three hundred guilders on the emancipation day. So we may suppose that this was done, as a profit upon his debit on the government account. Let us now see what became of that slave child Winst.

Cornelis Winst Blyd was born of slave parents, as stated above, on the plantation St. Barbara July 19, 1860. He was the son of Wilhelmina, a daughter of Father Dami. Besides Winst, his mother had two other sons. It came to pass that when Winst's mother Wilhelmina died, survived by her three sons, they were put under care of their Aunt Christina. Blyd, his brothers and Aunt afterward moved into town. His aunt placed Blyd in one of the Moravian mission boarding schools for boys, formerly known as "Amtri" School. It was desired that after he should finish his literary training he should be instructed in the handicraft of carpentry. So he was brought in to Mr. Ammon, the carpenter well renowned in the colony for furniture.

But this was not the way traced for him by our Lord. So they took him from Mr. Ammon to the "Central School" a former preparatory boarding school for teachers. Blyd, with his pious, gentle and sincere character, had won in no time the friendship of everyone who inhabited the institution. His educational instruction in the Bible was received from Rev. E. A. Renkemir. For song he was trained by Mr. Batenburg. In the classroom of the normal school for teachers, he was one of the beloved pupils of Dr. H. D. Benjamin, then the Inspector of the Board of Education in Surinam. Blyd had in competition among his fellow classmates held by his teachers, distinguished himself as a remarkable student in solving Bible questions. So we see he showed more inclination to the clergy and to become a minister than a school teacher. But in that time no natives were exalted to the order of preacher. So Blyd became a teacher.

Blyd followed his occupation as a teacher in several districts of the colony. His first field of operation was on the plantation, Berger Dal, one of the largest Negro settlements in Surinam. We may mention here an uproar that took place during his stay there. These will make us a little acquainted with his sincere and pious character. It came to pass, one day after school hours, two school boys got to quarreling about a pocket-knife. The quarrel became so noisy that the family of both the boys were coming up with hatchet, walking-stick and some more murderous weapons. So much feeling had then developed that the uproar would not have been prevented had not Mr. Blyd undertaken this difficult task and by his unusual moral power brought both parties to reflection. After a reprimand in well chosen words the quarrel was suppressed.

When Mr. Blyd later moved to plantation Wederzorg, situated on the Commewyne river, he then got permission from the Director of the Mission in Surinam, to lead now and then the church service. But these all were for Blyd merely as forerunner to reach his mile-stone. At the plantation Alkmaar, he came into touch with the Rev. Mr. Kersten, and it was not long before this man detected in Mr. Blyd a preacher of power. Blyd's impression made upon Rev. Mr. Kersten was so favorable that soon in 1899, the Mission Director in Surinam decided to appoint him as sub-preacher. And once the words spoken by the old Rev. Mr. Haller (white) became truth. He had said to Mr. Blyd "You should try to train yourself for the uplift of your fellow race-men, and to teach them the words of our living God." In the year 1902 Mr. Blyd was ordained to the order of deacon, and from that time, his name as a preacher was established.

Rev. Mr. Blyd had to wrestle with many storms that touched his social life. There came upon him the bad deportment of his two sons. He who knows the battle which he had to fight, brought upon him by his sons' evil deeds, will find in him, the preacher of God, a true and sincere knight of our Lord. Rev. Mr. Blyd sought in his hours of these temptations his refuge on his Savior knees and he always was consoled. Many had wondered at his patience and long suffering amid these storms of life. But this man, the preacher by the grace of God, the sincere Christian in the full sense of the word, had as his encouragement, that had been giving him consolation and confidence: "The Lord shall provide, be still my soul."

Rev. Mr. Blyd's sermons were of an uncommon sort. Never would one part from his service not being touched in the depths of his inner life. His sermons were delivered in Dutch and Negro-English. They were a splendor of oratory. In spite of all of these, however, Rev. Mr. Blyd still retained his humility, without overrating himself. His words won many hearts, even many a stranger. Among them we may count Bishop Hamilton, High Commissioner of the Moravian Board of Missions in England. In 1913, the year of the celebration of the Fifty Emancipation Anniversary, the Mission Director in Surinam decided to send Rev. Mr. Blyd to Europe, to the Netherlands, our mother country, to represent the black race. Rev. Mr. Blyd traveled also throughout Germany and Denmark. There in Europe, he came into touch with several notables.

He won many friends by his sermon preached at the celebration of the mission feast at Utrecht in the Netherlands as attested by H. M. Queen Wilhelmina of the Netherlands. Many ministers with the degree of Doctor of Divinity had addressed the audience on that occasion. After them Rev. Mr. Blyd rose from his seat to walk to the pulpit for he was being given a turn. When he was on the way to the pulpit, a white minister hastened to offer to him a minister's gown, but the man Blyd kept his simplicity and refused to accept it.[1] After the service everyone longed to cheer and greet the black minister. By hundreds and thousands they crowded themselves to see him pass. Photographers were busy taking his photo. To and fro they went to ask for a picture of the black minister. Rev. Mr. Blyd had made a deep impression upon H. M. Queen Wilhelmina, and under the emotion that Rev. Mr. Blyd had caused H. M. the Queen, he was invited by Her Majesty to deliver a sermon at the court, attended by all H. M. court representatives.

[1] Here in Surinam the Moravian preacher needs no gown by the church service. This offering was then for Rev. Blyd a sign of his worthiness, an honor and an acknowledgment of his true Christian soul.

Rev. Mr. Blyd was later invited to dinner at H. M. residence at Hagen, and he sat at the same table near by H. M. the Queen. This extraordinary event took place after his traveling from North Europe.

His love for his native land will be illustrated by the following event. It was at H. M. Queen Wilhelmina's residence that this took place. When the Queen put before him this question: "Reverend Mr. Blyd," H. M. turning to him, "which of the two places do you prefer? The Netherlands or Denmark?" And without hesitation he answered the Queen's question in his simple words: "Your Majesty, East, West, home is best!"

Rev. Mr. Blyd surrounded by all these courtesies has never forgot his race. He took the opportunity to bring before the Queen the needs of his people. He had made also his entrance at the courts of Germany and Denmark. In Denmark he was received with great enthusiasm and great homage. He had so impressed the clergy of Denmark that they made efforts to retain him for the order in that country. But the man with his humble character chose above all to serve among his own people. In Germany he had held several street meetings. A white eye-witness, now in the colony, told about the impression Rev. Mr. Blyd made upon his hearers. He said that the longer he lived the more he learned from Rev. Mr. Blyd.

During Rev. Mr. Blyd's sojourn in Europe the mission authorities were offered a better opportunity to study his character. And so this led to the conclusion to exalt him to the order of presbyter. This event took place before a large audience when he was returning to the Colony.

Alas! the poor slave boy, Cornelis Winst Blyd, with his unlimited energy traced his way from the slave cabin to kings and queens' palaces. From body bondage to liberty of spirit and body —raised to the highest order of Protestant dignity, the order which no man of his color in the Colony has since attained.

Of the literature which Rev. Mr. Blyd has left, we may mention here his well-styled booklet: "Superstition in Surinam." Therein he has showed a great capacity as a writer. In this booklet he warned his people of the devil's sacrifice—the fetishism and the belief in witchcraft, an African religion transplanted here in the colony by their ancestors from Africa. His effort in doing so was only as he has said, to release his people from the chains of such an empty religion.

It was on April 12, 1921, that the Colony was shocked from its foundation. People stood in groups, heads sadly bent. Black clouds now and then saluted in snow-white rainy cloud, to regain after a few moments their original ash-grey color. Rev. Mr. Blyd, nursed in the Military Hospital, had passed away. The sickness that had ended his life so suddenly had returned. It was known that physically his body was overpowered by a disease. But none had expected his end so suddenly. On Sunday he had delivered his last sermon. In the week when his sickness had become more serious they decided to take him to the Military Hospital at Paramaribo for a careful nursing. But his end was at hand.

The day of his burial, a funeral-service was conducted by the Rev. Dr. Muller. It would require too much space in this Journal to note here all that he spoke on that occasion. But I shall note here some passages. Dr. Muller said: "He was one of the most popular and loveliest personalities among our society. He was the first among his co-workers. Everyone respected his name with deep respect, the young as well as the aged. He stood for better days above all parties; above all difference of color, sect and confession. He was the man that won the general confidence of the Colony.

"Yea! he was a man loved by all, respected by his own people the black, as well as by white. His name will live forever in the hearts of his people, friends and all. His name is holy for young and old. His wandering upon this earth was a guide to and for many in this Colony. He was simplicity itself and his life ended the same."

A. P. Vrede,
Paramaribo, Surinam

The following communication from Captain T. G. Steward, U. S. A., retired, contains several statements of interest to students of Negro History:

Wilberforce, Ohio, January 13, 1923.

Mr. Carter G. Woodson,
Washington, D. C.

Dear Sir: Allow me to kindly refer you to page 67 of my book "Fifty Years in The Gospel Ministry" where you will find recounted the opening of the school in Marion, S. C., the names of the teachers, and a copy of their credentials, etc.

Also on page 47 of your "Negro in Our History" you mention one "Irish Nell." I am quite confident that the late Bishop James Theodore Holly, bishop of Haiti, was a descendant of the union of that lady with a black man. I do not know how the name Holly came in, but I may be able to cite you to the facts if you think it worth while to publish the matter.

I am glad to find you doing so much first hand work; and were I able I should be delighted to be engaged with you.

I suppose you are aware of the fact that the keeper of Fraunce's tavern or Faunce's tavern in New York where Washington took leave of his officers was a negro. Also his daughter was Washington's house-keeper when the latter lived on Murray Hill in New York.

I would think the Faunce hotel at that time was probably among the best, if not itself the best hotel in the country.

Yours truly,

T. G. STEWARD

BOOK REVIEWS

Das unbekannte Afrika (Unknown Africa). By Leo Frobenius. (O. Beck, München, 1923.)

The war has fettered Frobenius to his country and his desk, and he has found time to study his material, and the series of diaries, written every day while in Africa. Ten volumes of folklore, three volumes of *Atlas Africanus,* several philosophical books, and this one under discussion, have been the fruits of his unwelcome restraint. Frobenius is now preparing another book, "The dying Africa." Many of his collections have gone to the various museums, but he has a large number of interesting objects, and many thousands of pictures which are contained in his recent publications, and, at last, made known.

Each chapter of *Das unbekannte Afrika* is headed by small maps showing the distribution of the cultural elements treated in it. This is the form of registration which Frobenius has practiced for the last 25 years. Thus the enormous wealth of ethnological data is statistically fixed. The area, for instance, for a house type or a custom, when found in his travels, is compared with data found, in literature, on the same subject, and all the findings are, again, registered on a map. The results of seven expeditions, on which skilled artists accompanied him, have been kept under control in this manner. As soon as the center of a district which seemed of interest was reached, numerous trained assistants were sent in different directions. Each took notes and pictures on a given subject, so that a marvelous amount of work could be accomplished. Other data were gained by leaving questionnaires among the resident missionaries, merchants, or government officials, to whom letters were sent later, where matters did not seem sufficiently clear, when studied at home.

The deductions made are illustrated by the fascinating pictures contained in *The unknown Africa,* in which more than half of the space is devoted to illustrations. By them the interrelation between Neolithic European, Asiatic, Phoenician, Carthaginian, and the African cultures is shown, mainly in regard to art and architecture.

African art is nearer related to the prehistoric European than to the Asiatic and the American. On the whole, that of the south is historic, as compared with that of northwestern Africa. Linguistically the south African idioms are the oldest, while the illiterate eastern constitutes the second period, and the northwestern the youngest.

Racially the lighter Hamite in the northwest has displaced older types, which are now prevalent in the east. The Hamitic culture extends between the Canaries and the Indian Ocean, with extensions into Abyssinia and the southern apex. In the south dwell the Ethiopians. Originally there were two main points of cultural influx, one in Erythraea, and one on the western shores, having travelled through the Mediterranean and Gibraltar, around northwestern Africa. Some influence was also introduced from the north, and traversed the Sahara desert. There it did not survive, but penetrated the Soudan.

The two cultures are explained distinctly. The Hamitic contains remnants of the solar cult, while the Ethiopian shows that of the moon. The first has the matriarchal while the second has the patriarchal system. Hamitic inclinations are connected with the animal world, the Ethiopian with Mother Earth and the plant. Proofs for the entry of Hamitic elements by way of Erythraea are found in the fact that the matriarchate has existed on the eastern coast of India, and in southern Arabia, and that it still exists in northern Africa. Also, the ritual killing of the kings which exists near the White Nile, and in the eastern Soudan, was reported, by Diodorus, to have existed on the eastern coast of India and in Meroe.

The Nile kept Egypt in touch with the rest of the civilized world, while the western parts of northern Africa had no great stream to retain the ancient height of culture, but this tended to the guarding of traditions, and the preservation of ancient customs.

The same ritual procedure which is depicted on the rock-drawings, thousands of years old, prevails in these days in western Soudan. The same posture is taken by the supplicant huntsman, in regard to the cardinal points, while he traces similar images on the sand. The present-day pious Yoruba consults the replica of boards which were found in Ife, and which were thousands of years old. On them are carved the four main pairs of deities, or the sixteen cardinal points.

Frobenius found ancient terra-cotta heads and wood carvings which represented the same objects as those found in Benin. The latter must be considered as mediaeval. The pupils of the Benin heads are perforated, while the Ilife heads have blind eyes. This would affix, to the latter, a much greater age, as it is a feature of ancient Mediterranean sculpture. The Atlantic art of western Africa is highly developed, and has nothing in common with primitive Negro art. Some of the boards are exquisite, and rows of beautiful figures and mythological representations are carved on a door, in Yoruba, as shown in the book.

A very interesting theory is put forth, in this connection. So far, it was accepted that time, in archaeology, could be measured only by stone objects, as these were lasting. The author, however, is of the opinion that rock drawings and carvings may answer the aesthetic or ritual requirements of a region or a people for many centuries, while wooden implements and works of art must be replaced, being eminently perishable. Wood is available everywhere. The idea underlying a figure is renewed, with each generation of carvers, and the traditions are handed down as faithfully by wooden carvings as by folk-lore.

Drawings, in the strict sense of the word, are found, in Africa, only in ancient Egypt. They are more closely related to the Bushman paintings of South Africa than to the petrography of the western parts of the continent. Hamitic rock drawings, with depressed lines of contour, and tinted in the intervening surfaces, are seen in Egypt. Prehistoric and early historic figures were found in Egypt, Lesser Africa, and the Guinea Coast. In the east the lines are generally severe, while in the northwest they are rounded. The Hamitic culture zone has no plastic art, among Berber, Bisharin, Somali, Masai, and Hottentot. The Bushman who drew the beautiful rock ornaments has produced no plastic. What is found among this tribe must be considered as Carthaginian.

The primitive Hamite fears representations of the human and animal, from magic. Later the plastic representations have, however, penetrated the Hamitic boundaries, and reached the Nile. The peoples of Lesser and North Africa do not recognize what is on the rocks. The Negro is not gifted in this sense. The Hamite who does not readily see a drawing or picture, and never seems to have produced plastic art, draws well, realistically or ornamentally. The Negro is a good carver but draws very badly. Even those Negroes who recognize every photograph and carve excellently cannot draw.

Many deductions are made in studying the migration of cultures, and many parallels are shown up. One of the relationships found is that between the tattooing of the Neolithic Period of France and that of the living individual near the Niger. The lines run from the ear to the nose. Another well-known feature is the figure of the obese woman which extends from France to Malta. It is quite prevalent in Hamitic art, in the graphic productions of northern Africa, and in Egyptian plastic. Steatopygy, in the living, is natural to the South African tribes. The deduction made is that those models which seemed desirable to the artist, during the stone age of the northwest, still exist in the south. Therefore Hamitic culture must have wandered from the north, east and south.

Other stone-age elements, the stone graves, are found in the Hamitic regions. In Morocco the stone tumuli are explained as remnants of the houses of forebears. When food ran low, goes the tale, the head of the family collected all its members about him, and tore the home down, over them.

Two main types of dwellings are found in Africa, one a cave, the other a pile structure. The Hamitic culture prefers the first, the Ethiopian the latter. The oldest Hamitic "chthonic" bed is a pit. The oven and storehouse is built in the ground. The inhabitants of the Canary Islands, who are the descendants of the ancient Guanches, and most of the Kabyle tribes of Morocco, Algeria, and Tunis still have artificial caves, which are, however, not generally known. In Matamata, in the south of Tunis, tunnel-shaped, honeycomb dwellings constitute the newer type of cave dwelling.

Ethiopian "telluric" architecture uses the pile in the construction of beds, huts for guards, dwelling houses, and meeting places. The edifices are round or rectangular, and thatched. Later the thatch is covered with clay. Fortresses are constructed of clay and rafters. In parts of the Soudan the walls are beautifully ornamented with reliefs of humans and animals, or geometrical figures. In the interior of the houses the clay walls are tinted and polished, and the pictures show many beautiful decorative designs.

BEATRICE BICKEL

A History of the United States Since the Civil War. By Ellis Paxon Oberholtzer. In five volumes. Volume II, 1868–1872. (New York: The Macmillan Company, 1922. Pp. XI, 649. $4.00.)

This is the second of five volumes of a history of the United States since the Civil War to be completed by this author. Covering the period from 1868 to 1872, this treatise deals in detail with the Reconstruction, the Ku Klux Klan, international questions resulting from the Civil War, the building of railroads, and Oriental problems.

It is not usual, however, to find one publishing such a large and expensive volume as this for the purpose of giving merely the author's opinion about the problems of that day and the shortcomings of the men who were trying to solve them. Not unlike most writers on the Reconstruction, this author endeavored to commend those who achieved as he would have them and to condemn those who addressed themselves to these tasks in a different way. In most places, however, he found many to censure and few to praise. If the book has any purpose at all, it is intended not as a history of the period but a survey of the corruption and vice of the age. Very little of the malfeasance in positions of public trust escaped the attention of this writer.

Beginning with President Grant himself, the author has tried to show that there was little of virtue and efficiency among public functionaries of that time. He refers to Grant as being ignorant, stupid, and simple, holds up to scorn James G. Blaine, and questions Garfield's connection with Credit Mobilier in the style characteristic of the book. Other crimes to the credit of the leading statesmen of that day are given detailed treatment. The book abounds in so many recriminations and epithets belaboring the most distinguished men of the time that the uninformed reader would expect something like the fall of Rome to follow.

If the white people with all their advantages had degenerated to such a low level, the reader might wonder why the author should make any comment at all on the corruption of the Negroes in the South. Inasmuch as they had not been generally educated and had been denied participation in civic affairs, he might have excused them for abandoning work to enjoy their freedom, stealing from their former masters, and obtruding themselves socially upon haughty persons of the old regime. In the same style, however, the Negroes are given their share of vilification. "He refers to them as 'Sambo' and 'Cuffee' entering the halls of government, and a 'Coal Black' member made temporary chairman," " 'The Black Crook Convention,' 'Ring-tailed Coons,' 'Outlaws and Rag-a-muffins,' and a 'Gang of Jailbirds.' "

All of these expressions are not original with the author. They are taken from southern newspapers and books of the same sort of authorship. Instead of using such evidence only when known to be unconscious, the author has accepted this information as the truth. According to the requirements of modern historiography, newspapers are generally valuable only in determining the sentiment of the people except when the evidence obtained is unconscious. Furthermore, the author has too often accepted secondhand information, found in books of writers who have produced treatises on the Reconstruction for the express purpose of vilifying the Negroes who participated in that drama, and to justify the highhanded action of the whites who through such invisible powers as the Ku Klux Klan overthrew the liberal governments, and re-established the power of the aristocracy of the South. It is unreasonable to suppose that orators and editors interested in disfranchising and re-enslaving the Negroes would tell the truth about the freedmen.

It is most unfortunate that writers have accepted the point of view of these biased authors instead of making a research for the facts in the case. In too many instances, this author quotes Fleming for facts of Reconstruction in Alabama, Hamilton for North Carolina, Ficklen for Louisiana, Garner for Mississippi, Ramsdell for Texas, Reynolds for South Carolina, Davis for Florida, Eckenrode for Virginia, Thompson for Georgia, and the like. These "authorities" do not strengthen the claims of a work because of the very bias with which these books were written, for these writers accepted rumors, violent newspaper comments, and inflammatory speeches as reasons for their conclusions. Any history built upon such authority cannot be considered trustworthy.

From the point of view of the Negro himself, this book is not a history of the United States for the period which it purports to cover. It has very little to say about the Negroes except to refer to them as an ignorant, illiterate mass of thieves and rascals. In a work covering merely four years, a seeker of the truth would expect some information therefrom as to how the freedmen began their social and economic stride upward, what forces were set to work among them, and how susceptible they proved to be of the training offered in the schools and churches established for their special needs. Inasmuch as he found so much space for the Carpet-Baggers who went South to control the State governments through the Negro vote, it would have hardly been out of place for the author to mention that throng of apostles who came South as teachers to give their lives as a sacrifice in the uplift of these belated people. What these Negroes did, during these very years, to help themselves should have received some consideration. Every Negro of consequence in the South was not a politician or an office-seeker. What the race is accomplishing today is due in a large measure to the foundation laid at that time by Negroes of foresight, who acquired education and property and joined the missionary teachers from the North in the noble effort for the education and economic amelioration of the freedmen.

The Partition of Africa. By Sir Charles Lucas, K.C.B., K.C.M.G. (Oxford, Oxford University Press, 1922. Pp. 228.)

This book consists of the lectures given by the author at the Royal Colonial Institute to a circle of teachers of the London County Council in 1921. The author disclaims any pretension to exhaust the subject. He acknowledges that these lectures are somewhat discursive with the intention of suggesting diverse points of view and a variety of subjects for further study. With this purpose in mind he freely quotes a number of books and papers, evidently desiring to stimulate the reader to further study. It is admitted, moreover, that while these lectures have been awaiting publication there has taken place in Africa so many developments that this volume will not suffice to inform the reader.

The work begins with a survey of Africa in ancient times as it connected with the Mediterranean World. Unfortunately, in this chapter the author follows the well-beaten path of misrepresenting that land by referring to it as the "Dark Continent," which, from his point of view, was dependent and backward because it had no facilities of communication with Europe. In this chapter, therefore, he proves not that Africa had not made much advancement but that the European was merely ignorant of that part of the world.

In the chapter discussing "Africa from Ancient Times to the Nineteenth Century" there is little more than a casual sketch of the invasion of the Vandals, the Mohammedan conquest, followed by a rather brief and unscientific discussion of the natives of Africa. This chapter, however, presents in epitome the leading facts of the explorations of Europeans beginning with Prince Henry of Portugal, the forerunner of other adventurers from England, Italy, Spain and France.

Taking up the slave trade, the author becomes a little more interesting. He discusses the question from two points of view, distinguishing between the Mohammedan slave trade and the European traffic in men on the West Coast of Africa. He undertakes to give the causes of the West African slave trade in terms of the commercial revolution. Then follows a more detailed account of the participation therein by various European nations. In this connection is treated also the effort of philanthropic Europeans who exposed the horrors of the slave trade and finally abolished it. Further efforts for the improvement of the Negroes are traced to the establishment of Sierra Leone and Liberia.

The author then shows how this interest in the Negro, developing along with European expansion into Africa, led to further exploration and settlement and to the missionary enterprise of David Livingston. The interest in the uplift of the natives, however, as the book admits, was lost sight of after the Franco-German war, the prelude to the scramble for Africa. Then came the beginning of Belgian Congo, the Anglo-Portuguese treaty of 1884, the general acts of the Berlin Conference, the Congo atrocities, and the partition of the continent into Northeast-Africa, East-Africa, South-Africa, West-Africa and other spheres of influence. There followed also another sort of scramble in building African railways, tapping the wealth of the hinterland of Africa. The bearing of the Anglo-French Convention of 1904, the Franco-German Agreement of 1911 and other European treaties are all set forth.

Discussing North-Africa, the author first makes a comparison of the situation in the different parts of the continent, allowing for such influences as the proximity of that portion of the continent to Europe, the effect of the orientalization of Egypt, Tunis, Algeria, Tripoli, and Morocco. This discussion, however, is not carried out in all of its ramifications and the reader must make further investigation for adequate information.

In Chapter VIII the author reviews the settlements of the Dutch in South-Africa, the British occupation of the Cape, the conflict of the British and the Dutch, the rise of the Boer Republic, and the Kaffir wars. In keeping with so many writers who endorse almost anything which Europeans do, this author finds some justification for the intrusion of the Europeans in Africa. The cruel oppression visited upon the natives as a result of this conquest does not cause the author any grief. In the same way, he discusses the conquest and settlements of France and Great Britain in West-Africa, their dependencies, and methods of development. Treating the late campaigns in Africa, the author makes an effort to bring this information up to date as far as possible, trying to account for the territorial settlement in that continent as shown by the reconstructed map of Africa. The book closes with a discussion of such African problems as the elimination of Germany from Africa, the plurality of powers in Africa as an advantage to the Africans in bringing about mutual checks, and the effect of the World War upon the relation between whites and blacks.

A Boy's Life of Booker T. Washington. By W. C. Jackson, Vice President of the North Carolina College for Women, and Professor of History, Greensboro. (New York, The Macmillan Company, 1922. Pp. 147.)

The author does not pretend to add anything new to what is generally known about Booker T. Washington, or to what may be found in such works as *Up from Slavery, My Larger Education,* and *Booker T. Washington: Builder of a Civilization.* The aim is to tell this story in such simple language as to make it comprehensible for children. The author hopes that by reading this book some of them may be inspired to higher ambition and encouraged to nobler effort. While the reader may not agree with all of the observations made by the author, he must commend this effort to popularize the record of the distinguished citizen who by his achievement demonstrated that the race has within it the possibilities of other groups. This effort, then, has an important bearing on the dissemination of information concerning the Negro and on the preservation of the records of the race.

The details of the life of the subject of the sketch are omitted except that the interesting beginnings of Booker T. Washington as a boy, and his rise through poverty and ignorance to a position of leadership, are given with some degree of thoroughness. The author endeavors to impress upon the youth the bravery, courage, backbone, energy, fair-mindedness, honesty, wisdom, intelligence, judgment, modesty, patriotism, will power, self control, and love of humanity of Booker T. Washington. To do this, each important trait in the man is portrayed by reference to some achievement which served as a striking example of his character. In this way, the author draws upon his planning for an education, school days at Hampton, beginning life in the outside world, first efforts at teaching, the beginning of Tuskegee, early hardships, struggles to raise money, speech-making, leadership, political experiences, and travels abroad.

The book is well printed and neatly bound. It is also adequately illustrated so as to concentrate the attention of the youth on certain important achievements and events in the life of Washington. Among these illustrations appear the monument recently unveiled at Tuskegee, which constitutes the frontispiece of the book. Then follow various illustrations of the many activities of the institution. While there is not given a general view of the whole school, the various groups given will impress the reader with the magnitude of the work undertaken at Tuskegee. The cuts of Washington and his family show the home life of the man.

NOTES

Mr. A. A. Taylor, who during the last fiscal year devoted a part of his time to research under the direction of the Association, has been permanently employed as an Associate Investigator of the Association to make researches into Negro Reconstruction History. Mr. Taylor is an alumnus of the University of Michigan. He has recently done graduate work under Professors Abbott, Usher, Turner, Merk, and Channing at Harvard, where he obtained the degree of Master of Arts.

Miss Irene A. Wright, who has been employed by the Association to copy certain documents in the Archives of the Indies, Seville, Spain, reports that in the near future she will offer for publication in these columns interesting and valuable data giving the history of the Mose Settlement of Negroes in Florida.

Mr. Albert Parry, the contributor of the article in this number entitled "Hannibal, the Favorite of Peter the Great," is a former resident of Russia. He has been studying in this country two years.

The various aspects of German colonization in East Africa and the rôle played by that portion of this continent in the World War are treated in *Kumbuke; Erlebnisse eines Arztes in Deutsch Ostafrika* (Berlin, Dom-Verlag, 1922, pp. 502), by August Hauer.

Études sur l'Islam en Côte d'Ivoire (Paris, Leroux, 1922, pp. 502) by Paul Marty, *Au Congo: Souvenirs de la Mission Marchand* (Paris, Fayard, 1921) by General Baratier, and *Une Étape de la Conquête de l'Afrique Équatoriale Française* (Paris, Fournier, 1922, pp. 260) by the Ministry of War of France, cover altogether in a general way French colonization in Western and Central Africa.

The Associated Publishers will soon publish a work entitled *Negro Poets and Their Poems* by Robert T. Kerlin, Professor of English of the State Normal School, West Chester, Pennsylvania, former Professor of English at the Virginia Military Institute. This work will be an illustrated textbook for schools and will at the same time serve as a volume of general information on contemporary Negro poetry.

ANNUAL REPORT OF THE DIRECTOR

The fiscal year which ended June 30, 1923, was the most prosperous in the history of the Association. The efforts of the staff were directed toward carrying out the purposes for which the Association was organized, namely, to collect historical data and to promote studies bearing on the Negro. To attain these objectives the Director had to perform the two important tasks of soliciting funds to finance the Association and then to use the same in the employment of assistants to investigate the various aspects of Negro life and history.

Funds have been received and disbursed as follows:

COMPLETE FINANCIAL STATEMENT OF ALL DEPARTMENTS OF THE ASSOCIATION FOR THE STUDY OF NEGRO LIFE AND HISTORY *

July 1, 1922-June 30, 1923

Receipts		Disbursements	
Research Fund	$5,000.00	Printing and Stationery	$2,996.34
Interest on Reserve	78.77	Paid for Research	4,401.62
Subscriptions	1,798.91	Petty Cash (Incidentals)	900.00
Memberships	321.10	Stenographic Service	1,330.01
Contributions	6,727.99	Rent and Light	518.50
Advertisements	264.55	Salaries	2,733.37
Refunds	57.11	Traveling Expenses	300.39
Miscellaneous	107.80	Miscellaneous	520.47
Books	3.25		
Total Receipts	$14,359.48	Total Disbursements	$13,700.70
Balance on hand for Research June 30, 1922	5,000.00	Balance on hand, June 30, 1923, appropriated for Printing and Research	5,677.15
Balance on hand, General Expense Fund, June 30, 1922	89.46	Balance on hand, General Expense Fund, June 30, 1923	71.09
Grand Total	$19,448.94	Grand Total	$19,448.94

Respectfully submitted,
(Signed) S. W. RUTHERFORD,
Secretary-Treasurer.

* The books of the Association have been audited by a certified public accountant who reports that the receipts have been duly deposited, that all disbursements have been made through numbered voucher checks properly approved, and that the balances given in the records of the Association agree with the balances reported by the banks.

Various Interests

The Director, who is editor of the JOURNAL OF NEGRO HISTORY as well as the executive of the Association, has devoted some of his time to administrative duties, which, with the expansion of the work, are rapidly multiplying. It has been possible, however, to give much stimulus to all phases of the work in spite of arduous duties. That the additional assistants now associated with the Director will relieve him of some of these tasks is indeed gratifying.

THE JOURNAL OF NEGRO HISTORY has found its way into additional libraries and schools where it is becoming more and more to be regarded as a valuable aid in research. It is now used as such in the accredited colleges and universities of both races in the South and serves for similar purposes in centers of research in the North. A larger number of institutions abroad, moreover, are now subscribing to this publication, requiring, too, a complete file of the magazine in bound form. Briefly stated, then, while this publication has not a popular subscription list, it circulates throughout the civilized world as a library magazine of value for advanced students, investigators, and social workers.

The Director has spent some of his time in field work. Wherever there is a call to encourage a school or a club to do more for the study of Negro life and history, the Director generally responds. In this way the people of Kentucky, especially in Lexington and Louisville, were made acquainted with the purposes of the Association and induced to do something for the preservation of the local records of Negroes who have achieved well. Enterprising citizens of Lexington have organized for this purpose.

At Nashville, the Director availed himself of a similar opportunity to carry the work of the Association to the thinking people of the city, speaking to them for two days in their schools and churches. The interest aroused was most encouraging and resulted in the organization of a local club to co-operate with this national organization.

In addition to preserving the records of Negroes in that particular community, this group will engage in the actual study of the neglected aspects of Negro history, using the Branch Library as a center where numerous works on Negro life and history have been provided.

In Baltimore, where the Spring Conference of the Association was held, the citizens showed the same sort of interest in the work and pledged themselves to do more to save local records which are now being rapidly lost. Persons having an intelligent interest in the past of the Negro are now taking steps to organize there a Maryland Historical Society, to record and popularize the achievements of the Negroes of that commonwealth under the leadership of the teachers of history of the public schools and instructors at Morgan College.

RESEARCH

For the first time in the history of the Association its researches have taken a definite course. Up to the year just ended, the Association had the benefit of merely what investigations the Director's manifold duties permitted him to conduct, or of what others of their own will worked out in the interest of unearthing the truth. Thanks to the appropriations of the Carnegie Corporation and the Laura Spellman Rockefeller Memorial, however, the Association can now outline a definite program of investigation and systematically carry it out. For the present the staff is engaged in the study of the Free Negro prior to 1861 and Negro Reconstruction History.

With the assistance of a copyist, Mrs. C. B. Overton, the Director has been preparing a report on the Free Negro in the United States. This report will be decidedly statistical, giving the names of the persons of color who were heads of families in 1830, where they were living, how many were in each family, how many slaves each owned, and what relation these free Negroes sustained to the white people. This research covers also the statistics of absentee ownership of slaves by whites. The first volume of the report will be published within the next six months. Using it as a basis, the Director will make further investigation of the Free Negroes to determine their economic status, their social position, the attitude of the southern whites toward this class, and the opinion of the North with respect to them as citizens.

Working in this same field, but developing special aspects of this history, are Mr. George F. Dow and Miss Irene A. Wright. Mr. George F. Dow has been employed to read the 18th century colonial newspapers of New England for facts bearing on the Negro. Up to the present, however, he has been unable to finsh this task and does not promise to accomplish much until next fall. Miss Irene A. Wright is now extracting from the Archives of the Indies in Seville, Spain, some valuable documents showing the part the Negroes played in the early struggle between the British and Spanish in America and especially the records of the Mose Settlement of Negroes in Florida and the achievements of the Negroes in Louisiana. Miss Wright will also copy all accessible documents of Latin-America giving accounts of Negroes in higher spheres of usefulness. The Association is endeavoring to employ an investigator to render the same sort of service in the British Museum and the Public Record Office in London.

During the year the Association has had one worker in Negro Reconstruction History. This was Mr. A. A. Taylor, an alumnus of the University of Michigan, who has recently received the degree of Master of Arts for graduate work done at Harvard University under Professors W. C. Abbott, F. J. Turner, and Edward Channing. Although he has devoted only a part of his time to this research, he has produced one valuable dissertation, *The Social Conditions and Treatment of Negroes in South Carolina, 1865-1880*. He has also made a scientific study of the social and economic conditions of the Negroes in Virginia for the same period, but has not yet completed this treatise. It is expected that it will be ready for publication within the next twelve months. Mr. Taylor will continue this work as

Associate Investigator, permanently employed by the Association to devote all of his time to this effort.

The Association continues its interest in the work of training young men for scientific investigation. As far as possible it will follow its program of educating in the best graduate schools with libraries bearing on Negro Life and History, three young men supported by fellowships of $500 each from the Association and such additional stipends as the schools themselves may grant for their support. These students are assigned to different fields, one to make Anthropometric and Psychological measurements of Negroes, one to study African Anthropology and Archaeology, and one to take up history as it has been influenced by the Negro.

Closely connected with these plans, moreover, are certain other projects to preserve Negro folklore. In this effort the Association has the co-operation of Dr. Elsie Clews Parsons, the moving spirit of the American Folklore Society. She is now desirous of making a more systematic effort to embody this part of the Negro civilization and she believes that the work can be more successfully done by co-operation with the Association. As soon as the Director can obtain a special fund for this particular work, an investigator will be employed to undertake it. For the present the Association is endeavoring to stimulate interest in this field by offering a prize of $200 for the best collection of tales, riddles, proverbs, sayings, and songs, which have been heard at home by Negro students of accredited schools.

The interest in the result of these researches has become all but nation-wide. Most advanced institutions of learning now make some use of historical works on the Negro. *The Negro in Our History* has met with the general welcome as a much desired volume giving the essential facts of Negro achievement. It has been extensively used as collateral reading and has been adopted as a text in more than a score of schools and colleges. The demand for this book is so rapidly increasing that the second edition has been almost exhausted. The third edition, which is now in preparation, will be revised and enlarged so as to give more attention to the Negro in freedom, a period of more concern to most students than that of the Negro before the Civil War.

In almost every center of considerable Negro population and in most of the large schools of the race there are clubs or classes engaged in the study of Negro life and history. Some of these were organized under the supervision of the Association and others sprang up of themselves in response to the increasing desire among Negroes to know about themselves and to publish such information to a world uninformed as to what the race has thought and felt and attempted and done. These groups thus interested in the scientific study of the Negro, moreover, are not restricted to the schools and communities controlled by this race. The Association has found little difficulty in interesting advanced students in large northern universities, and this work has extended to some of the best white schools of the South.

THE STAFF

The staff has suffered one irreparable loss in that Miss A. H. Smith, who during the last seven years has served the Association as Office Manager and Assistant to the Secretary-treasurer, has recently retired from the service. The Association is immeasurably indebted to Miss Smith for the faithful service which she has rendered the cause, and it will be difficult to fill her position. Although offered opportunities for earning a larger stipend elsewhere, she remained with the Association because of her interest in the work which it has been prosecuting. The Association wishes her well and earnestly hopes that she may be welcomed in some other field of usefulness.

Respectfully submitted,
CARTER G. WOODSON,
Director

1538 NINTH ST., N. W.,
WASHINGTON, D. C.
Sept. 18, 1923

INDEX
JOURNAL OF NEGRO HISTORY
VOLUME VIII

A

A Negro Pioneer in the West, 333-335

Abram Hannibal, the Favorite of Peter the Great, 359-366

Africa and the Discovery of America, review of, 233-238

African Institution, the interest of, in colonization, 168, 169, 170, 178, 182, 200, 204, 215

African Methodist Episcopal Church, organization of, 303

African Methodist Episcopal Zion Church, the organization of, 303

African slave, the status of, in the colonies, 250, 251

Alabama, the movement of Negroes to, 367, 370, 373, 379-381; Cotton culture in, 372

Allen, Philip, owner of land near Dartmouth, 155

Allen, Richard, the work of 51; anti-colonization meeting in church of, 216

Allen, William, interest of, in African colonization, 174, 182, 186, 189, 195, 200, 201, 205, 206

Alvord, J. W., Assistant Commissioner of the Freedmen's Bureau, 13

American Catholic Historical Society, the prize offered by, 351

American Freedmen's Union Commission, 16

American Magazine, extract from, 91-92

American Missionary Association, the work of, in South Carolina, 7, 8, 15, 16, 25, 26

Anderson, Joseph, of Montreal, purchase of a slave by, 329

Anderson, Lymus, a teacher of Negroes at Port Royal, 38

André, a Negro, suit of, for freedom, 326, 327

Andrew, Governor, interest of, in Negro education, 35

Anna Murray-Douglass—My Mother As I Recall Her, 93-101

Antoine, C. C., sketch of, by W. O. Hart, 84-87; how he made money, 86

Arkansas, cotton culture in, 372

Arnett, Bishop B. W., the statistics of A. M. E. Church by, 310

Arnold, Thomas, a friend of Paul Cuffe, 184

Arthur, Stanley Cisby, sketch of Isaiah T. Montgomery by, 87-91

Asbury, Bishop, organizer of a mixed Sunday school, 302

Association for the Study of Negro Life and History, proceedings of the Annual Meeting of, 116-122; Spring Conference of, 353-357

Auger, Jean-Baptiste, a sale of a slave by, 322

Auguste, Tancrede, a ruler of Haiti, 138

Avery Institute, the establishment of, 19

B

Ba Mangwato, a native in South Africa, 288

Babcock, Colonel, effort of, to annex Santo Domingo, 145

Baganda, the morality of, 286-287, 288, 289; art of, 291

Index

473

Bailly, Augustin, a vendor of a slave, 321
Baltimore, Spring Conference in, 353-357; Negroes in domestic service in, 390; interest of, in training domestic workers, 399
Baptist Home Mission Society, the work of, 26
Baptists, the efforts of, among the freedmen, 18
Barahona, a plantation in Santo Domingo, 139, 140
Barbadoes, the progress of, 249
Beaufort, South Carolina, Negro schools at, 22, 24, 26
Beauvais, reference to, 286, 289
Bell, J. W., address of, at the annual meeting, 117, 122, 123-127
Benedict, Mrs., the gift of, 26
Benefit of clergy as applied to slaves, 443-447
Bent, reference to, and quotations from, 288, 292, 293, 294
Betty, a Negro servant, one of the first Methodists, 301
Bickel, Beatrice, review of *Das Unbekannte Afrika* by, 453-458
Bigelow, A. M., a teacher of a Negro school at Aiken, 31
Biography, Negro, by P. W. L. Jones, 128-133
Biron, an enemy of Abram Hannibal in Russia, 364
Bishop, Josiah, a preacher in Virginia, 51
Blaney, Mary, the owner of a slave in Montreal, 330
Blyd, Cornelius Winst, the achievements of, in Dutch Guiana, 448-453
Bond, James, participation of, in the annual meeting, 118
Book of American Negro Poetry, The, review of, 347-348
Booker, S. S., participation of, in the Spring Conference of the Association in Baltimore, 353
Border States, the movement of Negroes from, 367-383

Bornu, the kings of, 296; the rise of, 297
Boston Education Commission, 6
Boston, Negro servants in, 260, 261; Negroes in domestic service in, 429
Botume, Elizabeth Hyde, a teacher of Negroes in South Carolina, 11
Boutton, Louis Philippe, a sale of slaves by, 322
Bowles, Mrs. Emma Castleman, facts of, on the origin of Wilberforce, 335-337
Boyd, Wm. K., *Benefit of Clergy as applied to Slaves* by, 443-447
Boyer, a ruler of Haiti, 137
Boy's Life of Booker T. Washington, A, review of, 463-464
Bragg, George F., *The History of the Afro-American Group of the Episcopal Church* by, 107-109; remarks of, 355-356
Brass, a Negro held in Virginia, 258-259, 278
British America, the status of the Negro in, 276-277
Breeding of slaves for market, 374
Brooks, John, the purchaser of a slave in Montreal, 329
Brooks, W. H., a prominent Negro minister, 313
Brown, George W., an instructor in history, 115; *Haiti and the United States* by, 134-152
Brown, John, a vendor of a slave from Saratoga, 327
Brown, Moses, a friend of Paul Cuffe, 184
Brown, Thomas E., remarks of, 356
Brownell, David, the owner of land at Dartmouth, 154
Bryan, Andrew, a Negro preacher, 50
Bryan, Sampson, a preacher, 50
Bryan, William J., efforts of, to encroach upon Haiti, 143
Bryant, William Cullen, interest of, in freedom, 7
Buffum, a co-worker of Prudence Crandall, 74
Bulkley, Ichabod, an attorney against Prudence Crandall, 78

474　INDEX

Bureau of Refugees, establishment of, 3
Bush, W. O., a Negro farmer of fame in the West, 333
Bush, George, a Negro pioneer in the West, 333-335
Butler, B. F., at Fortress Monroe, 2-3
Byrne, William, disposal of slaves by, 329

C

Caesar, a slave sold in Montreal, 327
Campbell, William, the purchase of slaves by, 328
Came, Amable-Jean-Joseph, sale of a slave by, 319
Canada, slavery in, 316-330
Canal, a ruler of Haiti, 137
Canterbury, Connecticut, the people of, arrayed against Prudence Crandall, 76-80
Capers, Bishop, the missionary work of, 303
Carberry, Daniel, of Montreal, a purchaser of slaves, 329
Cardoza, F. L., an educator of Negroes in South Carolina, 39
Carter, Frank, a teacher of Negroes at Camden, S. C., 38
Carter, E. A., participation of, in the annual meeting, 116
Cary, Lott, a missionary in Africa, 304
Castor, John, a slave owned by Anthony Johnson, a Negro, 259, 278
Chaboille, Sir Charles, a purchaser of slaves, 329
Champlin, G. C., a supporter of Paul Cuffe, 184
Chavigny, Joseph, a vendor of slaves, 322
Channing, Walter, a supporter of Paul Cuffe, 184
Charleston, John, a Negro preacher, 302
Charleston, South Carolina, the Negro schools of, 18, 19, 20, 21, 22-40
Chase, Salmon P., interest of, in the freedmen, 7

Chêne, Mary Josephine, slaves of, by marriage, 329
Chicago, race commission of, 112-114; Negroes in domestic service in, 390, 422
Chicago Commission on Race Relations, *The Negro in Chicago* by, 112-114
Christophe, a ruler of Haiti, 136
Cincinnati, the treatment of Negroes in, 331-332
Clair, Bishop Matthew W., recognition of, by Methodists, 315
Claflin University, the establishment of, 26
Clark, Peter H., quotation from, 102-103
Clarkson, Thomas, interest of, in colonization, 168; efforts of, 193
Clifford, John R., the achievements of, 338-341
Coppin, Mrs. L. J., interest of, in training domestic workers, 399
Coggeshall, John, a supporter of Paul Cuffe, 184
Coker, Daniel, a friend of Paul Cuffe, 185
Collins, a friend of Paul Cuffe, 185
Colored Methodist Episcopal Church, the organization of, 312
Columbia, South Carolina, the Negro schools of, 18, 19, 20, 21
Columbus, Christopher, the discoverer of Haiti and Santo Domingo, 135
Colvis, Joseph, the record of, 132
Comparative Study of the Bantu and Semi-Bantu Languages, A, by Sir Harry H. Johnston, 241-242
Caucasians in domestic service in the United States, 386-387
Concerning the Origin of Wilberforce, 335-337
Congregationalists, educational efforts of, 15, 16
Connecticut, Negro servants in, 265-266, 280
"Contraband of War," at Fortress Monroe, 2-3
Cooke, Edward, quotation from letter of Paul Cuffe to, 221

INDEX

Cotterill, R. S., participation of, in the annual meeting, 118

Cotton, the rise of cotton culture, 370–374; the price of, 376–378; output of, 377–378

Cowan, Philip, petition of, for freedom, 279

Cox, a missionary to Africa, 304

Cramahé, Hector-Theophile, purchase of a slave by, 323–324

Crenshaw, David, a mixed Sunday School in the home of, 302

Croder, Josiah, a merchant connected with Paul Cuffe, 203

Cromwell, John W., letter of, 338–341

Cuffe, Paul, early life of, 153–156; a sea captain, 156–159; domestic affairs of, 159–161; protest of, against taxation, 162–166; a colonizationist, 167–210; trip of, to England, 174–181; life of, as a Quaker, 188–194; death of, 221–223; the will of, 230–232

Cuffe, John, a brother of Paul Cuffe, 155; protest of, against taxation, 162–166, 188

Cureux, Louis, purchaser of slaves, 319

Curry, Thomas, a purchaser of slaves in Montreal, 327

D

Daggett, Judge, decision of, in the Prudence Crandall case, 78–80

Daguille, Jacques-François, a vendor of a slave, 322

Damien, Jacques, sale of a slave by, 319

Das Unbekannte Africa, review of, 455–458

Dassier, Estienne, sale of slave by, 320

Davis, T. R., *Negro Servitude in the United States* by, 247–283

Davis, Jefferson, befriended by Isaiah T. Montgomery, 87–91

Dayly, Dennis, vendor of a slave, 324

Deane, Major E. L., work of, under the Freedmen's Bureau, 13

De Chalet, François, the hire of a slave by, 323

De Champigny, Intendant, proposal of, 316

De la Chevrotière, Joseph Chaviguy, purchase of an Indian slave by, 321

Decline of border States, 367–383

De Grasse, John V., the example of, 132

De la Tesserie, Joseph, the sale of a Negro by, 318

Delaware, Lord, the orders of, 267–268

Delaware, the movement of Negroes from, 367

Delaware River, status of Negroes along, 262, 263

Delzenne, Ignace-François, purchase of a slave by, 320

Denonville, Governor, proposal of, 316

Dessalines, the emperor of Haiti, 136

Detroit, Negroes in domestic service in, 390, 405

Detweiler, Frederick G., *The Negro Press in the United States* by, 238–239

De Vitre, Mathieu-Theodore, a purchaser of a slave, 322

Director of the Association, the annual report of, 466–471

Discovery of Gold in California, the result of, 377

Disfranchisement of Negro servants, 272

Disruption of Virginia, The, review of, 239–241

District of Columbia, the movement of the Negroes from, 367; Negroes in domestic service in, 390, 392, 393, 394, 395, 400, 401, 402, 403, 404, 407, 408, 409–413, 414, 415, 419, 425, 426

Dolgorukovs, friends of Abram Hannibal, 363

Dominican Republic, the history of, 135–142

476 INDEX

Domingue, a ruler of Haiti, 137
Domestic service in the United States, Negroes in, 384–442
Douglass, Frderick, story related by, 54; his wife, 93–101; in Ireland, 102–107
Dregis, Emanuel, a Negro servant, 260
Dumoulin, François, of Montreal, a vendor of slaves, 329
Dunière, Louis, sale of slaves by, 319, 320
Dutch frigate, slaves brought to Jamestown in, 249
Dutch law with regard to slavery, 253

E

Edie, Colonel J. R., Assistant Commissioner of the Freedmen's Bureau, 13
Educational Efforts of the Freedmen's Bureau and Freedmen's Aid Societies in South Carolina, 1862–1872, 1–40
Edwards, G. A., particiation of, in the Spring Conference in Baltimore, 354, 355
El Bekri, the author of Tarikh-es-Soudan, 296
Elizabeth, Empress, a friend of Abram Hannibal, 364
Elizabeth, Queen, the attitude of, toward slavery, 251, 256
Elkonhead, Jane, the owner of Francis Pryne, 259
Ellsworth, W. W., an attorney for Prudence Crandall, 78
Ely, General, daughters of, teachers of Negroes, 21
Embury, Philip, a meeting of Methodists at the home of, 301
Employment agencies as they concern Negro domestic workers, 436–440
Ethics of Africans, 286–290
Evans, Henry, a pioneer preacher, 51
Evening Bulletin (Philadelphia), extract from, 81–84

F

Farando, Bashasar, a Negro servant, 260
Fay, Thomas, inquiry of, into the affairs of Africa, 207
Featherstonhaugh, quotation from, 375
Fetishism, the religion of Africa, 43–45
Finley, Robert, the correspondence of, with Paul Cuffe, 212–213, 215
Fisher, Miles Mark, an instructor at Virginia Union University, 115
Fisher, Samuel R., proposal of, to establish a Negro school, 206
Flora, a slave sold in Montreal, 327
Forten, Charlotte S., a teacher in South Carolina, 10–11
Forten, James, correspondence of, with Paul Cuffe, 205–206, 207; attitude of, on colonization, 216, 217
Fouse, W. H., participation of, in the annual meeting, 118, 121
Free Negroes in Baltimore, 94
Free Society of Traders, attitude of, toward freedom, 263
Free Will Baptists, educational efforts of, in South Carolina, 15, 16, 18
Freedmen's Bureau, the work of, in South Carolina, 1–40
Freedmen's Aid Society of the Methodist Episcopal Church, the schools of, in South Carolina, 26
Frederick Douglass in Ireland, 102–107
French Canada, slavery in, 316–330
Friends, the work of, among freedmen in South Carolina, 27; interest of, in colonization, 170, 171
Friendly Society of Sierra Leone, the efforts of, 186, 193, 200, 206
Frobenius, Leo, reference to, 286, 287, 295; *Das Unbekannte Africa* of, 455–458
Furley, Benjamin, opposition of, to slavery, 263

G

Gainesville, Georgia, occupations of, graduates of schools of, 400

INDEX

Gannett, W. C., a teacher of Negroes in South Carolina, 8
Garneau, François-Xavier, quotations from, 316, 317
Garrettson, Freeborn, attitude of, toward slavery, 301
Garrison, William Lloyd, interest of, in the freedmen, 7; letter of Prudence Crandall to, 72; letter of Frederick Douglass to, 103-107
Gautier, Pierre, purchase of a slave by, 319
Gay, Sydney Howard, in the home of Frederick Douglass, 97
Geaween, John, a Negro servant, 260
Geffrard, a ruler of Haiti, 137
Georgia, restriction upon slavery in, 254-255; servants in, 279, 280; movement of Negroes from, 363
Germantown, Friends of, protest of, against slavery, 263
Ghana, the kings of, 296; the rise of, 296
Gibbons, William, inquiry of, into the affairs of Sierra Leone, 207-208
"Gideonites," the efforts of, 7
Gifford, Enos, owner of land near Dartmouth, 155
Gifford, Isaac, quotation from letter of Paul Cuffe to, 221-222
Gilbert, a settler from Antigua, 301
Gloucester, Duke of, interest of, in colonization, 169, 195
Goddard, Calvin, an attorney for Prudence Crandall, 78
Gold, the discovery of, in California, the effect of, 377
Grant, U. S., effort of, to annex Santo Domingo, 145
Guérin, Damelle Marie-Anne, vendor of a slave, 319
Guerrier, a ruler of Haiti, 137
Guillaume, a ruler of Haiti, 138
Gulf States, migration to, 367-383
Gummere, Amelia Mott, *The Journal of John Woolman* by, 349-350

H

Haiti, relations of, with the United States, 134-152; the occupation of, by the United States, 138; the commercial position of, 148-150
Haiti and the United States, by George W. Brown, 134-152
Hale, Edward Everett, interest of, in freedmen, 7
Hammond, Anna Eliza, a pupil of Prudence Crandall, 76; the arrest of, 76
Hammond, L. H., *In the Vanguard of a Race* by, 111-112
Hammond, John, of Saratoga, the sale of a slave by, 327-328
Hancock, Gordon B., *Three Elements of African Culture* by, 284-300
Hannibal, Ivan, a son of Abram Hannibal, 365
Hannibal-Pushkin, Nadejda, the mother of Alexander Pushkin, 365
Hannibal, Ossip, a son of Abram Hannibal, 365
Harris, Sara, a pupil of Prudence Crandall, 73
Harris, William, quotation from letter of Paul Cuffe to, 221
Hart, W. O., sketch of C. C. Antoine by, 84-87
Hartford, interest of, in the training of domestic workers, 399
Hartzell, Bishop J. C., *Methodism and the Negro in the United States* by, 301-315
Hawkins, Sir John, the trading of, 251; argument of, in favor of slavery, 255-256
Hawkins, M. A., participation of, in the Spring Conference of the Association in Baltimore, 353, 354
Hawkins, John R., address of, in Baltimore, 353-354
Hay-Pauncefote Treaty, 145-146
Haynes, Elizabeth Ross, *Negroes in Domestic Service in the United States* by, 384-442
Haynes, George E., *The Trend of the Races* by, 109-111
Health of Negro domestic workers, 432-433

Henrique y Carvajol, Frederico, nomination of, 144
Herard, a ruler of Haiti, 137
Hicks, Mrs. C. M., a teacher of Negroes in South Carolina, 37
Hicks, Jenkins, and Company, merchants connected with Paul Cuffe, 203
Higginson, T. W., quotations from, 55, 56, 57
Hill, L. P., address of, in Baltimore, 356-357
Hilton Head, capture of, 4; educational efforts at, 5
Hippolyte, a ruler of Haiti, 137
Hipp, George, sale of a slave by, 323
History, the teaching of, 123-127
History of the Afro-American Group of the Episcopal Church, review of, 107-109
History of the United States since the Civil War, A, review of, 458-461
Hodge, LeRoy, a letter of, 343-344
Holly, Bishop Theodore, the lineage of, 454
Hopkins, Charles, a teacher of Negroes in South Carolina, 37-38
Hopkins, Samuel D., interest of, in colonization, 168
Hosier, Harry, a Negro preacher, 49
Howard, Horatio P., the death of, 243; relation of, to Paul Cuffe, 243; the will of, 243
Howard, O. O., the head of the Freedmen's Bureau, 13
Howard School, the establishment of, 21
Hume, Naethan, the owner of slaves in Montreal, 330
Hunter, General David, in command in South Carolina, 8
Hunter, William, a friend of Paul Cuffe, 185
Hurst, Bishop John, participation of, in the Spring Conference in Baltimore, 356

Hutchinson, Samuel, a friend of Paul Cuffe

I

Importation of slaves, restriction on, 252-253, 375
Impostor posing as the relative of Paul Cuffe, 208-210
In the Vanguard of a Race, review of, 111-112
Indian slaves in Canada, 320-323
Indianapolis, occupations of graduates of schools of, 400, 401, 405, 434
Ireland, Frederick Douglass in, 102-107
Isabella, the slave of Hector-Theophilie Cramahé, Lieutenant-Governor of Quebec, 323, 324, 325
Isthmian Canal, the seizure of, 146; the completion of, 146

J

Jack, a pioneer Negro preacher, 50-51
Jackson, John H., the services of, 132
Jackson, L. P., *Educational Efforts of the Freedmen's Bureau and Freedmen's Aid Societies in South Carolina, 1862-1872* by, 1-40; an instructor at the Virginia Normal and Industrial Institute, 115
Jackson, W. C., *A Boy's Life of Booker T. Washington* by, 463-464
James, John, a friend of Paul Cuffe, 184; inquiry of, into the condition of Sierra Leone, 207
James, L. S., address of, in Baltimore, 355
Jamestown, the introduction of slavery at, 249
Jessop, Joseph, visit to, by impostor, 209
Johnson, Anthony, a Negro owner of slaves, 259, 278
Johnson, James Weldon, *The Book of American Negro Poetry* by, 347-348
Johnson, Richard, a Negro brought to Virginia, 260
Johnston, Sir Harry H., *A Compar-*

ative Study of the Bantu and Semi-Bantu Languages by, 241-242

Jones, Absalom, the opposition of, to colonization, 219

Jones, J. McHenry, the services of, 132

Jones, Laurence C., *Piney Woods and Its Story* by, 346-347

Jones, P. W. L., participation of, in the annual meeting, 117; *Negro Biography* by, 128-133

Jones, Bishop R. E., recognition of, by Methodists, 315

Jordan, L. G., participation of, in the annual meeting, 117

Journal of John Woolman, The, review of, 349-350

Judson, A. T., an opponent of Prudence Crandall, 75, 76, 77, 78

K

Keith, George, opposition of, to slavery, 263

Kentucky, Colonization Society of, the establishment of, 211; the culture of tobacco in, 368; breeding of slaves in, 374

Khama, an honest native of South Africa, 288

Kizell, John, a settler in Sierra Leone, 193

L

Labart, Guillaume, a vendor of slaves, 329

Ladoga Canal Commission, A b r a m Hannibal a member of, 364

Lane College, the establishment of, 312

La Promenade, Paul, a purchaser of a slave in Montreal, 328

Larger Canal Zone, a reality, 143, 146, 150, 151, 152

Larned, E. D., quotation from, concerning Prudence Crandall, 73

Lecompte Cincinnatus, a ruler of Haiti, 138

Lee, Barnard K., a founder of a school for Negroes, 8

Legitime, a ruler of Haiti, 137

Lepage Louis, a slave in Quebec, 322

Le Pailleur, Charles, a purchaser of a slave in Montreal, 327, 329

Levy, Gershon, owner of André, a Canadian slave, 326

Levy, Solomon, a purchaser of slaves, 327

Lewis, Edmonia, the achievements of, 132

Liberia, part played by Philadelphia in founding, 81-84

Lifland, Abram Hannibal in, 364

Light, George, an early owner of slaves in Virginia, 279

Living conditions of Negro domestic workers, 428-429

Locke, Perry, a minister going to Africa, 198, 201; interest of, in colonization, 217

London Freedmen's Aid Society, 15, 16

Los Angeles, domestic workers in, 435

Louisiana, the movement of Negroes to, 367, 370, 373, 379, 381; cotton culture in, 372

Louison, a slave in Canada, 319

Lucas, Charles, a slaveholder in Virginia, 279

Lucas, Sir Charles, *The Partition of Africa* by, 461-463

Lugard, Lady, quotation from, 294-295, 298-299, 300

Lurker, King, the grandson of, 205

M

McAdam, Hugh, a vendor of slaves in Saratoga, 327

McCoy, L. M., participation of, in the Spring Conference of the Association in Baltimore, 353

McGill, James, a vendor of slaves, 327

McGregor, James C., *The Disruption of Virginia* by, 239-241

McKinley and Roosevelt Administrations, The, review of, 348-349

INDEX

McLachlan, R. W., memorandum of, on the sale of slaves, 327
Macaulay, Zachariah, interest of, in colonization, 169-170
Madison, President James, visit to, by Paul Cuffe, 184-185, 186
Mansa Musa, a noble of Ghana, 296
Maryland, early slavery in, 260-261; treatment of servants in, 268-269, 271, 273, 274-275, 276, 280, 281, 282; movement of Negroes from, 367, 370; the culture of tobacco in, 368; breeding of slaves in, 374, 376
Martin, Governor Simeon, an endorser of Paul Cuffe, 184
Mashonaland, natives of, discussed, 288, 289, 292
Massachusetts, early slavery in, 252, 260, 261, 262; restrictions on servants in, 272, 273, 280
Mather, Mrs. Rachel C., the establishment of a school by, 26
Matthews, W. B., participation of, in the annual meeting, 117
May, Samuel, a coworker of Prudence Crandall, 74, 75, 76
May, Samuel J., in the home of Frederick Douglass, 97
Mazoe Valley, art in, 294
Meade, Bishop, interest of, in colonization, 217
Melle, a kingdom of Africa, 296
Methodist Churches, early difficulties of the races in, 302
Methodism and the Negro in the United States, 301-315
Menshikov, ruler of Russia, 363
Michaels, Myer, of Montreal, a purchaser of slaves, 329
Michigan Freedmen's Relief Association, 15
Migration to the lower South and Southwest, 367-383
Miller, Kelly, address of, in Baltimore, 354
Miller, Thomas E., Ex-Congressman, remarks of, at the Baltimore Spring Conference, 356

Mills, Samuel J., interest of, in colonization, 213-216
Miner Normal School, the occupation of the graduates of, 400, 401
Minich, Field Marshall, the friend of Abram Hannibal, 364
Minimum wage legislation, 424-425
Missionary efforts in the South, the success of, 304-305
Mississippi, the movement of Negroes to, 367, 373, 380, 379-381; cotton culture in, 372
Missouri, the culture of tobacco in, 368; breeding of slaves in, 374
Mole St. Nicholas, a prospective naval base, 143
Mona Passage, the, significance of, 148-150
Monroe Doctrine as it concerns Haiti and Santo Domingo, 135, 143, 144, 145, 146, 147, 148, 149, 150
Montgomery, Isaiah T., sketch of, 87-91
Monsaige, Jean, purchase of a slave by, 319
Morality of Africans, 286-291
Morgan, Peter G., the record of, 341-344
Morisseaux, Marie-Josephe, sale of a slave by, 322
Morrison, James, a vendor of a slave in Montreal, 327, 328-329
Morse, Dr. Jedekiah, inquiry of, into the affairs of Africa, 206
Morse, P. A., quotations from, 372
Moses, Ruth, an Indian girl, marriage of, to Cuffe Slocum, 154
Mossell, Mrs. N. F., remarks of, 355
Mtokoland, natives of, discussed, 294
Munro, Abby D., a teacher of Negroes in South Carolina, 27
Murray, Ella Spencer, remarks of, 356

N

Napier, Peter, the purchase of a slave called Isabella by, 324
Nat Turner's Insurrection, the results of, 375-376

Nassingh, Phillip Peter, employer of York Thomas, in Montreal, 330
Negro Biography, by P. W. L. Jones, 128–133
Negro folklore, interest in, 470
Negro in Chicago, The, review of, 112–114
Negroes in Domestic Service in the United States, 384–442
Negro Pioneer in the West, A, 333–335
Negro Press in the United States, The, review of, 238–239
Negro Servitude in the United States, 247–283
Neide, Major Horace, work of, under the Freedmen's Bureau, 13
Neptune, a Negro slave of the estate of De Beauvais, 323
New England Freedmen's Aid Society, 6, 15, 16, 17, 18, 19, 20, 21, 22, 23
New Jersey, memorial of citizens of, with respect to colonization, 212
New Netherlands, status of slaves in, 262–263
New York, the status of the slave in, 253, 262–263, 280; laws of, with respect to Negro schools, 344–345
New York National Freedmen's Relief Association, 6, 15, 16, 17, 18, 19, 20, 21, 22, 23
New York City, Negroes in domestic service in, 390, 391, 398, 406, 407, 418, 419, 420, 421, 427, 428
Nieboer, definition of *slave* by, 266
Nicolas, the sale of, 318
Nonomapata, a dynasty in Africa, 297
Nord, Alexis, a ruler of Haiti, 137–138
Normandin, Jean-Baptiste, a vendor of a slave, 321–322
North Carolina, early slavery in, 251–252, 260; treatment of Negro servants in, 271, 273, 279, 280, 281; the movement of Negroes from, 367, 374
Northern Methodist, the attitude of, toward slavery, 303, 304, 305, 306, 307, 311; statistics of, 309, 312; missionary work of, after the *Civil War*, 312–313; schools established by, 313–314; recognition given Negroes by, 314
Notes on the Slave in Nouvelle France, 316–330

O

Oberholtzer, Ellis Paxon, *A History of the United States since the Civil War* by, 458, 461
O'Connell, Pezavia, participation of, in the Spring Conference of the Association in Baltimore, 353, 354
Old Fort Plantation School, the establishment of, 11–12
Oreste, Michel, a ruler of Haiti, 138
Organizations of domestic workers, 435–436
Orleans, Duke of, proposal of, to Abram Hannibal, 362
Orr, Governor, interest of, in the uplift of Negroes in South Carolina, 32
Otis, James, quotation from, 249
Overton, C. B., an assistant in research, 468

P

Palapwe, an objective of Bent in South Africa, 288
Palmer, Alice Freeman, interest of, in training for domestic service, 398
Panama Canal, the building of, 143, 145, 146; the influence of, 145, 146, 147, 148
"Panis," Indian slaves among the French, 320–323
Parent, Louis, the petition of, 323
Paris, Abram Hannibal educated at, 361, 362
Park, Dr. R. E., quotation from, 45–46
Parker, Robert, a friend of John Castor, 278
Parry, Albert, *Abram Hannibal, the*

Favorite of Peter the Great by, 359-366

Partition of Africa, The, a review of, 461-463

Paul Cuffe, by H. N. Sherwood, 153-229

Péan, Hugues Jacques, sale of an Indian slave by, 321

Pécaudy, Claude, purchase of a slave by, 319

Peck Solomon, a teacher of Negroes in South Carolina, 8, 26

Pemberton, James, interest of, in African colonization, 169

Penn, William, in colonization dialogue, 218-220

Penn's Charter, with respect to slavery, 263

Pennington, J. W. C., the scholarship of, 132

Pennsylvania, early slavery in, 252, 262, 263; Negro servants in, 263, 264, 276, 279, 280, 281; value of lands of, compared, 370

Penn Normal and Agricultural Institute, the establishment of, 11

Pennsylvania Freedmen's Relief Association, 6

Perry, Heman E., sketch of, 91-92

Peter the Great, the favorite of, 359-366

Peter II, ruler of Russia, 363; Abram Hannibal, the instructor of, 363

"Peter's Negro," 359-366

Petion, a ruler of Haiti, 136-137

Philadelphia, the part of, in establishing Liberia, 81-84; Negroes in domestic service in, 390, 393, 398, 399, 414, 416, 418

Phillips, Wendell, in the home of Frederick Douglass, 97

Philleo, Rev. Calvin, the husband of Prudence Crandall, 80

Pierrot, a ruler of Haiti, 137

Pickens, William, address of, in Baltimore, 357

Pierce, E. L., efforts of, in South Carolina, 7, 8, 9, 10, 11, 12

Pierre, a slave sold in Canada, 320

Pinchback, P. B. S., partner of C. C. Antoine, 86-87

Piney Woods and its Story, review of, 346-347

Pioneer Negro, in the West, 333-335

Pitman, Thomas G., a supporter of Paul Cuffe, 184

Planters, migration of, from the border States, 367-383

Porter, Admiral, effort of, to lease Samaná Bay, 145

Porter, Rev. A. Toiner, the work of, among the freedmen, 27, 32

Port Royal, the education of Negroes at, 8, 9, 10, 11, 25, 26, 28, 32

Port Royal Experiment, the, 4-12

Port Royal Relief Committee, 6

Preobrajensky Guard-regiment, Abram Hannibal an officer in, 362

Presbyterian Church, the efforts of, to educate Negroes, 27

Proceedings of the Annual Meeting of Association for the Study of Negro Life and History, 116-122; of the Spring Conference, 353-357

Protest against slavery, 333

Potestant Episcopal Freedmen's Commission, the efforts of, in South Carolina, 27

Providence, attitude of, toward slavery, 261; interest of citizens of, in domestic service training, 399

Prudence Crandall, by G. Smith Wormley, 72-80

Punch, John, a Negro servant in Virginia, 282

Pushkin, Alexander, references of, to his grandfather, 359, 360, 361, 362

Pryne, Francis, a slave freed in Virginia, 259

Q

Quebec, slavery in, 316-330

R

Ragusinsky Savva, gift of Abram Hannibal to Peter the Great by, 360

Rathbone, William and Richard, merchants connected with Paul Cuffe, 203

INDEX

Rathbone Hodgson Company in communication with Paul Cuffe, 205

Réanme, Charles, a vendor of slaves, 315

Reed, E. E., participation of, in the annual meeting, 116

Reed, James, a colonizationist in Sierra Leone, 182

Reed, Lieut. Col. William N., services of, 131

Religion of the American Negro Slave: His Attitude toward Life and Death, 40–71

Research, the results of, 468–470

Reval, Abram Hannibal the commandant of, 364

Rhode Island, Negro servitude in, 264–265, 280

Rhodes, James F., *The McKinley and Roosevelt Administrations* by, 348–349

Richards, Ellen H., the experiment of, 398

Riché, a ruler of Haiti, 137

Riddell, William Renwick, *Notes on the Slave in Nouvelle France* by, 316–330

Rights of Negro servants, 271, 272

Rigot, Jean, a vendor of a slave, 329

Ripley, quotation from, 299–300

Robbins, Amasa, an attorney employed by Paul Cuffe, 184

Robert Gould Shaw School, the establishment of, 19–20

Rogers, Joel, quotation from letter of Paul Cuffe to, 222

Roman, C. V., address of, at the annual meeting, 122

Romana, La, a plantation in Santo Domingo, 138, 139, 140

Roscoe, references to, 287, 288, 290, 291, 292

Roth, William, a letter of, quoted, 193; interest of, in Paul Cuffe, 199, 203, 208, 224

Rotch, William, a friend of Paul Cuffe, 184

Rubin, a faithful slave of John Young in Canada, 325

Ruggles, David, the record of, 132

Russell, James S., letters of, 341–344

Russell, H. C., participation of, in the annual meeting, 121

Russell, J. H., quotations from, 258, 259, 260

Rust, R. S., a president of the original Wilberforce, 308

Rutherford, S. W., remarks of, at the Baltimore Spring Conference, 356

S

Saget, a ruler of Haiti, 137

Salnave, a ruler of Haiti, 137

Salomon, a ruler of Haiti, 137

Sam, a ruler of Haiti, 137

Samaná Bay, the desire of the United States for, 145

Santo Domingo, a brief account of, 138–142

Sara, a slave from Saratoga, sold in Canada, 327

Saxton, Major Rufus, work of, among the freedmen, 8, 9; Assistant Commissioner of the Freedmen's Bureau, 13

Schism in the Churches of the United States, 303, 304, 305, 306

Schofield, Martha, efforts of, for the uplift of Negroes, 27

Scott, Bishop I. B., mission of, to Africa, 314

Scott, General R. K., Assistant Commissioner of the Freedmen's Bureau, 13

Secretary-Treasurer, financial statement of, 466

Selenginsk, the flight of Abram Hannibal from, 363

Servitude distinguished from slavery, 247–260

Sewall, Judge, work of, against slavery, 262

Seward, F. W., efforts of, to secure Samaná Bay, 145

Sharp, Granville, interest of, in colonization, 168

Shaw, Francis G., interest of, in the freedmen, 7

Sherman, T. W., operations of, in South Carolina, 3
Sherman, W. T., field order of, 35–36
Sherbro, proposal to purchase land there, 208
Sherwood, H. N., *Paul Cuffe* by, 153–229
Sierra Leone, an objective of colonizationists, 168, 169, 182, 189
Slavery in the United States distinguished from servitude, 247–260; slavery in England, 250, 251; protest against, in the colonies, 333
Slocum, Cuffe, ancestor of Paul Cuffe, 153, 154
Slocum, Ebenezer, the owner of Paul Cuffe's ancestor, 153
Slocum, Ruth, the wife of Cuffe Slocum, the death of, 155
Smith, A. H., the retirement of, from the service of the Association, 351, 471
Smith, Georgine Kelly, participation of, in the Spring Conference of the Association in Baltimore, 353
Social life of Negro domestic workers, 434
Songhay, the civilization of, 295, 296, 297, 298, 299, 300
Soudan, the governments of, 295–300
Soulouque, a ruler of Haiti, 137
South, the movement of Negroes in, 367–383
South Carolina, refugees in, 1–6; education in, 1–40; early slavery in, 252, 280; missionary work in, 302, 304; movement of Negroes from, 368
Southern Methodists supreme over slavery, 306, 307, 308
Southwest, the movement of Negroes to, 367–383
Sowle, Jonathan, an owner of land near Dartmouth, 155
Spanish explorers, Negroes with, 249
Spencer, J. O., address of, in Baltimore, 353, 354
Spingarn, A. B., a letter of, 344–345

Sprague, Rosetta Douglass, *Anna Murray-Douglass—My Mother as I Recall Her* by, 93–101
Spring Conference of the Association for the Study of Negro Life and History, the proceedings of, 353–357
Springfield, Massachusetts, occupations of Negroes in, 405
St. Helena, Negro school at, 11
St. Louis, Negroes in domestic service in, 393–394
St. Petersburg-Moscow Canal, the plan for, submitted by Abram Hannibal, 365
Steward, T. G., extracts from *The Friend* supplied by, 331–333; a letter from, 453
Steward, W. H., participation of, in the annual meeting, 116
Stiles, Ezra, interest of, in colonization, 168
Stiles, Joshua, a vendor of slaves in Montreal, 329
Stoll, C. C., address of, at the annual meeting, 117
Strong, Henry, an attorney for Prudence Crandall, 78
Strouds, Giles, a sale of slaves by, 322
Sullivan, John, the purchaser of a slave in Montreal, 330
Sumner, Charles, quotation from, 262
Sumner High School, St. Louis, the occupations of the graduates of, 400
Survance, Antony, a native of Senegal, 199
Swedish Company, ordinance of, with respect to slavery, 263

T

Taber, Judge Constant, a supporter of Paul Cuffe, 184
Taber, Philip, a minister known to the Cuffes, 154
Tappan, Arthur, a supporter of Prudence Crandall, 78
Tarikh-es-Soudan, the author of, 296

Taylor, A. A., *The Movement of Negroes from the East to the Gulf States from 1830 to 1850* by, 367–383; a permanently employed investigator of the Association, 465, 469

Tennessee, the culture of tobacco in, 368; breeding slaves in, 374

Teaching of Negro History, The, by J. W. Bell, 123–127

Texas, admission of, stimulus to slave trade, 377

The Friend, extracts from, 331–333

The Item (New Orleans), extract from, 87–91

The Movement of Negroes from the East to the Gulf States from 1830 to 1850, by A. A. Taylor, 367–383

The States (New Orleans), extract from, 84–87

Thérèse, an Indian slave girl in Quebec, 321

Thomas, York, a Negro serving under an indenture, 330

Thompson, A. Eugene, participation of, in the annual meeting, 116

Thornton, William, interest of, in colonization, 168

Three Elements of African Culture, 284–300

Tillinghast, reference to, 286, 289

Tobacco, the production of, from 1830 to 1850, 368–369

Todd, Andrew, a purchaser of a slave, 329

Tomlinson, Reuben, work of, under the Freedmen's Bureau, 13; Assistant Commissioner, 13; report of, 34

Tomsk, the service of Abram Hannibal at, 363

Towne, Laura M., a teacher of Negroes in South Carolina, 11

Training of domestic service workers in England, 397; in the United States, 398–404

Transition from white servitude to slavery, 266–276; from Negro servitude to Negro slavery, 277–283

Treatment of Negroes in Ohio, 331–332

Trend of the Races, The, review of, 109–111

Turner, John, a vendor of a slave in Montreal, 329

Turner, George, a soldier, the owner of a slave in Canada, 330

Tyson, Elisha, a friend of Paul Cuffe, 185

U

Union American Methodist Episcopal Church organized, 303

Union Humane Society, the establishment of, 211

United States in the Larger Canal Zone, 145–146

V

Vallée, Jean Baptiste, a sale of slaves by, 322

Vase, John, an attorney employed by Paul Cuffe, 184

Vederique, François, purchase of a Negro by, 318

Venture, Thomas, the owner of a slave called Isabella, 324

Vernon, I., a supporter of Paul Cuffe, 184

Virginia, memorial of legislature of, 212; introduction of slavery in, 251, 254; Negro servants in, 256–260, 267; treatment of Negro servants in, 269, 270, 271, 272, 274, 275, 276, 278, 280, 282; movement of Negroes from, 367, 370, 374; tobacco culture in, 368, 369; breeding of slaves in, 374, 376

Von Sheberg, Christina Regina, the wife of Abram Hannibal, 364

W

Wallace, Henry A., the death of, 243; his services, 243–244

Ward, William, of Vermont, sale of slaves by, 328

Washington, Booker T., a quotation from, 49

Washington, D. C., Negroes in domestic service in, 390, 391, 393, 394, 395, 400, 401, 402, 403, 404, 407, 408, 409–413, 414, 415, 419, 425, 426

Webster, Dr. A., an educator in South Carolina, 26

Welch, Jonathan A., an attorney against Prudence Crandall, 78

Wesley, John, the baptism of a Negro by, 301

Wesleyan Methodists, educational efforts of, 15, 16

Westport, Friends at, 195

Wheatley, Phyllis, the story of, 44–45

Wheaton, Laban, presentation of Memorial of Paul Cuffe by, 196

White, Ned Lloyd, a teacher of Negroes in South Carolina, 39

Whittier, John G., interest of, in the Freedmen's education, 10–11

Wiener, Leo, *Africa and the Discovery of America* by, 233–238

Wilberforce, William, interest of, in colonization, 168, 174, 195

Wilberforce, the establishment of, 308, 335–337

Wilhelmina, Queen, a friend of Cornelius Winst Blyd, of Dutch Guiana, 451–452

Williams, Noah W., participation of, in the annual meeting, 117

Williams, Peter, inquiry of, into colonization prospects, 207; interest of, in colonization, 215; funeral sermon of, on Paul Cuffe, 224

Wilmington, Delaware, independent Negro Methodists of, 303

Wilson, G. R., *The Religion of the American Negro Slave: His Attitude toward Life and Death* by, 41–71

Wilson, Samuel, interest of, in colonization, 217

Windward Passage, the, significance of, 148–150

Woman's Home Missionary Society, the work of, 17, 26

Woodson, Carter G., quotation from, 47–48; address of, at annual meeting, 117; address of, in Baltimore, 354

World War and Negro domestic labor, 384–442

Wormley, G. Smith, *Prudence Crandall* by, 72–80; address of, in Baltimore, 355

Wyatt, Sir Francis, the owner of a Negro named Brass, 259

Wright, Irene A., the assistance of, in research, 465

Wright, John F., a founder of the original Wilberforce, 308

Wright, T. G., a founder of a Negro School, 20–21

Y

Yeamans, Sir John, introduction of slaves by, 252

Yoruban civilization, an estimate of, 286–287

Young, John, the purchaser of a Negro slave in Canada, 324

Z

Zamor, a ruler of Haiti, 138

Zimbabwe, a city of art in Africa, 292, 293

Zachas, John C., a teacher of Negroes in South Carolina, 8

Lightning Source UK Ltd.
Milton Keynes UK
UKHW011016210820
368606UK00002B/362